CISTERCIAN STUDIES SERIES: NUMBER SIXTY-TWO

THOMAS MERTON'S
SHARED CONTEMPLATION

A Protestant Perspective

CISTERCIAN STUDIES SERIES: NUMBER SIXTY-TWO

Thomas Merton's Shared Contemplation

A PROTESTANT PERSPECTIVE

Daniel J. Adams

CISTERCIAN PUBLICATIONS, INC.
Kalamazoo, Michigan
1979

...RIES

Bede Lackner O CIST
Jean Leclercq OSB
Louis J. Lekai O CIST
Bernard McGinn
Charles Dumont OCSO   Edmond Mikkers OCSO
E. Rozanne Elder   M. Basil Pennington OCSO
Anselm Hoste OSB   John R. Sommerfeldt
Elizabeth T. Kennan   James Wicksteed OCSO

Teresa Ann Doyle OSB
Editor of this volume

Available in the Commonwealth and Europe from:
A. R. Mowbray & Co Ltd
St Thomas House Becket Street
Oxford OX 1 1SJ

© Cistercian Publications, Inc. 1979
Kalamazoo, Michigan 49008

Library of Congress Cataloging in Publication Data

Adams, Daniel J.
     Thomas Merton's shared contemplation.

     (Cistercian studies series; no. 62)
     Bibliography: p. 347
     1. Merton, Thomas, 1915-1968. 2. Trappists in the United States—
Biography. I. Title.
II. Series
BX4705. M542A64   271'.125'024 (B)   78-6549
ISBN 0-87907-862-6

Typeset by the Contemplative Sisters of the Precious Blood
New Riegel, Ohio 44853

Printed in the United States of America

Cistercian Publications expresses its gratitude to the publishers of Thomas Merton's works for their permission to quote excerpts from their books.

Excerpts quoted by permission of the Seabury Press: Introduction the *Albert Camus' The Plague* by Thomas Merton.

Excerpts from *The Ascent to Truth, No Man Is An Island, The Seven Storey Mountain, The Sign of Jonas, The Waters of Siloe,* and *The Last of the Fathers* by Thomas Merton are reprinted by permission of Harcourt, Brace Jovanovich, Inc.; copyright © 1948, 1949 by Harcourt Brace Jovanovich, Inc.; copyright © 1951, 1953, by The Abbey of Gethsemani; copyright © 1976, 1977 by The Trustees of The Merton Legacy Trust.

TO

Carol Fang-Lan Chou
My Wife and
Finest Critic

TABLE OF CONTENTS

Foreword by Brother Patrick Hart   9

Preface   15

Author's Introduction   19

I.   Merton's Holy Worldliness: An Appraisal   29

II.   Merton's Social and Cultural Background   65

III.   The Spiritual Foundations of Merton's Thought   97

IV.   Religions of the East   145

V.   Concern for Social Justice   165

VI.   The Writer as Social Prophet   213

VII.   Contemplation in a World of Action   247

VIII.   The Union of Contemplation and Action   293

IX.   Directions for the Future   317

X.   A Sign of God   339

Bibliography   347

FOREWORD

THERE IS AN amusing episode in *The Abbess of Crewe* by Muriel Spark when the Abbess makes use of her private 'green line' to contact Sister Gertrude, who is in the Congo on an ecumenical safari. The Abbess explains that she has been questioned by Rome concerning the use of sophisticated electronic surveillance equipment in their abbey. How is such a technological control system to be reconciled with their ancient Rule? Sister Gertrude says it is a 'paradox', to which the Abbess replies that she should return to the abbey and give a seminar on the paradox. But Sister Gertrude wisely responds: 'A paradox you live with.'[1]

Throughout his life Thomas Merton struggled with the paradox that he faced within himself. Born of artist parents, his father an Anglican from New Zealand and his mother an American Quaker, he found himself at an early age at odds with the society around him. After he entered the Abbey of Gethsemani in 1941, his main preoccupation was how to reconcile the contemplative life with his creative writing, solitary prayer with poetry, being with doing. The yin-yang of the monastic life offered to his idealistic and artistic nature a life-long challenge from which he never completely escaped. In the end, it was by living out the paradox that he was able to transcend it and to make of it a fruitful tension in his life, and to share with the world something of his contemplative experience.

To understand the resolution Merton was working out shortly before his death, the following passage from one of his later journals, *Conjectures of a Guilty Bystander*, may shed light: "A personal crisis occurs when one becomes aware of apparently irreconcilable opposites in oneself...A personal crisis is creative and salutary if one can accept the conflict and restore unity on a higher level, incorporating the opposed elements in a higher

9

unity.''[2] This higher unity had to be attained by a realization that both the positive and negative elements were necessary to achieve an integrated and healthy spiritual life.

Daniel Adams, a Protestant churchman, who did his doctoral studies on the subject of ''contemplation and action in the spirituality of Thomas Merton'' has provided one of the best introductions available to the life and thought (and the paradox) of Thomas Merton. Beginning with an over-all appraisal, Adams moves on to the social and cultural background of Merton from his earliest years in France and America, tracing his steps through his college days at Cambridge in England and Columbia in New York. Finally, the author discusses Merton's conversion to Catholicism and his entrance into the monastic life at the Abbey of Gethsemani in Kentucky where he would live the next twenty-seven years of his life.

The spiritual foundations for Merton's development is detailed by Adams, who stresses the traditional Catholic teachings as found in St Augustine, St Thomas and the modern Thomists (notably Maritain and Gilson), St Bernard of Clairvaux and the early Cistercians of the 12th and 13th centuries. Merton's commentary on Pope Pius XII's encyclical on St Bernard, *Doctor Mellifluus*, entitled *The Last of the Fathers*, as well as an excellent commentary on St Bernard and interior simplicity, and two long essays which appeared serially in *Collectanea Cisterciensia* in the late forties and early fifties, bear this out.[3]

In the mid-fifties, Merton was studying and translating Guerric's sermons, and published a little volume with an introduction on *The Christmas Sermons of Blessed Guerric of Igny*. In the sixties he wrote a long article on Adam of Perseigne, entitled ''The Feast of Freedom: Monastic Formation according to Adam of Perseigne,'' which later appeared as an introduction to *The Letters of Adam of Perseigne*.[4] In the late sixties he provided an introduction to a study of St Aelred of Rielvaux by Amédée Hallier.[5]

The Biblical view of Merton is rightly stressed by Adams in this study. Merton's approach to the Scriptures was more devotional than exegetical, to which his writings bear abundant witness. Although he appreciated biblical scholarship, he was somewhat apprehensive in certain areas, and manifested a concern in regard to its over-emphasis on arid details. Merton wanted the Scriptures themselves to be read and savoured, rather than merely commentaries and critical studies of the sacred texts. He wanted the Word of God itself to be encountered in all its depth and richness.

The author explores Merton's abiding interest in the Christian mystical tradition, tracing his studies of the Desert Fathers, the platonic tradition, St Gregory of Nyssa, the sixteenth-century Spanish school of St John of the Cross and St Teresa of Avila. At the same time, he had a great love and respect for the Rhenish and English mystics, and contributed articles on both in the sixties. At the invitation of Sergius Bolshakoff he even wrote an introduction to *The Russian Mystics*, outlining the rich mystical tradition of the Russian school.[6] His studies of Mount Athos and the hesychastic tradition also appeared about this time.

Merton's interest in the Far East is not overlooked in this volume either. Adams notes Merton's growing fascination with the great Eastern traditions: Hinduism and his studies of Gandhi, the prophet of non-violence, whose life was to have such an influence on his own writings; his great attraction to Buddhism, Zen and the Tibetan variety in particular; the Sufis and the whole mystical tradition of Islam. Although he wrote mostly on Zen Buddhism, he delivered over twenty conferences to the Gethsemani community on the subject of Sufism during the last year of his life and spoke of how it could be related to Christian mysticism.[7]

Above all, Adams deals with the thorny problem of Merton's social concerns, which must find an important place in any competent study of Thomas Merton. His preoccupations with war and peace can be seen in his earliest autobiographical writings (*The Seven Storey Mountain* and *Secular Journal*), but they reached a peak during the Vietnam War. His leanings toward pacifism became more and more pronounced, and it can accurately be said that although he was not an absolute pacifist (he still maintained that a Christian nation could defend itself from an attack by means of conventional weapons), he certainly was a 'nuclear pacifist'. When it came to nuclear warfare, he was a total pacifist, and spoke out strongly on the issue when it was still an unpopular cause in this country. He felt that as a Christian and a monk, he had a moral obligation to 'cry out in the wilderness'.

Merton's writings on racism pre-date his writings on war and peace, but they soon converged to form a book, *Seeds of Destruction*. His anguish over the situation of the Black people in this country can be found in *The Seven Storey Mountain* where he writes of Harlem and the Black ghetto. Merton became involved in alleviating their sufferings and poverty by his work with Baroness Catherine DeHueck (Doherty) at Friendship House in Harlem in 1940 and 1941. With the Black

Revolution in the sixties, he became much more concerned about their cause, and began writing articles which appeared in *The Catholic Worker, Ramparts*, and other journals of social concern. Friends like Dorothy Day, the Berrigan brothers and John Howard Griffin kept him informed and the frequently frequently visited Gethsemani for retreat. Griffin was called to many large cities to arbitrate peaceful settlements betweent the Black and White communities during the summer of 1966. Black leaders and writers felt they had a friend and supporter in Merton. Martin Luther King was planning a retreat at Gethsemani with Merton shortly before his assassination. In *Soul on Ice*, Eldridge Cleaver documents his own appreciation of Merton's efforts and looked upon him as a brother.

Ishi Means Man,[8] a collection of essays on native American Indians, traces racism from our earliest days as a nation in our treatment of the Indian. Appearing in places like *The Catholic Worker* and *The Center Magazine*, these articles were part of Merton's effort to awaken consciences to the evil of racism. He pleaded for fair treatment of native Americans, whose land the colonists had confiscated.

Some Merton commentators have noted a radical shift in his thinking on social problems in the early sixties and attribute this orientation from an inward-looking to an outward-looking spirituality to his involvement in the Boris Pasternak affair. He had begun to correspond with Pasternak before *Doctor Zhivago* was published, and they exchanged six letters, as well as books and articles, at this time. Although this may have had some influence on Merton's later writings, I submit that the change came earlier, as part of a gradual development, more a matter of emphasis than an abrupt change. In the mid-fifties, Merton was beginning to correspond with a number of Latin American poets, and in 1957 Ernesto Cardenal, who had already published poetry in Nicaragua, entered the novitiate at Gethsemani. Merton, as his novice master, was able to get first-hand information of the social conditions in Latin America; and through these contacts with the poets of social change, he saw more clearly the great inequality of 'the good things of the earth', and the exploitation of the poor masses by the rich and powerful.

Yet Merton was committed to a 'spirituality of being'. He believed that for the monk as for the Christian, being must take precedence over doing (and having), and insisted that we must first *be* sons of the heavenly Father. This inward-looking spirituality which has been referred to as a 'spirituality of being', is actually intended to give direction and meaning not only to our understanding of God and the Mystery of our salvation in Christ, but also to our neighbor and our involvement in his history. A spirituality of being must give a new dimension to our own life and work in today's world.

The Christian, then, in Merton's view, must become acutely aware of the presence and action of God in his life, and must enter into an intimate relationship with Him. But this presupposes a true knowledge of self. In this respect as well as others, Merton was following a solid monastic tradition. Bernard of Clairvaux, writing of the Degrees of Truth, stressed the need for self-knowledge as the first essential degree of truth.[9] Before we can be compassionate or merciful to our neighbor, we must experience the presence of the living God within our own lives.

We must recognize our dignity as the object of God's redemption and then transcend ourselves in an intimate relationship with God. Merton expressed this well in his posthumously published volume, *The Climate of Monastic Prayer*, where he writes: 'We know [God] insofar as we become aware of ourselves as known through and through by him.'[10] Hence the continuity between self-knowledge and the awareness of God which is affective in Merton's spirituality: we are made essentially for a loving knowledge of God. Our whole being, including thought and feeling, must be brought into communication and ultimately into communion with God.

Thomas Merton firmly believed that every Christian should experience God as a living and personal reality in his life. To have a fully integrated Christian life, we must be so in contact with God that we experience a union with Him, and realize the end for which we were created: a personal and intimate union with God in Christ by love. Here Merton was fully within the Cistercian monastic tradition.

In this volume Daniel Adams rightly underscores the primacy of being to doing, of contemplation to action, in the spirituality of Thomas Merton and he clearly shows how Merton was able to share this vision with others. In an age of ecumenism, one can only be grateful to God for such a sympathetic and enlightened understanding of Merton and his work by a Protestant clergyman, theologian and missionary. Our hope is that it will reach the wide audience it deserves.

Brother Patrick Hart

Gethsemani Abbey

NOTES

1.   Muriel Spark, *The Abbess of Crewe* (N.Y.: Viking Press, 1974) p. 22.

2.   Thomas Merton, *Conjectures of a Guilty Bystander* (N.Y.: Doubleday Image Books, 1967) p. 208. See also, *Thomas Merton/Monk*, edited by Brother Patrick Hart, especially the chapters by John Eudes Bamberger and Tarcisius Conner (Doubleday Image Books, 1976).

3.   Thomas Merton, *The Last of the Fathers* (Greenwood Reprints). See also 'The Spirit of Simplicity', Texts from St Bernard of Clairvaux on Interior Simplicty. Translation and Commentary by a Cistercian Monk of Our Lady of Gethsemani (Thomas Merton), Trappist, KY., 1948. 'Transforming Union in St Bernard and St John of the Cross' published in five issues of *Collectanea Cisterciensia* (April and July of 1948, January and October of 1949 and January of 1950) and 'Action and Contemplation in St Bernard', published in three issues of *Collectania Cisterciensia* (January and July of 1953 and April 1954). I hope these articles will be re-published by Cistercian Publications in the not too distant future.

4.   *The Letters of Adam of Perseigne*, I, with an introduction by Thomas Merton, (Kalamazoo: Cistercian Publications, 1977).

5.   Amédée Hallier, *The Monastic Theology of Aelred of Rielvaux*, with an introduction by Thomas Merton (Kalamazoo: Cistercian Publications, 1969).

6.   Sergius Bolshakoff, *The Russian Mystics*, with an introduction by Thomas Merton (Kalamazoo: Cistercian Publications, 1976).

7.   Thomas Merton, *The Mystic Life* (Chappaqua, N.Y., Electronic Paperbacks), a series of 11 cassettes of Merton's conferences (22 conferences) on Sufism and Christian mysticism.

8.   Thomas Merton, *Ishi Means Man: Essays on Native Americans* (Greensboro, N.C.: Unicorn Press, 1976).

9.   St Bernard, *The Steps of Humility and Pride, 6*, in *Bernard of Clairvaux: Treatises II* (Washington, D.C.: Cistercian Publications, 1974) pp 34-5.

10.   Thomas Merton, *The Climate of Monastic Prayer* (Spencer, Mass.: Cistercian Publications, 1969). See also Thomas Merton's *The Monastic Journey* edited by Brother Patrick Hart (Kansas City: Sheed Andrews & McMeel, 1977), especially the chapters on 'The Humanity of Christ in Monastic Prayer' and 'Conversion of Life'.

PREFACE

I FIRST became acquainted with the thought of Thomas Merton in the summer of 1961, and from that time on I continued to read everything of his I could find. In 1967-68, while living in New York City, I began to build a collection of Merton's works, and by the time of my seminary graduation in 1969 this collection had grown to include close to fifty volumes. When I began work on my doctorate at the Aquinas Institute of Theology in Dubuque, Iowa, I chose Merton as the subject for my dissertation. Significantly, it was entitled 'Contemplation and Action In the Spirituality of Thomas Merton' and it reflected my own personal interest in developing a spirituality rooted in a personal relationship with God and yet also deeply committed to social justice.

As a Protestant, I was especially interested in Merton's thinking concerning the relation of monasticism and mysticism both to the spiritual life and to prophetic expressions of social action. Protestantism has always been suspicious of mysticism and has usually been extremely reserved in its evaluation of monasticism. To Protestant eyes, most mystics have appeared to be outside the mainstream of Christian theological thinking while monks are considered to be outdated and totally irrelevant to the modern world and its problems. Merton was an obvious exception, for he was not only orthodox in his theology, he was also a social prophet of unusual sensitivity and depth. Clearly then, my Protestant apprehensions of both mysticism and monasticism needed to be re-examined in the light of Thomas Merton's life and work. With this task in mind I have undertaken a thorough revision and rewriting of my dissertation and this book is the result.

The number of people who have had a part in making this book a reality is far too great to include mention of all their

names here; however, I wish to express my thanks to Dr Donald
G. Bloesch and Fr Alfred Wilder for providing direction and
guidance during the period of initial study upon which this book
is based, and I wish to thank Fr Cletus Wessels and Fr David
Hynous of the Aquinas Institute of Theology for making it
possible for me to teach a course on the life and thought of
Thomas Merton during the second semester of 1973. Many of
the ideas found in this book were clarified and enlarged upon as
a result of the stimulating dialogue in that class.

Many hours were spent in careful research prior to the
writing of this book and I am grateful to the many persons who
have provided me with research materials. These include Miss
Lillian Staiger of the University of Dubuque Theological
Seminary-Aquinas Institute Library, Mrs Charlaine Hays and
Miss Marquita Breit of the Bellarmine College Library, Br
Stephen Verbest of the library of New Melleray Abbey, Fr
Matthias Kerndt and Fr Thomas MacMaster of New Melleray
Abbey, and Mr and Mrs Frank E. O'Callaghan III of Louisville.
Br Patrick Hart of Gethsemani Abbey was most helpful in not
only providing research materials but, along with Fr Richard
McGuire of Mepkin Abbey, in reading the manuscript and
offering many helpful suggestions. Dr. E. Rozanne Elder of the
editorial staff of Cistercian Publications showed great patience
and wisdom in seeing the process of turning a dissertation into a
book through to completion, and to them I owe special thanks.

Mention should also be made of the Merton Legacy Trust, of
which Mrs O'Callaghan III is a trustee. The Merton Legacy
Trust administers the estate of Merton and all research carried
out in the Thomas Merton Collection at Bellarmine College is
done with their permission. I might add that because of the
restrictions of the Merton Legacy Trust I have been unable to
quote directly from any of Merton's unpublished writings.

Special thanks are also extended to the following persons
whose support and encouragement were always present: my
mother Mrs James B. Adams, Mr and Mrs Clarence Porter, Fr
Donald Goergen, and the congregations of the Golden Congre-
gational Church of Ryan, Iowa, and the Davies Memorial United
Church of Christ of Potosi, Wisconsin. There is one person to
whom my gratitude is deepest, so deep that it cannot adequately
be expressed. I wish to thank Carol, my wife, for her love and
encouragement during the long years of study and research that
have gone into the writing of this book. She not only aided me
in doing the research and in proofreading seemingly endless
pages, but she served to stimulate my mind when it was dry of
all creativity so that in a very real sense this book is hers as well

as mine. Her depth of love and understanding contributed more than any other factor to the completion of this work, and therefore to her it is dedicated.

Taipei, Taiwan
5 June 1976

AUTHOR'S INTRODUCTION

I N 1962 *Breakthrough to Peace* was published by New
Directions. It was a small book of twelve essays dealing
with the possibility of the extermination of the human race
by nuclear warfare. Contributors included scientists, sociolo-
gists, journalists, university professors, and a Trappist monk by
the name of Thomas Merton. A controversial book, it pointed in
no uncertain terms to the moral problems facing mankind as a
result of the discovery of nuclear energy and the building of
thermonuclear weapons capable of destroying entire civilizations. Its message was all too clear: the manufacture, stockpiling, and testing of nuclear weapons must cease if mankind is
to survive. In his introduction Merton wrote that 'we cannot
escape present reality. We cannot all offer ourselves to be
frozen up and comfortably hibernate through the critical years
that are to come, in order to wake up painlessly in a new
world.'[1] It was a call for concerted action to save humanity from
almost certain doom.

Thomas Merton not only wrote the introduction and
contributed an essay to the book, he was its editor as well. His
name did not appear as editor, for his superiors in the
Cistercian Order thought the book too controversial; it was not
the monk's place to speak out against the evils of modern
society, even when they could mean the complete extermination
of the human race. It was only with great difficulty that the book
was published at all.[2]

Only three years after the publication of this book, Merton
wrote to a friend: 'This week I officially begin the hermit life....
It is quite a step, and something that has not been done thus
officially in the Order since the Lord knows when, way back in
the Middle Ages.'[3] In the three remaining years of his life,
Merton lived alone in a small cabin in the woods on a hillside

overlooking his monastery, the Abbey of Gethsemani. He spent his days praying and meditating, writing and studying, and occasionally entertaining visitors. Once each day he would walk down the hill to the monastery to fill his water bottle and take care of such routine chores as returning books to the library and picking up supplies. This hermit existence seemed unlikely to lend itself to any kind of social action. Indeed, it would appear that the outspoken Merton of the early 1960s had chosen to withdraw his involvement from society and its concerns even as he had withdrawn from the world and entered the monastery twenty years earlier. Was Merton's withdrawal to the monastery and later to the hermitage a means of evading his responsibility to the world at large or, was his action a form of prophecy?

This question forms the rationale for my study. What is the relationship between contemplation and action in the spirituality of Thomas Merton? The conflict between the contemplative and the active life is an old one, and Merton was certainly not the first to deal with it. What is unique, however, is Merton's approach to this problem as a man of the twentieth century and, because he was a gifted writer, his ability to articulate it to others.

From his earliest days in the monastery Merton was convinced of his contemplative vocation. To a friend he wrote: 'My heart consents to nothing but God and solitude.'[4] His talent for writing was recognized by his abbot who instructed him to continue it, but young Merton himself felt that it only took time away from his real vocation, being a contemplative. As the years passed, however, he began to realize that writing itself could be a form of contemplation. He wrote so much, he later said, that 'people are now convinced that I secrete articles like perspiration.'[5] His writings grew from his life, and another monk observes that 'he could only write as he did about monasticism because he lived it first.'[6]

Merton's contemplative life was centered in knowing God and thereby knowing himself. For him 'contemplation is the awareness and realization, even in some sense *experience*, of what each Christian obscurely believes: "It is now no longer I that live but Christ lives in me."'[7] He believed that one's relationship to God also determined one's relationship to others. He explains:

> The whole problem of our time is the problem of love: how are we going to recover the ability to love ourselves and to love one another? The reason why we hate one another and fear one another is that we secretly or openly hate and

fear our own selves. And we hate ourselves because the depths of our being are a chaos of frustration and spiritual misery. Lonely and helpless, we cannot be at peace with others because we are not at peace with ourselves, and we cannot be at peace with ourselves because we are not at peace with God.[8]

Merton's emphasis upon contemplation, therefore, was not a turning against the world, but a rejection of those illusions which we so often mistake for reality: the illusions of war, racism, an uncontrolled technology, and power politics. For him there is only one reality: the union of God and man in contemplation. This is the essence of what it means to be human, and this union is the basis for all constructive social action.

The question still remains of the apparent contradiction between the life of contemplation and the life of action. To begin with, we must thoroughly understand that Merton did not think his vocation included action in the sense of actual personal involvement in struggles for social justice. Merton was a monk, and this in and of itself implied a separation from the world. In fact, Merton interpreted his being a hermit as a form of protest, 'for I live in the woods as a reminder that I am free not to be a number. There is, in fact, a choice'.[9] Isolation from the outside world can be a powerful protest against the evils of that outside world. Even though he lived alone in the woods, he heard the SAC bomber flying low overhead and he wrote: 'Meanwhile the metal cherub of the apocalypse passes over me in the clouds treasuring its egg and its message.'[10]

It is this choice of mankind that was so important to Merton and accounted for his intellectual dynamism and growth. Another Cistercian observes that 'his mind changed because it was intensely alive and therefore in constant development.'[11] He never ceased being open to choice: he chose between the world and the monastery, between the monastery and the hermitage. In one of his journals he wrote that his ideas 'are always changing, always moving around one center, always seeing that center from somewhere else.'[12] Yet there was a center around which he moved, the union of God and man in contemplation.

Merton was intensely aware that the more deeply one enters into union with God the more aware one becomes of those around him and the more one loves the world and those who live and work in it. His solitude and prayer naturally resulted in a concern for others and a desire to save them from dangers like nuclear war. He describes his vision of the monk's relationship to the world in these words:

> The monk belongs to the world but the world belongs to
> him insofar as he has dedicated himself totally to
> liberation from it, in order to liberate it....If you once
> penetrate by detachment and purity of heart to the inner
> secret of the ground of one's ordinary experience, you
> attain to a liberty which nobody can touch....I as a
> monk...can agree that we believe this to be the deepest
> and most essential thing in our lives, and because we
> believe this we have given ourselves to the kind of lives
> we have adopted. [13]

The monastic life, for Merton, was a withdrawal from the world
to God so that one could see the world as it really was. Then,
and only then, could one respond to the pressing social ills of
the world in constructive and compelling social action. It is this
monastic life, as Merton lived it, that forms the subject matter
for this study, a life of hidden wholeness. [14]

John Howard Griffin writes that Merton 'found no inconsis-
tency in seeming opposites.' [15] It did not bother him that he
lived as a hermit and had a boundless love for people. He was
not concerned that he wrote an article on war and peace a week
after affirming that he would make no further statements on
social issues. And it did not seem to disturb him that he could
speak in favor of renewal in the Church and yet continue to say
his own private Mass in Latin. [16] As a result he often appears to
make contradictory statements on contemplation and action and
indeed some scholars have suggested that there were really
several Mertons—an 'early' Merton, a 'middle' Merton, and a
'late' Merton. [17] We maintain, however, that this contradiction
is part and parcel of Merton's greatness, that because of it he
was able to develop a spiritual life of unity that is known to only
a very few. In the closing sentences of his introduction to
Breakthrough to Peace, Merton wrote:

> The perspectives in this book are, then, humanistic in the
> deepest and most spiritual sense of the word. They look
> beyond the interests of any restricted group toward the
> deepest and most critical needs of man himself. In so
> doing, they are, at least implicitly, faithful to the Judaeo-
> Christian tradition on which our civilization was built.
> There is no hope for us if we lose sight of these
> perspectives. There is no other human way out. [18]

In these words we hear the contemplative and the active elements of Christian faith expressed by a monk and a hermit who has become one of the truly great social prophets of our time. [19]

It is significant to me, a Presbyterian, that one of the first doctoral dissertations written on Merton's life and work was done by a Protestant. [20] It is also significant that one of the most influential Protestant theologians of our time, Paul Tillich, has also expressed deep concern over the relationship between contemplation and action. In his book *Theology of Culture* he wrote:

> Will there be a way to avoid a totalitarian reaction against the disintegration of which the Existentialist question is both a symptom and a possible remedy? To suppress this question is not a way out; to join the Eastern solution, even less. But the very nature of the Holy points the way out. It has two sides; the holiness of what ought to be, the sacramental and the personal, the mystical; and the social side, the mystery and reasonableness of being. Will we be able to find a new union of these elements in a creative synthesis in which we take the spiritual substance of the East into the personal and social forms of the West? This is our question. [21]

Although the context within which Tillich lived and worked was quite different from that of Merton, both men saw the need for a union of contemplation and action. And, even more importantly, both men understood that this was not a Protestant or a Catholic problem; it was a Christian, and a human, problem.

Protestants have traditionally been highly suspicious of what is usually called mysticism although there have been notable exceptions—Rudolf Otto and Paul Tillich, for example. [22] Protestants have also had numerous reservations about the monastic life, although here, as Merton pointed out, change is taking place and Protestants are now in the forefront of christian monastic renewal. I want to consider these Protestant hesitations in relation to Merton's works. It is my position that, in most instances, traditional protestant reservations toward both are dispelled by a careful reading of Merton. At the same time, areas of difficulty remain: those of an adequate conception of God and the problem of religious authority, both of which continue among Protestants to raise questions about mysticism. With an appraisal, from a protestant perspective, of

Merton's holy worldliness, we begin an examination of Thomas Merton's spirituality of Christian action and contemplation. We will look at his early life when many seeds were planted that later bore fruit in his monastic life.

We will follow the systematic study of Catholic theologians, mystical theology, Christian philosophy, and the Fathers of the Church in which he steeped himself. We will see his deepening interst in mysticism lead him to a study of the religions of the East—Hinduism, Islam and Buddhism. From this vast treasury of spirituality we will watch Merton construct a foundation from which he could regard the great social problems confronting mankind.

Merton's interests, though, lay primarily with war and peace, racism in America, the writer as a social prophet, and the quality of life in contemporary society. His social criticism was sharp, filled with insight, and generally ahead of its time. [23] In all cases, he was firmly convinced that social problems are an extension of personal problems and that meaningful action must be an outgrowth of contemplation.

No one was more convinced of the dynamic relationship between contemplation and action than Merton, for he knew by his own experience that he could not be *either* a contemplative *or* an activist. He had to be both:

> The prayer of the heart must penetrate every aspect and every activity of Christian existence....But it cannot flourish where an activist spirit seeks to evade the deep inner demands and challenges of the Christian life in personal confrontation with God. This inner personal quest does not conflict with the mediating power of the Church, for the dread and guilt of the sinner show him more clearly than anything else his desperate need *for reconciliation with God in and through reconciliation with his brother.* [24]

The contemporary Christian, in Merton's view, should be a contemplative in a world of action.

Several areas Merton pioneered hold great promise for the future. Much work remains to be done on the need for contemplation in today's world, the ecumenics of spirituality, the Marxist-Christian dialogue, and the importance of the inner man. In all these areas Merton demonstrated to all, Protestant and Catholic alike, that true mysticism and a renewed monasticism result in a spirituality that is both contemplative and active, for action finds its source in the deep wellsprings of contemplation.

It is difficult to assess the importance of a man like Thomas Merton. Ten years after his death, his work is coming into greater prominence than ever before, both in the academic world and in the life and work of the Church at large. Beyond this, however, was Thomas Merton the man, who lived as a monk at the Abbey of Gethsemani and there 'achieved his identity as a man, a monk, a priest, a man of God, a poet, and a prophet'.[25] Basil De Pinto, writing in memory of Merton, eloquently states that his spirit continues to live: 'Genius is rare, holiness even rarer, but when they make their appearance as they unquestionably did in Merton, they have the power to pass beyond the last frontier; death itself can lay no claim on them.'[26]

1. *Breakthrough to Peace*, p. 10. [Bibliographic information is contained in the bibliography of Merton's works, which are cited here by title alone.] See pp. 347-52.

2. . The difficulties are related by Edward Rice in *The Man in the Sycamore Tree: The Good Times and Hard Life of Thomas Merton* (Garden City: Doubleday, 1970) pp. 81, 86 and by Gordon Zahn in 'The Peacemaker', *Continuum* 7 (1969) 268.

3. Quoted by James P. Shannon, 'Thomas Merton's New Mexico', *New Mexico* 49 (May-June 1971) 21.

4. Ibid., p. 19.

5. Quoted by Anne Saword *ocso*, 'A Tribute to Thomas Merton', *Cistercian Studies* 3 (1968), 267; rpt. as 'A Nun's Tribute' in Brother Patrick Hart, ed., *Thomas Merton/Monk: A Monastic Tribute*, p. 198. Edward McCorkell, 'Towards Conclusions: A Pre-position Paper', in M. Basil Pennington *ocso*, ed., *The Cistercian Spirit: A Symposium in Honor of Thomas Merton*, Cistercian Studies Series 3 (Spencer, Mass.: Cistercian Publications, 1970) p. 257, states that 'according to his abbot [Merton] devoted about two hours a day to writing....'

6. Basil De Pinto *osb*, 'In Memoriam: Thomas Merton, 1915-1968' in *The Cistercian Spirit: A Symposium*, p. vii.

7. *New Seeds of Contemplation*, p. 4.

8. *The Living Bread*, pp. xii-xiii.

9. *The True Solitude: Selections from the Writings of Thomas Merton*, ed. Dean Walley (Kansas City, Mo.: Hallmark, 1969) p. 48.

10. Saword, 'A Tribute', p. 270; rpt. in *Thomas Merton/Monk*, p. 202.

11. Quoted by Dennis Quentin McInerny, 'Thomas Merton and Society: A Study of the Man and His Thought Against the Background of Contemporary American Culture', Dissertation, University of Minnesota 1969, p. 5.

12. *The True Solitude*, p. 61.

13. Quoted by John Eudes Bamberger OCSO, 'The Cistercian', *Continuum* 7 (1969) 240; rpt. in Hart, *Thomas Merton/Monk*, p. 56.

14. See John Howard Griffin and Thomas Merton, *A Hidden Wholeness: The Visual World of Thomas Merton* (Boston: Houghton Mifflin, 1970). On p. 1 Griffin comments: 'His religious life formed a single arc. From the beginning he sought to lose himself in God and the silence of Trappist contemplative life. Through all the intrusions of his celebrity as a writer and prophetic figure, that initial religious passion remained paramount and growing. At the end of his life he was in search of deeper silence and solitude and more perfect contemplation.'

15. Ibid., p. 101. See James F. Andrews, 'Was Merton a Critic of Renewal?' *National Catholic Reporter* 6 (February 11, 1970) Lenten Supplement, 13.

16. Ibid., p. 14, Andrews points out that 'Merton's problem with *aggiornamento* was not change itself but with the basic orientation of the people involved: they too often assume cultural standards and fads rather than distancing themselves from them.' In his *Spiritual Direction and Meditation*, p. 85, Merton stated that 'tradition is the *renewal*, in each Christian generation and society, of the experiential knowledge of the mysteries of the faith.'

17. See John J. Higgins SJ, *Merton's Theology of Prayer*, pp. xv-xvii.

18. *Breakthrough to Peace*, p. 14.

19. For an indication of the wide scope of Merton's Influence see the Merton memorial issue of *Continuum* 7 (1969) 226-332; Colman McCarthy, 'Thomas Merton', *The Critic* 31 (July-August 1973) 35-39; Jack Wintz *ofm*, 'Thomas Merton Lives!' *St Anthony Messenger* 82 No 3 (1974) 18-27) and Hart, ed., *Thomas Merton/Monk*.

20. James Thomas Baker, 'Thomas Merton: The Spiritual and Social Philosophy of Union', Dissertation, Florida State University 1968. Baker, a Southern Baptist, sent a copy of this dissertation to Merton for correction and approval. Found by Baker after Merton's death with his corrections and notations carefully written in the margins, it was revised and published as *Thomas Merton Social Critic* (Lexington: University Press of Kentucky, 1971). See also E. Glenn Hinson, 'Merton's Many Faces', *Religion in Life* 42 (1973) 153-67. Hinson is on the faculty of the Southern Baptist Theological Seminary in Louisville and was a frequent visitor to both the monastery and the hermitage.

21. Paul Tillich, *Theology of Culture*, ed. Robert C. Kimbell (1959; rpt. New York: Oxford Galaxy, 1964) p. 187.

22. See ibid., pp. 188-99 for a discussion of mysticism in religion. See also Rudolf Otto, *The Idea of the Holy*, trans. John W. Harvey (1923; rpt. New York: Oxford Galaxy, 1958).

23. This is seen most vividly in Merton's writings on the racial problem in the United States. See Martin E. Marty, 'To: Thomas Merton. Re: Your Prophecy', *National Catholic Reporter* 3 (August 30, 1967) 6.

24. *The Climate of Monastic Prayer*, pp. 146-7.

25. John Eudes Bamberger OCSO, 'A Homily', *Continuum* 7 (1969) 226.

26. De Pinto, 'In Memoriam: Thomas Merton, 1915-1968', in Pennington, ed., *The Cistercian Spirit*, p. ix.

I

MERTON'S HOLY WORLDLINESS: AN APPRAISAL

CONTEMPORARY American society can be characterized as a society of problems. Indeed Merton says that 'in our age everything has to be a "problem". Ours is a time of anxiety because we have willed it to be so. Our anxiety is not imposed upon us by force from the outside. We impose it on our world and upon one another from within ourselves.'[1] Man is not a victim of outside forces which determine his behavior; rather, man can determine his own future and create whatever lifestyle he chooses. The root of man's problem, in Merton's view, is that 'our mentality is involved in deep illusions, most of all about itself'.[2] He writes:

> The problem as I see it is no longer merely political or economic or legal or what have you (it never was merely that). It is a spiritual and psychological problem of a society which has developed too fast and too far for the psychic capacities of its members, who can no longer cope with their inner hostilities and destructiveness. They can no longer really manage their lives in a fully reasonable and human way—only by resort to extreme and possibly destructive maneuvers. A nuclear arms race. A race to get on the moon. A stupid war in Asia that cannot be won by either side. An affluent economy depending on built-in obsolescence and the ever increasing consumption of more goodies than anyone can comfortably consume. A bored, ambivalent over-stimulation of violence and sex. We are living in a society which for all its unquestionable advantages and all its fantastic ingenuity just does not seem to be able to provide people with lives that are fully human and fully real.[3]

These illusions have alienated man from himself, from his fellowmen, and from God. This 'lack of interest in the desperate fate of man,' says Merton, 'is a sign of culpable insensitivity, a deplorable incapacity to love! It cannot in any sense claim to be Christian. It is not even genuinely human.'[4]

This is not to say that there is not a great deal of activism aimed at solving the various social problems of mankind; but 'action is not governed by moral reason but by political expedience and the demands of technology.'[5] The choices that are made 'have nothing to do with reasoned moral action, even though they may appeal to apparent moral values.'[6] What really counts in contemporary society is big business, big government, and power politics. Man's optimistic claims to a better life ring hollow, for personal meaning in life eludes him:

> We live at the precise moment when the exorbitant optimism of the materialist world has plunged into spiritual ruin. We find ourselves living in a society of men who have discovered their own nonentity where they least expected to—in the midst of power and technological achievement. The result is an agony of ambivalence in which each man is forced to project upon his neighbors the burden of self-hatred which is too great to be tolerated by his own soul.[7]

And so man creates still more illusions to protect himself from the reality within his own soul—a reality which he cannot face.

Contemplation is Merton's answer to modern man's problem. By this he does not mean a withdrawal from the world, history, society, and problems but something much more than going off into the woods by oneself and thinking. In fact, he avers that 'a purely mental life may be destructive if it leads us to substitute thought for life and ideas for actions.'[8] He cautions against exercising discretion to a point where nothing at all gets done.[9]

'What we really ought to do,' he writes, 'is what the first monks did: go off somewhere into the wilderness. . .and see how long and how well we can stand it—either with or without companions—and then go on to build upon a foundation of experience.'[10] The purpose is twofold: to discover self and to develop an understanding of one's relationship to society and the world. In contemplation one responds to reality.[11] At a new level of awareness, one experiences 'the intuitive perception of life in its Source',[12] which in turn provides a new perspective on the world. As Merton puts it: 'In order to understand even the trivial events of our own lives, we need to *create a religious perspective* in which to view everything that happens.'[13] The contemplative views himself, his society, and the world as they really are—united together in God.

A certain degree of solitude and silence are basic to contemplation. Merton was of the opinion that silence is a basic human need for the fulfillment of personhood.[14] Existence, he says, is noisy; being is silent.[15] If we are to make distinctions clearly we must be able to separate ourselves from the hustle and bustle of modern life. A certain distance, or detachment, permits objectivity; 'by renouncing the world we conquer the world, rise above its multiplicity and recapitulate it in the simplicity of a love which finds all things in God'.[16]

Merton felt strongly that 'in [our contemporary] situation it is no longer permissible for Christians seriously and honestly to devote themselves to a spirituality of evasion, a cult of other-worldiness that refuses to take account of the *inescapable implication of all men* in the problems and responsibilities of the nuclear age'.[17] All 'men must collaborate sincerely in solving their difficulties. This is a basic Christian obligation.'[18]

The spiritual life is both contemplative and active. One looks first within himself. Illusions must be stripped away until ultimate reality is found in God. One's life thus becomes centered in the Center of being and one develops a new consciousness of himself and of God and a new and unique perspective on the world. 'Without the deep root of wisdom and contemplation,' Merton believed 'Christian action would have no meaning and purpose.'[19]

Merton proposes a kind of 'holy worldliness'.[20] Christianity involves being *in* the world but not being *of* the world. One's life is centered in the reality of God and not in the illusions of the world, yet at the same time one's love is extended to the world in action. Merton recommended meditation on *both* the Passion of Christ and the extermination camps of Dachau and Auschwitz if we are to enter fully into the experience of Christianity in our time.[21] If the extermination camps are to have any meaning, the Christian must first of all meditate on the Incarnation of God in Christ.

> If I allow the Holy Spirit to work in me, if I allow Christ to use my heart in order to love my brother with it, I will soon find that Christ loving in me and through me has brought to light Christ in my brother. And I will find that the love of Christ in my brother, loving me in return, has drawn forth the image and the reality of Christ in my own soul.[22]

For Merton, the contemplative life is basic to Christian life and action and it is imperative for modern man as he faces the problems of living in the latter half of the twentieth century.

The question that Merton felt must be faced today is: 'Is the contemplative life finished?'[23] There are, of course, those who say that there is no place today for monks, hermits, and contemplatives.[24] Ours is a time of action, secularism, and scientific discovery. And so, says Merton: '"Contemplative" is a bad word. . .we belong to a Christianity so deeply implicated in a society which has outlived its spiritual vitality'.[25] Contemplation is finished for anyone who defines contemplation as withdrawal from the twentieth-century world into a twelfth-century church. At the same time we are experiencing a rebirth of interest in the contemplative life today. New ventures in monastic and communal life are springing up, and there seems to be a turning inward among many young people.[26] Here again the contemplative life may be finished, for much of the interest in contemplation today is undisciplined and theologically unsound.[27] There is the additional possibility that, like other religious fads that come and to, this too shall pass.

One of the changes of our changing time, Merton makes it clear, involves monastic life, but 'in its essentials—solitude, poverty, obedience, silence, humility, manual labor, prayer and contemplation—monastic spirituality does not change'.[28] This list in itself would eliminate many who would call themselves contemplative; a life directed toward contemplation is never easy.

To isolate any one factor as the chief hallmark of the contemplative life is difficult. Yet Merton, in his later writings, spoke explicity of one element of contemplation that he felt had increasing significance for today: sacrifice of security. In Merton's words it is: '*sacrificing the psychological stability we have built on foundations that we do not dare to examine.*'[29] At first glance such a sacrifice may seem excessive and, indeed, almost impossible. Careful consideration will reveal, however, that the sacrifice of security is basic to contemplation, for contemplation is primarily concerned with stripping away all illusion and finding reality in God. Modern man's security is a false security, for it is based on nuclear weapons, material possessions, power politics, technology, and even religion. Real security can be found only in God, and so the false security of the world must be renounced. To become secure, one must first experience insecurity.[30]

As a monk, Merton could be critical of the illusions surrounding modern secular man. But his criticism went beyond the secular world to include the so-called religious world. Many monastic foundations seemed to Merton false havens of security whose structures needed to be shaken radically and changed.[31] Ideally such changes come from within. But in the modern world such changes often come from without, from the powerful political and military structures that determine so much of how modern life is lived. In his last talk at Bangkok, just hours before his death, Merton referred specifically to the political situation in Tibet, where the communists have eliminated all monastic structures and institutions.[32] 'You cannot rely on structures,' he warned. 'The time for relying on structures has disappeared.'[33]

Merton related this idea to the Zen question: 'Where do you go from the top of a thirty-foot pole?'[34] When all structures and institutions, all forms of security and all illusions have been removed, where do we turn? Replies Merton: 'What is essential in the monastic life is not necessarily embedded in buildings, is not embedded in clothing, is not necessarily embedded even in a rule. It is somewhere along the line of something deeper than a rule. It is concerned with this business of total inner transformation.'[35] If structures are taken away, how will monasticism survive? Merton's answer:

> The essential thing. . .is the formation of spiritual masters who can bring [a belief in freedom and transcendence] out in the hearts of people who are as yet unformed. Wherever you have somebody capable of giving some kind of direction and instruction to a small group attempting to do this thing, attempting to love and serve God and reach union with him, you are bound to have some kind of monasticism. This kind of monasticism cannot be extinguished. It is imperishable. It represents an instinct of the human heart, and it represents a charism given by God to man. It cannot be rooted out, because it does not depend upon man. It does not depend on cultural factors, and it does not depend on sociological or psychological factors. It is something much deeper.[36]

We can see the importance of Merton's understanding of monasticism as *being* rather than *doing*. He views prayer as one's *orientation* toward God, and the 'dark night of the soul'— what God is *not*—becomes charged with meaning for the future. True security lies within, and from it is formed the union of contemplation and action.

While Merton writes as a monk within a monastic

framework, what he has to say concerning contemplation and the spiritual life applies to other religious institutions as well. He is saying that the Christian life can be lived wherever there is a small group of believers seeking communion with each other and union with God. At the center of Merton's spirituality lies the belief that being takes precedence over doing, that responsible action is always preceded by a right relationship with God, oneself, and others which begins within one's own innermost being.

The spiritual life for Merton is a now, firmly rooted in the past, which looks toward the future. It is as easy to cling to the past and retreat from the insecurities of the future as it is to become attached to each futuristic fad and cut oneself off from one's spiritual roots. According to Merton, contemplation is for today. Action is for today. The spiritual life is to be lived today, 'for only in the present can man come in full contact with the truth willed for him and in him by God'.[37] With his feet planted deep in the tradition of the desert fathers and his eyes fixed upon the secular world of tomorrow, Merton espouses a spirituality of contemplation and action for today.

A Protestant Appraisal of Contemplation and Action

A BIBLICAL VIEW

A Protestant appreciation of Merton's contemplation-and-action must necessarily begin with the Bible, for here Protestantism has its foundation. Merton was not a biblical scholar or exegete. His training was in literature, theology, philosophy, and church history, and his approach reflects this background. Yet this does not mean that Merton was not biblical nor does it imply that he was not familiar with the biblical view of contemplation and action.[38] As a monk, he approached the Bible more devotionally than exegetically. He appreciated biblical scholarship, yet he was well aware of its dangers:

> Curiously, the most serious religious people, or the most concerned scholars, those who constantly read the Bible as a matter of professional or pious duty, can often manage to evade a radically involved dialogue with the book they are questioning. In fact (we know it too well!) there is such a thing as studying the isolated words and other details

with such intense application that one loses all interest in
their meaning.

We are fortunately living in an age of theological
ferment and of biblical renewal. All of us—scholars,
simple believers or mere interested readers—stand in
immense debt to the specialists who have done so much to
really open the Bible to us. Nevertheless, in all the
thousands of pages of Biblical scholarship that have been
printed in the last hundred years we must admit...that a
high proportion of it is an arid, exhausting desert of futile
detail which wearies the mind by distracting it from the
meaning of the Bible....

Good Biblical scholarship is essential for a serious
understanding of the Bible, but this scientific itch for arid
and pointless investigations which throw no new light on
anything whatever has deadened our sensitivity to the
existential reality of Biblical experience. [39]

These are the words of someone who is poetic in temperament
and not given to long hours of detailed study of ancient
manuscripts. Many biblical scholars might have similar feelings
toward Merton's interest in monasticism, which they would
consider an arid subject. In spite of his obvious personal bias,
Merton is making an important point: biblical scholarship must
never allow itself to become separated from the meaning and
message of the Bible.

Merton also warns against the dangers of approaching the
Bible secondhand. Too often, he says, we are told 'what the
Bible demands of us before the Bible itself has a chance to
make known its own claims'. [40] He says:

We should not consider ourselves obliged to accept *all*
official or sectarian claims uncritically. As a matter of fact,
we should be courageously ready to distinguish between
the claims which believers make for the Bible and the
perhaps even greater claims they make for *themselves*
because of the Bible. [41]

Merton's approach to the Bible is not unlike that of many
Protestants who understand the Bible as a basic authority which
speaks for itself. [42]

To understand the interplay of contemplation and action in
the Bible, we must distinguish between the point of view of the
ancient Hebrews and of the New Testament Christians. To
begin, we must emphasize that mysticism is alien to the Old

Testament—as W. R. Inge points out:

> In the first place, the religion of Israel, passing from what
> has been called Henotheism—the worship of a national
> God—to true Monotheism, always maintained a rigid
> notion of individuality, both human and Divine. Even
> prophecy, which is mystical in its essence, was in the early
> period conceived as unmystically as possible. Balaam is
> merely a mouth-piece of God; his message is external to
> his personality, which remains antagonistic to it. And,
> secondly, the Jewish doctrine of ideas was different from
> the Platonic. The Jew believed that the world, and the
> whole course of history, existed from all eternity in the
> mind of God, but as an unrealised purpose, which was
> actualized by degrees as the scroll of events was unfurled.
> There was no notion that the visible was in any way
> inferior to the invisible, or lacking in reality....Moreover,
> the Jew had little sense of the Divine *in* nature: it was the
> power of God *over* nature which he was jealous to
> maintain. [43]

In the Old Testament man's sinfulness was contrasted to
God's holiness, and the relationship between God and man took
the form of a covenant. 'The basic theme of the Old Testament
is God's movement in history. Destiny and doom are epitomized
in the giving and the breaking of the covenant.' [44] The
contemplatives were the prophets, and as prophets they were
vitally active. Rabbi Abraham Heschel contrasts their role with
the mystics':

> Unlike the mystic experience, the significance of prophecy
> lay not in those who perceived it but in those to whom the
> word was to be conveyed....The purpose was not in the
> perception of the voice but in bringing it to bear upon the
> reality of the people's life. Consequently, the substance of
> prophecy was in the content rather than in the act, and
> revelation was a prelude to action. [45]

According to Merton 'the whole idea of covenant, dialog,
reciprocity, mutual respect—and above all the idea that God
respects man's liberty, dignity, and rights—is brought out by
giving the exchange a frankly human character.' [46] The
exchange between God and Moses is not a mystical experience
but a conversation. God speaks and Moses replies. Moses
brings God's word to the Hebrew people and they respond by

acting. Merton emphasizes that 'the message of the Bible is above all a message preached to the poor, the burdened, the oppressed, the underprivileged.'[47] The prophets received God's word, which demanded concrete action in human society. Time and time again the overriding message is that of judgment; a call is extended for repentance and a return to the ways of God. This is especially significant since the Hebrew people were oppressed and in bondage during much of their history.

Of all the Old Testament books the Psalms and the wisdom literature have appealed most to mystics, and Merton is no exception. As a monk he recited the entire Psalter each week, and he wrote at least two books on the Psalms.[48] They are, he maintained 'the songs of men who *knew who God was*'.[49] Of the wisdom literature, the *Song of Songs* has been most popular among mystics, who have interpreted it allegorically as the mystical marriage between God and man.[50] In *The New Man*, first published in 1962, Merton attempted by an allegory of the first Adam in the Garden of Eden and the second Adam in the person of Christ, to show how the Fall brought about a separation between contemplation and action and how this breach was healed in the person of Christ.[51] Merton's interpretation is certainly mystical and largely based upon Augustine's interpretation of the fall. Yet in such later works as *Life and Holiness* and *Opening the Bible*, his approach was more prophetic.[52]

In the Gospels contemplation and action are brought together in the life of Jesus. He was not a mystic who spent his time in the desert in contemplation, ignoring the problems in the world around him, yet he spent much time alone in the wilderness fasting and praying. These periods of solitude and prayer were especially significant for Jesus prior to times of crisis, as his entry into Jerusalem and his arrest, trial, and crucifixion.

Jesus' contemplation was always coupled with compelling action. He spoke of the Kingdom of Heaven as being within and then as being in the midst of men with all their problems and sin. Jesus himself acted and he constantly emphasized repentance and a change in one's way of living as a necessary part of salvation.[53] His active ministry was in the tradition of the Old Testament prophets, as Georgia Harkness points out when she says that Jesus 'is best viewed, not as a mystic, but as a prophet of Israel and a rabbinical teacher with a marvelously fresh and life-giving outlook on the nature of both God and man'.[54]

The most problematic of Jesus' teachings on contemplation and action is the story of Mary and Martha.[55] Mary sat at

Jesus' feet listening to his teaching while Martha was busy preparing the meal. The symbolism here is obvious: Mary represents the contemplative and Martha represents the active. On this passage Merton comments:

> Traditionally this has been explained by the fathers of the Church, in a way that we all know, to justify a certain renunciation of good, productive, healthy social activity in order to simply listen to the words of Christ, to be silent and listen to God. Of course this really doesn't solve any problems, yet the use of this text as a justification of the contemplative life does rest on a solid psychological basis, on a basis of real experience which can be verified in the lives of those who have tried to put it into practice and know what it means.
>
> When someone has an authentic call to the contemplative life or to the monastic life, that call can be understood in terms of this gospel text and experienced in the way that is suggested by it. Our vocation can be understood as the resolution of a conflict which is expressed in this story, a conflict in ourselves. Now the important thing is that the conflict is *in ourselves* rather than projected outward into *institutions*. It is one thing to experience in our own lives the difference between the action of Martha and the listening of Mary—but quite another to 'prove' that Trappists are 'better' than Dominicans.[56]

In Merton's view this conflict is not between contemplation and action as such: it is an expression of our own inner preferences. 'Where the conflict resolves itself,' says Merton, 'is in our own hearts as individual persons or small groups, called to this particular life of quiet, of *freedom to listen* to the Word of God in our hearts.'[57]

A careful examination of the text reveals that the problem with Martha was not action in itself but her distraction and anxiety. It implies that Martha's action was a sign of her inner anxiety. Jesus does not condemn action nor does he hold contemplation to be superior to action. He does, however, emphasize that action must be an outgrowth of one's inner relationship with God.[58] For Jesus contemplation and action are dynamically related and cannot be separated. Undoubtedly Merton appreciated this in his reading of the Bible, for his own life was a rare combination of contemplation and action.

The union of contemplation and action is also found in the life of St Paul, for he was not only converted to Christianity by a mystic vision but he also spent time in the desert where he was taught through a revelation of Jesus Christ.[59] Following his conversion, Paul withdrew into the desert to prepare himself for his vocation. Georgia Harkness expands upon this withdrawal:

> Following the traumatic upsurge of long-suppressed emotions which resulted in Paul's conversion, there is a period of withdrawal into Arabia. Like Jesus in the wilderness after his baptism, Paul needed to think through what had occurred, search out God's leading, and gather spiritual energy for what might lie before him. Then came years of service at Antioch as a subordinate to Barnabas, a service of teaching that was useful but not much acclaimed, probably restrictive and humbling to Paul's restive spirit. In the language of mysticism this was a time of purgation. Only after the call to missionary service does Saul become Paul and assume real leadership. Then, filled with the Holy Spirit, he spoke boldly for his faith.[60]

To compare Paul and Merton is irresistible, for Merton entered the monastery following his conversion, spent a number of years studying for the priesthood, served as a teacher of novices, and often encountered restrictions upon his restless spirit. Only after these many years of preparation was he allowed to become a hermit, a vocation to which he felt called soon after entering the monastery.

Both Jesus and Paul withdrew apart from society for a time after their baptism and conversion. Perhaps today new converts should take this time to reflect on what has happened to them and what this new presence of God means for them as persons in the world. New seeds, once planted, need time to germinate, take root, and grow into tender young shoots before they are ready to develop to maturity and bring forth fruit. The fruits of contemplation cannot reach maturity without time given to contemplation, in some cases, many years' time.

Contemplation served Paul as a preparation for a life of action which included extensive missionary travels and theological dispute. As the first great theologian, Paul made an important contribution to mystical thought in emphasizing being-in-Christ rather than being-in-God. In Paul's thinking, 'the transcendent God of Hebrew faith is still the high and holy one, though no longer the God of Israel only, for in Christ those who were far off have now been brought near.'[61] Paul added the dimension of the Incarnation.[62] Georgia Harkness comments at length on what she refers to as Paul's Christ-mysticism:

Christ is the incarnate Lord, who had lived, died, risen again, and returned to the Father, yet as Spirit still lives eternally. To be in Christ, then, is to live a transformed life in faith, hope and love through the enabling grace of this incarnate, indwelling Christ. Paul states it perfectly in the cryptic words, 'I am crucified with Christ: nevertheless I live; yet not I, but Christ liveth in me' (Gal 2:20). A mystery? Yes. But an actuality in Paul's life, and in that of many others.[63]

For Paul the authentic, full Christian life was both contemplative and active.

Throughout the Bible, then, a mixed life of contemplation and action is the norm. The Old Testament prophets spoke God's word in order to call the Hebrew people to repentance. The life of Jesus and his teachings exemplified and emphasized action flowing from one's relationship to God. Paul stressed the incarnate Christ present among us on both a contemplative inner level and an active outer level. Thomas Merton's uniting of contemplation and action is in accord with the biblical witness.

PROTESTANT SUSPICION OF MYSTICISM

What is the religious experience of mysticism? For Merton the contemplative experience is mystical and therefore very difficult to define. Even so classic a definition as that of W. R. Inge, *'the attempt to realise, in thought and feeling, the immanence of the temporal in the eternal, and of the eternal in the temporal'*[64] is extremely vague, and it raises almost as many questions as it seeks to answer. These questions, with certain historical factors, have aroused among many Protestants a strong suspicion of mysticism from the very beginning of the Reformation to the present day.

It must be kept in mind that the Reformers reacted against what were considered excesses within the Catholic Church. Luther's ninety-five theses, which sparked the Reformation, were largely concerned with the question of indulgences which involved a theology of salvation in which man took an active role. Luther's understanding of salvation was radically different:

For Luther, in fact, the assertion of God's unique sanctity involves necessarily the denial of any participated sanctity. The affirmation of Christ as the only Savior of men

> involves the denial of any active participation on the part
> of any creature other than Christ in the salvation of the
> human race, and especially the denial of any active part
> played by any man in the accomplishment of his own
> personal salvation. Finally, the recognition of faith as the
> unique source of justification necessitates the rejection of
> works.[65]

To Luther mystics often seemed to be attempting to gain their
salvation through works. His failure to differentiate between
Catholic ascetic theology and mystical theology further clouded
the issue, for in actual fact the mystic often took a passive role
in his union with God.

Of crucial importance to both Protestants and Catholics is the
issue of authority. The great mystics of the Catholic Church
were for the most part subject to ecclesiastical approval or at
least toleration. They operated within the structure of the
Church and most were members of religious orders. Mystic
excesses were kept in check by the authority and traditions of
the Church. By the Protestants, however, the entire structure of
authority within the Catholic Church was called into question.

Within Protestantism itself the issue of authority was
resolved by the concept of *sola scriptura*—scripture alone was
considered authoritative. The mystics, however, placed the locus
of authority chiefly in personal experience. This caused not only
theological but social and political difficulties.[66]

Franklin H. Littell points out that 'Luther wrestled against
the spirit of "inspirationalism" and "enthusiasm" (*Schwärm-
geisterei*) among the radical reformers. He feared the
consequences of their subjectivism; when they asserted an
infallible inner authority he declared that the hidden God is
revealed only in the objective word and not by vision.'[67]
Luther's criticism flared into open antagonism during the
Peasant Revolts of 1524-1525 and he 'thought that the revolt
was the logical outcome of the confused and excited prophetism
with which he had earlier contended'.[68] In 1534-1535 the tragic
Münster rebellion convinced most Protestants that the radicals,
many of whom claimed mystic visions, were heretical,
schismatic, and downright dangerous.[69] As a result, Protestant
opinion turned more and more against the radical reformers,
and against mysticism.

The Reformation was a revolution; the Protestants were
struggling for an identity separate from Rome and attempting to
preserve some unity and cohesion within their own ranks. Anything that tended toward Catholicism or seemed excessive to the

point that it threatened Protestantism was automatically suspect. Mysticism in its most visible forms—Catholic monasticism and Anabaptist radicalism—fit squarely into both categories.

Perhaps even more threatening was the relationship between contemplation and action manifested among the radical reformers. Luther and the other major reformers soon discovered that this particular kind of mystical spirituality has dangerous social and political implications. Unlike Catholics, Protestants lacked any built-in ecclesiastical structure, such as monasticism, to hold mystics and radicals in check. Any denial of the authority of Scripture soon gave way to a denial of the necessity of a visible church structure, which in turn led to the founding of autonomous city-states under radical control. When the leaders of some of these city-states justified excesses on the basis of the inner light of God, the reformers felt that intervention, armed if necessary, was entirely justified. These radical reformers demonstrated, in a negative manner, the importance of a proper relationship between contemplation and action.[70] Unlike them, Merton always understood the mystical experience within the context of the Christian community of believers, the Church, and daily Scripture reading formed a vital part of his contemplative life.

Mysticism also poses a number of theological problems to most Protestants. Donald G. Bloesch sums up this Protestant attitude:

> Evangelical theologians have always sought to distinguish faith from mystical religion. Even where the mystical element in Christian spirituality is acknowledged, they have taken pains to point out that Christianity is not mysticism. John Wesley wrote that 'all the other enemies of Christianity are triflers: The mystics are the most dangerous of its enemies. They stab it in the vitals.' In the words of Benjamin Warfield: 'We may be mystics, or we may be Christians. We cannot be both. And the pretension of being both usually merely veils a defection from Christianity.' Among other evangelically oriented scholars who have taken a forthright stand against mysticism are Karl Barth, Anders Nygren, Reinhold Niebuhr, Emil Brunner and Friedrich Heiler.[71] Protestantism has produced very few mystics, and most of these have been considered to be outside the mainstream of general Protestant Christianity.[72]

Bloesch lists nine points on which Protestants and mystics

may differ; briefly enumerated these are:

1. The foundation of faith is an objective historical revelation....The foundational criterion in mysticism is religious experience.
2. Faith is a gift of God whereas mystical rapture is to some degree a work of man.
3. Faith speaks of the descent of God to man, while the concern in mysticism is man rising to God.
4. Faith is rational as well as experiential....Mystical experience, on the other hand, is ineffable or inexplicable.
5. Faith is based on an exclusive message; mystical religion, on the other hand, is almost always syncretistic.
6. Whereas faith is dualistic and personalistic, mystical religion is monistic and pantheistic.
7. Mysticism can take the form of pantheism, in which God and the world are depicted as mutually dependent rather than identical.
8. Whereas the mystic way leads from purgation to illumination and finally to union, the way of faith consists in daily repentance under the cross on the basis of a prior union with Christ through his Spirit.
9. The soul of faith is supplication, heartfelt petition to a personal God. Mystical prayer, on the other hand, consists in meditation and contemplation upon the being of God. [73]

Each of these points could become a difficulty in a Protestant appraisal of Merton. I am of the opinion, however, that Merton does not follow a rigid mystical position on most of these and that a thorough examination of his writings would dispel most Protestant apprehensions. [74] Additional questions can be raised as to the validity of these nine points, especially in the sharp divisions between mystical religion and the so-called way of faith. Three points do present definite difficulties for Protestants, particularly those of an evangelical orientation. These are: the foundational criterion in mysticism is religious experience; mysticism is almost always syncretistic; and mystical religion is monistic and pantheistic. The last two points, syncretism, monism and pantheism, will be discussed under 'The Ecumenics of Spirituality', so we need only concentrate here on the first.

The basic, perhaps the most crucial, point of conflict between Protestants and mystics centers in the area of

authority. Because one's theology has a vital influence upon
one's social ethics, it is crucial to determine the authority from
which one's theology derives. Evanglical Protestantism has
always affirmed that faith is based upon the objective historical
revelation of God in Jesus Christ witnessed in the Scriptures.
Revelation is in Jesus Christ and in him alone. This is not
always so in mysticism, as Sidney Spencer explains:

> In mystical experience there is implicit a claim to
> immediate revelation. Philo interpreted the experience of
> the prophets on the basis of mental ecstasy; and whether
> or not his interpretation is justified in its details, it rests
> upon a certain essential insight. The experience of the
> great leaders of religion, whose teaching is enshrined in
> the Scriptures, is at least comparable to that of the
> mystics. Religious authority, in other words, rests in the
> last resort on personal insight and experience. In so far as
> authority is externalized and identified with the written
> words of Scripture or the dogma of the Church, while it
> may be accepted by the mystic, there is always the
> possibility of conflict between its dictates and his inner
> vision. For the mystic, whatever his professed creed, final
> authority lies in his own experience.[75]

Spencer goes on to point out that 'for the mystics the essential
feature of religion is its inner quality. Doctrines, observances,
institutions are secondary, and if unduly stressed, they may
become a positive hindrance to the life of the spirit.'[76] The
mystic is always in potential conflict with the religious
orthodoxies of his day.

A withdrawal from the cares of the world and the fellowship
of the Church might be justified on the basis of one's own inner
light, but Merton would not have considered this authentic
mysticism for, in his words: 'The highest vocation in the
Kingdom of God is that of sharing one's contemplation with
others and bringing other men to the experimental knowledge of
God that is given to those who love Him perfectly'.[77]

Merton was aware of the potential conflict,[78] but he was
very careful to express his loyalty to the Church and to the
Cistercian Order, and his mystical statements were always sub-
stantiated by liberal quotations from the great mystics of the
past and from renowned theologians of the Church. A gradual
shift in emphasis occurs in Merton's writings, however. In *The
Ascent to Truth*, written in 1951, he emphasizes what he calls
the dangers of false mysticism:

In the abstract, false mysticism can fall under two characteristic headings. Both of these situate the private mystical experience in an incorrect relation to the Truth which God has revealed publicly to the Church. One of these incorrect definitions says that the mystic has no need whatever of any conceptual knowledge of God, revealed or otherwise....

The second kind of false mysticism is much more common: it claims to arrive at special supernatural knowledge by means other than those normally ordained by God....The most common illusion of well-meaning religious souls is to imagine that they hear heavenly voices, see visions, fall into ecstasies and swoon away with rapture when in actual fact they are fabricating these experiences by the work of their own imagination.[79]

He concludes a lengthy discussion of false mysticism with these signs:

Clearly, a prominent place among them must be assigned to a contumacious rejection of reason, of philosophy, of theological truth, and of the dogmatic authority of the teaching of the Church.[80]

By Merton's definition, true mysticism does not reject the authority of the Church or the objective and historical revelation of God in Jesus Christ.

In his later writings Merton never rejects this position, but he does not give it the same emphasis he had in earlier works. This is particularly true in his writings on Zen. In *Zen and the Birds of Appetite*, published in 1968, he writes:

We repeat: Zen explains nothing. It just sees. Sees what? Not an Absolute Object but Absolute Seeing.

Though this may seem very remote from Christianity, which is definitely a message, we must nevertheless remember the importance of *direct experience* in the Bible. All forms of 'knowing', especially in the religious sphere, and essentially where God is concerned, are valid in proportion as they are a matter of experience and of intimate contact.[81]

He continues by relating this emphasis upon direct experience to the cross of Christ:

Here it is essential to remember that for a Christian 'the word of the Cross' is nothing theoretical, but a stark and existential experience of union with Christ in His death in order to share in His resurrection. To fully 'hear' and 'receive' the word of the Cross means much more than simple assent to the dogmatic proposition that Christ died for our sins. It means to be 'nailed to the Cross with Christ' so that the ego-self is no longer the principle of our deepest actions, which now proceed from Christ living in us. 'I live, now not I, but Christ lives in me.' (Gal 2:19-20; see also Romans 8:5-17) To receive the word of the Cross means the acceptance of a complete self-emptying, a *Kenosis*, in union with the self-emptying of Christ's 'obedience unto death.' (Phil 2:5-11) It is essential to true Christianity that this experience of the Cross and of self-emptying be central in the life of the Christian so that he may fully receive the Holy Spirit and know (again by experience) all the riches of God in and through Christ. (John 14:16-17; 15:26-27; 16:7-15).[82]

Experience, for Merton, is not divorced from theology, for theology 'must be theology as experienced in Christian contemplation, not the speculative theology of textbooks and disputations'.[83]

Merton was well aware that an emphasis upon experience can be dangerous. In the foreword to William Johnston's *The Mysticism of the Cloud of Unknowing: A Modern Interpretation,* he writes:

Even when properly understood, and treated with perfect orthodoxy—as in this present book—mysticism tends to inspire apprehension even in religious minds. Why? Because the mystic must surrender to a power of love that is greater than human and advance toward God in a darkness that goes beyond the light of reason and human conceptual knowledge.[84]

We must always keep it in mind that Merton was thoroughly grounded in theology and the teachings of the Church and so he was less prone to error than are many so-called mystics who have cut all ecclesiastical ties. Merton's monastic vocation also helped him to blend his mysticism with traditional theology and doctrine. Probably most significant is Merton's willingness to admit the dangers inherent in mysticism and thus to be constantly on his guard against them.

At the point of experience Merton's mysticism and his expressions of social concern are directly related. He observed that Christians who supported war and racism were often perfectly orthodox and theologically correct in their thinking,[85] but many of them had had no kind of contemplative or mystical experience whatsoever. He stressed experience in the hope of producing concrete results in the social sphere.

From a Protestant perspective Merton's emphasis upon mysticism is to be commended, providing, of course, that one always keep in mind the possible dangers of mysticism. For too long Protestants have turned their backs on the mystical and contemplative experience—yet it does exist as part of mankind's religious experience and it is perhaps showing itself in a somewhat changed form within contemporary Protestantism in the charismatic movement and the widespread interest in various forms of eastern religion. By providing a balanced approach to mysticism, Merton has much to offer the Protestant reader.

Merton's understanding of mysticism, contemplation and action is not unlike the view of Friedrich Schleiermacher, although their contexts are quite different. Schleiermacher contended that 'the heart of religion was and has always been feeling, not rational proofs and discussions. The God of religion is not, as much speculation seemed to imply, a theory dragged in to explain the universe. God, to the religious man, is an experience, a living reality.'[86] He viewed religion as based upon personal experience,[87] and from this experience he derives his ethics, as William E. Hordern explains:

> For Schleiermacher religion is essentially ethical because when one becomes aware of his dependence upon the universe he is immediately aware of his relationship with his fellow men, who are likewise bound to the source of their being. In all religions we find this primary experience of man, and it is expressed in various doctrines and forms. But if the forms become too important we must get rid of them in order that we can once more find the experience of religion in all of its purity and power.
>
> Sin occurs when man tries to live by himself, isolated from the universe and his fellow men. He lives for his own selfish interest, but in so living he finds that he is miserable. This misery of man in his isolation is proof, to Schleiermacher, of man's oneness with God. It can be overcome only when one loses himself in the service of God and man.[88]

The strand of Protestant liberalism that originated with Schleiermacher is sympathetic to mysticism and would likely find Merton's views compatible.

A second strand of Protestant liberalism originated with Albrecht Ritschl who has been characterized as 'the great theologian of practicality'.[89] He was concerned with facts, values, and practical consequences and, as a result, he rejected many of Schleiermacher's views. He 'had no patience with metaphysics or with theological discussions that did not appear to him to have practical consequences.'[90] Consequently he had no sympathy with mysticism. The Ritschl strand of liberalism tends to be value and action oriented, and to place its emphasis upon social ethics with little concern for personal religious experience.[91]

Evangelical Protestantism, stressing intellectual assent to correct theology after an initial personal conversion experience, has almost completely neglected the mystical.[92] There are, however, signs of renewal among evangelical Protestants in both personal religious experience and expressions of social concern.[93] It remains true, for the most part, that evangelical Protestants are highly suspicious of mysticism because it emphasizes subjective personal experience rather than objective revelation.[94] There is a feeling among many evangelicals that an emphasis upon experience would seriously undermine what they consider to be the historic Christian faith. If, however, Protestantism were to develop a kind of monastic structure that would assure protection from excesses, it is possible that mysticism could develop. As it stands now, Protestants who call themselves mystics usually end up founding new sects, cults, or denominations.

Merton's mysticism involves what he calls a *metanoia*—a radical change in one's personal self-understanding. It is religious in nature and has implications for one's relationships with others. *Metanoia* in Merton's view, is what mysticism and contemplation are all about, for such *metanoia* necessarily involves action, not merely as a by-product, but as an essential part of the experience. Mysticism is a part of the total Christian life, which involves the person both as an individual and as a part of society. His insistence that contemplation and action necessarily belong together should be heeded by all Christians today, including Protestants.

PROTESTANT RESERVATIONS CONCERNING MONASTICISM

Merton himself was the first to admit that Protestants have been hostile to monasticism.[95] He traced this hostility back to Luther:

> The crisis and collapse of Luther's life under religious vows (Luther was not strictly a 'monk' since he was an Augustinian) marked a decisive point in the Reformation. Luther's 'monastic' experience was in fact quite central to his whole view of the Church and Christian life, and his repudiation of religious vows was a critical point in his theology of *fides sola*. He challenged the whole medieval ethos, dominated by the monastic order as reformed and incorporated into the cultural and political life of Europe since Charlemagne.
>
> The defensive reaction of the Catholic Church was to reject the challenge and to reaffirm without question the essentials of the medieval monastic structure.[96]

Merton did not think all Luther's criticism of monasticism lacked justification, for abuses were certainly present and needed reform which the Catholic Church had failed to bring about.

Luther published his strongest criticism of monasticism in 1522 under the title *De votis monasticis Martini Lutherii judicium*. Biot summarizes Luther's case against monasticism:

1. The vows are contrary to the word of God; they have no scriptural support in their favor.
2. The vows are contrary to faith, since they are held by the monks to be sources of sanctification.
3. The vows are contrary to evangelical liberty—liberty of conscience—which should be bound by no obligation.
4. The vows are contrary to the commandments of God, for they suppose the existence of 'counsels', which in Luther's eyes were additions to the commandments. Especially are they contrary to charity in creating within the Church a state wherein the aim is to be served rather than to serve.
5. The vows are contrary to reason because of their irrevocability.[97]

Luther was speaking of monasticism as he saw it, in obvious need of reform. He was not speaking of the ancient monasticism of the desert fathers but of wealthy monasteries deeply involved in the social and political life of his time. To his eyes monasticism was spiritually corrupt. Action was not a sharing of the fruits of contemplation. Indeed, monastic vows were seen by many sixteenth-century monks as a means of obtaining their own salvation rather than as the fruit of a salvation already achieved.

Calvin was also critical of monasticism, although unlike Luther he had never been a member of a religious community and his comments on the matter were not laid out in systematic form. Using his *Institutes of the Christian Religion* and his *Commentary on the First Epistle to the Corinthians*, Biot shows that Calvin considered 'monastic vows are unlawful and therefore do not bind in conscience, moreover, being abominable to God, they should be abrogated; God save us from remaining in them'.[98] Calvin was emphatic on the following points:

1.   Marriage is a divine institution, obliging in principle, which binds man and woman mutually; it is at once a blessing from God and a remedy for human weakness, preventing disorders of the flesh.
2.   Man must obey God and remain ever ready to answer any divine call. Hence, he has no right to bind himself by a commitment which mortgages the future instead of yielding its free and entire disposition to the Holy Spirit.
3.   The vows create a state of servitude, opposed to the spiritual liberty of a Christian, in matters which God has left open to human choice.[99]

Celibacy, obedience, and Christian liberty were Calvin's main concerns and he saw monasticism fall short in all three.

Behind the criticisms of both Luther and Calvin lay their concern for the relationship between contemplation and action. Both saw monasticism as something legalistic restricting one from acting according to his conscience and the call of God. Both believed that salvation was achieved through faith alone and that monasticism was neither a means to salvation nor a necessary result of salvation. Most importantly, however, both Luther and Calvin saw that the monasticism of their day was to a large extent so corrupted that the balance between contemplation and action had been lost. The monasteries had become so involved in the social, political and economic life of the times that the spiritual foundations of the life were either lost or all but unrecognizable.

Writing from a modern Reformed viewpoint, Karl Barth

raised significant questions about monasticism, especially poverty, chastity and obedience.[100] He questions whether property and sexuality can be singled out as more serious than other areas of possible temptation, and he asks whether any man—as an ecclesiastical superior—can properly represent divine authority within an institution such as a monastery. Barth was not totally opposed to monasticism, however, and he conceded that because with God all things are possible, the Holy Spirit can be at work even within the confines of a monastery.[101] He was willing to distinguish between the monastic vocation and the institutional forms to which it has given rise.

> We may have many serious objections to the ancient and modern theory and practice (and sometimes the *usus* and *abusus*) of Eastern and Western monasticism, and we may be constrained to voice them, yet without invalidating in any way the underlying will and intention—even if there is reason to think that this, too, is not altogether free from error. The serious repudiation of a Macarius the Great or a Basil the Great, a Benedict of Nursia, a Francis of Assisi or Dominic, a Thomas à Kempis, even an Ignatius Loyola or a Teresa of Avila, is not quite such a simple matter—either in their own time or today—as many good Protestants have supposed, not only because they have been conscious of at least some of the things that we think we know better, but also because they have given us other things at least to think about. It is advisable to advance very cautiously at this point, not at all in a censorious spirit, but for all our firmness with a definite anxiety to learn.[102]

Such a distinction is of the utmost importance, and Thomas Merton was among the first to admit that the institution of monasticism all too often becomes so corrupted by the culture which surrounds it that it can easily degenerate into a form of legalism devoid of a living and vital spirituality.[103] At the same time Merton was aware of the dynamic spiritual roots of monasticism and pointed out that the only reason for the monastic life at all is that it enables one to abandon oneself entirely to God's good pleasure. If it does not do this, it is useless.[104]

According to Merton, the essence of monasticism does not live in structures or institutions; the monastic vocation is essentially a charism and not simply a call to special work in and for the Church. When the familiar monastic structures frustrate this true purpose, it becomes a serious error to regard these structures as the norm. His major emphasis is not upon the vows. He asserts that the monastic apostolate should not be subject to unusual pressures and constant demands, but should be rather a life of silence and prayer. Here the emphasis upon *being* rather than *doing* takes primary importance.[105]

Contemporary Protestantism tends to be activistic and is therefore critical of monasticism's withdrawal from the world. Merton points out that while there is a certain degree of withdrawal involved, there is a social dimension as well:

> The monastic life is a life wholly centered upon this tremendous existential silence of God which nobody has ever been able to explain and which is, nevertheless, the heart of all that is real....The monastic life is not dedicated to a sounding communication among men. It lives by a soundless communication in mystery between man and God, between man and his brother, and between all created things. [106]

Monasticism begins with God and the individual person, and then it moves outward to include not only other people but the whole of creation. Tensions arise because monks are out of touch with the everyday world in its secular realities, but Merton maintains that this is just a fact to be accepted.[107] He makes no apologies nor does he try to defend or explain away this aspect of monastic life.

Merton does take issue with the view that monks are withdrawing from the world to escape their responsibilities in it. He says that monks 'have not come to the monastery to escape from the realities of life but to find those realities: they have felt the terrible insufficiency of life in a civilization that is entirely dedicated to the pursuit of shadows.'[108] It is necessary, in his view, to withdraw from the illusory world of society in order to find the realities of the world in contemplation. It is equally imperative to share with the world the fruits of contemplation, a task which Merton accomplished so well through his writings.

The monk, according to Merton, is a man who has no established place in society. 'He is a marginal person who withdraws deliberately to the margin of society with a view to deepening fundamental human experience.'[109] Merton compares him to poets and hippies:

> Are monks and hippies and poets relevant? No, we are

deliberately irrelevant. We live with an ingrained irrelevance which is proper to every human being. The marginal man accepts the basic irrelevance of the human condition, an irrelevance which is manifested above all by the fact of death. The marginal person, the monk, the displaced person, the prisoner, all these people live in the presence of death, which calls into question the meaning of life. He struggles with the fact of death in himself, trying to seek something deeper than death; because there is something deeper than death, and the office of the monk or the marginal person, the meditative person or the poet is to go beyond death even in this life, to go beyond the dichotomy of life and death and to be, therefore, a witness to life. [110]

This is the point at which Protestants have perhaps their greatest difficulty with monasticism, for Protestants cannot bear to be irrelevant. For this reason monasticism has something unique to offer them: Protestants need to learn how to be irrelevant.

When most Protestants think of monasticism, unfortunately, they think of a secluded cloister filled with robed men or women who cannot speak to one another and who have absolutely no contact with the outside world. It is no wonder they see monasticism as irrelevant, for they see it primarily as an institution. Merton's monasticism is entirely different; he sees it as a charism, a vocation, a manner of being. Its irrelevance has little or nothing to do with institutional structures and forms, but stems from its emphasis on *being* within a society almost totally oriented towards *doing*. Protestants need to discover monasticism as *being* rather than *doing*—or not-doing—for it is here, in this discovery, that one learns the relationship between contemplation and action. One must *be* before one can really *do*, and those irrelevant monks have much to offer worldlings in putting this important distinction into perspective.

PROTESTANT VENTURES IN THE CONTEMPLATIVE LIFE

Contemporary Protestantism is rediscovering the contemplative life in various forms, particularly the monastic. To be sure, Protestant monasticism is experienced on a very small scale among a limited number of people, and the average church member is still probably suspicious of such ventures, if he is even aware of their existence.

Merton was in full sympathy with Luther's revolt against 'the limitation of religious life in a community that was, if not totally corrupt, at least subject to serious deficiencies. Sterile devotionalism, attachment to trivial outward forms, forgetfulness of the essentials of the Christian faith, and obsession with accidentals....'[111] He consistently distinguishes between rigid institutionalism and monasticism. From the Reformation on 'one might assume that "Protestantism" and "monasticism" were mutually exclusive and that such a thing as "Protestant monasticism" was inconceivable.'[112] He considered the very existence of Protestant monasticism therefore significant.[113]

One Catholic who has studied the rise of Protestant monasticism thinks that *'the rediscovery of the religious life in Churches born of the Reformation is but one aspect of a general reawakening that has been going on in all the Churches since the beginning of the century.'*[114] Signs of this reawakening include the reaction against liberal theology, especially by theologians such as Barth; a renewed interest in biblical studies, not only among Protestants but also among Catholics; a developing concept of the Lord's Supper; liturgical renewal; a gradual shift of emphasis from individualism to community; the growth of Christian ecumenism. To this list should also be added the reforms brought about by Vatican II. Protestants and Catholics are now viewing each other in a positive light, whereas formerly their relationship was almost entirely negative.

That Protestants are beginning to re-examine the value of mysticism and the contemplative life is due in part to the ecumenical dialogue with both Catholics and Orthodox and to increasing contact with the eastern religions of Hinduism and Buddhism, both of which have a strong mystical and contemplative tradition. Protestants are becoming increasingly aware of their historical roots, including the mystical and contemplative. As a result, they are beginning to take the monastic life style seriously.[115]

Protestant monasticism is not an attempt to recover the structures and institutional forms of medieval Catholic monasticism. Protestant monasticism, says Merton, combines 'a traditional form of Christian monastic life with a welcome flexibility and with a strong ecumenical emphasis. The combination of these elements is even more significant than the fact that a "Protestant monastery" should exist.'[116] He felt that Protestants are on the cutting edge of monastic renewal today: 'It is perhaps in Protestantism that the more general monastic movement has gathered the strongest momentum and displayed the greatest vitality in the shortest time. One might even hazard the opinion that these Protestant communities are the most telling and hopeful signs of life in the monastic revival today.'[117] This vitality and creativity comes from Protestant monasticism's return to the earliest forms of monastic life. Not primarily concerned with medieval monasticism and its institutional forms,[118] Protestant monasticism balances contemplation and action.

Protestant monasticism emphasizes freedom. This, says Merton, gives these communities 'the flexibility in meeting crucial needs of our time, not in stereotyped institutional ways (schools, clubs, etc.), but with an apostolic spontaneity nourished by monasticity of life'.[119] This freedom has resulted in a number of different life styles among Protestant communities. Some, like the Taizé Community, are monastic in structure while others, like the Reba Place Fellowship, admit entire families to membership.[120] Many of these communities maintain active missions in cities while others are noted for their contributions to theology and liturgical renewal. All are relatively recent in origin, and most are contemplative in orientation.[121]

Many of these Protestant communities admit married couples into their membership, thereby removing the barrier of celibacy which prevents many from entering the Catholic monastic orders. Some Protestant communities are loosely organized and have a large turnover in membership.[122] Although this may be a disadvantage in terms of stability it does allow persons to maintain their freedom to follow the call of God wherever that call may lead. Even the more traditionally-structured monastic groups such as the Taizé Community exercise Christian freedom in letting their members serve in various jobs away from the community.

Donald Bloesch avers that these Protestant communities challenge the Church because 'they remind the churches, particularly those that have been acclimated to the culture, that there is a frontier between the truth of the gospel and the values of the world'.[123] An article in *The Christian Century* echoes this theme by comparing the counter-culture of American youth to monasticism. The author maintains that monasticism and the counter-culture both refuse to make dualistic compromise and that conversion must be acted out as cultural alternative.[124] This emphasis, greatly needed among Protestants today, can be and is being recovered in the monastic life.

Merton considered the monastic life one of the essential treasures of the Church, and he says:

> There is certainly great significance in the lesson which is being taught us by an apparently ironic Providence: that the Reformation which began by demolishing a whole segment of a tottering monastic fabric should now be seeking to help us rebuild it according to its primitive lines. [125]

It is important that the primitive lines along which Protestant monasticism is built are drawn from a dynamic relationship between contemplation and action. [126] Roger Schutz, the founder and prior of Taizé, has said that 'experience of the needs of our times and the meditation in common of the Gospels led the brothers to give definite form to their original vocation.' [127] This vocation is the essence of monasticism.

It is this vocation which formed the center around which Merton's life and work revolved for the twenty-seven years he was a member of the Gethsemani community. It shaped his views on the spiritual life, gave form and content to his social concern, provided him with a deep sense of personal identity and calling in a world of shifting values and insecurity, and it served as the stimulus for him to chart new and exciting directions for the future. We live in a time when contemplation and action are often seen as antitheses and when the tension between the spiritual and the social have become divisive for many Christians. Therefore it is entirely fitting that we give serious consideration to the life and work of this man who sought to bring unity to a world of diversity. In the words of John Thomas Baker: 'Merton was a Catholic, but he was more Christian than Catholic, more religious than Christian, more human than religious.' [128]

1.   *Thoughts in Solitude*, p. 105. Cf. *Redeeming the Time*, p. 11: 'The world is not something static and established—it is in the process of becoming. It is *being made* by man.'

2.   From a Merton letter quoted by Leslie Dewart, 'A Post-Christian Age?' *Continuum* 1 (1964) 559.

3.   *Faith and Violence: Christian Teaching and Christian Practice*, p. 174.

4.   *Life and Holiness*, pp. 136-37.

5.   *Conjectures of a Guilty Bystander*, p. 53.

6.   Ibid. J.M. Cameron in his introduction to Max Picard's *The Flight From God* (Chicago: Henry Regnery, 1951) p. xxi, states that today 'there is a complete "transvaluation of values"; the hierarchy of being is inverted; contemplation is for the sake of action, not action for the sake of contemplation.'

7.   *The Living Bread*, p. xiv.

8.   *Thoughts in Solitude*, p. 37.

9.   Ibid., p. 37, Merton states that 'laziness and cowardice are two of the greatest enemies of the spiritual life. And they are most dangerous of all when they mask as "discretion." '

10.   *Disputed Questions*, p. 70. Merton's understanding of the wilderness includes both a literal physical wilderness and an inner spiritual wilderness.

11.   See *No Man is an Island*, p. 40.

12.   *Selected Poems of Thomas Merton*, p. 111.

13.   *Spiritual Direction and Meditation*, pp. 89-90. An important element of this religious perspective is its independence from political ideology. See Donald G. Bloesch, 'The Ideological Temptation', *Listening: Current Studies in Dialog* 7 (Winter, 1972) 45-54.

14.   *The Silent Life*, pp. 166-68.

15.   See 'Notes From Meeting of Contemplatives,' mimeographed, p. 5.

16.   *Thoughts in Solitude*, p. 68. This detachment also aids in the way in which we view others as Merton points out on p. 111: 'It is necessary that we find the silence of God not only in ourselves but also in one another.'

17.   *Life and Holiness*, p. 136.

18.   *Seeds of Destruction*, p. 113.

19.   *Faith and Violence*, p. 222.

20.   The term 'holy worldliness' originates with Dietrich Bonhoeffer, as Donald

G. Bloesch points out in *The Christian Witness in a Secular Age: An Evaluation of Nine Contemporary Theologians* (Minneapolis: Augsburg, 1968) pp. 84-85: 'This is not to be confused with the unholy this-worldliness that characterizes the godless man, but it is also to be distinguished from the otherworldliness that has plagued pietism and revivalism. Discipleship means to be conformed to the incarnate one; it means to become truly human. Sanctity and true humanity are thereby closely allied.' Bonhoeffer explains what he meant by this in *Letters and Papers from Prison*, trans. Reginald H. Fuller (New York: Macmillan, 1962), pp. 237-38.

21.   *Spiritual Direction and Meditation*, pp. 88-89. See Merton, 'Marxism and Monastic Perspectives' in Moffitt, ed., *A New Charter for Monasticism*, p. 80; rpt. in *The Asian Journal of Thomas Merton*, edd. Naomi Burton, Brother Patrick Hart, James Laughlin (New York: New Directions, 1973) pp. 341-42.

22.   *Disputed Questions*, p. 101.

23.   See Merton's essay 'Is the Contemplative Life Finished?' in his *Contemplation in a World of Action*, pp. 331-84.

24.   Not all critics of the contemplative life are necessarily opposed to contemplation as such, but their opposition stems from the fact that contemplative living is for many another way of shirking their responsibilities in the world.

25.   *Contemplation in a World of Action*, p. 331.

26.   See Theodore Roszak, *The Making of a Counter Culture: Reflections on the Technocratic Society and Its Youthful Opposition* (Garden City: Doubleday Anchor, 1969).

27.   That Merton was critical of much of what passes for renewal in the Church is shown by James F. Andrews, 'Was Merton a Critic of Renewal?' *The National Catholic Reporter*, 6 (Feb. 11, 1970) Lenten Supplement 1, 12-15.

28.   *Basic Principles of Monastic Spirituality*, p. 31; rpt. *The Monastic Journey*, ed. Brother Patrick Hart (Sheed Andrews & McMell, 1977) p. 36.

29.   *Contemplation in a World of Action*, p. 337.

30.   This is an extension of the mystical experience where one must pass through the dark night of the soul before experiencing union with God.

31.   See *Contemplation in a World of Action*, p. 337.

32.   'Marxism and Monastic Perspectives' in Moffitt, ed., *A New Charter*, pp. 76-79; rpt. in *The Asian Journal*, pp. 336-40. See also Chogyam Trungpa, as told to Esme Cramer Roberts, *Born in Tibet* (Baltimore: Penguin, 1971). This book was highly recommended by Merton for its vivid account of the Chinese invasion of Tibet and the hardships of Buddhist monks.

33.   'Marxism and Monastic Perspectives' in Moffit, ed., *A New Charter*, p. 78; rpt. in *The Asian Journal*, p. 338.

34.   Ibid.

35.　Ibid., p. 79/p. 340.

36.　Ibid., p. 81/p. 342.

37.　*Seasons of Celebration*, p. 162.

38.　Merton drew heavily from biblical material in the following books: *Bread in the Wilderness, Life and Holiness, Opening the Bible, Praying the Psalms,* and *The New Man.* He referred to it in all of his books and his writings give an eloquent testimony to his knowledge of Scripture.

39.　*Opening the Bible*, pp. 24-25.

40.　Ibid., p. 2.

41.　Ibid.

42.　This is undoubtedly due, at least in part, to the influence of Karl Barth upon Merton's thought. The first chapter of *Conjectures of a Guilty Bystander*, pp. 1-49 is entitled 'Barth's Dream'. In *Opening the Bible*, Merton makes use of material from Karl Barth, *The Word of God and the Word of Man*, trans. Douglas Horton (1928; rpt. New York: Harper & Row Torchbook, 1957). In this same work Merton also shows that he is acquainted with the work of Rudolf Bultmann.

43.　W. R. Inge, *Christian Mysticism* (1899; rpt Cleveland/New York: Living Age Meridian, 1956) pp. 39-40.

44.　Georgia Harkness, *Mysticism: Its Meaning and Message* (Nashville/New York: Abingdon, 1973) p. 37.

45.　Abraham Joshua Heschel, *God in Search of Man: A Philosophy of Judaism* (New York: Farrar, Straus and Cudahy, 1955) pp. 225-26.

46.　*Opening the Bible*, p. 34.

47.　Ibid., p. 41.

48.　*Bread in the Wilderness* and *Praying the Psalms.*

49.　*Praying the Psalms*, p. 3.

50.　St Bernard of Clairvaux wrote extensively on the *Song of Songs*. Inge spoke strongly in his opposition to an allegorical intepretation in *Christian Mysticism*, p. 43: 'As to the Song of Solomon, its influence upon Christian Mysticism has been simply deplorable.'
See also Harkness, *Mysticism: Its Meaning and Message*, p. 39.

51.　See *The New Man*, pp. 82-83.

52.　In *Opening the Bible* Merton quotes extensively from such modern-day prophets as Karl Barth, Dietrich Bonhoeffer, Erich Fromm, and William Faulkner. The very title of his book *Life and Holiness* shows the relationship between contemplation and action.

53.   Zacchaeus (Lk 19:1-10) is an outstanding example. After his conversion experience he gave half of his goods to the poor and repaid fourfold those whom he had cheated, and then Jesus said, 'Today salvation has come to this house'.

54.   Harkness, *Mysticism*, p. 42.

55.   See Lk 10:38-42.

56.   *Contemplation in a World of Action*, pp. 361-62.

57.   Ibid., p. 362.

58.   Jesus condemned the activism of the Scribes and the Pharisees because their actions did not flow from their relationship to God, but from their desire for social status in the community.

59.   See Gal 1:12. Inge comments on this in *Christian Mysticism*, p. 60.

60.   Harkness, *Mysticism*, pp. 44-45.

61.   Ibid., p. 49.

62.   Much has been written concerning the Gospel of John and its relationship to mysticism. See Inge, *Christian Mysticism*, pp. 44-60. On pp. 47-48 Inge states that 'in St John, as in mystical theology generally, the Incarnation, rather than the Cross, is the central fact of Christianity.' Merton placed the Incarnation at the center of his mystical thought. See *The New Man*, pp. 92-139 and *New Seeds of Contemplation*, pp. 123-29. For a unique point of view see J. Edgar Burns, *The Christian Buddhism of St John: New Insights into the Fourth Gospel* (New York/Paramus, N.J./Toronto: Paulist Press, 1971).

63.   Harkness, *Mysticism*, p. 49.

64.   Inge, *Christian Mysticism*, p. 5.

65.   Francois Biot OP, *The Rise of Protestant Monasticism*, trans. W. J. Kerrigan (Baltimore/Dublin: Helicon, 1963) p. 27.

66.   For an example see Williston Walker, *A History of the Christian Church*, rev. ed. (New York: Scribner's, 1959) p. 329.

67.   Franklin H. Littell, *The Anabaptist View of the Church: An Introduction to Sectarian Protestantism*, Studies in Church History, 3 (New York: American Society of Church History, 1952) p. 22.

68.   Ibid., p. 24. See pp. 24-25 for a discussion of the Peasant Revolt.

69.   See Walker, *A History of the Christian Church*, p. 336, for a brief description of the Münster rebellion and its tragic consequences.

70.   The role of authority here is very important. Today many conservative Protestants are in sympathy with conservative Catholics over the implications of the decline of authority. See Harvey Cox, *The Secular City: Secularization and*

Urbanization in Theological Perspective (New York: Macmillan, 1965) p. 160: 'The real ecumenical crisis today is not between Catholics and Protestants but between traditional and experimental forms of church life.'

71.   Donald G. Bloesch, *The Ground of Certainty: Toward an Evangelical Theology of Revelation* (Grand Rapids: Eerdmans, 1971) p. 140. Bloesch also cites Catholic reservations concerning mysticism, p. 140, quoting Baron Friedrich von Huegel, *The Life of Prayer* (London: Dent, 1960) p. 34.

72.   Among them would be Emmanual Swedenborg, founder of the Church of the New Jerusalem, numerous founders of sects and cults such as Joseph Smith, founder of the Mormons, and Ellen G. White, founder of the Seventh-Day Adventists, many of the founders of the communitarian religious communities which sprang up in the United States in the nineteenth century. Although not mystical in the strict sense of the word, certain groups of Quakers, Pentecostals, and those in the Holiness movement place a strong emphasis upon the personal experience of God and the guidance of the Holy Spirit in one's everyday life.

73.   Bloesch, *The Ground of Certainty*, pp. 142-43. See also Friedrich Heiler, *Prayer: A Study in the History and Psychology of Religion*, trans. Samuel McComb (New York: Oxford University Press, 1932) pp. 135-71.

74.   See especially *The Ascent to Truth, New Seeds of Contemplation, The New Man, Basic Principles of Monastic Spirituality,* and *The Climate of Monastic Prayer.* See also John J. Higgins, sj, *Merton's Theology of Prayer,* Cistercian Studies Series, 18 (Spencer, Mass.: Cistercian Publications, 1971)

75.   Sidney Spencer, *Mysticism in World Religion* (Baltimore: Penguin, 1963) p. 337.

76.   Ibid., p. 339.

77.   *New Seeds of Contemplation*, p. 210.

78.   While Merton did come into conflict with his superiors in areas of social concern, he avoided controversy in areas of doctrine and theology. After his death however numerous unfounded rumors circulated about him being a heretic or converting to Buddhism, and even one to the effect that God took him before he could do further harm to the Church.

79.   *The Ascent to Truth*, pp. 66, 67.

80.   Ibid., p. 73.

81.   *Zen and the Birds of Appetite*, p. 73. Merton's stress on experience did not mean a neglect of the Bible, for he read and meditated on the Bible daily, usually for several hours, which is certainly more than most 'biblical Protestants' (or Catholics) are able to say for themselves.

82.   Ibid., pp. 55-56.

83.   Ibid., p. 58.

84.   (New York: Desclee, 1967) p. ix.

85.   Merton cited a particularly glaring example of this in *Conjectures of a Guilty Bystander*, pp. 94-95. He says, on p. 95 'that one can think himself a "good Catholic" and be thought one by his neighbors, and be, in effect, an apostate from the Christian faith.'

86.   William E. Hordern, *A Layman's Guide to Protestant Theology*, rev. ed. (New York: Macmillan, 1968) p. 44.

87.   Barth vigorously protested against this view. See Karl Barth, *The Humanity of God* (Richmond: John Knox, 1960) pp. 25-27. True religious experience, he argues, begins not with man but with God.

88.   Hordern, *A Layman's Guide*, p. 45. For an excellent introduction to Schleiermacher's views see Paul Tillich, *Perspectives on 19th and 20th Century Protestant Theology*, ed. Carl E. Braaten (New York: Harper & Row, 1967) pp. 90-114.

89.   Hordern, *A Layman's Guide*, p. 46. See also pp. 46-49.

90.   Ibid., p. 47.

91.   See Richard R. Hicks, 'The New Mood of College Students: A Black Viewpoint', *The Christian Century* 90 (1973) 539, where he says of liberal, activist students of the 1960s: 'White students are affluent, and their anxiety is directly related to that affluence. Their crisis is an identity crisis. Theirs is not a struggle for physical survival but a struggle to make sense out of their existence and find purpose and meaning for their lives.'

92.   The Pentecostals are a notable exception in that they place the major emphasis upon experience.

93.   Renewal is taking place in small encounter groups, experiments in communal living, and the practice of the charismatic gifts in local churches. An increasing sense of social concern and responsibility is shown by many evangelicals. See the following books by Donald G. Bloesch: *The Reform of the Church* (Grand Rapids: Eerdmans, 1970) and *The Evangelical Renaissance* (Eerdmans, 1973).

94.   See Karl Barth, *Church Dogmatics*, I/2, trans. G.T. Thomsom and Harold Knight (Edinburgh: T. & T. Clark, 1956) pp. 318-25. Barth speaks of mysticism and atheism as two forks of one road which seeks to put forth an inadequate conception of an internalized God rather than an external 'wholly other' known only through His revelation in Jesus Christ.

95.   'Monastic Experience and the East-West Dialogue' in Finley P. Dunne, Jr., ed., *The World Religions Speak on the Relevance of Religion in the Modern World* (The Hague: Dr. W. Junk N. V. Publications, 1970) p. 73; rpt. in *The Asian Journal*, p. 311.

96.   *Contemplation in a World of Action*, p. 181.

97.   Biot, *The Rise of Protestant Monasticism*, pp. 14-15.

98.   Ibid., p. 35. Biot discusses Calvin's views on monasticism on pp. 29-46.

99.   Ibid., p. 45.

100.   See Karl Barth, *Church Dogmatics*, IV/2, trans. G. W. Bromiley (Edinburgh: T. & T. Clark, 1958), pp. 11-19.

101.   Ibid., p. 17.

102.   Ibid., p. 12.

103.   See *Contemplation in a World of Action*, pp. 3-234, for Merton's suggestions for monastic reform.

104.   'Conference on Contemplative Living in the Contemporary World', mimeographed, p. 13. Cf. *Seeds of Destruction*, p. 184.

105.   This does not mean that Merton swept away all forms and structures nor did he advocate weakening monastic discipline. In *Contemplation in a World of Action*, p. 108, he stated that 'the idea of discipline implies a clear recognition of an elementary human fact: permissiveness is all right if you are content to drift along with a stream that carries you more or less safely by itself.' On p. 109 he pointed out that 'the real function of discipline is not to provide us with maps, but to sharpen our own sense of direction so that when we really get going we can travel without maps.'

106.   *Silence in Heaven: A Book of the Monastic Life*, p. 126.

107.   'Notes From Meeting of Contemplatives', p. 11. All vocations have their unique problems, contradictions, and unresolved questions. This is not reserved to the monastic vocation.

108.   *The Waters of Siloe*, p. xviii.

109.   'Monastic Experience and the East-West Dialogue' in Dunne, ed., *The World Religions Speak on the Relevance of Religion in the Modern World*, pp. 79-80; rpt. as 'Thomas Merton's View of Monasticism' in *The Asian Journal*, p. 305.

110.   Ibid., p. 80/p. 306.

111.   *Mystics and Zen Masters*, p. 188.

112.   Ibid., p. 189. Merton points out that Anglicans are strictly speaking not Protestant. Therefore he excludes their monasteries from his discussions. For an excellent account of Anglican monasticism see Peter F. Anson, *The Call of the Cloister: Religious Communities and Kindred Bodies in the Anglican Communion* (London: SPCK, 1964).

113.   Several attempts at establishing Protestant religious communities were made before this century. See Biot, *The Rise of Protestant Monasticism*, pp. 65-82.

114. Ibid., p. 109.

115. See *Mystics and Zen Masters*, p. 191 where Merton quotes Barth on the need for the solitary life.

116. *Contemplation in a World of Action*, p. 181. In *Mystics and Zen Masters*, p. 191, Merton points out that 'Protestant monasticism is not interested in merely *imitating* Catholic communities, but in discreetly helping and encouraging monastic reform wherever it is needed and possible'.

117. *Mystics and Zen Masters*, p. 189.

118. See ibid., p. 189.

119. Ibid., p. 190.

120. For a description of a number of the new Protestant communities see the following books by Donald G. Bloesch: *Centers of Christian Renewal* (Boston/Philadelphia: United Church Press, 1964), *Wellsprings of Renewal: Promise in Christian Communal Life* (Grand Rapids: Eerdmans, 1974), and *Servants of Christ: Deaconesses in Renewal* (Minneapolis: Bethany Fellowship, 1971). See also Lydia Praeger, ed., *Frei für Gott und die Menschen* (Stuttgart: Quell-Verlag, 1959), Siegfried von Kortzfleisch, *Mitten im Herzen der Massen* (Stuttgart: Kreuz-Verlag, 1963), and Olive Wyon, *Living Springs* (Philadelphia: Westminster, 1964).

121. During the nineteenth century the United States was the home of hundreds of utopian and sectarian communities, most of which were religious, although not contemplative or monastic, in orientation. These included the Amana Colonies, the Icarians, the Oneida Community, and the Shakers. Today few remain.

122. This is especially true of many conservative Protestant groups and various small independent mission boards. Often they function much like a religious order with farms, houses in a community, daily worship, assigned tasks, and communal living. Many people pass through these groups for training.

123. Bloesch, *Centers of Christian Renewal*, p. 6.

124. W. Paul Jones, 'Monasticism as Counterculture', *The Christian Century* 89 (1972) 628-30.

125. *Mystics and Zen Masters*, p. 192.

126. See ibid., p. 189: 'Protestant monasticism implies a rediscovery of the contemplative patterns of life characteristic of the ancient Catholic orders. Active works of charity have an important place in the life of the new communities, but it may be said that they are predominantly contemplative.'

127. Quoted by Merton, ibid., p. 189.

128. James Thomas Baker, *Thomas Merton Social Critic* (Lexington: University Press of Kentucky, 1971) p. 148.

II

MERTON'S SOCIAL AND CULTURAL BACKGROUND

The Early Years

THOMAS MERTON was born on 31 January, 1915, in the village of Prades, France 'under the sign of the Water Bearer, in a year of great war, and down in the shadows of some French mountains on the borders of Spain....'[1] His parents were both artists, a fact which Merton later considered significant, especially in terms of his interest in contemplation and action.

> Not many hundreds of miles away from the house where I was born, they were picking up the men who rotted in the rainy ditches among the dead horses and the ruined seventy-fives, in a forest of trees without branches along the river Marne.
> My father and mother were captives in that world, knowing they did not belong with it or in it, and yet unable to get away from it. They were in the world and not of it—not because they were saints, but in a different way: because they were artists. The integrity of an artist lifts a man above the level of the world without delivering him from it.[2]

His parents were both wanderers, and their travels took the family throughout Europe as well as to the United States. Indeed their stay in Prades, although planned as permanent, lasted only a few short years.

Merton's religious training in those early years was all but nil. He was baptized in the Anglican Church mainly because of his father's wishes, for his mother had little interest in formal religion as practised by the established churches of the day. And yet Merton was influenced by religion, for the mountains around Prades contained the ruins of many ancient monasteries.

As a boy he spent a great deal of time wandering among these ruins drinking in the atmosphere and imagining what life must have been like centuries before when those monasteries were inhabited. Years later he wrote of those ancient ruins:

> There were many ruined monasteries in those mountains. My mind goes back with great reverence to the thought of those clean, ancient stone cloisters, those low and mighty rounded arches hewn and set in place by monks who have perhaps prayed me where I am now. St Martin and St Michael the Archangel, the great patron of monks, had churches in those mountains. Saint Martin-du-Canigou; Saint Michel-de-Cuxa. Is it any wonder I should have a friendly feeling about those places?[3]

While one cannot attach too much importance to these early experiences and memories, there is little doubt that the young Merton possessed a vivid imagination and was highly impressionable.

This vivid imagination bothered Merton's mother especially when he did such things as show 'a deep and serious urge to adore the gas-light in the kitchen with no little ritualistic veneration, when I was about four.'[4] His mother was concerned undoubtedly lest he show an undue interest in religion, for she did not attach much importance to religious training. Says Merton: 'My guess is that she thought, if I were left to myself, I would grow up into a nice, quiet Deist of some sort, and never be perverted by superstition.'[5] His mother did occasionally attend services at a Quaker meeting house but there was no pressure put upon her son to attend. He was left more or less to himself in the working out of his early religious understanding and had virtually no religious guidance or direction during his early years.

Merton's mother was a strong believer in progressive education and she taught young Merton at home. Among the books she used were a geography book and a collection of stories entitled *Greek Heroes*.[6] From these he developed a desire to travel and unconsciously picked up a fragmentary religious and philosophical background.

> In a sense, this was intended as the fruit of my early training. Mother wanted me to be independent, and not to run with the herd. I was to be original, individual, I was to have a definite character and ideals of my own. I was not to be an article thrown together, on the common bourgeois pattern, on everybody else's assembly line.[7]

Although he did not realize it at the time, this independent streak was to be with him throughout his entire life and play an important role in his later life as a monk.[8]

Merton's first encounter with social action took place while his family was living in Flushing, New York. The Mertons rented a small house and with it a small garden which Merton's father considered theirs. The landlord thought otherwise, and one night during supper he helped himself to some rhubarb from it. Harsh words were exchanged, and when supper resumed the young Merton tried to work out the morality of the situation by attempting to persuade his father that it was perfectly all right for the landlord to help himself to what was in the garden any time he liked. Merton later wrote: 'I mention this with the full consciousness that someone will use it against me, and say that the real reason I became a monk in later years was that I had the mentality of a medieval serf when I was barely out of the cradle.'[9]

During these years the family had to struggle to make ends meet; unknown artists were anything but wealthy. Merton's mother developed cancer of the stomach. It was her wish, as she lay dying in the hospital, that the boys, Tom and his younger brother John Paul, not visit her and all knowledge of her sickness was kept from them. Merton's father took on extra work to pay the medical bills. He worked by day as a gardener and by night he played the piano in a small movie theatre. Later the family moved to the grandparents' home in Douglaston and the elder Merton took a job as organist at an Episcopal church. During this time Merton attended church every Sunday, but this early religious influence was without either context or direction, and he later wrote that 'one came out of the church with a kind of comfortable and satisfied feeling that something had been done that needed to be done, and that was all I knew about it'.[10]

The death of his mother hit Merton especially hard, for he was informed of her impending death by a note in her own hand-writing. Once his mother was gone, all semblance of family life began to disappear; 'he was not to know again a completely settled and secure existence until he became a monk.'[11] The next few years of Merton's life were confused, unsettled, and yet very wonderful, for he traveld throughout Europe with his father and lived a life of freedom, independence and wandering. Edward Rice describes those years:

Owen Merton was a wanderer: when possible he took the children with him, to Provincetown and Bermuda where they lived briefly. Eventually he returned to Europe, leaving the children with Pop and Bonnemaman. In 1925, Owen Merton was sufficiently at ease to bring his sons to France to live....The Mertons travelled at lot in western Europe, occasionally meeting Pop and Bonnemaman, and the boys went to school in France, boarding at a lycée, and after two years they moved to England: more schools and shifting around. John Paul was sent to Douglaston to live with his grandparents, and Merton went ot Oakham, a boarding school in Scotland. And his father became ill, very ill, and was confined to the hospital, and here, after many months of suffering, he died. There was a trip home—which was now Douglaston—in the summer of 1931, another rather longish year at Oakham and then Merton took the Grand Tour to Italy. He had just turned eighteen. [12]

During this period Merton lived in southern France not far from his birthplace, and while his father painted he wandered around the mountains visiting the ancient ruins of monasteries and churches. 'When I went to France, in 1925, returning to the land of my birth, I was also returning to the foundations of the intellectual and spiritual world to which I belonged.' [13] He was also returning to the only part of the world which he could call home.

While there, in southern France, Merton began to be attracted to the contemplative life. He was not consciously interested in the religious life as such, but the ancient abbeys and monasteries held a certain fascination for him. He explains that 'I had no curiosity about monastic vocations or religious rules, but I know my heart was filled with a kind of longing to breathe the air of that lonely valley and to listen to its silence'. [14] He wrote these words after he had seen pictures of the Grande Chartreuse in a book. His fascination with ancient monastic ruins may have been increased by the fact that Merton's father bought an abandoned thirteenth or fourteenth century chapel from a farmer and used the stones in the construction of their house in the village of St Antonin. [15] The very house in which Merton lived was literally a part of this monastic atmosphere. The entire countryside was 'so steeped in Catholic history that he seemed to enter into the Sacraments just by breathing the air.' [16]

In 1928, following an exhibition of his paintings in London, Merton's father decided to leave France and move to England. The new house at St Antonin had only recently been completed, and Merton was sad at the thought of not being able to live there for long. He enrolled at Ripley Court School and there was exposed to the Church of England, an exposure which slowly began to dull any religious sensitivities he had had up to that time. On Sundays he attended church dressed in an Eaton jacket and in the evenings he listened to the English teacher read from *Pilgrim's Progress*. Each night he knelt by his bed and said his prayers, and for about two years went through what he called 'my religious phase'.[17]

In time, however, he realized that most of this religion was more social than spiritual. He saw the Church of England as 'a class religion, the cult of a special society and group, not even of a whole nation, but of the ruling minority in a nation....The Church of England depends, for its existence, almost entirely on the solidarity and conservatism of the English ruling class.'[18]

> I got mixed up in all this as soon as I entered Ripley Court, and it was strong enough in me to blur and naturalize all that might have been supernatural in my attraction to pray and to love God. And consequently the grace that was given me was stifled, not at once, but gradually. As long as I lived in this peaceful hothouse, I was pious, perhaps sincerely. But as soon as the frail walls of this illusion broke down again—that is, as soon as I went to a Public School and saw that, underneath their sentimentality, the English were just as brutal as the French—I made no further effort to keep up what seemed to me to be more or less manifest pretense.[19]

As a Catholic, he later explained the spiritual and social implications of this class religion:

> Perhaps one explanation of this sterility and inefficacy of Anglicanism in the moral order is, besides its lack of vital contact with the Mystical Body of the True Church, the social injustice and the class oppression on which it is based: for, since it is mostly a class religion, it contracts the guilt of the class from which it is inseparable.[20]

Already, while still a comparatively young man, Merton was beginning to think in terms of the relationship between the spiritual and the social, a relationship that would later be expressed in terms of contemplation and action.

During his early years Merton was searching for a kind of religious experience which was concerned with being rather than doing. He found, however, that attending church was doing something and had little or no relation to his being. Only as he walked through the mountains of southern France and admired the ruins of ancient monasteries did he feel a spiritual presence which touched his life. During these crucially important years of his spiritual and religious formation he was led to believe that religion in its formal sense was something to *do*—it was not something to *be*. It was, in a very real sense, action with no contemplative base. Such a religion would be unable to sustain him in times of crisis.

The death of Merton's father was such a crisis. Owen Merton died of a brain tumor after a long illness and hospitalization. Merton relates his reaction when he heard of his father's impending death:

> I hung up the receiver and the bottom dropped out of my stomach. I walked up and down in the silent and empty house. I sat down in one of the big leather chairs in the smoking room. There was nobody there. There was nobody in the whole huge house.
> I sat there in the dark, unhappy room, unable to think, unable to move, with all the innumerable elements of my isolation crowding in upon me from every side: without a home, without a family, without a country, without a father, apparently without any friends, without any interior peace or confidence or light or understanding of my own— without God, too, without God, without heaven, without grace, without anything.[21]

The slow deterioration and eventual death of his father affected Merton deeply, but he took some comfort in the fact that his father was a man of deep religious faith even though it was not expressed in conventional pietistic or religious terms. As a result Merton was able to affirm his faith in the resurrection of the dead. 'For I hope that, in the living Christ, I shall one day see my father again.'[22]

Curiously Merton's father played an important part in his later conversion, for it was he who introduced him when he was only ten to the writings of William Blake. Shortly after his father's death Merton rediscovered Blake and began to take a serious interest in his writings. This interest remained with him throughout his life. He not only wrote his master's thesis at Columbia University on Blake, but continued to write occasional articles and essays on Blake even while in the monastery. He later wrote that it was the providence of God that led him to

Blake and the consequent reawakening of his dormant faith. He declared: 'I have to acknowledge my own debt to him, and the truth which may appear curious to some, although it is really not so: that through Blake I would one day come, in a round-about way, to the only true Church, and to the One Living God, through His Son, Jesus Christ.'[23]

During his last year at Oakham, Merton was accepted by Cambridge University. Prior to beginning his studies there, however, he made a trip to Italy and passed along the French Riviera, stopping at various places along the way. Upon reaching Florence he stayed with an artist friend, but only one night. 'I was tired of passing through places. I wanted to get to the term of my journey, where there was some psychological possibility that I would stop in one place and remain.'[24] He was experiencing a deep need for a home, for a sense of 'being-in-the-world' and having a place he could call his own, both spatially and vocationally. Although he was a free man he was unhappy and he found that the pursuit of pleasure was destined by its very nature to be self-defeating and to end in frustration. By the time he reached Rome he was totally aware of the emptiness within himself. The stage was being set for two very significant events: his own pilgrimage among the churches of Rome, and a mystical experience in which his father appeared to him in his hotel room.

While in Rome, Merton began to discover the Christian past through the frescoes and mosaics of the churches and chapels of the city. At first he was merely visiting museums and other places of interest, which of course included a number of churches. He was especially drawn to the Byzantine mosaics and soon began to visit all the churches where they were found. Before he realized it he was also visiting other churches of the same period.

> And thus without knowing anything about it I became a pilgrim. I was unconsciously and unintentionally visiting all the great shrines of Rome, and seeking out their sanctuaries with some of the eagerness and avidity and desire of a true pilgrim, though not quite for the right reason. And yet it was not for the wrong reason either. For these mosaics and frescoes and all the ancient altars, thrones and sanctuaries were designed and built for the instruction of people who were not capable of immediately understanding anything higher.[25]

For the first time in his life he began to discover something about the real person of Christ. He started reading the New Testament and studying the Gospels. In the next few weeks Merton spent a great deal of time in the churches of Rome, not only viewing the great works of art, but also heeding an inner compulsion. In his words: 'I loved to be in these holy places. I had a strong conviction that I belonged there: that my rational nature was filled with profound desires and needs that could only find satisfaction in the churches of God.'[26]

Until this time Merton had not had any particularly important religious experience, but while in Rome something happened to him which he made no attempt to explain. It deserves to be told in detail.

> I was in my room. It was night. The light was on. Suddenly it seemed to me that Father, who had now been dead more than a year, was there with me. The sense of his presence was as vivid and as real and as startling as if he had touched my arm or spoken to me. The whole thing passed in a flash, but in that flash, instantly, I was overwhelmed with a sudden and profound insight into the misery and corruption of my own soul, and I was pierced deeply with a light that made me realize something of the condition I was in, and I was filled with horror with what I saw, and my whole being rose up in revolt against what was within me, and my soul desired escape and liberation and freedom from all this with an intensity and an urgency unlike anything I had ever known before. And now I think for the first time in my whole life I really began to pray— praying not with my lips and with my intellect and with my imagination, but praying out of the very roots of my life and being, and praying to the God I had never known, to reach down towards me out of his darkness and to help me get free of the thousand terrible things that held my will in their slavery.[27]

This experience made a deep and lasting impression upon Merton, and throughout his life he never wavered from the firm belief that it really was his father's presence in the room that night.

Almost immediately he began to pray in the various churches that he visited—something he had never done before. During his last week in Rome he made a visit to the Cistercian monastery of Tre Fontane in the countryside outside the city. As he walked among the trees on the monastery grounds he thought of becoming a monk. At the time, he was expressing himself on an emotional level and was not giving the matter serious consideration. Yet the desire for the religious life was there and little did Merton know that he would not only become a monk, but he would also become the best-known Cistercian of the twentieth century.

Slowly but surely Merton's religious fervor ebbed away. At first he read the Bible in secret, afraid of being ridiculed. Later he tried attending Quaker meetings and even investigated the teachings of the Mormons. Within the space of three months he was once again a modern secular man. He was searching for a religious faith, but he had no direction. He would attend services here and there, read books and pamphlets about the various denominations, and try reading his Bible and praying on his own. At the same time he continued to search for a home— both in a physical and spiritual sense. He was attracted to the artistic, the poetic, and the mystical. The various Protestant denominations and religious groups which he investigated failed to provide him with what he needed during times of heightened spiritual awareness and he would lapse back again into a life of routine secularity. He also rejected Catholicism during this period because he associated it with Tammany Hall and political corruption.

Merton's personal faith developed through an informal exposure to Christianity, ancient ruins of chapels and monasteries, the reading of William Blake, the viewing of great works of Christian art, and his relationship with his father. While this may be a less than ideal form of spiritual development, it made Merton sensitive to the needs of those who are either marginally connected with or altogether outside the established Church—the poets, artists, writers, and intellectuals. Some of his best books were written with this audience in mind and even today Merton is appreciated by many who appear to be outside the household of faith. These early years were a time when seeds were planted which would bear fruit in his later work, and many of his early experiences influenced him throughout his life. Most important, however, was that the great quest for meaning and inner peace and ultimately for God, which began in those early years, continued throughout his life and never decreased in intensity.

Student Years

In the fall of 1933 Merton entered Clare College at Cambridge University. At first he was impressed by the beauty and the setting of Cambridge, but behind the facade of ancient buildings, sprawling lawns, and youthful exuberance there lurked another world—wild parties, campus capers, and of course, girls. 'But for me, with my blind appetites, it was impossible that I should not rush in and take a hugh bite of this rotten fruit. The bitter taste is still with me after not a few years.'[28] He began to spend his time with a crowd whose interests centered in such activities.

He also became deeply involved in the study of psychology, particularly that of Freud, and he came to the conclusion that the reason for his unhappiness was the repression of his sexual desires. This led him into a serious and painful relationship with a girl he met at Cambridge. Although he never disclosed the exact nature of the relationship, there can be no doubt that it was very delicate. Edward Rice states that Merton often spoke of this girl while at Columbia University, and that after leaving Cambridge he frequently mentioned returning to England to see her 'but he was never able to go back to England, and the girl and her son were killed in the Blitz'.[29] In a review of Rice's book, *The Man in the Sycamore Tree*, Mayo Mohs interprets this passage as implying that the romance produced a child.[30] Merton himself never gave any details of the relationship, and all speculations are merely that—speculations. Indeed, Rice points out that 'no one can recall all the details today, and there is no need to speculate on them, except to say that it was a serious situation and in retrospect clearly one that had a lot to do with his eventual conversion and vocation'.[31]

Merton's campus behavior came to the attention of his guardian in London and he was called to account.[32] Yet, things did not change for the better and Merton was later called in by his tutor for failing to attend class lectures. He was able to pass his examinations, however, and thus assure himself a place at Cambridge for the following year. But while he was in New York during the summer his guardian informed him that he had best remain in the United States and not return to England.

Merton left Europe for good in November of 1934, after returning briefly to take care of immigration details and obtain a permanent visa to enter the United States. Europe was under the threatening clouds of war and Merton made a connection between this and his own behavior.

> I speak of what I remember: perhaps the war that grew out of all this did something to cure it or to change it.
> For those who had nothing but this emptiness in the middle of them, no doubt the things they had to do and to

suffer during the war filled that emptiness with something stronger and more resilient than their pride—either that or it destroyed them utterly....

I had seen enough of the things, the acts and appetites, that were to justify and to bring down upon the world the tons of bombs that would someday begin to fall in millions. Did I know that my own sins were enough to have destroyed the whole of England and Germany? There has never yet been a bomb invented that is half so powerful as one mortal sin—and yet there is no positive power in sin, only negation, only annihilation: and perhaps that is why it is so destructive, it is a nothingness, and where it is there is nothing left—a blank, a moral vacuum. [33]

It is significant that Merton made a connection between his own inner being and the war, for this was a concern that was to grow and become more important as his thought matured and developed. He was able to see that the great social problems of the world were the result of an emptiness within men. At the same time he held a powerful view of sin in which sin was understood as pure negation with no positive power whatsoever. This too, was to be important in his later thinking on issues related to war and peace, for he saw war not as a means used by humankind to achieve its ends, but as an evil which dominated man and brought about his own end. In spite of this feeling of negation Merton still believed that there was hope, for each time man seemed ready to destroy himself there were those who rose up in protest and tried to live lives of goodness, love, charity, and sanctity.

In January of 1935 Merton entered Columbia University, and was immediately attracted to communism. He was open to almost anything that could fill the void left by his Cambridge experience, yet well aware that his personal life was far from what it ought to be. Therefore he came to the conclusion that the problem was not within himself, but within the society in which he lived.

So, now, when the time came for me to take spiritual stock of myself, it was natural that I should do so by projecting my whole spiritual condition into the sphere of economic history and the class-struggle. In other words, the conclusion I came to was that it was not so much myself that was to blame for my unhappiness, but it was the society in which I lived.

I considered the person that I now was, the person that I

had been at Cambridge, and that I had made of myself,
and I saw clearly enough that I was the product of my
times, my society and my class. [34]

A good deal of his attraction to communism came from his
realization that society was evil and corrupt and his conviction
that the communists were the only ones trying to do something
about it. It was, as he explains, the beginning of his social
consciousness:

> It was, I suppose, my acknowledgement of my selfishness,
> and my desire to make reparation for it by developing
> some kind of social and political consciousness. And at
> that time, in my first fervor, I felt myself willing to make
> sacrifices for this end. I wanted to devote myself to the
> causes of peace and justice in the world, I wanted to do
> something to interrupt and divert the gathering momen-
> tum that was dragging the whole world into another war—
> and I felt there was something I could do, not alone, but
> as the member of an active and vocal group. [35]

Merton read a great deal of communist literature, attended
protest rallies, saw numerous Russian propaganda movies, and
defended the communist cause in campus bull-sessions. His
involvement was not very deep, however, and he soon became
disillusioned. He was especially disturbed when the communists, who had all signed the Oxford Pledge, later turned
from pacifism to fight for the Loyalist cause in the Spanish Civil
War. [36] Merton found it difficult to understand how one's views
could change so radically on such an important issue and he
began to question the motivations of the communists.

Merton was deeply involved in the campus life at Columbia,
and a schedule of studies, two part-time jobs, and running on
the cross country team, without going into training, became too
much for him. At the same time both his grandparents died and
he found himself more and more on his own. Finally in 1937 he
suffered what he later described as 'a sort of nervous breakdown'. [37] Among his other symptoms, he found himself
contemplating suicide and he developed gastritis, a condition
which remained with him throughout his life. Undoubtedly he
remembered the death of one of his fraternity brothers who
disappeared and whose body was found two months later in
Brooklyn's Gowanus Canal. He also remembered a class trip to
the Bellevue Morgue and he grew concerned that a similar fate
awaited him. [38] For the first time in his life Merton knew that he

was really in danger and he began to see that, 'In filling myself, I had emptied myself. In grasping things, I had lost everything. In devouring pleasures and joys, I had found distress and anguish and fear.'[39] He had reached his own personal dark night of the soul.

It was at this point in his life that Merton was decisively influenced from three different directions. The first came from Mark Van Doren, a Columbia professor under whom he studied. Merton was impressed with his sincerity and his desire to get to the bottom of things and not deal only with illusion. Perhaps the most important aspect of Van Doren's influence upon Merton was his acquaintance with scholastic philosophy and such modern Neo-Thomists as Jacques Maritain, Etienne Gilson, Mortimer Adler, and Richard McKeon. Van Doren was, in Merton's words, 'profoundly scholastic in the sense that his clear mind looked directly for the quiddities of things, and sought being and substance under the covering of accident and appearances'.[40] As he continued his studies Merton's attentions were drawn more and more to the period of the Middle Ages, and he wrote that his mind 'was turning back, in a way, to the things I remembered from the old days in Saint Antonin. The deep, naive, rich simplicity of the twelfth and thirteenth centuries was beginning to speak to me again.'[41]

A second decisive influence upon Merton began when he bought a copy of Etienne Gilson's book *The Spirit of Medieval Philosophy*. Merton came upon the book quite by chance and later admitted that he would not have bought the book had he known it was Catholic in its orientation. However, he read the book carefully and was especially struck by the concept of *aseitas:*

> This notion made such a profound impression on me that I made a pencil note at the top of the page: 'Aseity of God—God is being *per se*.' I observe it now on the page, for I brought the book to the monastery with me, and although I was not sure where it had gone, I found it on the shelves in Father Abbot's room the other day, and I have it here before me.[42]

The fact that he took this book with him to the monastery is indicative of the importance of it to him in general and the concept of *aseitas* in particular.

Writing about statements in the book which he had underlined, Merton says: 'I think the reason why these statements, and others like them, made such a profound impression on me, lay deep in my own soul. And it was this: I had never had an adequate notion of what Christians meant by God.'[43] In his younger days Merton had never received a clear understanding of who God was, and so these words of Gilson were like a new revelation to him. He comments as follows:

> I think one cause of my profound satisfaction with what I now read was that God had been vindicated in my own mind. There is in every intellect a natural exigency for a true concept of God: we are born with the thirst to know and to see Him, and therefore it cannot be otherwise....
> What a relief it was for me, now, to discover not only that no idea of ours, let alone any image, could adequately represent God, but also that we *should not* allow ourselves to be satisfied with any such knowledge of Him.
> The result was that I at once acquired an immense respect for Catholic philosophy and for the Catholic faith. And that last thing was the most important of all. I now at least recognized that faith was something that had a very definite meaning and a most cogent necessity.[44]

It is significant, especially from a Protestant perspective, that Merton was attracted to Catholic philosophy, which in turn laid the intellectual foundations necessary for Christian faith. He was not able to find this kind of philosophical basis in the Protestantism of his day and he was not satisfied with simplistic appeals to faith and a vague form of religious humanism.[45] What Merton was seeking were clear definitions which would explain his religious longings and experiences. These he found in the writings of Gilson, Maritain, and others of the Neo-Thomist school.

Almost at once Merton felt the need to attend church on a somewhat regular basis, and he began going to the old Zion Episcopal Church where his father had once played the organ. He found that the liberal theology of the rector did not appeal to him, especially when he said that the doctrine of the Incarnation was too much for a reasonable man to believe. He had struggled in order to come to religious belief and now he found the pastor of the church labeling that very belief unreasonable. He continued to attend services occasionally, and later wrote that God was teaching him a lesson by having him attend the Episcopal Church which he had earlier come to despise because of his experiences in England.

During his years at Columbia, Merton became involved with a group of students, many of whom remained his lifelong friends. This group, which included Robert Lax, Edward Rice, Seymour Freedgood, Bob Gibney, Robert Giroux, and others, became the third decisive influence on Merton during his college years. Looking back, he saw God working in the midst of this group, for all of them were having crises of faith and all were disillusioned with what Merton called 'the world'. They were bound together by such common things of life as books, ideas, music, cities, places, and the basic feeling of fear. Merton elaborates:

> The coming war, and all the uncertainties and confusions and fears that followed necessarily from that, and all the rest of the violence and injustice that were in the world, had a very important part to play. All these things were bound together and fused and vitalized and prepared for the action of grace, both in my own soul and in the souls of at least one or two of my friends, merely by our friendship and association together. And it fermented in our sharing of our ideas and miseries and headaches and perplexities and fears and difficulties and desires and hangovers and all the rest. [46]

Like Merton, they were involved in a life-style that could lead only to misery and unhappiness. They were aware of their plight and were seeking answers in philosophy, including scholastic philosophy, and they were all interested in the literary world and expressed talents in this area. Thus Merton found that he was not alone in his disillusionment, searchings, and discoveries. Indeed, several members of the group were seriously discussing becoming Catholics. Merton found that this group partially satisfied his need for community; a need which had not previously been satisfied by the churches which he had attended.

In November of 1937, Merton and Robert Lax, one of this group, were discussing the book *Ends and Means* by Aldous Huxley. [47] Merton had read Huxley several years before and had found his earlier works espousing a philosophy of pleasure, but something different was coming through in *Ends and Means*: Huxley was now showing an interest in mysticism. Merton found this very important in his own spiritual development. He writes:

> The point of his title was this: we cannot use evil means to attain a good end. Huxley's chief argument was that we were using the means that precisely made good ends impossible to attain: war, violence, reprisals, rapacity. And

he traced our impossibility to use the proper means to the fact that men were immersed in the material and animal urges of an element of their nature which was blind and crude and unspiritual.

The main problem is to fight our way free from subjection to this more or less inferior element, and to re-assert the dominance of our mind and will; to vindicate for these faculties, for the spirit as a whole, the freedom of action which it must necessarily have if we are to live like anything but wild beasts, tearing each other to pieces. And the big conclusion from all this was: we must practice prayer and asceticism. [48]

At first he found asceticism revolting and totally foreign to his thinking. After further study he realized that there was much more to it than mere mortification of the flesh and masochism. 'Out of it all,' he writes, 'I took these two big concepts of a supernatural, spiritual order, and the possibility of real, experimental contact with God.' [49]

In the winter of 1937-1938 Merton graduated from Columbia University and immediately enrolled in the graduate school of English. At the time he saw himself becoming a college professor who would spend his time on a peaceful campus teaching and writing books. After a great deal of indecision, he decided to write his master's thesis on the religious ideas in the poetry of William Blake. With this he entered into a new beginning which ended in his conversion to Catholicism.

Conversion to Catholicism

What was needed was the planting of a seed, and that seed came in the life and work of William Blake. The next year was an exciting one for Merton as he studied and read Blake's works, for by now his interest was more than academic. He writes: 'But oh, what a thing it was to live in contact with the genius and the holiness of William Blake that year, that summer, writing the thesis!' [50] Merton found that Blake's problem was really his own:

It was Blake's problem to try and adjust himself to a society that understood neither him nor his kind of faith and love. More than once, smug and inferior minds con-ceived it to be their duty to take this man Blake in hand and direct and form him, to try and canalize what **they** recognized as 'talent' in some kind of a conventional channel. And always this meant the cold and heartless disparagement of all that was vital and real to him in art and faith. There were years of all kinds of petty persecution, from many different quarters, until finally Blake parted from his would-be patrons, and gave up all hope of an alliance with a world that thought he was crazy, and went his own way.[51]

At that time Merton was not consciously giving serious consideration to leaving the world and becoming a monk, but on the personal level he was coming to realize that he must part from his 'would-be patrons' and give up all hope of an alliance with 'the world' to go his own way no matter where that way might lead.

In the process of writing his thesis, entitled 'Nature and Art in William Blake', he found that he was being driven to the realization of his need for a vital faith: 'I was to become conscious of the fact that the only way to live was to live in a world that was charged with the presence and reality of God.'[52] He found Blake's reaction against naturalism and realism in art basically mystical and supernatural. This orientation of Blake struck a responsive chord in Merton, for his artist father had always taught him that it was not the function of art merely to reproduce some pleasure or to stir up one's emotions. Since childhood Merton had 'always understood that art was contemplation, and that it involved the action of the highest faculties of man'.[53]

As he worked on his thesis Merton discovered the works of the Neo-Thomist philosopher Jacques Maritain, particularly his book, *Art and Scholasticism*.[54] In reading it, Merton became more and more aware that, like art, the moral order was not meant to be naturalistic, and that while he had always been anti-naturalistic in art he was totally naturalistic in the moral order. For the first time in his life he learned that nature, when understood in terms of the supernatural, took on a new meaning and significance and that this could be clearly seen in the works of Blake. Merton wrote in his thesis:

One of the most important ideas in Blake is that nature, simply as the eye sees it, is utterly unimportant to art.... He found it literally impossible to draw directly from nature. We have seen what confusion and despair he fell into when he tried to do so. Yet once nature had been assimilated and transformed by his imagination, it blazed before him in a vision fired with the glory of God. Nature, for Wordsworth, was God's greatest and most important creation and so he, too, saw God in nature. But for Blake, nature is only the hem of God's garment. [55]

Merton could now apply this to life. Once nature has been assimilated and transformed by the virtues—which bring about man's unity of nature with itself and with God—one becomes immersed in the vision of the glory of God. The groundwork for Merton's conversion had been more or less laid.

In the middle of his first year of graduate study Merton had a memorable encounter with a Hindu monk, Bramachari, who was visiting New York. Merton was immediately impressed by the simplicity of his life. Bramachari spoke harshly of the missionaries whose standard of living was so far above that of most Hindus that no meaningful relationship could possibly develop. He pointed out that most Christians ate meat, a practice Hindus abhorred. His basic criticism seemed to be that Christians did not know the meaning of asceticism and sacrifice. He was especially critical of Protestant liberal theology, but he also reacted negatively to a large Catholic monastery which he had visitied, for it seemed to him as if their primary interests were in their machinery, printing presses, and physical plants. In the course of his discussion with Merton, Bramachari remarked: 'There are many beautiful mystical books written by Christians. You should read St Augustine's *Confessions*, and *The Imitation of Christ*.' [56] Merton always considered it providential that a Hindu monk should have come all the way from India to tell him to read St Augustine.

Merton was strongly attracted to Catholicism as a philosophy but not as a religion, for he was very fearful of the Catholic Church as an institution. Undoubtedly this feeling could be traced to his childhood when Catholicism conjured up images of political corruption and power politics. He could well have heard some of the frightful tales of the alleged indiscretions between priests and nuns which commonly circulated in Protestant circles. Merton had once visited St Bonaventure College near Olean, New York and refused to get out of the car, unable to endure being in the presence of so many priests and nuns. As a Protestant, this writer can well appreciate Merton's fear, for a childhood memory of running, terrified, from a Catholic church in Quebec in fear of being kidnapped by the priests remains very vivid. Yet despite these fears, Merton found himself being drawn to the Catholic Church and nothing he could do was able to free him from this attraction.

In August 1938, Merton attended Mass for the first time in his life at the Church of Corpus Christi near the Columbia campus. The service impressed him deeply and he was particularly moved at hearing the preacher say that one cannot believe on his own volition but must first be the recipient of God's grace. His reading became more Catholic in orientation, thereafter, and he began reading everything he could about the Jesuits. He even considered entering a seminary to study theology. Still he was not yet ready to take the final step and become a Catholic.

On a muggy summer evening Merton heard the news that World War II had begun with the German occupation of Czechoslovakia. He was shaken to his very roots and became depressed over the entire world situation—a seemingly impossible political impasse, the internal contradictions of American society, a future obscured by a war, and the terrible feeling that no one knew what was to happen. In his mind's eye he envisioned his own death on a battlefield and he knew that he would soon have to come to a decision concerning the Catholic faith. He made it one dreary afternoon as he sat in his room reading about the Jesuit poet Gerard Manley Hopkins. The chapter he was reading concerned Hopkins' own indecision about becoming a Catholic and as he read, a voice seemed to be urging him to decide. Finally he could stand it no longer. He went to the Church of Corpus Christi and told the priest he wanted to become a Catholic.

At last he had taken the greatest step of all toward his conversion and he immediately began taking instruction from the same priest who had preached the day he first attended Mass. He was a good student and never missed a class session. Soon he grew eager to set the date of his baptism. On 16 November 1938, Merton was baptized in the Catholic Church. His close friends from Columbia attended, and the only Catholic among them, Edward Rice, stood up as his godfather. Looking back on that memorable occasion Merton reflected:

> For now I had entered into the everlasting movement of that gravitation which is the very life and spirit of God: God's nature, His goodness without end. And God, that center Who is everywhere, and whose circumference is nowhere, finding me, through incorporation with Christ, incorporated into this immense and tremendous gravitational movement which is love, which is the Holy Spirit, loved me.
>
> And he called out to me from His own immense depths. [57]

After a long and sometimes terrible search, Merton had at last found his spiritual home.

While he was still taking instruction, Merton felt a vague desire to become a priest. To keep this separate from his conversion he said nothing about it to anyone. At the same time, he heard of an instructor at Columbia, Dan Walsh, who taught scholastic philosophy, and he decided to enroll in his class and perhaps speak to him about the priesthood. This encounter with Walsh was the beginning of a friendship between the two that lasted until Merton's death.[58] Through Walsh, Merton was also introduced to Jacques Maritain, whose works had influenced him earlier, and again a lifelong friendship developed.[59] While attending Walsh's class Merton became acquainted with the varieties of Catholic thinking. At one point Walsh called him an Augustinian, a label which pleased Merton greatly. He later wrote: 'From the tenor of his course, I realized that he meant my bent was not so much towards the intellectual, dialectical, speculative character of Thomism, as towards the spiritual, mystical, voluntaristic and practical way of St Augustine and his followers.'[60] Although he enjoyed the course and found Walsh easy to converse with, Merton decided to say nothing to him about his desire to become a priest.

In January 1939, Merton received his MA degree and began working on his doctorate. He planned to write his dissertation on Hopkins and he cherished hopes of becoming a writer himself. These were difficult times, for while he was happy in his new-found faith, he lacked a sense of purpose and thus tended to live an aimless and undisciplined life. At a time when he needed it most, immediately following his conversion, he had no spiritual direction. He was unable to grow and to develop in spiritual isolation. We should note here that while Merton was attracted to contemplation and solitude, he also had a strong need for friends and community. Undoubtedly this was an important factor in his decision to become a monk.

Merton still had said nothing to anyone about his desire to become a priest, but it continued to grow stronger no matter how he tried to put it out of his mind. After a sleepless night in September of 1939 he made his decision. James Thomas Baker describes it as follows:

> Merton's still-fresh religious conversion, his even more recent baptism into the church, and his failure to see any positive hope for the strife-torn world led him in 1939 to make what would prove to be the most important decision of his life. After a sleepless night he told some of his

friends that he intended to become a priest and maybe even enter a monastery. All that day he thought about this abrupt decision, and in the evening he entered a church and promised God that he would indeed be a monk.[61]

This was, for Merton, not only *a* decisive moment, but it was *the* decisive moment of his life. 'And then it suddenly became clear to me that my whole life was at a crisis. Far more than I could imagine or understand or conceive was how hanging upon a word—a decision of mine.'[62] He later speculated that this moment was really his last chance, and that if he had decided not to become a prist his entire life might have been vastly different. With this, Merton's conversion was complete. He had given God everything, including his life.

Monastic Life

Once Merton had made the decision he went to Dan Walsh for advice. As a result of their conversations Merton applied to enter the Franciscan Order. While awaiting an answer, he continued to work on his doctorate, taught some classes at Columbia University, and took a short trip to Cuba where he visited a number of religious shrines.

While in Cuba, Merton had a mystical experience similar in its intensity and reality to the experience which had taken place in Rome several years previously. Merton was attending Mass. The priest was leading the congregation in the beginning words of the creed, 'I believe'. Then it happened:

> I knew with the most absolute and unquestionable certainty that before me, between me and the altar, some-where in the center of the church, up in the air (or any other place because in no place), directly before my eyes, or directly present to some apprehension or other of mine which was above that of the senses, was at the same time God in all His essence, all His power, all His glory, and God in Himself and God surrounded by the radiant faces of the uncountable thousands upon thousands of saints contemplating His glory and praising His Holy Name. And so the unshakable certainty, the clear and immediate knowledge that heaven was right in front of me, struck me like a thunderbolt and went through me like a flash of lightning and seemed to lift me clean up off the earth.[63]

Merton mentions that though this experience lasted only a few moments, it was vivid, and it was an experience he always remembered. In reflecting upon it, he pointed out that such experiences are common to all people everywhere, regardless of their religious beliefs, so long as they believe in God. 'These movements of God's grace are peculiar to nobody, but surely stir in everybody, for it is by them that God calls people to Him, and He calls everybody.'[64] Here again, Merton was laying the groundwork for his later emphasis upon the common elements of mystical experiences of Muslim Sufis, Hindu gurus, Zen Buddhists, and Christian contemplatives like himself.

Merton's experiences with and interest in mysticism were also an important element in his rejection of Protestantism. Protestants, as a whole, have generally been extremely suspicious of mysticism, and this was especially true during the 1930s when the major Protestant denominations in the United States were involved in the fundamentalist-liberal controversy. The fundamentalists, on the one hand, were concerned with a strict orthodoxy and a rigid biblical literalism which left no room for such subjective elements as mysticism. The liberals, on the other hand, tended toward naturalism and humanism and often denied such traditional manifestations of the supernatural as miracles and religious experiences. Merton's exposure to liberal Protestant theology convinced him that it would not satisfy his needs. Had he come into contact with fundamentalist Protestant theology the result would no doubt have been the same. Roman Catholic thought, however, was able to combine the rational and the mystical he read in such thinkers as Thomas Aquinas, St John of the Cross, and Jacques and Raissa Maritain. Perhaps even more important, from Merton's point of view, was the Catholic Church's ability to accommodate mysticism within the framework of monastic orders. During the 1930s Protestant monasticism could only be found in the Anglican/Episcopal tradition and Merton's unhappy experiences in England precluded any serious consideration of this option. In a very real sense, the Catholic Church was the only religious tradition which Merton could call his spiritual home.

Following his return from Cuba Merton spent a few weeks with friends at a cabin near Olean. He spent some time at the Franciscan school, St Bonaventure College, and he began to think seriously about his motivation in asking to become a Franciscan. The rule was fairly simple for him to keep, and he would probably spend his days teaching on a peaceful college campus, perhaps even at St Bonaventure. As he thought about his call he was struck by a realization that no one knew what kind of a person he really was. He had told no one about his past, and the more he thought about it the more constrained he felt to return to New York and tell the Franciscans everything. Upon arriving in the city Merton went straight to the Franciscans and told them. After a day's reflection he returned again and voiced his doubts concerning his motives for wanting to enter the order. At the same time he was overwhelmed with a deep sense of homelessness and was troubled by the knowledge that his brother, John Paul, was suffering at Cornell many of the same things that he had endured at Cambridge. After a second interview he was advised to reconsider his application, and a priest who did not understand the situation, told him he should never enter a monastery and should not become a priest. Says Merton, 'When I came out of that ordeal, I was completely broken in pieces.... The only thing I knew, besides my own tremendous misery, was that I must no longer consider that I had a vocation to the cloister.'[65]

At this point Merton again made a very important decision. He could have easily become discouraged and remained content to live as an ordinary layman or perhaps even given up his faith altogether, but he was convinced that there 'could be no more question of living just like everybody else in the world. There could be no more compromises with the life that tried, at every turn to feed me poison. I had to turn my back on these things.'[66] He bought four breviaries and resolved that if he could not enter the cloister he would at least say the office daily and live as much like a monk as he could. He later remarked that a special grace had inspired him to buy those breviaries, for they helped him to discover the importance of daily prayer in his life.

Following his disappointment at being rejected by the Franciscans, Merton was given a position teaching English at St Bonaventure College and in September 1940 he moved to the campus. Slowly he noticed that his life was improving. He found teaching enjoyable and he continued to say the office daily. His sense of security was rudely shattered, however, when he registered for the draft. Although it did not bring the war very close, it served to remind him that the peaceful life of a college professor would not be his forever:

> Yet it was enough to remind me that I was not going to enjoy this pleasant and safe and stable life forever. Indeed, perhaps now that I had just begun to taste my security, it would be taken away again, and I would be cast back into the midst of violence and uncertainty and

blasphemy and the play of anger and hatred and all passion, worse than ever before. It would be the wages of my own twenty-five years: this is what I had earned for myself and the world. I could hardly complain that I was being drawn into it. [67]

This insecurity was to be with Merton until the very last day of his life, and in his last talk, given in Bangkok just a few hours before his death, he pointed out that in an increasingly politically unstable world even the monastery was insecure.

While at St Bonaventure Merton began to experience a profound love of solitude. He was writing poetry, something that he had not done successfully before becoming a Catholic, and when the snow came he would walk alone by the woods and read his breviary. 'No one would ever come and disturb me out there in all that silence, under the trees, which made a noiseless, rudimentary church over my head, between me and the sky. It was wonderful out there....' [68] In February 1941, realizing his great need for silence, Merton wrote to the Abbey of Gethsemani asking to make an Easter retreat. The mere thought of going to the monastery filled him with happiness, and he was overjoyed when in March he received a letter stating they would be glad to have him come.

About three weeks before his trip to Gethsemani, Merton read in the *Catholic Encyclopedia* about the contemplative orders: the Cistercians, the Carthusians, and the Camaldolese. 'What I saw on those pages,' he wrote, 'pierced me to the heart like a knife.' [69] In the depths of his heart, he grew convinced that he was to enter a monastery and remain there for the rest of his life. He said nothing publicly, but he knew he had found his vocation.

Merton arrived at Gethsemani filled with anticipation, and he was not disappointed, for the life there was all that he had hoped it would be. For him the Abbey of Gethsemani was the center of the universe:

> I should tear out all the other pages of this book, and all the other pages of anything else I have written, and begin here.
>
> This is the center of America. I had wondered what was holding the country together, what has been keeping the universe from cracking in pieces and falling apart. It is places like this monastery—not only this one: there must be others....
>
> It is an axle around which the whole country blindly

turns, and knows nothing about it. Gethsemani holds the
country together the way the underlying substrata of
natural faith that goes with our whole being and can
hardly be separated from it, keeps living on in a man who
has 'lost his faith'—who no longer believes in Being and
yet himself *is*, in spite of his crazy denial that He who IS
mercifully allowed him to *be*.[70]

The majestic liturgy, the prayer, and the solitude of the
monastic life made so deep an impression upon Merton that
when he returned to Louisville the frantic hustle and bustle of
the world disgusted him. 'I turned and fled from the alien and
lunatic street, and found my way into the nearby cathedral, and
knelt, and prayed, and did the Stations of the Cross.'[71]

After visiting Gethsemani, he had little doubt as to what he
should do, and yet he had been told by the Franciscans that he
had no religious vocation. His confusion increased even more
when he heard Baroness Catherine de Hueck speak about her
work in Harlem. Her description of Friendship House caught his
attention and for a time he seriously thought that perhaps this
might be his vocation. He went to Harlem and began working at
Friendship House. The conditions there touched him deeply and
never left his mind. Until then, Merton's attitudes toward the
world had been twofold: outright approval and participation, as
during his college days; and loathing and withdrawal, as
followed his retreat at Gethsemani. His involvement at Friendship House added a new dimension to his attitude toward
society—one of concern and an attempt on his part to alleviate
the sufferings of the victims of a corrupt social system. Merton
made a connection between the social conditions of Harlem and
the conditions in society at large. His social conscience was
filled with both insight and biting social criticism. In Harlem
began what would later make him one of the most significant
social prophets of our time.

During another retreat, this time at the Cistercian Abbey of
Our Lady of the Valley near Providence, Rhode Island, Merton
came to an important realization of his own needs. He writes:

I felt for Friendship House a little of the nostalgia I had
felt for Gethsemani. Here I was, once again thrown back
into the world, alone in the turmoil and futility of it, and
robbed of my close and immediate and visible association
with any group of those who had banded themselves
together to form a small, secret colony of the Kingdom of
Heaven in this earth of exile. No, it was all too evident: I

> needed this support, this nearness of those who really
> loved Christ so much that they seemed to see Him. I
> needed to be with people whose every action told me
> something of the country that was my home: just as
> expatriates in every alien land keep together....[72]

No matter what his vocation, he knew that he could not make
the choice alone—he needed the support and guidance of
others. No longer could he be content with reading his breviary
alone as he walked in solitude through the woods. The active
life of Friendship House and the contemplative life of
Gethsemani both promised him the guidance and support he
needed.

As time passed, he came to accept what he had known all
along deep in his heart: he must become a Trappist. After
talking if over with one of the friars at St Bonaventure whom he
trusted and admired, Merton said that he wanted to give God
everything.

His decision was given further impetus by a notice from his
draft board telling him to come in for another physical
examination and possible reclassification. A few days later the
United States entered the war. Merton knew that he could put
off his decision no longer. He wrote his draft board that he was
entering a monastery and he resigned his teaching position at St
Bonaventure College. Once he had made the decision he acted
with haste to settle his affairs and be on his way to Gethsemani.
In so doing he cut himself off from his past involvement in the
world. He writes:

> I took the manuscripts of three finished novels and one
> half-finished novel and ripped them up and threw them in
> the incinerator. I gave away some notes to people who
> might be able to use them, and I packed up all the poems
> I had written, and the carbon copy of the *Journal of My
> Escape from the Nazis*, and another *Journal* I had kept,
> and some material for an anthology of religious verse, and
> sent it all to Mark Van Doren. Everything else I had
> written I put in a binder and sent to Lax and Rice who
> were living on 114th Street, New York. I closed my
> checking account at the Olean bank, and collected a check,
> with a bonus, for my services in the English Department
> from the bursar who couldn't figure out why a man should
> want to collect his wages in the middle of the month. I
> wrote three letters—to Lax, the Baroness and my
> relatives—and some postcards, and by the afternoon of the

following day, Tuesday, with an amazing and joyous sense
of lightness, I was ready to go. [73]

By evening of the next day Merton was knocking on the door of
the gatehouse at Gethsemani.

Merton's decision to become a monk was not accepted with
joy by many of his friends. Rice reports that 'one of his friends
thought he had gone into an ecclesiastical Devil's Island'. [74] An
editor who had read some of Merton's early works was
infuriated as she thought that a writer with so much promise
was now forever lost to the world. [75] Merton, however, had no
doubt that he had at last found his true vocation.

The journey from the little village of Prades, France, to the
Abbey of Gethsemani in Kentucky was a long one, and when
Merton entered the monastery he made what he thought would
be a clean break with the world. He had experienced the
corruption of the world and his 'decision to become a monk put
a seal of seriousness upon his rejection of American culture'. [76]
And yet, at the same time, he was in a very real sense tied to
the world, and he could not break completely from it. Indeed, it
can be argued that he was tied to American culture in that his
entry into the monastery was within the American tradition of
communitarianism. [77] In later years Merton would discover that
many of the things he rejected that cold December of 1941
would be rediscovered and appreciated anew: his love of
writing, a concern for the world and its problems, and perhaps
most ironic of all, the development within Protestant monasticism of a community life even more authentic than that found
in much of traditional Catholic monasticism. As the years passed
by, Merton found that the monastery, and even the hermitage,
were not far removed from the world after all. At the time,
however, he saw the monastery as 'a school—a school in which
we learn from God how to be happy. Our happiness consists in
sharing the happiness of God, the perfection of His unlimited
freedom, the perfection of His love'. [78]

NOTES

1.   *The Seven Storey Mountain*, p. 3.

2.   Ibid.

3.   Ibid., p. 6.

4.   Ibid., p. 5. Merton learned many details of his childhood from a diary kept by his mother.

5.   Ibid.

6.   Merton's early interest in geography and travel may have provided the foundation for his long poetic work *The Geography of Lograire* (New York: New Directions, 1969). Throughout his life he retained an interest in other countries, cultures, and customs.

7.   *The Seven Storey Mountain*, p. 11.

8.   See Bamberger 'The Cistercian,' *Continuum* 7 (1969) 227-41, rpt. as 'The Monk' in Hart, ed., *Thomas Merton/Monk*, pp. 37-58.

9.   *The Seven Storey Mountain*, p. 7.

10. Ibid., p. 13.

11. Baker, *Thomas Merton Social Critic*, p. 2.

12. Rice, *The Man in the Sycamore Tree*, p. 18.

13. *The Seven Storey Mountain*, p. 30.

14. Ibid., p. 43.

15. Ibid. Merton comments on this incident at length on pp. 42-43.

16. Baker, *Thomas Merton Social Critic*, p. 3.

17. *The Seven Storey Mountain*, p. 65.

18. Ibid.

19. Ibid., p. 66.

20. Ibid.

21. Ibid., pp. 71-72. The experience of his father's death had a great deal to do with Merton's emphasis upon interior peace when all outside supports fail or are removed.

22. Ibid., p. 85.

23. Ibid., p. 88.

24. Ibid., p. 105. When he entered the monastery Merton thought that he had finally found a home, especially as he was obliged to take a vow of stability. In later years, however, he frequently spoke of the monk as a wanderer and a pilgrim.

25. Ibid., p. 108.

26. Ibid., p. 110.

27. Ibid., p. 111. See Rice, *The Man in the Sycamore Tree*, pp. 18-19; and Baker, *Thomas Merton Social Critic*, pp. 4-5.

28. *The Seven Storey Mountain*, p. 118.

29. Rice, *The Man in the Sycamore Tree*, p. 19.

30. Mayo Mohs, *Time* December 7, 1970, p. 59.

31. Rice, *The Man in the Sycamore Tree*, p. 19.

32. *The Seven Storey Mountain*, p. 125.

33. Ibid., pp. 127-28.

34. Ibid., pp. 132-33.

35. Ibid., p. 136.

36. Ibid., pp. 144-45. The Oxford Pledge was a resolution passed by the Oxford Union stating that those Oxford undergraduates who signed the pledge would refuse to fight for king and country in any war whatsoever. As the clouds of World War II gathered this pledge was signed by hundreds of thousands of students on campuses around the world, including Columbia University.

37. Ibid., pp. 161-64. Merton had a similar kind of breakdown while in the monastery which he describes briefly in *The Sign of Jonas* (1953; rpt. Garden City: Doubleday Image, 1956) p. 226.

38. *The Seven Storey Mountain*, pp. 152-53.

39. Ibid., p. 164.

40. Ibid., p. 140.

41. Ibid., p. 171.

42. Ibid., p. 173. Merton refers to Etienne Gilson, *The Spirit of Medieval Philosophy*, trans. A.H.C. Downes (New York: Scribners, 1936) pp. 42-63. The concept of *aseitas* is similar to the Zen Buddhist concept of 'suchness' or 'pure consciousness' and Merton elaborates on this similarity in the essay 'The New Consciousness' in *Zen and the Birds of Appetite*, pp. 15-32.

43. *The Seven Storey Mountain*, p. 174.

44. Ibid., pp. 174-75.

45. During the late 1920s and early 1930s a school of Christian philosophy arose in the Netherlands which attempted to provide a philosophical basis for Protestant thought. Herman Dooyeweerd and D.H. Th. Vollenhoven were the originators of this philosophical movement which has had considerable influence in Europe, North America, South Africa, and to a lesser extent in Asia. Merton was unaware of this school since the original works were not available in English at that time.

46. *The Seven Storey Mountain*, p. 178.

47. Aldous Huxley, *Ends and Means: An Inquiry into the Nature of Ideals and into the Methods Employed for Their Realization* (New York: Harper, 1937).

48. *The Seven Storey Mountain*, p. 185.

49. Ibid., p. 186.

50. Ibid., pp. 189-90. See also Merton, 'Nature and Art in William Blake: An Essay in Interpretation,' Thesis, Columbia University, 1939.

51. *The Seven Storey Mountain*, p. 190.

52. Ibid., p. 191.

53. Ibid., p. 203.

54. Jacques Maritain, *Art and Scholasticism*, trans. J.F. Scanlan (New York: Scribners, 1930).

55. Merton, 'Nature and Art in William Blake,' p. 94.

56. *The Seven Storey Mountain*, p. 198.

57. Ibid., p. 225.

58. Dan Walsh became a Catholic priest at the age of sixty. For a number of years he lived in Bardstown, Kentucky, only a few miles from Gethsemani. He died on 28 August 1975 and was buried at Gethsemani.

59. Jacques Maritain taught philosophy for many years at Princeton University. Following his retirement he returned to France and joined the Little Brothers of Jesus in Toulouse. He died there on 28 April 1973.

60. *The Seven Storey Mountain*, p. 221.

61. Baker, *Thomas Merton Social Critic*, pp. 11-12.

62. *The Seven Storey Mountain*, p. 255.

63. *The Secular Journal of Thomas Merton*, p. 71. See Carl G. Jung, et al., *Man and His Symbols* (Garden City: Doubleday, 1964), p. 226, for a fifteenth century French miniature that is remarkably similar to Merton's description of his mystical vision. Merton believed that mystical experience and artistic experience are closely related. He expands on this in his *Raids on the Unspeakable*, pp. 179-82.

64. *Secular Journal*, p. 72.

65. *The Seven Storey Mountain*, p. 298.

66. Ibid., p. 300.

67. Ibid., pp. 308-09.

68. Ibid., p. 309.

69. Ibid., p. 318. The Cistercians who in the seventeenth-century reformed their life-style to primitive ideals are also known as the Trappists, a name derived from La Grande Trappe, the French Cistercian Abbey which led the reform.

70. *Secular Journal*, p. 154.

71. *The Seven Storey Mountain*, p. 332.

72. Ibid., p. 349.

73. Ibid., p. 368. The *Journal of My Escape from the Nazis* was published after Merton's death as *My Argument with the Gestapo: A Macaronic Journal* (Garden City: Doubleday, 1969). The *Journal* was published as *The Secular Journal of Thomas Merton* (New York: Farrar, Straus and Cudahy, 1959) with the copyright assigned to Madonna House, founded by Baroness Catherine de Hueck Doherty.

74. Rice, *The Man in the Sycamore Tree*, p. 51.

75. See Naomi Burton, 'A Note on the Author and This Book' in Merton, *My Argument with the Gestapo*, p. 10.

76. Dennis Quentin McInerny, 'Thomas Merton and Society', Dissertation, University of Minnesota 1969 p. 40.

77. Ibid., pp. 214-16.

78. *The Seven Storey Mountain*, p. 373.

III

THE SPIRITUAL FOUNDATIONS OF MERTON'S THOUGHT

The Modern Thomists

MARK VAN DOREN introduced Merton to scholastic philosophy and to such modern scholastic thinkers as Etienne Gilson, Jacques Maritain, and the American Neo-Thomists Mortimer Adler and Richard McKeon. Van Doren was 'profoundly scholastic...and sought being and substance under the covering of accident and appearances'.[1] Merton's previous orientation had been more toward appearances than substance, he had tended to see God in immature conceptions which he had held as a child or he had equated God with various forms of institutional religion which he had rejected as inadequate.[2] Because he rejected these conceptions, he rejected God. His introduction to scholastic philosophy brought him face to face with the reality of God, a reality that went much deeper than childish conceptions and institutional religion.

In reading Gilson's book, *The Spirit of Medieval Philosophy*, Merton was struck in particular by the concept of *aseitas*, a concept that revolutionized his thinking.

> *Aseitas*—the English equivalent is a transliteration—simply means the power of a being to exist absolutely in virtue of itself, not as caused by itself, but requiring no cause, no other justification for its existence except that its very nature is to exist. There can be only one such Being: that is God. And to say that God exists *a se*, of and by reason of Himself, is merely to say that God is Being Itself. *Ego sum qui sum*. And this means that God must enjoy 'complete independence not only as regards everything outside but also as regards everything within Himself.'[3]

Or, as Gilson puts it, 'When God says that He is being, and if what He says is to have any intelligible meaning for our minds, it can only mean this: that He is the pure act of existing.'[4] For Merton, *aseitas* meant that 'there is in every intellect a natural exigency for a true concept of God: we are born with the thirst to know and to see Him, and therefore it cannot be otherwise.'[5]

Such a concept of God is not without certain practical implications, as Gilson indicates:

> Since in fact God is being *per se*, and since our conception of God absolutely excludes all non-being, and all that dependence that would result from non-being, it follows that in Him the fulness of existence must be completely realized. God is thus pure being in its state of complete fulfillment and realization, as that being alone can be which can receive no addition either from within or from without.[6]

The average man or woman of the twentieth century does not realize the fullness of existence in God. Merton was no exception. This new understanding of God was a turning point not only in his thinking but in his actions as well. A number of years after becoming a monk he remarked, 'Everything you love for its own sake, outside of God alone, blinds your intellect and destroys your judgment of moral values.'[7]

Even as Merton became interested in Catholic culture and scholastic philosophy, the Catholic Church conjured up in his mind images of political corruption and totalitarian thinking. By reading Gilson he was able to see within the Catholic tradition someone who had a deep respect for freedom and basic human liberties. He comments concerning Gilson's interpretation of Duns Scotus:

> According to Gilson, Duns Scotus says of God that He is free 'to set up any moral code He pleases so long as it deals with rules of human conduct whose relations to His own essence are not necessary ones.' This is against those who assume that all moral relationships with God are necessary ones, excluding spontaneity; that to serve God is not to be free but finally and irrevocably bound. A moral code does not suppress choice, but educates and forms liberty. But for some, morality is opposed not only to evil choice (sin) but to *any* choice at all, any personal act of the will, and initiative, and obedience is therefore compulsion, not a matter of love. For them God is not love but power, obedience is not freedom but submission and inertia.[8]

As Merton's thought matured, Gilson's interpretation of Duns Scotus provided a background for many of his own comments on contemporary forms of monasticism and the religious life.[9]

Merton was struck by the ability of the modern Thomists to get to the heart of whatever matters were under consideration, whether it was the being and existence of God or the place of freedom in morality. He always paid tribute to Mark Van Doren and Dan Walsh, who introduced him to scholastic philosophy.[10]

Jacques Maritain's thought was an important influence on Merton from the days when he was writing his master's thesis to his last few years at the hermitage. He was first struck by Maritain's understanding of 'virtues' not in a negative sense, but as 'the powers by which one can come to acquire happiness'.[11] Maritain distinguished between two kinds of virtues: those of the speculative order where the sole end is knowledge, and those of the practical order where one's knowledge is put to use with a goal of making or doing something.[12] For Maritain art was a part of the practical order, and since it was concerned with action it was also concerned with morality. Beyond this, however, 'all our values depend upon the nature of God'.[13] This had special significance for Merton; his thesis was on 'Nature and Art in William Blake', and his own father had been an artist. In addition, Maritain pointed out that 'the Contemplative and the Artist...both prefected by intellectual habit binding them to the transcendental order, are in a position to sympathise'.[14] Reading this, Merton was reminded that his father had taught him 'that it was almost blasphemy to regard the function of art as merely to reproduce some kind of sensible pleasure or, at best, to stir up the emotions to a transitory thrill. I had always understood that art was contemplation, and that it involved the action of the highest faculties of man.'[15] Merton was, in a sense, already predisposed to appreciate what contemplation was all about, and he understood art in terms of a higher purpose than mere sensual pleasure. From a scholastic point of view, art found its ultimate purpose and fulfillment in God, and from his study of Maritain, Merton was able to make a transition from art to the religious life, for he 'understood that the artistic experience, at its highest, was actually a natural analogue of mystic experience'.[16] He was able to write, 'It has taken little more than a year and a half, counting from the time I read Gilson's *The Spirit of Medieval Philosophy* to bring me up from an "atheist"—as I considered myself—to one who accepted all the full range and possibilities of religious experience right up to the highest degree of glory.'[17]

Maritain's work, particularly his *The Degrees of Knowledge*, provided the foundation for much of Merton's thinking on contemplation and the importance of the inner life. In fact he stated that the second part of *The Degrees of Knowledge*, along with *Prayer and Intelligence* by Maritain and his wife Raïssa, form the necessary groundwork for his own book *The Ascent to Truth*.[18] In reading Maritain one can see how he influenced Merton.[19] He was largely responsible for Merton's interest in St John of the Cross, as he was deeply impressed with the concept of *Todo Y Nada*—all and nothing—as it pertains to the life of contemplation and mystical union with God.[20]

Raïssa Maritain also exercised a great influence upon Merton, for like him, she was a poet. Jacques and Raïssa worked closely together and their love for each other was evident in their work. Merton says of her:

> Raïssa Maritain was perhaps one of the greatest contemplatives of our time, great in her humility, her simplicity, her angelic purity of heart, her utter devotion to truth. Her whole life, all her thought and love were centered in the supernatural, that is to say in the Three Divine Persons considered as a source and finality more intimate and more ultimate to her than her own natural and contingent individuality.[21]

Merton found Raïssa's poetry so immediate and vivid that he thought 'instinctively of visual analogies for her poetic experience precisely because it is so immediate and so pure. It has the direct impact of painting....'[22] It was this sense of immediacy, this stripping away of all illusion, that strongly appealed to Merton.

Able to read and speak French, Merton was fascinated by French thinkers, particularly by Maritain and his Thomist circle at Meudon.[23] To him Paris was always *the* city:

> It means Baudelaire, it means Valéry, Péguy. It means Leon Bloy and the Maritains (not to forget Bergson!). It means Manet and Monet, Renoir, Toulouse-Lautrec, Eric Satie. It means Braque and Picasso and Chagall, Jean Cocteau, Max Jacob and Proust...once you start this litany there is no end to it. Through these words, plays, paintings, and poems Paris has kept reaching out and grabbing hold of me in London, in Cambridge, in Rome, in New York, and in this monastery lost in Kentucky.[24]

The most significant of the French thinkers for Merton were the Thomists—Gilson, Maritain, Leon Bloy, and Garrigou-Legrange, especially important for his synthesis of Thomism with St John of the Cross. Twentieth century Thomism and scholasticism provided Merton with a philosophical framework. For the first time in his life he was exposed to what he saw to be clear thinking; ideas not only logical and well thought out but totally orientated toward God.

St Augustine

At the same time Merton was studying Neo-Thomists, he was also reading in mysticism and related subjects. The Hindu monk Bramachari had told him, 'There are many beautiful mystical books written by Christians. You should read St Augustine's *Confessions....*'[25] At the time he failed to take the advice but when he later did, Augustine became very much a part of his study. Augustine's greatest influence came to Merton more or less indirectly, by way of Catholic theology and spirituality. In any serious study of mysticism one encounters the insights of Augustine, whose spirituality has left a lasting impression upon Catholic thought.[26]

While Aquinas was relatively optimistic and viewed grace as fulfilling the nature of man, Augustine was more pessimistic and saw man as fallen from grace. According to Augustine, man in his original state of paradise was able to will and do good and at the same time was sustained by the general assistance of divine grace. However, as a result of the fall, man found himself unable to attain spiritual union with God without being given a special grace from God.[27] This theological doctrine has direct implications for the spiritual life, and in this respect Augustine made a new contribution to Christian thought, especially in his concept of love. In his book *Agape and Eros*, Anders Nygren comments:

> Augustine's view of love has exercised by far the greatest influence in the whole history of the Christian idea of love. It even puts the New Testament view of love in the shade. New Testament texts continue to form the basis of discussion, but they are *interpreted* in accordance with Augustine. Ever since his time the meaning of Christian love has generally been expressed in categories he created, and even the emotional quality which it bears is largely due to him. Not even the Reformation succeeded in

making any serious alteration. In Evangelical Christendom to the present day, Augustine's view has done far more than Luther's to determine what is meant by Christian love.[28]

Nygren points out that Augustine's influence had been possible because he lived on the frontiers of two religious worlds, 'Hellenistic Eros and primitive Agape, and his significance lies chiefly in the fact that *these worlds really meet in his person and form a spiritual unity.*'[29] This alone reminds one of Merton, who took spiritual unity and union as one of his major themes. In a written statement presented on the occasion of the opening of the Thomas Merton Studies Center at Bellarmine College in Louisville, he declared, 'Whatever I may have written, I think it all can be reduced in the end to this one root truth: that God calls human persons to union with Himself and with one another in Christ, in the Church which is His Mystical Body.'[30] Merton, like Augustine, was concerned with unity.[31]

Augustine was able to unite the Hellenistic concept of *eros* with the primitive Christian concept of *agape* to form a synthesis which he called *caritas*. *Eros* is a love that ascends and seeks to satisfy its needs, while *agape* descends so that it can bring help and give to others.

> Eros, left to itself, can see God and feel drawn to Him. But it sees God only at a remote distance; between Him and the soul lies an immense ocean, and when the soul imagines it has reached Him it has simply entered, in self-sufficiency and pride, into the harbour of itself. But for pride, Eros would be able to bring the soul to God. Here Agape must come to its assistance: God's *humilitas* must vanquish man's *superbia*. For even if all other ties that bind the soul to things earthly and transient are broken, its ascent will not succeed so long as it is infected with *superbia*. By *superbia* the soul is chained to itself and cannot ascend to what is above itself. *It is the task of Agape to sever this last link of the soul with things finite.* When a man has been freed from himself under the influence of God's *humilitas*, then the ascent succeeds. There is no longer anything to drag the soul down. The humility of Christ, the Cross of Christ, bears it over the ocean to its fatherland.[32]

Augustine realized that man could not ascend to God on his

own, since this ability had been lost in the fall. Man could, however, ascend to God when given God's grace to do so in the form of *agape*. While it is true that modern Catholic theology rejects some points of Augustine's thought on grace, 'in its idea of grace as "infused love" which makes our ascent to God possible, it has faithfully continued the course Augustine began'.[33]

Dom Cuthbert Butler, in his book, *Western Mysticism*, says that 'Augustine is for me the Prince of Mystics, uniting in himself, in a manner I do not find in any other, the two elements of mystical experience, viz. the most penetrating intellectual vision into things divine, and a love of God that was a consuming passion.'[34] Beyond Augustine's theme of union, however, is an understanding of mysticism that has become part and parcel of Catholic mystical theology and certainly played an important role in the development of Merton's understanding of it. Louis Bouyer gives this explanation:

> Immersed in the world by its senses, the soul must begin by withdrawing itself from the world, by re-entering into itself, and thus rediscovering itself. Thus it will rediscover the image of God to which it was made. But God is not His image: He is the model of it. And so, having re-entered into itself, the soul must still go beyond itself in order to find Him. Yet it cannot accomplish this return except by hearing the Word of God which made all things and which, by the Incarnation, now resounds in this world where the soul has forgotten Him in forgetting itself. Thereby the soul is recalled from lust ('the love of self carried to contempt of God') to charity ('the love of God carried to contempt of self').[35]

'The Augustinian idea of charity, in which love of self is not so much renounced or transcended as purified by again becoming love of self as the image of God' was basic to Aquinas.[36]

Augustine and others of his time saw contemplation purely as a gift from God, a special grace necessary for this total love of God. An important aspect of this contemplative process was the purification of the soul. Through purification one could go beyond the self and ascend to God. This idea is reflected when Merton says, 'To enter into the realm of contemplation one must in a certain sense die: but this death is in fact the entrance into a higher life. It is a death for the sake of life, which leaves behind all that we can know or treasure as life, as thought, as experience, as joy, as being.'[37]

It is possible to refuse this grace of God and thus never to ascend beyond the mundane existence of everyday life. One can reject the *agape* of God and not cut oneself off from the world of the finite. As Merton points out, *'The seeds that are planted in my liberty at every moment, by God's will, are the seeds of my own identity, my own reality, my own happiness, my own sanctity'*.[38] Augustine pointed out that basic to every human life is desire and that desire can only find its meaning in God—'God *is the only right and natural correlate to man's desire.'*[39] If man fails to desire God he is failing to realize his full humanity and to find his true identity, and thus he cannot realize the fruits of contemplation and enjoy the mystical experience. Man realizes himself through the ascent to God which is made possible by God's grace and which results in love not only for God but for others.

The young Merton was deeply concerned with the purification of his soul, forsaking the world, and making the ascent to God. While his interests were primarily mystical, he did not reject theology, and he studied not only Augustine but Aquinas as well.

St Thomas Aquinas

Merton first became acquainted with the thought of Aquinas through Dan Walsh, whose opinion that Merton was basically Augustinian delighted Merton, especially since it was made while he was taking a course on the philosophy of Aquinas. He writes:

> To be called an 'Augustinian' by Dan Walsh was a compliment, in spite of the traditional opposition between the Thomist and Augustinian schools, Augustinian being taken not as confined to the philosophers of that religious order, but as embracing all the intellectual descendants of St Augustine. It is a great compliment to find oneself numbered as part of the same spiritual heritage as St Anselm, St Bernard, St Bonaventure, Hugh and Richard of St Victor, and Duns Scotus also. And from the tenor of his course, I realized that he meant that my bent was not so much towards the intellectual, dialectical, speculative character of Thomism, as towards the spiritual, mystical, voluntaristic and practical way of St Augustine and his followers.[40]

There is little doubt that Walsh's classification of Merton was basically correct: Merton was not then and never became a theologian in the strict sense of the word, and he had certainly a spiritual and mystical bent. At the same time, however, the major theological influence upon Merton came not so much from Augustine as from Aquinas, for it was through the modern Thomists that he came to know and understand mysticism.

In the mid-thirteenth century there had arisen a theological conflict between three forces—the rationalists who followed Averroes, the traditionalists who followed Augustine, and a third group, in the center, which included Albert the Great and Aquinas. The Averroists stressed the importance of the intellect and placed authority in the realm of human reason. The Augustinians went to the other extreme and affirmed the transcendence of God to the point where they often elevated faith and mystical intuition at the expense of reason. Aquinas took a middle position and emphasized one supremely important ideal: 'To defend the autonomy of man's intelligence and of the human personality against the extremists on both sides who threatened to submerge man in God, on the one hand, and in a universal active intellect on the other.'[41] Aquinas' emphasis upon the intellect Merton saw as a safeguard against extremism and as a protection of true mysticism, for Aquinas was not only a great theologian but a mystic as well, as Merton points out:

> Saint Thomas, like all Christian theologians, knows perfectly well that the consummation of man's destiny is in love and that the way to divine union is the way of the theological virtues, through the night of faith. Hence the paradox that the intellectualism of Thomas Aquinas turns out, after all, to be the supreme criterion of true mysticism, because there is no such thing as a sanctity that is not intelligent.[42]

This stress upon the intellect is very important, for Merton always cautions against a false mysticism of emotionalism, fanaticism, and the occult.[43]

Merton contends that for Aquinas 'theology was an organic whole, his mysticism is not merely centered in the questions of the *Summa* devoted to the contemplative life but in all his discussions of the relations of men with their God'.[44] His own emphasis is much the same:

> Contemplation, far from being opposed to theology, is in fact the normal perfection of theology. We must not

separate intellectual study of revealed truth and contemplative experience of that truth as if they could never have anything to do with one another. On the contrary they are simply two aspects of the same thing. Dogmatic and mystical theology, or theology and 'spirituality' are not to be set apart in mutually exclusive categories, as if mysticism were for saintly women and theological study were for practical but, alas, unsaintly men. This fallacious division perhaps explains much that is actually lacking both in theology and in spirituality. But the two belong together. Unless they are united, there is no fervour, no life and no spiritual value in theology, no substance, no meaning and no sure orientation in the contemplative life.[45]

For Merton as for Aquinas spirituality is always closely united with theology. The two always go together.

Today we think of Aquinas as the foremost authority in the Catholic Church, but Aquinas himself never accepted any such role. In fact he had little respect for the 'argument of authority' in philosophical matters, and Merton states that 'the whole difficulty of St Thomas arises, not from Thomas himself, but (as has been said so often) from Thomists.'[46]

Merton, in his studies, attempted to get back to Aquinas himself. While he was introduced to Aquinas by the modern Thomists, he was not content to read only interpretations of Aquinas, he went back to the sources. Here he found that Aquinas' study of Aristotle—considered ill-advised by his contemporaries—brought out one major truth of utmost importance: 'Aristotle gave to Christian thought in the thirteenth century its *"turning to the world"*, its respect for nature, for the physical, for the concrete reality of the universe.'[47] Merton comments at length:

> The theology of St Thomas is a reaction against a theology that denatures nature by engrossing itself in allegorical and symbolic systems. St Thomas returned to the realities that the symbols were intended to signify....
>
> This was the result of the action of theology as aware of itself *in the world*, not out of it or above it. The theology of St Thomas was fully rooted in the Christian culture of his time, but also in the culture that was resulting from the encounter between Christianity and Islam, which did so much to create the modern Western world....
>
> There is first of all that 'turning to the world'—that

awareness of the modern world, the world of poor people, of cities, of politically minded burghers and artisans, of men more interested in the authority of reason than of ecclesiastics. But there is also the Bible. And there is the turning to the non-Christian world—to Aristotle and to Islam.[48]

This understanding of Aquinas provided a theological framework for a change in Merton's own thinking. In his early works he had rejected the physical world in preference for that which was spiritual. In his later works, he turned to the world for his inspiration.

Finally, Aquinas was concerned with going beyond allegory and symbol to that which was real, as was Merton. He declares: 'We are all too prone to believe in our own programs and to follow the echo of our own slogans into a realm of illusion and unreality....I am not merely a spokesman for a contemplative or monastic movement, and I am not purely and simply a "spiritual" writer.'[49]

This desire to avoid illusion and unreality means that one must be cautious in speaking about the intimate union with God that is the goal of the Christian life. Merton points out that the Catholic Church, in following the very heart of Aquinas' *Summa Theologica*, refuses to let man divide himself:

> The sanity of Catholic theology will never permit the ascetic to wander off into the bypaths of angelism or gnosticism. The Church does not seek to sanctify men by destroying their humanity, but by elevating it, with all its faculties and gifts, to the supreme perfection which the Greek Fathers call 'deification'. At the same time, the Church does not leave man under any illusion about himself. She clearly shows him the powerlessness of his natural faculties to achieve Divine Union by their own efforts.[50]

Maritain contends that such union is only partially achieved in this life: 'For St Thomas Aquinas and the whole Christian tradition, the final end of human life is transformation in God, "to become God by participation," which is fully achieved in heaven by the beatific vision and beatific love, and fulfilled here below, in faith, by love.'[51] Man, then, may desire union with God but he can achieve this union only by God's grace.[52] It was of utmost importance to Merton that these two points be kept in their proper balance; otherwise the humanity of man is destroyed or the divinity of God is sacrificed.

Aquinas influenced Merton greatly on the very personal question of the active and contemplative life. In an essay entitled 'Poetry and Contemplation: A Reappraisal' Merton states that 'contemplation is the fullness of the Christian vocation—the full flowering of baptismal grace and of the Christ-life in our souls.'[53] Aquinas put forth a similar view when he said that 'the contemplative life is more excellent than the active'.[54] An examination of Aquinas' utterances on contemplation clearly shows his influence on Merton.[55] Aquinas makes a distinction between the two kinds of contemplation: 'The contemplation of God in this life is imperfect in comparison with the contemplation of heaven.'[56] Merton also distinguishes between these two levels in holding that what God begins in this life will be finally consummated in the final union with God of the life to come.

Although Aquinas considers the contemplative life superior to the active life, he points out that a mixed life is superior to either the contemplative or the active life, and that when taken together each serves to strengthen the other.

> Consequently those who are more adapted to the active life can prepare themselves for the contemplative by the practice of the active life; while none the less, those who are more adapted to the contemplative life can take upon themselves the works of the active life, so as to become yet more apt for contemplation.[57]

Aquinas goes on to say that 'it would seem that prudence belongs neither to the active nor to the contemplative life, but...to a kind of life which is betwixt and between.'[58] For Aquinas the contemplative life grows from an active life, yet the contemplative life is deepened by the actions which spring from it. Merton found that a purely contemplative life was an impossibility for him and that his own life was in reality a mixed life, even though he considered himself a contemplative.

There is yet another, although rather indirect, area in which Aquinas had an influence upon the development of Merton's thought. Merton carried on an extensive correspondence with a number of Asian scholars, among them the great Zen Buddhist authority D.T. Suzuki. Merton was greatly impressed with Suzuki's ability to communicate with westerners in terms that were familiar, particularly in discussions dealing with mysticism and the contemplative tradition. Suzuki was thoroughly familiar with the western mystical tradition, especially with the thought of Meister Eckhart.[59] Eckhart's master was Aquinas, as Merton points out, so Suzuki's ability to communicate with western Christians is in part due to his familiarity with the basic principles of Aquinas as they came to him through Eckhart. In their dialogue together Merton and Suzuki were able to speak a common language on two fronts—Merton understood Buddhism and Suzuki understood Christianity—and this communication was in part due to Aquinas.

Aquinas has probably left a greater imprint upon Catholic theology than any other single person, and it is no surprise to find his theology present in the background of all of Merton's writings. Merton considered Aquinas the greatest of all the theologians and a great mystic: 'His mystical theology fits into the apophatic tradition...but is not confined to it. Nor is his mystical doctrine formally separated from his dogma and moral theology.'[60] Like Aquinas, Merton attempts to be open to the world, to respect the integrity of the human person, and yet he maintains firmly and without apology that union with God is the highest state to which man can attain.

St Bernard of Clairvaux

Bernard of Clairvaux has been called the last of the Church Fathers. Although he does not actually belong to the Patristic Age, he was loyal to the spirit of patristic theology during the period of great intellectual ferment that immediately preceded the development of medieval scholasticism. Bernard defended monastic theology against the speculative innovations of Abelard and Gilbert of Poitiers. He condemned Abelard's notion of faith and Gilbert's distinction between God and Divinity, and in doing so he helped prepare the way for scholasticism and the thought of Aquinas. Merton came into contact with the thinking of Bernard of Clairvaux only after his acquaintance with scholasticism.

It was only natural that Merton should find Bernard a foundation stone in his own thinking, for Bernard was both a Cistercian and troubled by the question of contemplation and action. He was also very like Merton in his personality and interests. Bernard was a man of great literary ambition, and upon entering the monastery he did all that he could to escape this ambition and completely focus his attention upon God. Merton elaborates:

It seems that one of the things Saint Bernard wanted to

get away from, when he entered Cîteaux, was literary
ambition. Profoundly affected by the humanistic renaissance of the twelfth century, his works still bear witness,
by their quotations from Ovid, Persius, Horace, Terence,
and other classical authors, to the influence he met with
when he studied the liberal arts with the canons of Saint
Vorles at Chatillon-sur-Seine. He seems to have become
afraid of poetry and rhetoric, and to have run away from
them....He was not one who wrote because he had to. His
treatises were usually composed at the request of some
fellow monk, some abbot, some other churchman, to
answer a question or to meet some particular need.[61]

Merton expressed a similar sentiment in his journal, *The Sign of
Jonas*: 'At that time I was upset by the fact that Dom Frederic,
who was then Abbot, wanted me to write a lot of books. Perhaps
I was less upset than I thought. But in any case, I did have to
write a lot of books, some of which were terrible.'[62] Merton was
a gifted writer, and although some of his early works may have
been 'terrible' there can be no doubt that most of what he wrote
was unique in its style and content. Merton has similar things to
say concerning Bernard's works:

Bernard is never abstract....His sermons are alive with
images and figures out of the Scriptures. Color, music,
movement, fire, contrasts of light and darkness, impas-
sioned dialogue between the poverty of man and the
greatness of God, between the mercy of God and His
justice, flights of allegory, realistic examples sketched
from life in the cloister—all these elements make
Bernard's sermons extraordinarily alive. Indeed the very
wealth of them sometimes oppresses the reader who has
lost his sense of symbolism, or never had one. All the
opulence that Bernard criticized in the plastic arts here
runs riot in his prose....[63]

It is not difficult to understand how Merton could be so
attracted to Bernard.

Merton shared the accepted view that Bernard was a great
mystic, and he writes that 'he is spiritual indeed, and a great
mystic. But he is a speculative mystic; his mysticism is
expressed as a theology'.[64] Bernard believed that man is made
solely for the purpose of loving God, but this love must be
expressed in freedom; the progress of the spiritual life must
take place in an atmosphere of liberty. According to Bernard it

is liberty that constitutes God's image in man. At the same time, he emphasizes God's presence in bringing about the soul's transformation: it 'is an *ordinatio caritatis*, that is to say the elevation, disciplining, and redirection of all the soul's capacity for love by the actual motion of the divine spirit.'[65] In the inner soul of man the struggle between sin and the love of God takes place. Merton explains Bernard's understanding of sin:

> Now St Bernard puts this *sapor mortis*, this taste for death, at the very heart of original sin. It is the exact opposite of the wisdom, the *sapida scientia* of existential ('tasting') knowledge of the divine good. The two are incompatible with one another. They cannot exist together. Consequently, having acquired the one, Adam necessarily lost the other.[66]

For both Bernard and Merton, the arena of spiritual conflict lies not in the outside world but within the soul of man himself.

A concept common to much of Catholic thought, and coming from Augustine, is that man has an innate desire for God which sin cannot eradicate. According to Merton, Bernard maintains that man's soul retains the image of God—for Bernard, liberty—in spite of sin:

> For after all, human nature in its essence was not ruined, only weakened by original sin. St Bernard sees the fall not as a descent from the supernatural to the natural, but as a collapse into ambivalence in which the historical 'nature' in which man was actually created for supernatural union with God is turned upside down and inside out, and yet *still retains its innate capacity and 'need' for divine union.*
>
> The human soul is still the image of God, and no matter how far it travels away from Him into the regions of unreality, it never becomes so completely unreal that its original destiny can cease to torment it with a need to return to itself in God, and become, once again, real.[67]

Two things stand out: First, Merton sees human sinfulness in terms of unreality. Reality is God and the further one becomes separated from God, the more unreal one becomes. Second, the real—the image of God—is never completely stamped out or lost. It is always possible to return to reality, to return to the ground of one's own being, to return once again to God and to love God with all one's heart, soul and mind.

Within the soul of man there are in opposition two elements that must be reconciled and united: the human and the divine. According to Merton 'this conflict counters the other, cuts across it at right angles, and even lifts it upwards into a new dimension. But here everything takes place in mystery. We cannot see what happens, because no man can see into another man's soul. He can barely see a little into his own.'[68] The conflict between the real and the unreal—between love for God and love for sin—is only part of the problem, for the conflict between the human and the divine is also expressed in the division between the sacred and the secular and between the contemplative and the active. This conflict reached epic proportions in the life of Saint Bernard, for his life was very active and his involvement in the affairs of the world very deep.

> It was because he was at once so much a person and so much a mystic, that Bernard was also essentially a man of the Church—*Vir Ecclesiae.*
> We shall glance presently at some details of his tremendously active life. Although the tension between these two apparently conflicting powers does not account for that life, or for its achievements, or for its sanctity, it was most certainly a factor in his sanctification, because, as we have said, all sanctity is born of conflict.[69]

The conflict in Bernard's life came to a head in 1145 when he and Pope Eugene III planned the second Crusade.

The second Crusade was largely Bernard's work, for it was he who organized and preached it. At first he refused, but when asked to do so by Pope Eugene III, he accepted and gave the crusade his blessing. 'It is here,' says Merton, 'that we see Bernard, the saint, as a most provoking enigma, as a temptation, perhaps even as a scandal.'[70] It is fashionable in some circles to say that Bernard the crusader is not the real Bernard, the Bernard of mystical contemplation, the Bernard who wrote the masterful sermons on the *Song of Songs.* Merton, however, considered such a view as illusion and says that 'we cannot see the "true" Bernard by dividing him against himself, and the truth is that the Bernard of Vézelay is the very same man who is prepared, within a short time, to preach the magnificent last sermons on the Canticle of Canticles, sermons which have nothing to do with war but with the sublime peace of mystical marriage.'[71]

Merton himself was often accused of this same kind of ambivalence by those who, having read his more spiritual writings, supposed him to be something of a saint or holy man. John Eudes Bamberger, then a fellow monk at Gethsemani, relates how a nun misunderstood Merton's criticism of his own community:

> Fr Louis [Merton] had been asked about the renewal of monasticism. Had it been accepted at Gethsemani, was there evidence of understanding of aggiornamento there? Fr Louis: 'Oh sure, they're doing great. They now have cornflakes for breakfast.'
> 'How,' she wrote, 'could he be the holy mystic she had come to respect so deeply through his books and go around speaking in this vein about his own community?'[72]

Like Bernard, Merton was not a holy man living in another world of spiritual perfection. He saw no conflict in drinking beer whenever he had an opportunity and in rising at 3:15 each morning to spend several hours in prayer. For Merton being a contemplative did not mean giving up one's humanity.

Merton's constant quest for reality enabled him also to appreciate the good in a person while not being embarassed about those aspects which were not good or with which he did not agree. The stimulus for much of his writing came from those with whom he did not entirely agree: French existentialists, American Marxists, Buddhist philosophers, and Reformed theologians. Merton was able to maintain a relationship of openness and dialogue with people of many diverse points of view, and to enrich his own life and work. He could admire Bernard while not agreeing with his war aims in the second Crusade.

Bernard was, as his involvement in the Crusade shows, very much a part of the contemporary Church. His contemplation was not the kind that is withdrawn from the world and its concerns. For Bernard 'sanctity is supernatural life. The saints not only have life, but they give it. Their sanctity is best known to those who have received life from them.'[73] The union between the human and the divine begins within, but it has implications for the world without, as Merton explains:

> The mystical union of the Word with the individual soul is simply an extension of the union of the Incarnate Word with His Church. And this...brings us to the inner unity that binds everything together in the life and work of Bernard of Clairvaux. In all that he writes, in all that he says, in all that he does, Bernard has only one end in

view: the integration of nations, dioceses, monasteries, and individuals into the life and order of the Church.[74]

This is also true of Merton: 'Very few men are sanctified in isolation. Very few become perfect in absolute solitude....Far from being essentially opposed to each other, interior contemplation and external activity are two aspects of the same love of God.'[75] The contemplative must always remain in relationship with the Church. 'The more I become identified with God,' says Merton, 'the more will I be identified with all the others who are identified with Him.'[76]

Bernard taught that there are several stages in the spiritual life: conversion through penitence, good works, prayer, contemplation, and spiritual fecundity. This last, spiritual fecundity, is very important since the 'effect of contemplation is to generate a love that makes such a one a good and worthy pastor of souls.'[77] In his sermons on the Song of Songs, Bernard explains how contemplation and action are related:

> For rightly is the Bride called 'love', in that by preaching, advising, ministering, she zealously and faithfully seeks to make gain for the Bridegroom. Rightly she is called 'dove', in that she ceases not in prayer to win the divine mercy for her sins. Rightly too is she called 'beautiful', in that, radiant with heavenly desire, she takes on herself the beauty of divine contemplation, but only at the hours when it may be done conveniently and opportunely.[78]

True contemplation, for Bernard, produces the fruit of action.

There are those, however, who choose—or are chosen—to live a life primarily of contemplation, often within the framework of monastic enclosure. Bernard had a great deal to say concerning the monastic life, and he believed that the 'most complete of all vocations, the union of action and contemplation in the care of souls, also finds a place in the monastery....'[79] To those both inside and outside the enclosure 'the apostolate without virtues and without a deep interior life is of no value'.[80] Yet Bernard also made a place for the apostolate of contemplation, as Merton points out:

> In principle, as St Bernard has told us all through the present study, it is the *contemplative life* which we have come to seek in the monastery. The monastery is for contemplatives. A certain amount of action is necessary to make the contemplative life easier and freer and more

accessible. If there be an apostolate within the monastery, it must be a contemplative apostolate—it must form souls not to lives of action but of humility and prayer. If Martha has the highest calling, it is only by reason of her contact with Mary and for the sake of Mary. St Bernard's teaching fully vindicates the primacy of contemplation.[81]

Bernard saw the monastery as a school of Christ where one sought Christ, not merely subjective experiences. The monk's vocation was to seek Christ in contemplation, and this meant that 'contemplation should always be desired and preferred. Activity should be accepted, though never sought.'[82] In reflecting on this, one must keep in mind that Bernard was writing primarily to monks and not to those living outside the enclosure, who by necessity would be living active lives.[83]

Bernard's life and work made a difference in the world at large. The spread of the Cistercian Order throughout Europe, the importance of the Abbey of Clairvaux under Bernard's leadership, the significant though ill-fated second Crusade, the writings and sermons of Bernard, and his own colorful life[84] all made a lasting impression on Merton and served as a major building block in his spiritual formation. For him, Bernard represented a spiritual revival:

> Clairvaux and Bernard both meant one thing above all: the great renaissance which had its effects in all the other renaissances of the time. For Bernard was to influence everything from politics to the *roman courtois* and the whole humanistic trend to 'courtly love'. He left his mark on schools of spirituality, on Gregorian chant, on the clerical life, and on the whole development of Gothic architecture and art. One of the signs of a spiritual revival that is really spiritual is that it affects every kind of life and activity around it, inspires new kinds of art, awakens a new poetry and music, even makes lovers speak to one another in a new language and think about one another with a new kind of respect.[85]

Here one can make a comparison between Bernard and Merton, for Merton also has had an influence on the modern world, an influence that goes far beyond the monastery walls, and indeed, far beyond the confines of the Christian Church.[86]

In his Foreward to Daniel-Rops' book *Bernard of Clairvaux: The Story of the Last of the Great Church Fathers*, Merton notes that 'Bernard, the contemplative, was a great man of action because he was a great contemplative. And because he was a contemplative he never ceased fearing to be a mere man of action.'[87] Bernard's sanctity is, according to Merton, a kind of sanctity needed in our world today:

> Because he is so much a man, readers who forget that saints must be men may here and there be inclined to question his sanctity. That would be a great pity in an age which needs saints as badly as ours. Bernard is sent to instruct us how human a saint must be, to forge out the will of God in the heat of the affairs of men. In his Sermons on the Canticle he can be as lyrical as St Francis. In his letters he is too busy upbraiding the bishops to have time for a sermon on the birds.[88]

Merton concludes with these words:

> Perhaps our own century needs nothing so much as the combined anger and gentleness of another Bernard.[89]

Platonic Mysticism

No discussion of mysticism can avoid the problem of reality and unreality, the sacred and the secular, the relationship between spirit and matter. There are many different terms to describe this problem, and contemplation and action are two of them. Underlying any such set of terms is a basic dualism; a concept of reality that posits two levels of reality, one of which is more real than the other. In *Thoughts in Solitude*, Merton illustrates this very well: 'For the "unreality" of material things is only relative to the *greater* reality of spiritual things.'[90] In his early works Merton clearly rated the contemplative life vastly superior to the active life. He made this especially clear in commenting on Aquinas' views: '*Vita contemplativa*, he remarks, *simpliciter est melior quam activa* (the contemplative life in itself, by its very nature, is superior to the active life).... The contemplative life directly and immediately occupies itself with the love of God, than which there is no act more perfect or meritorius.'[91] While Aquinas says that a mixed life of action and contemplation is to be preferred, Merton says that this is possible only if one is a 'supercontemplative'. The early Merton considered contemplation more desirable than a life of action.

This dualism can be traced directly to Plato, and Platonism provided the foundation not only for western mysticism but also

for much of Christian theology. And those who influenced
Merton most were also greatly affected by Platonic thought. The
basic problem of mysticism has been somehow to break through
this dualism either by a union of the two elements or by a
mortification of the physical and an emphasis upon the spiritual.
In the *Republic*, Plato posits this dualism in his famous story of
the cave, which Sidney Spencer retells as follows:

> In the analogy of the Cave (in Book VII) he illustrates the
> position of those who are unawakened to the truth—those
> whose outlook is confined to the world of the senses. Such
> men are prisoners in a dark underground cavern. A fire is
> burning behind them, and between them and the fire is a
> road along which people pass. The prisoners are shackled,
> so that all they can see is the shadows cast by the fire on
> the wall of the side of the cavern. Such, Plato says, is our
> situation in the physical world: the things that we see are
> only shadows; the realm of truth and reality lies beyond.
> The prisoners can only see things as they are, if they
> emerge into the light of the sun. So, if we are to see the
> truth, our souls must be illuminated by the light of
> supreme Reality, which is the sun of the eternal world.[92]

According to Plato, the soul can ascend to the vision of
divine Reality because the essential nature of the soul enables it
to do so. This divine Reality is called the Good, and it is the
highest form of that which constitutes the sphere of reality.
Plato's mysticism emphasizes vision rather than union, and such
vision is capable of totally changing a person's outlook on life.
Spencer explains:

> They no longer care for the things which men commonly
> prize. The man who looks to eternal things has no desire
> to take part in men's quarrels, or to catch the infection of
> their jealousies and hates; he seeks to fashion himself in
> likeness of the eternal realm, where all wrong is done
> away; he reproduces that order in his soul, and becomes
> god-like, as far as man may.[93]

The nature of the Good is 'the singly transcendent Reality of
absolute perfection which is the ultimate cause and explanation
of the universe'.[94] In this Good one finds Reality and
fulfillment.

This basic dualistic understanding of Plato has been nowhere
more manifest in western thought than in mysticism. 'Christian

mysticism is a result of the fusion of evangelical biblical faith with Platonic and Neo-Platonic (and perhaps also Oriental) philosophy.'[95] Augustine leaned heavily upon Plato and the Neo-Platonists, especially Plotinus, so that 'he accepted the main principles of the Neo-Platonic philosophy, and his whole intellectual outlook, his mysticism included, was coloured by it to the end.'[96] Although Aquinas broke partially with Platonism through his study of Aristotle, he was still greatly influenced by Platonic and Neo-Platonic thought.[97] Indeed, Plato's influence totally pervaded Christian mysticism, and continues to do so to the present day.

Merton's first direct contact with Plato came during his years at Columbia University where he read a huge volume of Plotinus' *Enneads* in spite of what he called his 'almost congenital dislike for Platonism'.[98] He was aware at the time that there were important philosophical differences between Plato and Plotinus, but he was not knowledgeable enough in philosophy to understand them. In time, especially after he entered the monastery, Merton found that Plato's influence upon him grew, both directly and indirectly via Neo-Platonism and the platonic thought of mystical writers. After reading and commenting on the moral and poetic beauty of Plato's *Phaedo*, Merton remarked: 'One does not have to agree with Plato, but one must hear him. Not to listen to such a voice would be unpardonable: like not listening to conscience, or to nature itself. I love this great poem, this purifying music of which my spirit has need and with which my mind does not agree.'[99]

While grateful for the contributions of Platonism, Merton parts with Plato on his concept of man. According to Plato, the soul of man once existed in the higher world where it enjoyed the immediate vision of Reality, but when the soul descends into the body it becomes 'fettered to the body "as an oyster to his shell"—tied to its limitations and its narrow range of vision.'[100] Thus there is a constant struggle between the soul, which is spiritual, and the body, which is physical. Because of its nature the soul constantly struggles toward the Good and must therefore break free from the body and those physical things which hinder it in its ascent to the Good. Merton strongly disagrees with this element of platonic thought:

> We must try to distinguish the Biblical concept of man from the Platonic view which has become almost inseparable from it in Western thought. The Bible does not divide man into a spiritual essence (soul) and an accidental body made of existence and neither of course

does Orthodox Christian theology. Yet in the tradition of Christian Platonism, magnificent though it may be, Biblical anthropology has tended to take on a Greek coloring. The true life of man is said to be the life of the soul as *distinct from and opposed to* the life of the body. Christian asceticism comes to be seen as the liberation of the soul from a kind of 'imprisonment' in the body. Temporal things, belonging to the realm of the body, are either evil or at best inferior to the spiritual things in the realm of the soul and of eternity. The 'spiritual life' of man is then a withdrawal from time into eternity, and this in turn implies neglect of or contempt for the ordinary temporal active life of everyday. 'Spirituality' then seems to demand the negation of everyday reality and a withdrawal into a realm of angels and pure essences, where eventually 'union with God' will be attained outside time and beyond the contamination of all that is bodily and temporal.[101]

Merton was careful to avoid the dualism of body and soul and the resulting spirituality which is by necessity abstract and withdrawn from the physical and temporal world.

According to Merton, body and soul may be distinguished but not separated. The Christian life is concerned with both body and soul as well as with an outreach to the rest of the world. Merton questioned the Platonic position:

Is this a genuinely Christian perspective? Is the function of self-denial merely to 'liberate the soul' and withdraw it from temporal distractions and cares? Is not Christianity rather a humble and realistic acceptance of everyday life and of God's will in a spirit of obedience and liberty? Is not the true function of our self-denial the *clarification* of God's will in our regard, and the *unification* of our whole being, body and soul, in His service?[102]

Merton contends that we must seek to unify the physical and the spiritual, and that the function of self-denial is clarification, getting to the cause of our problems. For him, the root of the problem is not in the difference between the physical and the spiritual; it lies in our own understanding of the physical and the spiritual. We must renounce 'the illusory reality which created things acquire when they are seen only in their relation to our own selfish interest. Before we can see that created things (especially material) are unreal, we must see clearly that they are real.'[103] For Merton, then, the unreality of the physical is of our own making, and the task of the contemplative is to break through the illusions of this unreality and see all reality unified in God. Significantly, it is against the background of Platonic thought—both in dialogue and opposition—that Merton is able to develop his own ideas of what the spiritual life is all about.

The Desert Fathers

Basic to an understanding of asceticism is the concept of wilderness or desert, for it is often the stage for the purification of self and the perception of reality in the light of God. Plato, in his analogy of the cave, taught that to catch the vision of the Real one must first leave the cave. For many Christians in different situations and places this has meant going into the wilderness to be purged of falsehood and illusion. In his book *Wilderness and Paradise in Christian Thought*, George Williams remarks: 'We shall find that in the positive sense the wilderness or desert will be interpreted variously as a place of protection, a place of contemplative retreat, again as one's inner nature or ground of being, and at length as the ground itself of the divine being.'[104] Many of the early ascetics believed that the desert was the haunt of demons and at the same time the realm of bliss and harmony with the natural world. This dualism is important in the development of spirituality, for the concepts of wilderness and paradise are often closely related, as Williams avers: 'In the East one strove contemplatively to recover primordial manhood before the Fall. In the West one sought the promised land through mystical elevation in the covenanted company of pilgrims in the wilderness.'[105] Eastern mysticism focused on *paradeisos* while western mysticism was more concerned with *desertum*.

Merton was deeply impressed by the spirituality of the desert fathers, who in the fourth century lived in the deserts of the Middle East. The most famous of them, St Anthony, became well-known as a wise and saintly spiritual master whose counsel attracted countless disciples and visitors. As Anthony's fame spread, others joined him in the desert, and soon there were hundreds of hermitages and tiny monastic communities springing up there. Asceticism took on many forms, some aberrant:

> In Syria St Ephrem (306-73), theologian and poet, founded the school of Edessa with a monastic framework of vowed

students and the task of spiritual service for the surrounding hermits. It was Syria also that witnessed the appearance of strange classes of solitaries chained to rocks either in a cave or in the open air, and still stranger 'solitary monks' who remained standing motionless either on the ground or on a pillar. Of these last the most celebrated was Symeon the Elder (389-459), who remained for more than thirty years on his column thirty feet high near Antioch, a true saint who gave to those who pressed round his pedestal wise and temperate advice on spiritual and human problems. [106]

Most of the desert fathers, we should note, were not so extreme in their asceticism.

The desert fathers, even those who were considered hermits, did not completely forsake the world and their responsibility to their fellowmen. The historian M. Henri Marrou has pointed out 'that of the dozen or so outstanding "Fathers", Greek and Latin, of the fourth century, all save Ambrose were monks. This fact alone is evidence that monasticism, while in a true sense a flight from the world, is also profoundly Christian and catholic in its orientation.' [107] This is further borne out by the vital concern that these monks of the desert showed for the spiritual and social welfare of those around them. Merton says:

> They knew that they were helpless to do any good for others as long as they floundered about in the wreckage. But once they got a foothold on solid ground, things were different. Then they had not only the power but even the obligation to pull the whole world to safety after them. [108]

Originally these monks fled to the desert to escape the pagan society of their day; a society that was corrupt to its very core. In Merton's words, 'These were men who believed that to let oneself drift along, passively accepting the tenets and values of what they knew as society, was purely and simply a disaster.' [109] The interesting thing is that when the emperor became a Christian and the known world was 'christianized' these desert fathers resolved even more to turn from society, for they believed that there was no such thing as a truly Christian state. 'They seem to have doubted that Christianity and politics could ever be mixed to such an extent as to produce a fully Christian society', Merton says. 'In other words, for them the only Christian society was spiritual and extramundane: the Mystical Body of Christ.' [110] At first such a view seems an extreme form of negativism and withdrawal, but Merton avers that such was not really the case:

> The Desert Fathers did, in fact, meet the 'problems of their time' in the sense that *they* were among the few who were ahead of their time, and opening the way for the development of a new man and a new society. They represent what modern social philosophers (Jaspers, Mumford) call the emergence of the 'axial man,' the forerunner of the modern personalist man. [111]

In other words, 'what the Fathers sought most of all was their own true self, in Christ. And in order to do this, they had to reject completely the false, formal self, fabricated under social compulsion in "the world."'[112]

It is this kind of rejection of the false self, and consequently of the falsehood of the world, that provides the foundation for monasticism. 'The monk is a man...who seeks the naked realities that only the desert can reveal.'[113] Yet this flight is not an evasion of the world nor is it a negation of matter, as Merton explains: 'It is one thing to live *in* the flesh, and quite another to live *according to* the flesh.'[114] In fact he cautions against the idea that all men should become monks and that people should always observe fasting, since there must be married men and we must eat if we are to live. According to Merton, 'we cannot become saints merely by trying to run away from material things. To have a spiritual life is to have a life that is spiritual in all its wholeness...' and that includes the physical.[115] The desert fathers were primarily concerned not with negation, but with purification.

Going into the desert—literally in the case of the desert fathers, and figuratively in the case of contemporary monks—forces one to face himself and God with no support from the outside. This rejection of outside support has two important results; the first is contemplative and personal and the second is active and social. Merton explains:

> The real meaning of faith is the rejection of *everything that is not Christ in order that all life, all truth, all hope, all reality may be sought and found 'in Christ.'*...To reject the 'world' is not to reject people, society, the creatures of God or the works of man, but to reject the perverted standards which make men misuse and spoil a good creation, ruining their own lives in the bargain.[116]

One finds reality first in Christ and then in turn finds himself, not in terms of society or the world, but in terms of his relationship to Christ. Yet the desert experience has a social dimension as well:

> We cannot use created things for the glory of God unless we are in control of ourselves. We cannot be in control of ourselves if we are under the power of desires and appetites and passions of the flesh. We cannot give ourselves to God if we do not belong to ourselves. And we do not belong to ourselves if we belong to our own ego....Self denial is useless unless it opens up the ears of our heart to obey the will of God commanding us to take our place in time, in history and in the work of building His Kingdom of Love and Truth.[117]

In a sense then, one goes to the desert to find himself. Having done this he is able to help society find itself and, if need be, he will even return again to the world.

One must accept the reality of the desert, for it can become a paradise only when it is accepted as desert, and it can never be anything but desert if we try to escape it. In *Raids on the Unspeakable*, Merton gives this further explanation:

> It is in the desert of loneliness and emptiness that the fear of death and the need for self-affirmation are seen to be illusory. When this is faced, then the anguish is not necessarily overcome, but it can be accepted and understood. Thus, in the heart of anguish are found the gifts of peace and understanding: not simply in personal illumination and liberation, but by commitment and empathy, for the contemplative must assume the universal anguish and the inescapable condition of mortal man. The solitary, far from enclosing himself in himself, becomes every man. He dwells in the solitude, the poverty, the indigence of every man.[118]

As one probes more deeply into the implications of this desert experience, and as one seeks reality, one soon discovers that the reality was there all the time; the difference is that now it has been made known to us.[119]

It is impossible for everyone to become a hermit in the desert, yet we must not neglect the message of the desert fathers and others who have followed in their path, for their voices come across the centuries to speak to us today. Merton compared the desert fathers with similar contemporary figures:

> In many respects, therefore, these Desert Fathers had
> much in common with Indian Yogis and with Zen Buddhist
> monks of China and Japan. If we were to seek their like in
> twentieth-century America, we would have to look in
> strange, out of the way places. Such beings are tragically
> rare. They obviously do not flourish on the sidewalk at
> Forty-Second Street and Broadway. We might perhaps find
> someone like this among the Pueblo Indians or the
> Navahos: but there the case would probably be entirely
> different. You would have simplicity, primitive wisdom:
> but rooted in a primitive society. With the Desert Fathers,
> you have the characteristic of a clean break with a con-
> ventional, accepted social context in order to swim for
> one's life into an apparently irrational void. [120]

There must be such people in every age, for—according to
Williams—'this outer wilderness, both as savage and as benign,
as the mystics knew, is also within. It is our true creaturely
estate.' [121]

It is a characteristic of the desert experience that it moves
from one stage to another. 'Once God has called you into
solitude, everything you touch leads you into further solitude.' [122]
For Merton the new stage was compassion. His self-denial and
asceticism filled him with compassion for others and for the
world outside the monastery walls. Little wonder then that
Merton's strongest social criticism was written during the years
he was a hermit. There is little doubt that the desert fathers
provided yet another of the cornerstones for Merton's thinking
on contemplation and action. He summarized his feelings toward
the desert fathers by saying:

> We cannot do exactly what they did. But we must be as
> thorough and as ruthless in our determination to break all
> spiritual chains, and cast off the domination of alien com-
> pulsions, to find our true selves, to discover and develop
> our inalienable spiritual liberty and to use it to build, on
> earth, the Kingdom of God. This is not the place in which
> to speculate what our great and mysterious vocation might
> involve. That is still unknown. Let it suffice for me to say
> that we need to learn from these men of the fourth century
> how to ignore prejudice, defy compulsion and strike out
> fearlessly into the unknown. [123]

St Gregory of Nyssa

St Gregory of Nyssa was born in Cappadocia about 335 AD, at the time when the activity of the desert fathers was at its peak. He was a man of literary tastes and before becoming a monk had been married and very much a man of the world. He entered a monastery which had been founded by his brother, St Basil. Gregory, Basil, and their friend, Gregory, the bishop of Nazianzen, played decisive roles in defending the Church against Arianism. Gregory of Nyssa, in fact, exerted such an important influence at the Second Council of Constantinople that he was thereafter looked upon as a strict defender of orthodoxy and became known as a great dogmatic theologian. According to Merton, Gregory's defense against Arianism was vital to the survival not only of the Church, but also of mysticism, for the Arians denied the divinity of Christ, and, in consequence, the doctrines of the Incarnation and of the Trinity. Merton held that 'the consequence of such a denial, in mysticism, reduces contemplation to the level of poetry or, at best, of pantheism.'[124]

Gregory's mystical writing has remained relatively unknown in the western Church even though his ascetical and mystical works have been well-known in the eastern Church for centuries. He is the founder of the apophatic tradition of Christian mysticism, although his contribution is often overshadowed by the later works of the Pseudo-Dionysius. Merton explains how this came about:

> The *Pseudo-Dionysius*, as he is called, was a follower of Proclus, the last of the great Neo-Platonists (fifth-century, A.D.), but in his reconciliation of Platonic ideas with Christian faith he was also following in the footsteps of Saint Gregory of Nyssa, who had died at the end of the fourth century. Since they were supposed to spring from the Apostolic Age, the works of Pseudo-Dionysius acquired such prestige that all subsequent apophatic Christian mysticism has rested on him. In actual fact, Gregory of Nyssa was not only the true fountainhead of this mystical tradition but was also perhaps a greater philosopher and theologian than Pseudo-Dionysius.[125]

Gregory saw two kinds of human movement, both of which involve change. The first is a cyclical movement of the flesh, and the second is the transformation from glory to glory. He has several analogies by which he seeks to explain the cyclical movement of the flesh. He likens it to blindfolded animals on a treadmill, to a man climbing a hill of sand, and to children's sand castles which are destroyed by the advancing tide. In each case man is locked in the prison of a perpetual cycle from which there is seemingly no escape. Jean Daniélou points out that 'a final characteristic of this movement is its insubstantial, illusory, quality. It is a motion without progress....'[126] Merton also describes this cyclical movement:

> A life based on desires is like a spider's web, says Saint Gregory of Nyssa. Woven about us by the father of lies, the Devil, the enemy of our souls, it is a frail tissue of vanities without substance, and yet it can catch us and hold us fast, delivering us up to him as his prisoner. Nevertheless, the illusion is only an illusion, nothing more....
>
> A life immersed in matter and in sense cannot help but reproduce the fancied torments which Greek mythology displays in Hades—Tantalus starving to death with food an inch from his lips, Sysiphus rolling his boulder uphill though he knows it must escape him and roll down to the bottom again, just as he is reaching the summit.[127]

This first kind of movement results in one repeatedly putting his whole self into values that do not in fact exist, and this in turn leads one to a situation where 'the measure of illusion is the very intensity of activity itself. The less you have, the more you do. The final delusion is movement, change, and variety for their own sakes alone.'[128]

To escape this endless cycle of movement, Gregory avers that there is a second kind of movement, which he calls a transformation from glory to glory. Daniélou explains:

> Gregory shows us—and this....is one of his greatest contributions—that it is characteristic of this spiritual movement not to produce any satiety, precisely because it is a continual discovery of what is new. Here it is not a question of instability, but of growth. Only the flesh can know satiety: the Spirit never wearies....Such spiritual activity develops by being exercised.[129]

Gregory himself says that we must ever become more perfect through daily growth yet we never arrive at a limit of perfection since 'that perfection consists in our never stopping our growth in good, never circumscribing our perfection by any limitation.'[130] One is in a continual state of ascending toward God and deepening the spiritual life.

In the Christian mystical tradition there are two major lines: a theology of light and a theology of darkness. Among the theologians of light Merton numbered Origen, St Augustine, St Bernard of Clairvaux and St Thomas Aquinas; among the theologians of darkness St Gregory of Nyssa, the Pseudo-Dionysius, and St John of the Cross. The theologians of darkness emphasize the importance of nothingness or the void.[131] To rid oneself of falsehood and illusion one must pass through a period of nothingness or a 'dark night of the soul'. One must be emptied of illusion in order to be filled with reality and to possess the 'ascetic gift of discernment which, in one penetrating glance, apprehends what creatures are and what they are not'.[132] Merton carefully pointed out that this experience of nothingness is not the same thing as a denial of the physical world or of other realities:

> But we must remember that when a Christian mystic speaks of the created world as an illusion and as 'nothingness', he is only using a figure of speech. The words are never to be taken literally and they are not ontological....
> When Creation appears to us in the false light of concupiscence, it becomes illusion. The supreme value that cupidity seeks in created things does not exist in them. A man who takes a tree for a ghost is in illusion. The tree is objectively real: but in his mind it is something that it is not. A man who takes a cigar coupon for a ten-dollar bill is also in illusion. It is a real cigar coupon, and yet, considered as a ten-dollar bill, it is a pure illusion. When we live as if the multiplicity of the phenomenal universe were the criterion of all truth, and treat the world about us as if its shifting scale of values were the only measure of our ultimate good, the world becomes an illusion. It is real in itself, but it is no longer real to us because it is not what we think it is.[133]

Gregory and those of the apophatic mystical tradition were speaking basically of the same thing as the desert fathers, although on a different level. The desert fathers retreated from the world to discover within themselves, away from all outside influences, what was illusion and what was reality. They literally went into the deserts of the world and symbolically into the desert of their own inner being to discover reality. Gregory did not retreat into the physical desert. He was saying that one must retreat into the nothingness of one's own soul—one's inner desert if you will—and distinguish between illusion and reality, and thus discover the ultimate reality of God. This is similar to Aldous Huxley's idea of 'cleansing the doors of perception'.[134] After this experience of the desert, this nothingness, and this cleansing, one is able to say, 'Now I see through a glass darkly, but then face to face...' (1 Cor 13:12). In order to see clearly one must first pass through the darkness. This is why Gregory uses the terminology of purification, for the apophatic tradition is concerned with doing away with all that stands in the way of reality, a reality which is God. This mystical tradition is 'known as "apophatic"' William Johnston says, 'because of its tendency to emphasize that God is best known by negation: we can know much more about what God is *not* than about what He is.'[135] When one is in the midst of darkness and there is nothing left, something appears that cannot be grasped or identified, yet it is there. Asks Merton: 'What is it? It is hard to say: but one feels that it is somehow summed up in "the will of God" or simply, "God"'.[136]

In Gregory's passage from 'glory to glory' there is more than one experience of darkness, one time of nothingness, and one dark night of the soul. The spiritual journey is from darkness to light and from light to darkness. According to Merton: 'The ascent from falsity to Truth begins when the false light of error (which is darkness) is exchanged for the true but insufficient light of elementary and too-human notions of God. Then this light must itself be darkened.'[137] In terms of Gregory's symbolism, Merton explains:

> These degrees of the ascent to God were symbolized, thought Saint Gregory, in the degrees of illumination and darkness through which Moses journeyed to God. Moses first saw God in the burning bush. Then he was led by God across the desert in a pillar of cloud. Finally he ascended Sinai, where God spoke to him 'face to face' but in the divine darkness.[138]

One does not see God in pure light until one is with God in eternity, for then a true vision and a total union will be achieved. Merton gleaned from Gregory ideas which remained with him throughout his life and underwent numerous transformations not at all unlike Gregory's movement 'from glory to glory'. In his later writings Merton saw a relationship between apophatic mysticism and the Zen Buddhist concept of the void.

St Teresa of Avila

Merton was profoundly influenced by the sixteenth century Spanish mystics whose roots could be traced to apophatic mysticism, for there is a 'long tradition stretching from Gregory of Nyssa and the Pseudo-Dionysius to the Rhineland mystics whence it later crosses the Pyrenees to reach a great climax with St John of the Cross in sixteenth century Spain'.[139] Although the time and places are different, one detects the same themes in sixteenth-century Spanish mysticism as in Gregory, as well as new ideas which played a significant role in the development of Christian mysticism and in the formation of Merton's thought.

Teresa of Avila, that remarkable reformer of the Carmelite nuns, is regarded both as an outstanding contemplative and as an able administrator who was filled with energy and enthusiasm for whatever she was doing. Born in Avila in 1515, she entered a Carmelite convent at the age of twenty-one. Her first twenty years of religious life were not only uneventful, but were, in Merton's words, 'years of religious mediocrity' when she was 'neglecting the graces of interior prayer and living aimlessly from month to month without serious ideals, with no one to direct her along the paths of religious perfection.'[140] Not until she was forty did Teresa begin to understand what the spiritual life was really all about, and this was largely the result of her coming into contact with the Jesuit, Franciscan, and Dominican spiritual directors who taught her the ways of the spiritual life. The insight and direction which she received from these men was crucial for her spiritual development; without them it is doubtful she would have ever become anything more than a mediocre Carmelite nun of less than average spirituality.[141]

Teresa is best known for her reform of the Carmelites that grew out of her spirituality: 'her whole aim in returning to the original Carmelite Rule was to enable persons like herself to find the solitude and spiritual liberty upon which the contemplative life depends.'[142] 'Her idea of contemplation was clearly one of an apostolate, and 'she believed that her nuns, by their lives of prayer and sacrifice, would do much to atone for the religious confusion of sixteenth-century Europe, to save souls, and to preserve the unity of the Catholic Church.'[143] Teresa saw her work as part of the total activity of the whole Church and not as something removed from its life and work. For Merton, this emphasis upon the apostolate was important; it clearly showed that contemplation was not only an end in itself but it results in a renewal of the active life as well. Teresa's reform genuinely brought about change that was based upon a reorientation of values in the inner being. It is little wonder that Merton describes Teresa's life as one of 'high contemplation, prodigious activity, and unbelievable suffering'.[144]

'The chief characteristic of Saint Teresa's spirituality is her realization of the importance of mental prayer. It was this that inspired her plans for the Carmelite reform.'[145] Bouyer in his book *Introduction to Spirituality* also stresses the significance of Teresa's understanding of prayer, and he points out that she was the first to make a 'radical distinction between contemplation and the meditation that precedes it'.

> Meditation, laborious by nature, is the activity of beginners in the spiritual life, or of those who have not yet progressed very far in it. But normally, one ought to attain a phase of spiritual progress in which meditation no longer adds anything, or even becomes psychologically impossible to carry out. Then, it would seem, contemplation will flower of its own accord.[146]

This crucial distinction has far-reaching implications for the spiritual life. Meditation is of vital importance, but it is not the same thing as contemplation. Merton states that 'the life of contemplation implies two levels of awareness: first, awareness of the question, and second, awareness of the answer'.[147]

Meditation is concerned with the first level, the awareness of the question. Merton elaborates further:

> Meditaton is almost all contained in this one idea: the idea of *awakening* our interior self and attuning ourselves inwardly to the Holy Spirit, so that we will be able to respond to His grace. In mental prayer, over the years, we must allow our interior perceptivity to be refined and purified. We must attune ourselves to unexpected movements of grace, which do not fit our own preconceived ideas of the spiritual life at all, and which in no way flatter our own ambitious aspirations.[148]

Meditation is a deliberate exercise by which one opens oneself to God's grace. It is extremely difficult and demands much time, effort, and determination. Merton holds that sincere meditation cannot fail to be rewarded by grace, a direct reference to St Teresa who 'believed that no one who was faithful to the practice of meditation could possibly lose his soul'.[149]

Contemplation involves the second level, the awareness of
the answer. Contemplation must be understood as a grace from
God; it 'is not and cannot be a function of this external self'. [150]
Contemplation is the opening of the self totally to the grace of
God and to total experience. Merton explains:

> Contemplation...is the experiential grasp of reality as
> *subjective*, not so much 'mine' (which would signify
> 'belonging to the external self') but 'myself' in existential
> mystery. Contemplation does not arrive at reality after a
> process of deduction, but by an intuitive awakening in
> which our free and personal reality becomes fully alive to
> its own existential depth, which opens out into the mystery
> of God. [151]

Contemplation always comes of the grace of God freely
bestowed upon those persons who have, through meditation,
awakened themselves to God's grace active in their lives.

The impact of Teresa upon Merton's thought is obvious, but
it is most felt through the works of that other great Spanish
mystic, Ho John of the Cross. St John of the Cross was only
twenty-six when he met Teresa in 1568. He had been a member
of the Carmelite Order for five years but had become
disillusioned; he was planning to leave and become a
Carthusian. [152] Teresa persuaded him to remain with the
Carmelites and told him that 'all he needed to do was return to
the original Carmelite ideal and he would find plenty of
opportunity for solitary communion with God, along with the
mortification which protects the "purity of heart" without which
no man can "see" God.' [153] John also became an important
reformer and while Teresa reformed the nuns, he reformed the
friars.

St John of the Cross

St John of the Cross left a decisive mark upon Merton's
thought, so great a mark in fact, that Merton wrote an entire
book, *The Ascent to Truth*, his only strictly theological work,
based on the theology of the Spanish saint. Merton did not
consider it one of his better books, as he was not a theologian
by training or temperament. Like Merton, John of the Cross
was informed by the teachings of Aquinas and was, in Merton's
words, 'a true Thomist' who received the basic structure of his
doctrine from Aquinas. The principles upon which he 'builds his

doctrine of complete detachment from creatures in order to arrive at union with God, are sometimes quoted word for word from Saint Thomas....' [154] Merton states that 'practically the whole of *The Ascent of Mount Carmel* can be reduced to these pages of the Angelic Doctor' dealing with beatitude in his *prima secundae.* [155] Aquinas took a theological approach to contemplation while John of the Cross tended to be more mystical. This was more a difference in form then in substance; the two had similar ideas which they expressed in different ways. It was this mystical and experiential emphasis that distinguished John of the Cross and gave his spirituality its uniqueness and vitality.

John of the Cross, says Merton, 'has never been a very popular saint, outside of his native Spain. His doctrine is considered "difficult", and he demands of others the same uncompromising austerity which he practiced in his own life.' [156] John of the Cross sums up his concept of asceticism in the following lines:

> *In order to have pleasure in everything*
> *Desire to have pleasure in nothing.*
> *In order to arrive at possessing everything*
> *Desire to possess nothing.*
> *In order to arrive at being everything*
> *Desire to be nothing.*
> *In order to arrive at knowing everything*
> *Desire to know nothing.*
> *In order to arrive at that wherein thou hast no pleasure*
> *Thou must go by a way in which thou hast no pleasure.*
> *In order to arrive at that which thou knowest not*
> *Thou must go by a way that thou knowest not.*
> *In order to arrive at that which thou possessest not*
> *Thou must go by a way that thou possessest not.*
> *In order to arrive at that which thou art not*
> *Thou must go through that which thou art not.* [157]

Merton was careful to point out that John of the Cross did not ask the ascetic to give up the material world in the sense of denying its existence:

> The key word in each of his rules for entering into the ascetic night is the word 'desire'. He does not say: 'In order to arrive at the knowledge of everything, *know* nothing', but *'desire to know* nothing'. It is not pleasure, knowledge, possession or being as such that must be 'darkened' or 'mortified', but only the passion of desire for these things. [158]

Behind this stands Gregory of Nyssa: desire, when considered as a passion, is by necessity directed toward a finite object and therefore has a limit. Hence, if one is to go beyond these limits one must escape the passions which tie one down.

The theology of John of the Cross can be summarized in the phrase *Todo y Nada*, all and nothing. *Todo*—all—is God and in God, and in him alone we possess all things, but in order to reach this we must first of all give up the possession of all that is not God—nothing—*Nada*. In Merton's words, 'the *nada* of Saint John of the Cross is simply a drastically literal application of the Gospel, "If anyone of you renounce not all that he possesses, he cannot be my disciple" (Luke 14:33).'[159] This renunciation of all that one possesses, John of the Cross taught, is a total renunciation which involves two aspects, submission to authority and a turning away even from genuine religious experiences.

Submission to authority requires humility, obedience, interior detachment, and engenders a certain amount of conflict. When one seems totally defeated and crushed, then victory will come. In Merton's view 'the cross is the only way to mystical prayer. Christian contemplation is precipitated by crisis within crisis and anguish within anguish.'[160] The 'final step on the way to holiness in Christ is then to completely abandon ourselves with confident joy to the apparent madness of the cross.'[161] Even as Christ was submissive to the authority of his Father, so we too, must be submissive to authority. John of the Cross advises one to 'turn away even from genuine visions, revelations, raptures, locutions and so on in order to rest in "pure faith", which is the only proximate means of union with God.'[162] Following in this tradition Merton asserts that 'the mystical knowledge of God...is above concepts. It is a knowledge that registers itself in the soul passively *without an idea*.'[163] Merton comments further on this in *The New Man:*

> This is the existentialism of the 'apophatic' tradition: which contemplates spiritual realities not in light, not under clear objective forms, but in darkness, without form and without figure, apprehended only in the intimacy of the most personal and incommunicable experience. This night is brighter and clearer than any intellectual light that can appeal to our natural and unaided intelligence. It is the night of which it is written: 'And the night shall become as bright as day'—the dark night of St John of the Cross....[164]

Merton concludes that 'in the deepest spiritual darkness, in the most profound night of unknowing, in the purity of naked faith, God unites the soul to Himself in mystical union'.[165]

Merton viewed the uncertainty principle of the German physicist Werner Heisenberg as being in tune with the unknowing of John of the Cross:

> As God in the highest eludes the grasp of concepts, being pure Act, so the ultimate constitution of matter cannot be reduced to conceptual terms. There is, logically speaking, *nothing there that we can objectively know....*
> This seems to me to be the end of conventional nineteenth-century materialism—which, funny enough, now appears exactly for what it was: a 'faith,' and not science at all. To be more precise, let us say a 'myth', which was accepted on the 'authority of science'.[166]

Merton is careful, however, to show that one cannot become a detached observer of the so-called material world while living in a world of spiritual bliss, for we 'are part of nature and our knowledge of nature as known by us, who are parts of it'.[167] We must live with material realities, but we must not allow them to obscure our knowledge of God. The *Todo y Nada* of John of the Cross is a means by which we can see the material world for what it is in and of itself—*nada*—nothing. At the same time we can see God for what he is—*Todo*—all. It was his almost ruthless dedication to this end that Merton admired in John of the Cross, and it became a dominant theme in his own life and work. In *New Seeds of Contemplation* he wrote: 'We experience God in proportion as we are stripped and emptied of attachment to His creatures.'[168] This idea was given added depth and meaning as Merton broadened his spiritual and theological studies to include the religions of the East.

1. *The Seven Storey Mountain*, p. 140.

2. Baker, *Thomas Merton Social Critic*, p. 10. *The Seven Storey Mountain*, pp. 65-66, 85, 115-16, and 174-77.

3. *The Seven Storey Mountain*, pp. 172-73.

4. Etienne Gilson, *The Spirit of Medieval Philosophy*, trans. A.H.C. Downes (New York: Scribners, 1936) p. 52.

5. *The Seven Storey Mountain*, p. 174.

6. Gilson, *The Spirit of Medieval Philosophy*, p. 54.

7. *New Seeds of Contemplation*, p. 158.

8. *Conjectures of a Guilty Bystander*, p. 19.

9. Merton comments at great length on moral codes and monasticism in *Contemplation in a World of Action*, pp. 98-116, 117-28.

10. See Merton, 'Mentors' in *A Thomas Merton Reader*, ed. McDonnell, pp. 253-66.

11. *The Seven Storey Mountain*, p. 204.

12. Jacques Maritain, *Art and Scholasticism*, trans. J.F. Scanlan (New York: Scribners, 1930) p. 3.

13. Ibid., p. 62. Merton comments extensively on the relationship between virtues, art, and morality in *The Seven Storey Mountain*, pp. 203-04.

14. Maritain, *Art and Scholasticism*, p. 66.

15. *The Seven Storey Mountain*, pp. 202-03.

16. Ibid., p. 202.

17. Ibid., p. 204.

18. *The Ascent to Truth*, p. x.

19. See Jacques Maritain, *The Degrees of Knowledge*, trans. Gerald B. Phelan (New York: Scribners, 1959), Part II 'The Degrees of Suprarational Knowledge,' pp. 247-383.

20. See ibid., pp. 352-83.

21. *Emblems of a Season of Fury*, p. 105.

22. Ibid., p. 5.

23. See Maurice Sachs, *Witches' Sabbath and The Hunt*, trans. Richard

Howard (New York: Ballantine Books, 1965), pp. 84-105, for an account of Maritain and his circle at Meudon.

24.   *Conjectures of a Guilty Bystander*, p. 164. On the same page Merton says: 'Two more names must be mentioned—Paris in the twentieth century means Camus and it means Sartre. For Camus I always had great sympathy. He was one with whom my heart agreed. Sartre I can read, sometimes with excitement, sometimes with a superficial agreement....Both Sartre and Camus are inconceivable outside the tradition of Christendom, even though they reject it!'

25.   *The Seven Storey Mountain*, p. 198.

26.   Augustine has also left a lasting impression upon Protestant theology, especially certain varieties of Calvinism. See Bernard Zylstra, 'Introduction' in L. Kalsbeek, *Contours of a Christian Philosophy: An Introduction to Herman Dooyeweerd's Thought* (Toronto: Wedge Publishing Foundation, 1975) p. 15.

27.   For a concise summary of Augustine's theology see Karl Rahner and Herbert Vorgrimler, *Theological Dictionary*, trans. Richard Strachan (New York: Herder and Herder, 1965), pp. 43, 93. A study in-depth of Augustine's theology may be found in Eugene TeSelle, *Augustine the Theologian* (New York: Herder and Herder, 1970).

28.   Anders Nygren, *Agape and Eros*, trans. Philip S. Watson (Philadelphia: Westminster, 1953) p. 450. Nygren's study is a classic in the field along with two other studies: M.C. D'Arcy, *The Mind and Heart of Love* (New York: Meridian Books, 1956) and Denis de Rougemont, *Love in the Western World*, trans. Montgomery Belgion, rev. ed. (Greenwich, Conn.: Fawcett, 1956). See also Daniel Day Williams, *The Spirit and Forms of Love* (New York: Harper & Row, 1968).

29.   Nygren, *Agape and Eros*, p. 451.

30.   Merton, 'Concerning the Collection in the Bellarmine College Library', *The Thomas Merton Studies Center*, 1 (Santa Barbara: Unicorn Press, 1971) p. 14.

31.   A further development of this theme is found in James Thomas Baker, 'Thomas Merton: The Spiritual and Social Philosophy of Union,' Dissertation, Florida State University 1968.

32.   Nygren, *Agape and Eros*, p. 474. D'Arcy differs with Nygren concerning Augustine's understanding of *caritas*. Cf. D'Arcy, *The Mind and Heart of Love*, pp. 88-89.

33.   Nygren, *Agape and Eros*, p. 531.

34.   Dom Cuthbert Butler, *Western Mysticism* (New York: E.P. Dutton, 1924) p. 20.

35.   Louis Bouyer, *Introduction to Spirituality*, trans. Mary Perkins Ryan (New York: Desclee, 1961) pp. 150-51.

36. Ibid., p. 152.

37. *New Seeds of Contemplation*, p. 3.

38. Ibid., p. 26.

39. Nygren, *Agape and Eros*, p. 493.

40. *The Seven Storey Mountain*, pp. 220-21.

41. *The Ascent to Truth*, p. 324.

42. Ibid., p. 325.

43. See *The Ascent to Truth*, pp. 14-16, 59-73 and *New Seeds of Contemplation*, pp. 194-202.

44. *The Ascent to Truth*, p. 323.

45. *New Seeds of Contemplation*, pp. 197-98.

46. *Conjectures of a Guilty Bystander*, p. 186.

47. Ibid., p. 185.

48. Ibid., pp. 185-86.

49. 'First and Last Thoughts: An Author's Preface', *A Thomas Merton Reader*, p. viii.

50. *The Ascent to Truth*, pp. 15-16.

51. Maritain, *The Degrees of Knowledge*, pp. 320-21.

52. For a further discussion of man's response to grace see the following works: Karl Rahner, *Theological Investigations*, 6 (Baltimore: Helicon, 1969), pp. 390-98 and Karl Barth, *Christ and Adam: Man and Humanity in Romans #5*, trans. T.A. Smail (New York: Macmillan, 1956/1957).

53. *Selected Poems of Thomas Merton*, p. 114.

54. St Thomas Aquinas, *Summa Theologica*, 2, trans. Fathers of the English Domincan Province (New York: Benziger, 1947) p. 1943.

55. Merton's *The Ascent to Truth* is based largely on the Thomism of Maritain's *The Degrees of Knowledge*. Similar ideas are found in Merton's *New Seeds of Contemplation*.

56. Aquinas, *Summa Theologica*, 2, p. 1438.

57. Ibid., p. 1946. See pp. 1929-46 for Aquinas' views on the relationship between the active and contemplative life.

58.   St Thomas Aquinas, *On Prayer and the Contemplative Life*, ed. Hugh Pope *op* (London: Washbourne, 1914) p. 226.

59.   A comparison of Meister Eckhart with Zen Buddhism is found in D.T. Suzuki, *Mysticism: Christian and Buddhist, The Eastern and Western Way* (1957; rpt. New York: Macmillan, 1969). See *Zen and the Birds of Appetite*, pp. 63-64, for Merton's comments on Suzuki and Aquinas.

60.   *The Ascent to Truth*, p. 323.

61.   Merton, *The Last of the Fathers* p. 47.

62.   *The Sign of Jonas*, pp. 23-24. An analysis of Merton's struggle concerning his writing and his monastic vocation is found in Alice Mayhew, 'Merton Against Himself', *Commonweal* 91 (1969-70) 70-74.

63.   *The Last of the Fathers*, p. 65.

64.   Ibid., p. 48.

65.   Ibid., p. 49.

66.   *The New Man*, p. 75.

67.   Ibid., pp. 78-79.

68.   *The Last of the Fathers*, p. 26.

69.   Ibid., pp. 25-26.

70.   Ibid., p. 40.

71.   Ibid.

72.   Bamberger, 'The Cistercian', *Continuum* 7 (1969) 233, rpt. as 'The Monk' in Hart, ed., *Thomas Merton/Monk*, p. 46.

73.   *The Last of the Fathers*, p. 27.

74.   Ibid., pp. 66-67.

75.   *New Seeds of Contemplation*, pp. 149, 150.

76.   Ibid., p. 50.

77.   Butler, *Western Mysticism*, p. 249.

78.   Bernard, *On the Song of Songs, Sermon* 57, cited by Butler, p. 254.

79.   *The Last of the Fathers*, p. 13.

80.   Merton, 'Action and Contemplation in St Bernard,' *Collectanea Ordinis Cisterciensium Reformatorum* 15 (1953) 31.

81. Ibid., p. 121.

82. *The Climate of Monastic Prayer*, p. 76.

83. See *The Last of the Fathers*, pp. 43-44.

84. The scope of Bernard's influence can be seen in H. Daniel-Rops, *Bernard of Clairvaux: The Story of the Last of the Great Church Fathers* (New York: Hawthorn, 1964).

85. *The Last of the Fathers*, p. 29.

86. See *Continuum* 7 (1969) Merton memorial issue. Most of these articles have been reprinted in Hart, ed., *Thomas Merton/Monk*.

87. 'Foreword' in Daniel-Rops, *Bernard of Clairvaux*, pp. 5-6.

88. Ibid., p. 6.

89. Ibid., p. 7.

90. *Thoughts in Solitude*, p. 17.

91. *The Seven Storey Mountain*, p. 414.

92. Sidney Spencer, *Mysticism in World Religion* (Baltimore: Penguin, 1963) p. 128.

93. Ibid., pp. 131-32.

94. Ibid., p. 135. Quoted from A.H. Armstrong, *An Introduction to Ancient Philosophy* (London: Methuen, 1947) p. 39.

95. Donald G. Bloesch, *The Ground of Certainty: Toward an Evangelical Theology of Revelation* (Grand Rapids: Eerdmans, 1971) pp. 141-42.

96. Butler, *Western Mysticism*, p. 19.

97. The influence of Platonic thought upon Aquinas is shown in R.J. Henle, *Saint Thomas and Platonism: A Study of The Plato and Platonic Texts in the Writings of Saint Thomas* (The Hague: Martinus Nijoff, 1956).

98. *The Seven Storey Mountain*, p. 137.

99. *Conjectures of a Guilty Bystander*, p. 46.

100. Spencer, *Mysticism in World Religion*, p. 129.

101. *Seasons of Celebration*, pp. 126-27.

102. Ibid., p. 127.

103. *Thoughts in Solitude*, pp. 17-18.

104. George H. Williams, *Wilderness and Paradise in Christian Thought* (New York: Harper, 1962) p. 5. See also p. 41.

105. Ibid., p. 50.

106. David Knowles, *Christian Monasticism* (London: Weidenfeld & Nicolson, 1969) pp. 20-21.

107. M. Henri Marrou quoted in Knowles, *Christian Monasticism*, p. 24.

108. *The Wisdom of the Desert: Sayings from the Desert Fathers of the Fourth Century*, p. 23.

109. Ibid., p. 3.

110. Ibid., p. 4.

111. Ibid. See also Karl Jaspers, *Man in the Modern Age*, trans. Eden and Cedar Paul (London: Routledge & Kegan Paul, 1951).

112. *The Wisdom of the Desert*, pp. 5-6.

113. *Silence in Heaven*, p. 19.

114. *No Man is an Island*, p. 84.

115. Ibid., p. 85.

116. *Life and Holiness*, p. 100.

117. *Seasons of Celebration*, p. 138.

118. *Raids on the Unspeakable*, p. 18.

119. The advantage of the desert is that its simplicity and loneliness enable one to find reality since all illusion is stripped away. The reality which one seeks is at the center of one's being and thus always present. See Merton's essay, 'Christ in the Desert' in *Monastery of Christ in the Desert*.

120. *The Wisdom of the Desert*, p. 9.

121. Williams, *Wilderness and Paradise*, p. 137.

122. Merton in *The Sign of Jonas*, p. 323, speaks of the desert of compassion.

123. *The Wisdom of the Desert*, p. 24.

124. *The Ascent to Truth*, p. 319. Merton's view changed considerably in later years, especially in relation to Zen Buddhism. His approach toward contemplation in non-Christian religions was very open on an experiential level and less critical on a theological, dogmatic level. Cf. Merton, 'Contemplation and the Dialogue Between Religions', *Sobornost* 5 (Winter-Spring 1969) 562-70.

125. *The Ascent to Truth*, p. 320.

126. Jean Daniélou, *From Glory to Glory: Texts from Gregory of Nyssa's Mystical Writings*, trans. and ed. Herbert Musurillo (New York: Scribners, 1961) p. 50. [See also *Gregory of Nyssa, The Life of Moses* (Paulist Press, Cistercian Publications, 1978].

127. *The Ascent to Truth*, pp. 22-23.

128. Ibid., p. 23.

129. Daniélou, *From Glory to Glory*, p. 70.

130. Ibid., p. 52.

131. In *The Ascent to Truth*, pp. 25-26, he discusses the theology of light and the theology of darkness.

132. Ibid., p. 28.

133. Ibid., p. 26.

134. Aldous Huxley provides an interesting and informative treatment of perception as it relates to mysticism in *The Doors of Perception and Heaven and Hell* (Harmondsworth: Penguin Books in association with Chatto & Windus, 1959). See R.C. Zaehner, *Mysticism Sacred and Profane: An Inquiry into Some Varieties of Praeternatural Experience* (New York: Oxford Galaxy, 1961) for a rebuttal to Huxley.

135. William Johnston, *The Mysticism of The Cloud of Unknowing*, p. 1. Merton, *Faith and Violence: Christian Teaching and Christian Practice*, pp. 259-87, relates apophatic mysticism to the God-is-dead movement in modern theology.

136. *New Seeds of Contemplation*, p. 184. He puts forth a similar concept in *Faith and Violence*, pp. 272-73.

137. *The Ascent to Truth*, p. 50.

138. Ibid., pp. 50-51.

139. Johnston, *The Mysticism of The Cloud of Unknowing*, p. 1.

140. *The Ascent to Truth*, p. 327.

141. Ibid., p. 328. Merton emphasizes the importance of spiritual direction in *Spiritual Direction and Meditation*.

142. *The Ascent to Truth*, p. 328.

143. Ibid.

144. Ibid.

145.   Ibid. See also Merton's essay 'The Primitive Carmelite Ideal' in *Disputed Questions*, pp. 167-99.

146.   Bouyer, *Introduction to Spirituality*, p. 68. F.C. Happold, *Prayer and Meditation: Their Nature and Practice* (Harmondsworth: Penguin, 1971) pp. 81-151, makes a distinction between meditation and contemplation.

147.   *New Seeds of Contemplation*, p. 3.

148.   *Spiritual Direction and Meditation*, p. 98.

149.   Ibid., p. 99.

150.   *New Seeds of Contemplation*, p. 5.

151.   Ibid., p. 7.

152.   Merton also considered becoming a Carthusian on several occasions. He describes this in *The Seven Storey Mountain*, pp. 327-28, 282-86 and in *The Sign of Jonas*, pp. 27-28.

153.   *The Ascent to Truth*, p. 329.

154.   Ibid., p. 132. See pp. 127-37 for details of the influence of Aquinas on John of the Cross.

155.   Ibid., p. 132.

156.   Ibid., p. 330.

157.   Ibid., pp. 52-53, quoted by Merton from St John of the Cross, *The Ascent of Mount Carmel*, Vol. 1 of *The Complete Works of St John of the Cross*, trans. Allison Peers (London: Burns & Oates, 1934) p. 260.

158.   *The Ascent to Truth*, p. 53.

159.   Ibid., p. 55.

160.   Ibid., p. 107.

161.   *Life and Holiness*, p. 162.

162.   *The Ascent to Truth*, pp. 249-50. See also pp. 52-55. It is important to distinguish between natural and supernatural mystical experiences. See Zaehner, *Mysticism Sacred and Profane*, pp. 153-207 and Maritain, *The Degrees of Knowledge*, pp. 247-77.

163.   *The Ascent to Truth*, p. 83. William Johnston, *Christian Zen* (New York: Harper & Row, 1971) p. 4, asserts that a mystical knowledge of God can result in imageless prayer among some who are devoted to meditation.

164.   *The New Man*, p. 173.

165. *The Ascent to Truth*, p. 257.

166. *Conjectures of a Guilty Bystander*, pp. 271-72.

167. Ibid., p. 272.

168. *New Seeds of Contemplation*, p. 208.

IV

THE RELIGIONS OF THE EAST

Gandhi

WITHOUT DOUBT the major influence upon Merton from the Hindu tradition, to which he was introduced at Columbia by Bramachari, came from the great Indian teacher and leader Mohandas Gandhi.[1] He was, for Merton, a man who coupled profound spiritual depth with unparalleled social concern. This spirituality and social concern manifested itself in three ways: a belief in a universally valid spiritual tradition common to both east and west; the conviction that nonviolence is the fruit of an inner freedom already achieved; and the crucially important principle that the spiritual life is not an exclusively private affair.

Of special importance is the fact that Gandhi first discovered his Indian heritage because of his western education and experience. It was commonplace during Gandhi's time for students from India to go to England or the United States to study, and they were expected to become westernized and give up their 'primitive' ways in favor of the vastly 'superior' ways of the West. Gandhi did not do this. He recognized the good in the West, not because it was western, but because it was universally human and thus compatible with what was universally human in the East. He was able to return to India and appreciate his Indian heritage and his western education. Merton elaborates:

> One of the great lessons of Gandhi's life remains this: through the spiritual traditions of the West he, an Indian, discovered his Indian heritage and with it his own 'right mind'. And in his fidelity to his own heritage and its spiritual sanity, he was able to show men of the West and of the whole world a way to recover their own 'right mind' in their own tradition, thus manifesting the fact that there

are certain indisputable and essential values—religious, ethical, ascetic, spiritual and philosophical—which man has everywhere needed and which he has in the past managed to acquire, values without which he cannot live, values which are now in large measure lost to him so that, unequipped to face life in a fully human manner, he now runs the risk of destroying himself entirely. [2]

Gandhi was not a syncretist who believed in merging all religions regardless of belief, Merton points out, nor was he indifferent to the obvious conflicts between the world religions. He did believe that certain values were basically human, that they were found in both east and west, that such values were transmitted by different religions, and that one purpose of these religions and values is to help one find his 'right mind' or *satyagraha*. [3] Thus it was not necessary to give up one's own spiritual heritage to realize these values, nor was it necessary to reject the spiritual heritages of others.

Gandhi's emphasis upon these basic human values grew from his concept of the nature of man which Merton describes in these words:

Gandhi's religio-political action was based on an ancient metaphysic of man, a philosophical wisdom which is common to Hinduism, Buddhism, Islam, Judaism, and Christianity: that 'truth is the inner law of our being'. Not that man is merely an abstract essence, and that our action must be based on logical fidelity to a certain definition of man. Gandhi's religious action is based on a religious intuition of *being* in man and in the world, and his vow of truth is a vow of fidelity to being in all its accessible dimensions. His wisdom is based on experience more than logic. Hence the way of peace is the way of truth, of fidelity to wholeness and being, which implies a basic respect for life not as a concept, not as a sentimental figment of the imagination, but in its deepest most secret and most fontal reality. The first and fundamental truth is to be sought in respect for our own inmost being, and this in turn implies the recollectedness and awareness which attune us to that silence in which alone Being speaks to us in all its simplicity. [4]

Gandhi's spirituality was based not in any particular religious or cultural tradition, but in the nature of man. He sought what was human in both east and west while expressing these human values within the Indian context.

Gandhi also believed that one's outward social actions were a direct result of one's inward spiritual condition. His nonviolence was more than a political tactic: it was the logical expression of his beliefs. In Merton's words: 'The spirit of non-violence sprang from *an inner realization of spiritual unity within himself.* The whole Gandhian concept of non-violent action and *satyagraha* is incomprehensible if it is thought to be a means of achieving unity rather than as *the fruit of inner unity already achieved.*'[5] At this point Gandhi's perspective was radically different from that of the majority, for he saw nonviolence as much more than a technique for gaining independence from Britain. For Gandhi 'most important of all was the inner unity, the overcoming and healing of inner division, the consequent spiritual and personal freedom, of which national autonomy and liberty would only be consequences.'[6] Gandhi failed in the realm of politics, as he acknowledged: 'Non-violence is my creed, It never was of the Congress. With the Congress it has been a policy.'[7] The Congress understood *satyagraha* as a technique to be used and then discarded when it no longer proved useful politically. As a result, 'no inner peace was achieved, no inner unity, only the same divisions, the conflicts and the scandals that were ripping the rest of the world to pieces' remained, so that the situation was really not changed.[8] For Gandhi, *swaraj*—the Sanskrit term for independence meaning literally 'one's own rule'—began with one's self and then spread outward to society.[9]

Gandhi believed that the spiritual life was not lived individually, but contained a definite social dimension. 'His approach to these problems was *inseparably* religious and political at the same time'.[10] Merton explains this in detail:

> For Gandhi...political action had to be by its very nature 'religious' in the sense that it had to be informed by principles of religious and philosophical wisdom. To separate religion and politics was in Gandhi's eyes 'madness' because his politics rested on a thoroughly religious interpretation of reality, of life, and of man's place in the world....Political action therefore was not a means to acquire security and strength for one's self and one's party, but a means of witnessing to the truth and the reality of the cosmic structure by making one's own proper contribution to the order willed by God. One could thus preserve one's integrity and peace, being detached from results (which are in the hands of God) and being free

from the inner violence that comes from division and untruth, the usurpation of someone else's *dharma* in place of one's own *svadharma*. These perspectives lent Gandhi's politics their extraordinary spiritual force and religious realism. [11]

Gandhi's *satyagraha* was 'not simply ascetic or devotional indulgences that may possibly suit the fancy of a few religious pacifists and confused poets.' [12] It was a way in which man could recover his right mind, individually, communally, and nationally. In his book *Resistance and Contemplation*, James Douglass quotes from Gandhi the following lines which show clearly the social dimension of his life and work: 'Recall the face of the poorest and the most helpless man whom you have seen and ask youself if the step you contemplate is going to be of any use to him. Will he be able to gain anything by it? Will it restore him to control over his own life and destiny?' [13] Little wonder that Merton observes that 'the liberation of India was to Gandhi a *religious* duty because for him the liberation of India was only a step to the liberation of all mankind from the tyranny of violence in others, but chiefly in themselves'. [14]

The original Sanskrit meaning of *satyagraha* implies a 'vow of truth'. Thus *satyagraha* becomes a matter 'of worship, adoration of the God of truth, so that his whole political structure is built on this and other vows...and becomes an entirely religious system. The vow of *satyagraha* is the vow to die rather than say what one does not mean.' [15] Once Gandhi had found his 'right mind' nothing could deter him from his course. This understanding of spirituality and political action provided the basis for much of Merton's own conviction of the relationship between spirituality and social action. It is not surprising then, to read in his essay 'A Tribute to Gandhi' the following words:

> Gandhi is, it seems to me, a model of integrity whom we cannot afford to ignore, and the one basic duty we all owe to the world of our time is to imitate him in 'disassociating ourselves from evil in total disregard of the consequences.' [16]

Zen Buddhism

The most significant Eastern influence on Merton came from Zen Buddhism. [17] His interest grew from his study of the

Christian mystics and their search for reality, their understanding of contemplation and action, and the dualism between
the physical and the spiritual. In Gandhi, Merton began to see
how this dualism could be overcome, at least in the case of
religious and political life, and this problem fascinated him. He
was particularly impressed with the Taoist concept of the
yin-yang where the opposites are smoothly run together and
not in direct opposition to each other. [18] It was in Zen, however,
that Merton found that 'experience is a direct grasp of the
unity of the invisible and the visible, the noumenal and the
phenomenal, or, if you prefer, an experiential realization that
any such division is bound to be pure imagination'. [19]

As a contemplative, Merton had difficulty with much of
traditional western thought, primarily concerned with what are
called the basic facts of existence. According to Merton, 'we
tend immediately to conceive these facts as reducible to certain
austere and foolproof propositions—logical statements that are
guaranteed to have meaning because they are empirically
verifiable'. [20] In other words, the West is concerned with
explanation while the East is concerned with experience, and so
often the explanation is substituted for the experience itself.
Merton's contemplative life was his attempt to live as much as
possible within the realm of experience rather than of
explanation. Zen also attempts this and Merton found an affinity
between Zen and his own life.

> Buddhist meditation, but above all that of Zen, seeks not
> to *explain* but to *pay attention*, to *become aware*, to *be
> mindful*, in other words to develop a certain *kind of con-
> sciousness that is above and beyond deception* by verbal
> formulas—or by emotional excitement. Deception in what?
> Deception in its grasp of itself as it really is. Deception
> due to diversion and distraction from what is right there—
> consciousness itself. [21]

One is reminded of Gregory of Nyssa or John of the Cross, and
one can see that they were saying something similar in stripping
away all illusion and all unreality until the reality that had
always been there could be perceived. It is very akin to the
biblical words describing Paul after his conversion: 'And
immediately something like scales fell from his eyes and he
regained his sight' (Acts 9:18).

Reality is obscured and often superseded by the explanation
of that reality. Merton points out that 'for Zen, from the
moment the fact is transferred to a statement it is falsified. One

ceases to grasp the naked reality of experience and one grasps a form of words instead'.[22] One is reminded of how impressed Merton was by Gilson's discussion of the *aseitas* of God, and how Merton had previously found statements about God to be inadequate. Such a concern with being—true reality—is much needed in today's world, Merton contended, and Zen is one way of arriving at it:

> I believe that Zen has much to say not only to a Christian but also to a modern man. It is nondoctrinal, concrete, direct, existential, and seeks above all to come to grips with life itself, not with ideas about life, still less with party platforms in politics, religion, science or anything else.[23]

The real problem of modern life is to be solved not by a correct understanding of religious or political doctrines, but only through a direct experience of the reality of life.

Zen was particularly influential when Merton came to the problem of dualism, especially that between the sacred and the secular and the spiritual and the physical. William Johnston, in *Christian Zen*, comments on a letter from Merton dealing with this problem:

> What he states well and with rough clarity is that Zen goes beyond all categories and all duality and that Christianity can do the same. In certain areas of apophatic experience (the Rhineland mystics make it clear) the subject-object relationship disappears, and this is no mere Christian atheism or denial of God but simply another way of experiencing God.[24]

Merton explains this quality of Zen by pointing out that Zen 'neither affirms nor denies, it simply *is*. One might say that Zen is the ontological *awareness of pure being beyond subject and object*, an immediate grasp of being in its "suchness" and "thusness"'.[25] He went so far as to say that there is no dualism in Zen, nor is there a division of man into body and soul. The Zen concept of *prajna*, according to Merton, is not merely self-realization but it is 'realization pure and simple, beyond subject and object. In such realization, evidently "emptiness" is no longer opposed to "fullness", but emptiness and fullness are One. Zero equals infinity.'[26]

Such a concept of being raises questions concerning man and the 'otherness' of God, and Zen is often accused of being atheistic or pantheistic. Yet Zen does not deny the existence of a supreme being; it just refuses to make any speculations at all.

> When asked, 'If all phenomena return to the One, where does the One return to?' The Zen master Joshu simply said: 'When I lived in Seiju, I made a robe out of hemp and it weighed ten pounds.'
>
> This is a useful and salutary *mondo* (saying) for the Western reader to remember. It will guard him against the almost irresistible temptation to think of Zen in Neo-Platonic terms. Zen is *not* a system of pantheistic monism. It is not a system of any kind. It refuses to make any statements at all about the metaphysical structure of being and existence. Rather it points directly to being itself, without indulging in speculation.[27]

Merton was thus able to apply Zen to his own life as a Christian contemplative without compromising his belief in God.

Basic to the Zen experience is *satori* or enlightenment. This usually comes after years of study under a Zen master who teaches one to meditate on *koans* or riddles. Eventually enlightenment or illumination will come and one will accept himself as he is, 'as a riddle *without an answer that is communicable to others in an objective manner*'.[28] According to Merton *satori* may be an unconscious demand for grace:

> If he is capable of 'illumination', he will at that moment taste the delight of recognizing that his own incommunicable experience of the ground of his being, his own total acceptance of his own nothingness, far from constituting a problem, is in fact the source and center of inexpressible joy: in Christian terms, one can hardly help feeling that the illumination of the genuine Zen experience seems to open out into an unconscious demand for grace—a demand that is perhaps answered without being understood. Is it perhaps already grace?[29]

Merton was open to the possibility that the Zen experience of *satori* was a vehicle for grace and thus also revelatory in nature.

Merton also compared the Zen doctrine of the void with the dark night of the soul of St John of the Cross, and pointed out that in both Zen and John of the Cross 'there must be a "death" of that ego-identity or self-consciousness which is constituted by a calculating and desiring ego.'[30] In addition,

Merton showed how Zen can aid in approaching the Bible by helping us 'distinguish carefully between faith in dogmatic propositions about God and faith as a personal, inscrutable *event and encounter* which revolutionizes one's entire sense of being and identity'.[31] Zen, if seen as something other than only a religion, can be helpful to the Christian, particularly if he is already familiar with christian mysticism. Merton was able to say: 'It is quite possible for Zen to be adapted and used to clear the air of ascetic irrelevancies and help us to regain a healthy natural balance in our understanding of the spiritual life.'[32]

A significant aspect of Zen thought is its ethics. It is concerned with 'the existential *present* of life here and now'.[33] There is no heaven, no hell, no future life, and thus no concern for a better life in the next world. Zen faces squarely the problems of this life in this world. Zen's concerns with this life, according to Merton, are two: 'one, the penetration of the meaning and reality of suffering by meditation, and two, the protection of all beings against suffering by nonviolence and compassion.'[34] The first of these concerns is contemplative and rises out of the Zen quest for being. The second, however, is active and pertains to the social order. Zen enlightenment is not found alone in utter solitude, but 'is found in action (though not necessarily as activity, still less in *activism*). Zen is a full awareness of the dynamism and spontaneity of life, and hence it cannot be grasped by mere introspection, still less by dreaming.'[35]

Buddhism in general and Zen in particular seek to be in touch with human experience and the suffering of mankind.[36] *Nirvana* is not an escape from the world and its problems, rather, it is found in the midst of the world. Says Merton: 'The problem of human suffering is insoluble as long as men are prevented by their collective and individual illusions from getting directly to grips with suffering in its very root within themselves.'[37] One must break through these illusions and face suffering first in oneself and then in others. Then, says Merton, 'on the basis of a correct *perception* (not a correct *interpretation*, please note), one may proceed then to correct— that is to say, *realistic*—action.'[38] In so much of western ethical thought there is no correct perception and hence no realistic action. Merton asks: 'Is there not an "optical illusion" in an eschatological spirit which, however much it may appeal to *agape*, seeks only to transform persons and social structures *from the outside*?'[39] Here is a basic principle of Zen, a principle that became fundamental to Merton's ethical thought and to his thinking on contemplation and action.[40]

The Sufis of Islam

'Merton had also a "Muslim period," H. Mason points out, which is to say, a period in which meditation on Islamic faith, as introduced to him by Louis Massignon, brought into his own language and spiritual life an element which stimulated an expression of his own deepest concerns and longings.'[41] Merton was deeply impressed by the life and work of Massignon, especially with his attempts to bring about a Muslim-Christian dialogue, the need for which was evident in light of the christian crusades and later missionary efforts.

As a result of the traditional Christian antagonism toward Islam, there has been little study of Islamic theology among western theologians and scholars, and consequently the importance of Sufism has often been overlooked. However, as Sidney Spencer indicates:

> The growth of Islamic mysticism (or Sufism) is a significant illustration of the strength of the mystical tendency in religion. On the face of it, the religion of Mohammed can scarcely be regarded as of itself providing fruitful soil for the growth of that tendency. Yet within a comparatively short time after the Prophet's death a movement arose among his followers which has given birth to some of the greatest of the mystics.[42]

This development did not occur in isolation, and 'there is no doubt that Christian and Neo-Platonic influences played an important part in the development of Sufism.'[43] Indeed, Merton refers to the belief among some scholars that the Sufi mystic Ibn Abbad of Ronda exercised at least an indirect influence upon the thought of St John of the Cross:

> Ibn Abbad taught that it is in the night of desolation that the door to mystical union is secretly opened, though it remains tightly closed during the 'day' of understanding and light.[44]

While questions may remain concerning the influence of Sufism upon Christian mysticism, there is no doubt that there was misunderstanding between the Sufis and Muslim philosophers. Merton speaks of the anguish (the *angustia*, the pain and frustration caused by confinement within limitations) which Averroes experienced when he was not able to grasp what the young Sufi mystic, Ibn al' Arabi, had seen as a divine gift.[45]

Averroes was a philosopher and Ibn al' Arabi was a mystic. Averroes was concerned with explanation and Ibn al' Arabi was concerned with experience, and Averroes trained in his methods, was unable to understand the depth of the Sufi mystical insight.

Most significant for Merton's thought is the Sufi understanding of the nature of man. The Sufis divide man in terms of his knowledge of God and his faculty for knowing God. The innermost man, what Sufism calls the 'secret of man', is in God and one's secret is God's innermost knowledge of man—which only God possesses. This 'secret of man' or the heart is 'the faculty by which man knows God and therefore Sufism develops the heart'.[46] In other words, the emphasis is not upon the outward actions of man, but upon the inner man, the center of man's being. This understanding of man has important implications for both the contemplative life and the active life. Sufism is concerned with final integration of man so that the person becomes himself as he is intended to be. In Sufi terms this means that 'real maturity is for a person to become a mystic. This is what man is made for.'[47] Merton saw this as a very unusual concept, especially among theologians who 'are fighting over controversial ideas that really don't touch the heart of man so deeply'.[48] The possibilities for religious life are obvious, and Merton states that 'it is unfortunate that there should be so many contemplative and monastic communities in which ... everything gets pushed over into some other aspect of the life, whereas this is the real aspect of life, the real contemplative and prayerful aspect of the life.'[49]

The Sufi concept of man is also very important for the active life. This has been pointed out by Reza Arasteh, a Persian psychoanalyst, in his book *Final Integration in the Adult Personality*.[50] Merton believed that Arasteh's most important contribution came from the insights he borrowed from Sufi mysticism. Most psychoanalysts have as their goal the adaptation of the patient to the society so that the patient can become normal. Merton declares that 'Dr Arasteh holds that adaptation to society at best helps a man "to live with his illness rather than cure it," particularly if the general atmosphere of the society is unhealthy because of its over-emphasis on cerebral, competitive, acquisitive forms of ego-affirmation.'[51] In other words, in many cases psychoanalysis becomes a technique for making people conform to a society that prevents them from growing and reaching their full capabilities as human beings. Merton applies this concept to the religious life and maintains that there is a kind of spirituality that 'frustrates and stifles growth beyond a median level. It makes no provision for anything but formal adaptation to a rather narrow and limited communal pattern. Within that pattern it tolerates "safe" moderate growth and blesses lack of growth.' [52] It results in a spiritual mediocrity. Its goal is not to attain a mystic union with God, but rather to conform the person to whatever happens to be the prevailing spirituality of the day. The implications of this idea go far beyond the spiritual life and provide the basis for a critique of contemporary society.

The important breakthrough of Sufism is that man should be understood in terms of his highest development. Rather than attempting to raise people up to a median standard, one should strive to raise people up beyond that standard to attain their highest possible development. In the spiritual life this 'peak experience' [53] is a mystical union with God that leads one to an integration not only with God, but also with oneself and with others. This demands that the religious person look beyond the society for his goals, for society's goals are nothing more than an expression of the median standard. Merton asks:

> Where are we to look for the true solutions? Precisely from the Spirit who will speak clearly at the right time through a renewed ecclesiastical and monastic community. The path to a final integration for the individual, and for the community lies, in any case, beyond the dictates and programs of any culture ('Christian culture' included). [54]

Our decisions must be more than merely historical; they must be eschatological. For Merton the insights of Sufism provide a basis for making such eschatological decisions.

The Quest for Authentic Spirituality

The quest for an authentic spirituality was a dominant goal of Merton's life and work. Even the questions of contemplation and action are basic to his understanding of spirituality and form a part of that quest. It was not until his college years that Merton's spiritual life began to take on shape and direction. Until then he had been confused, unsure of himself, and what little spirituality he possessed had been largely unrelated to his everyday life. Many years later he wrote: 'If you want to have a spiritual life you must unify your life. A life is either all spiritual or not spiritual at all. No man can serve two masters. Your life is shaped by the end you live for. You are made in the image of what you desire.'[55] He says elsewhere that one must possess '*the ability to make a firm decision* to embrace a certain state of life and *to act on that decision.*'[56]

The spiritual foundations of Merton's thought were vitally important in bringing him to the point where he could make a decision concerning his life and then act on it. His encounter with the modern Thomists was instrumental in providing him with a framework in which to grow and develop spiritually. Gilson's concept of the 'aseity of God—God is being *per se*' gave Merton a new understanding of God which he could accept.[57] Maritain's thinking on the virtues and morality enabled Merton to see for the first time the relationship between his belief in God and his personal actions.[58] Augustine played an important role in Merton's quest for an authentic spirituality with his emphasis upon human desire and its relationship to God. Since human desire can find meaning only in God, man is incomplete without God and must therefore become a new creature living by the Spirit of God.

Merton is careful to emphasize that ontologically the source of this new life is in God, and therefore outside and above ourselves. At the same time, however, 'both the supernatural life and God Himself Who gives it are in the centre of our own being'.[59] He clarifies this by saying:

> Since we are made in the image and likeness of God, there is no other way for us to find out who we are than by finding, in ourselves, the divine image. Now this image, which is present in every one of us by nature, can indeed be known by rational inference. But that is not enough to give us a real experience of our own identity. It is hardly better than inferring that we exist because other people act as if we existed....
>
> Self-realization in this true religious sense is then less an awareness of ourselves than an awareness of the God to whom we are drawn in the depths of our own being.[60]

Here we find the theological basis for Merton's understanding of contemplation. He goes on to affirm that there is a natural striving in man for union with God:

> He cannot rest unless he rests in God....This alone is the reality for which we are made. Here alone do we finally 'find ourselves'—not in our natural selves but out of ourselves in God. For our destiny is infinitely greater than our

own poor selves: 'I said: You are Gods, all of you sons of
the Most High.' (Psalm 81:6) The spiritual *anguish of
man* has no cure but mysticism.[61]

There is a danger that spirituality may become what Merton
calls 'damnable abstractness'.[62] For Merton an authentic
spirituality must take into account the humanity of man and the
reality of the world in which man lives. He drew heavily from
Aquinas and Bernard of Clairvaux's emphasis upon man and the
larger community beyond the individual and his experience.

For Merton a true spirituality must make a difference not
only in one's personal spiritual life but also in the world at
large. It must be more than mere revivalism:

> This means going a little further than the vapid preach-
> ments of that popular religion which has led some to
> believe that a 'religious revival' is taking place among us.
> Let us not be too sure of that! The mere fact that men are
> frightened and insecure, that they grasp at optimistic
> slogans, run more frequently to Church, and seek to pacify
> their souls by cheerful and humanitarian maxims, is surely
> no indication that our society is becoming 'religious'. In
> fact, it may be a symptom of spiritual sickness. It is cer-
> tainly a good thing to be aware of our symptoms, but that
> does not justify our palliating them with quack medi-
> cines.[63]

Revivals come and go but true spirituality places an indelible
mark upon society. Merton takes the spirituality of Aquinas and
Bernard of Clairvaux seriously, for their spirituality resulted in
changes in the Church, philosophy, and theology, politics and in
the society at large.[64]

Mysticism and the inner spiritual struggle of man was also
vitally important as Merton sought to develop an authentic
spirituality, for he saw this inner struggle as basic to all of
mankind's struggles. His study of the Desert Fathers, Gregory
of Nyssa, Teresa of Avila, and John of the Cross taught him
something of the depth of the mystical experience. The idea of
stripping away all that is illusory impressed Merton and he
sought to face himself and God without evasion. Says Merton:
'The religious answer is not religious at all if it is not fully real.
Evasion is the answer of superstition.'[65] The concept of *Todo y
Nada* had a special meaning for Merton as he came to realize
that one must renounce one's concepts of God. 'As soon as we
try to verify the spiritual presence as an object of exact

knowledge,' he wrote, 'God eludes us.'[66]

Merton's interest in non-christian religions deepened only after he was thoroughly grounded in christian theology, church history, and mysticism. Merton's dialogue with eastern religions was not faddish nor was it an attempt to syncretize all religious faiths. He approached the non-christian with a profound understanding of his own faith balanced by years of experience as a Cistercian monk. As a result, his dialogue with such men as D.T. Suzuki was viewed by scholars as a serious attempt at religious understanding, for it was the fruit of years of study, meditation, and prayer. Perhaps most important of all is that this encounter with the religions of the East was a way by which Merton deepened his own spiritual life. He points this out in remarks prepared for an interfaith meeting held in Calcutta just a few weeks before his death:

> I speak as a Western monk who is pre-eminently concerned with his own monastic calling and dedication. I have left my monastery to come here not just as a research scholar or even as an author (which I happen to be). I come as a pilgrim who is anxious not just to obtain information, not just facts about other monastic traditions, but to drink from ancient sources of monastic vision and experience. I seek not only to learn more (quantitatively) about religion and monastic life, but to become a better and more enlightened monk (qualitatively) myself.[67]

Merton was not only willing to give to others; he was willing to receive.

By all of this Merton came more and more to realize that there was a relationship between contemplation and action, between the spiritual life and the active life. Thus he wrote that 'the spiritual life is first of all a *life*. It is not merely something to be known and studied, it is to be lived.'[68] If the spiritual life is to have any meaning the western emphasis upon explanation must be enriched by the eastern emphasis upon experience, and the dualistic tendency in western spirituality must be overcome. In addition, Merton came to understand the concept of the integration of the individual in terms of mysticism rather than in terms of social acceptance, for it does little good to become integrated into a society, an ecclesiastical structure, or a religious order that is itself in need of healing. 'Perhaps', he wrote, 'we ought to be a little more critical of this whole concept: "the spiritual life."'[69] Spirituality involves the whole person and his relationships with others and with his world. A morbid self-hatred of the body and the world has no place in true mysticism, for sanctity affirms, it does not deny, one's humanity:

> Hence sanctity is not a matter of being *less* human, but *more* human than other men. This implies a greater capacity for concern, for suffering, for understanding, for sympathy, and also for humor, for joy, for appreciation of the good and beautiful things of life. It follows that a pretended 'way of perfection' that simply destroys or frustrates human values precisely because they are human, and in order to set oneself apart from the rest of men as an object of wonder, is doomed to be nothing but a caricature. And such a caricaturing of sanctity is indeed a sin against faith in the Incarnation. It shows contempt for the humanity for which Christ did not hesitate to die on the cross. [70]

The spiritual life, for Merton is incarnational. Man retains his full humanity, yet at the center of his being God is present, and man can achieve full meaning only in union with this center, with God.

Merton's quest for an authentic spirituality was a long one, stretching from the hills of France to New York and Gethsemani and finally to Bangkok. It was quest that prepared Merton for his role as an American social prophet who would become famous the world over for his incisive critique of contemporary society. Most important of all, it was a quest that never really ended throughout Merton's life. In his last talk, presented just hours before his death, Merton said: 'I believe that our renewal consists precisely in deepening this understanding and grasp of what is most real.' [71]

NOTES

1.   The facts of Gandhi's life are too well known to need recital here. See Merton, ed., *Gandhi on Non-Violence: Selected Texts from Mohandas K. Gandhi's 'Non-Violence in Peace and War'* (New York: New Directions, 1964) pp. 1-20. See also Merton's essay 'A Tribute to Gandhi' in his book *Seeds of Destruction*, pp. 221-34. 'A Tribute to Gandhi' also appears in *Thomas Merton on Peace*, ed. Gordon C. Zahn (New York: McCall, 1971) pp. 178-84. For the life of Gandhi see M.K. Gandhi, *Gandhi's Autobiography: The Story of My Experiements with Truth*, trans. Mahadev Desai (Washington, D.C.: Public Affairs Press, 1948) and Robert Payne, *The Life and Death of Mahatma Gandhi* (New York: E.P, Dutton, 1969).

2.   *Gandhi on Non-Violence*, p. 4. Cf. Paul Tillich, *The Future of Religions*, ed. Jerald C. Brauer (New York: Harper & Row, 1966) pp. 80-94. Here Tillich speaks of what he calls 'The Religion of the Concrete Spirit' consisting of universally human values which point to the ultimate meaning of life.

3.   See *Gandhi on Non-Violence*, p. 4, where Merton defines *satyagraha* as a 'term coined by Gandhi. Its root meaning is "holding on to truth," and, by extension, resistence by non-violent means.'

4.   *Seeds of Destruction*, pp. 231-32.

5.   *Gandhi on Non-Violence*, p. 6.

6.   Ibid.

7.   Ibid., p. 75.

8.   Ibid., p. 6.

9.   See James W. Douglass, *Resistance and Contemplation: The Way of Liberation* (Garden City: Doubleday, 1971) pp. 90-91.

10.   *Seeds of Destruction*, p. 226.

11.   Ibid., pp. 226-28. [*Svadharma* means, in fact, one's own *dharma*—ed.]

12.   *Gandhi on Non-Violence*, p. 20.

13.   Douglass, *Resistance and Contemplation*, p. 136. These words of Gandhi are taken from Eileen Egan, 'Crossing India', *The Catholic Worker* 37 No. 2 (1971), 7.

14.   *Gandhi on Non-Violence*, p. 7.

15.   *Seeds of Destruction*, p. 230.

16.   Ibid., p. 234.

17.   See Sr M. Thérèse Lentfoehr, 'The Spiritual Writer', *Continuum* 7 (1969), p. 253, rpt. in Hart, ed., *Thomas Merton/Monk*, p. 120.

18. *The Way of Chuang Tzu,* pp. 30-31.

19. *Zen and the Birds of Appetite,* p. 37.

20. Ibid., p. 36.

21. Ibid., p. 38.

22. Ibid., p. 37.

23. Ibid., p. 32.

24. William Johnston, *Christian Zen,* p. 23. See also pp. 21-22. A somewhat different interpretation is given by R.C. Zaehner, *Concordant Discord: The Interdependence of Faiths* (Oxford: Clarendon Press, 1970) pp. 130-31.

25. *Mystics and Zen Masters,* pp. 13-14.

26. "The Zen Revival', *Continuum* 1 (1964) 535.

27. *Mystics and Zen Masters,* p. 14. See also *The True Solitude: Selections from the Writings of Thomas Merton,* ed. Dean Walley (Kansas City, Mo.: Hallmark, 1969) pp. 54-55.

28. *Mystics and Zen Masters,* p. 228.

29. Ibid.

30. Ibid., p. 242.

31. *Opening the Bible* (Collegeville, Minn.: Liturgical Press, 1970) pp. 52-54.

32. *Zen and the Birds of Appetite,* p. 58. Cf. William Barrett in the introduction to D.T. Suzuki, *Zen Buddhism: Selected Writings of D.T. Suzuki,* ed., William Barrett (Garden City: Doubleday Anchor, 1956) p. vii.

33. *Mystics and Zen Masters,* p. 25.

34. *Zen and the Birds of Appetite,* p. 93.

35. *Mystics and Zen Masters,* p. 222.

36. Ibid., p. 286, Merton points out that traditional Buddhism is often not in touch with human experience. One must be careful to distinguish between a traditional Buddhism which is largely a folk religion and the living Buddhism of a number of monks and scholars.

37. *Mystics and Zen Masters,* p. 286.

38. Ibid., p. 287.

39. Ibid., pp. 287-88.

40. See Chalmers McCormick, 'The Zen Catholicism of Thomas Merton', *Journal of Ecumenical Studies* 9 (1972) 802: While Merton progressively deepened his understanding of Oriental religions and was generally well-informed, he was at times guilty of overstating and oversimplifying their positions, and erred in overconceptualizing their beliefs. While Merton himself did not develop fully the implications of Zen for ecumenism within Christianity, the author finds hope in the move toward a more contemplative and less conceptual approach to religion. The somewhat paradoxical combination in Merton's later career of an interest in Zen and in social concerns seems to suggest that Merton found the two not only compatible but complementary.'

41. H. Mason, 'Merton and Massignon', *Muslim World* 59 (1969) 317-18. Merton comments on Massignon in his *Conjectures of a Guilty Bystander*, p. 132.

42. Sidney Spencer, *Mysticism in World Religion* (Baltimore: Penguin, 1963) p. 299.

43. Ibid. See pp. 299-325 for a discussion of Islamic mysticism.

44. *Raids on the Unspeakable*, p. 141. For an extensive discussion of Islamic thought and its influence upon Christian philosophy see Etienne Gilson, *History of Christian Philosophy in the Middle Ages* (New York: Random House, 1955) pp. 181-246, 387-402.

45. *Conjectures of a Guilty Bystander*, pp. 188-89. Averroes' problem was one of limitation rather than error. Merton was so moved by this incident that he wrote a poem entitled 'Song for the Death of Averroes' in Thomas Merton, *Emblems of a Season of Fury* (New York: New Directions, 1963) pp. 23-27.

46. 'The Life That Unifies', ed. Naomi Burton Stone, *Sisters Today* 42 (1970) 71. Cf. Herman Dooyeweerd, *A New Critique of Theoretical Thought* (Amsterdam: H.J. Paris, and Philadelphia: Presbyterian and Reformed, 1953-58) for a Protestant philosopher's understanding of the importance of the heart, note especially Vol. 1 of this 4 vol. work.

47. 'The Life That Unifies,' p. 67.

48. Ibid.

49. Ibid., p. 66.

50. Reza Arasteh, *Final Integration in the Adult Personality* (Leiden: E.J. Brill, 1965).

51. *Contemplation in a World of Action*, pp. 208-09.

52. Ibid., p. 215.

53. See 'The Life That Unifies,' p. 67. For an informative discussion of peak experiences see also Abraham H. Maslow, *Religion, Values and Peak Experiences* (Columbus: Ohio State University Press, 1964).

54. *Contemplation in a World of Action*, p. 217.

55. *Thoughts in Solitude*, p. 67.

56. *No Man is an Island*, p. 125.

57. *The Seven Storey Mountain*, p. 173. See also pp. 174-75.

58. See Gary Wills, *Bare Ruined Choirs: Doubt, Prophecy, and Radical Religion* (Garden City: Doubleday, 1972), pp. 45-48, for a discussion of Maritain's understanding of the virtues and his influence upon Merton and other liberal Catholics. Wills contends that the influence of Gilson and Maritain was due in part to their status as laymen.

59. *The New Man*, p. 116.

60. Ibid., pp. 85-86.

61. Ibid., pp. 79-80.

62. *Conjectures of a Guilty Bystander*, p. 254. Merton is speaking here of a spirituality which is so totally separate from the physical body and the physical world that a kind of schizoid situation exists. See also *The True Solitude*, p. 51 where he states that a schizoid spirituality results in the kind of spiritual life 'people worry about when they are so busy with something else they think they ought to be spiritual. Spiritual life is guilt.'

63. *Life and Holiness*, p. 14.

64. See *The Last of the Fathers*, p. 9, where he writes of Bernard of Clairvaux: 'One of the dominant figures in the history of the Church, and by all odds the greatest in his own century, he had tremendous influence on the political, literary, and religious life of Europe.' See also *The Ascent to Truth*, p. 323, where he speaks of St Thomas Aquinas: 'The vast scope of his theological and philosophic synthesis, the logic and serene clarity of his thought, and above all the combination of order, simplicity, and depth which characterize his *Summa Theologica* are a monument to his genius and to his sanctity.'

65. *No Man is an Island*, p. 12.

66. *The Climate of Monastic Prayer*, p. 109. See also Merton, 'Prayer, Tradition, and Experience,' ed. Naomi Burton Stone, *Sisters Today* 42 (1971) 286, where Merton asserts that a theology which seeks to prove God's existence or justify God by the use of reason alone is not only bad theology but 'it is the theology of Job's friends.'

67. *The Asian Journal*, pp. 312-13.

68. *Thoughts in Solitude*, p. 55.

69. *Conjectures of a Guilty Bystander*, p. 254.

70. *Life and Holiness*, p. 21.

71. 'Marxism and Monastic Perspectives, in Moffit, ed., *A New Charter for Monasticism*, p. 81, rpt. *The Asian Journal*, p. 343.

V

CONCERN FOR SOCIAL JUSTICE

Pacifism and the Just War

N O AREA of social concern moved Merton as deeply as war. During his student years the subject was often the topic of late-night discussions and, like many of his fellow students, he protested the Italian invasion of Ethiopia.[1] When called up for the draft Merton registered as a noncombatant and entered the monastery without serving in World War II.[2] In 1943, his only brother, John Paul, was killed when his bomber crashed into the North Sea. John Paul had visited Merton at Gethsemani, and while there had become a Catholic. New, spiritual ties drew them closer than before. His death was a great loss for Merton, who felt responsible for having a part in it: 'John Paul had at last come face to face with the world that he and I helped to make!'[3]

Although this statement is one of Merton's earliest on the subject of war, it contains one of his basic assumptions: wars do not just happen, they are caused by people, persons like himself. Merton made a connection between the individual and society. He thought that man is afraid to face his real self so he tries to account for his wrongdoings by 'seeing an equivalent amount of evil in someone else. Hence I minimize my own sins and compensate for doing so by exaggerating the faults of others.'[4] The solution to the problem of war begins with the individual:

> So instead of loving what you think is peace, love other men and love God above all. And instead of hating the people you think are warmakers, hate the appetites and the disorder in your own soul, which are the causes of war. If you love peace, then hate injustice, hate tyranny, hate greed—but hate these things in *yourself*, not in another.[5]

Merton was able to recognize, in his past life, his inability to see himself as he was and to admit his contribution within society's misperception of itself, to the war in which his brother died, to Americans' minimization of their own sins and exaggeration of the sins of Germany and Japan.

Wars do happen and one finds one must make a decision. Accepting personal responsibility for what is happening in no way postpones or cancels the decision. His draft notice made Merton face such a decision. He writes:

> For a war to be just, it must be a war of defence. A war of aggression is not just. If America entered the war now, would it be a war of aggression? I suppose if you wanted to get subtle about it, you could work out some kind of argument to that effect. But I personally could not see that it would be anything else than legitimate self-defence. How legitimate? To answer that, I would have to be a moral theologian and a diplomat and a historian and a politician and probably also a mind reader. And still I would not have had more than a probable answer. And since there was such strong probable evidence that we were really defending ourselves, that settled the question as far as I was concerned....
>
> The men in Washington presumably knew what was going on better than we did, and if, in a situation as obscure as this one was, and as perilous, they thought war was getting to be necessary—what could we do about it? If they called us to the army, I could not absolutely refuse to go. [6]

But at the same time Merton was concerned about the methods of war, the bombing of cities, so he registered as a noncombatant. He took a middle position: while he did not refuse to register for the draft, he did refuse to serve in a capacity which might require him to take a human life.

Within traditional Catholic legalism, the just war was legitimate. Merton explains that 'all Catholics who defend the just war theory are implicitly following Augustine. *Saint Augustine is, for better or for worse, the Father of all modern Christian thought on war.*'[7] Augustine's teaching on war, according to Merton, rests upon three basic assumptions:

> First, that it's impossible for man to live without getting into violent conflict with other men.
> Second, if one's interior motive is purely directed to a

just cause and to love of the enemy, then the use of force is not unjust. This distinction between the external act and the interior intention is entirely characteristic of Augustine.

Third, the Christian may join the non-Christian in fighting to preserve peace in the earthly city. But suppose that the earthly city itself is almost totally made up of Christians. The cooperation between the 'two cities' takes on a new aspect, and we arrive at the conclusion that a 'secular arm' of military force can be called into action against heretics, to preserve not only civil peace but the purity of faith.[8]

Although over the years Merton's thinking on the war question underwent numerous changes, he never lost sight of the connection between the individual and the society at large. In one of his earliest works, *Journal of My Escape from the Nazis*, Merton not only showed an anti-war bias but seemed to be in opposition to society in general. By 1951, he realized that his earlier solution to war had been a false one, and he corrected the anti-war view that he had expressed in the *Journal*:

One of the problems of the book was my personal relationship to the world and to the last war. When I wrote it I thought I had a very supernatural solution. After nine years in the monastery I see that it was no solution at all. The false solution went like this: the whole world, of which war is a characteristic expression, is evil. It has therefore to be first ridiculed, then spat upon, and at last formally rejected with a curse.[9]

Merton found that his primary purpose for entering the monastery had not been to escape the world but to find his place in the world. He discovered that 'wars are evil but the people involved in them are good, and I can do nothing whatever for my own salvation or for the glory of God if I merely withdraw from the mess people are in....'[10] His experience in the monastery was the right kind of withdrawal: 'It has given me perspective. It has taught me how to live. And now I owe everyone else in the world a share in that life.'[11] He began to look again at the question of war and to share his insights with the world.

Once again Merton approached the question of the just war, but now he looked beyond the legality to the morality of war. The most important question to answer became: *What are our real intentions?*[12] While he still held to the *possibility* of a just war, his answers to this question make him virtually a pacifist,[13] for our real intentions are a total destruction of the enemy and even a just war—a defensive war—soon loses its justness because it turns into a war of obliteration and destruction that goes far beyond the necessities of defense. Merton points out how Machiavelli changed the concept from 'a "just war" to a *victorious war*. For Machiavelli the important thing was to *win.'*[14] In a quotation from Clausewitz, Merton clarifies this point:

> *'To introduce into the philosophy of war a principle of moderation would be absurd. War is an act of violence pursued to the uttermost.'*
>
> And this of course was a philosophy which guided the policies of Hitler. The rest of the world, for all its good intentions, was forced to learn it from Hitler in order to beat him.[15]

The just war is theroetically possible, but in actual practice it becomes impossible, Merton is saying, since the goal of defense soon gives way to a goal of complete victory which can be won only if the defenders use the same methods as the aggressors.

Merton never claimed to be a complete pacifist, but in practice he was much more a pacifist than he would admit. Gordon C. Zahn comments:

> His was a relative pacifism, a position which always left room, in theory at least, for even a defensive nuclear war. Absolute pacifism, that is pacifism 'in a completely unqualified form,' had, he felt, been officially reproved. 'A Catholic may not hold,' he wrote, 'that all war under no matter what conditions is by its very nature unjust and evil. A Catholic may not formally deny that a community has the right to defend itself by force if other means do not avail....'
>
> Viewed in retrospect...it would appear that Merton's attachment to the 'just war' formulations was formal and academic, almost, one might say, a 'hang-up' on traditional theology with little or no foundation in intellectual conviction.[16]

We can little doubt Merton firmly believed that no current war, especially the Vietnam war, could by any stretch of the imagination fit into the category, a just war. He was, in addition, totally opposed to obliteration bombing, the use of nuclear weapons, chemical and biological warfare, and the bombing of civilians. It is no surprise to find that almost all of his statements on the question are pacifistic and anti-war.

One cannot doubt either that he favored nonviolence as a means of effecting social change. He declared that *'there exists in the American mind today an image of non-violence which is largely negative and completely inadequate....* Non-violence is based on principles which call into question the popular self-understanding of the society in which we live.'[17] Contemporary American society, he thought, is oriented toward violence and war, and by skillful use of the mass media Americans have been convinced that this orientation is based on the ideals of democracy and even Christianity. Nonviolence, however, differs from this popular view:

> Non-violence does not attack the ideals upon which democratic society is built, still less the ideals of Christianity. It claims on the contrary to be a genuine fulfillment and implementation of those ideals. And in so claiming, it rejects the counter claim of that popular self-understanding which is in fact a myth and betrayal of democracy and of Christianity.[18]

What is needed therefore is a breaking-down of the myths and illusions surrounding both nonviolence and democracy until people see that 'the chief argument in favor of non-violent resistance is that it is, per se and ideally, *the only really effective resistance to injustice and evil'.*[19]

Basic to Merton's proposal is the conviction that whatever change occurs cannot take place on a superficial level. One must begin with one's inner self, with one's attitudes and intentions, and then one must break through the myths and illusions to an understanding of what is happening. One must move beyond mere abstractions:

> I have learned that an age in which politicians talk about peace is an age in which everybody expects war: the great men of the earth would not talk of peace so much if they did not secretly believe it possible, with *one more war,* to annihilate their enemies forever. Always, 'after just one more war' it will dawn, the new era of love: but first everybody who is hated must be eliminated. For hate, you see, is the mother of their kind of love.
>
> Unfortunately the love that is to be born of hate will

never be born. Hatred is sterile; it breeds nothing but the image of its own empty fury; its own nothingness. Love cannot come of emptiness. It is full of reality. Hatred destroys the real being of man in fighting the fiction which it calls 'the enemy'. For man is concrete and alive, but 'the enemy' is a subjective abstraction. A society that kills men in order to deliver itself from the phantasm of a paranoid delusion is already possessed by the demon of destructiveness because it has made itself incapable of love. It refuses *a priori*, to love. It is dedicated not to concrete relations of man with man, but only to abstractness about politics, economics, psychology and even, sometimes, religion. [20]

By having faced himself one may face others as they really are, as persons. This, of course, makes Merton's reservations concerning the just war almost an impossibility. At the same time, however, it lends strength to the validity of his statement that he entered the monastery to find his place in the world, for one cannot deal with the place of others until one has first of all found his own place, and one cannot truly love others until one has first rooted the hatred out of his own life.

I doubt that Merton's conflicting opinions on pacifism and the just war will ever be reconciled. The conflict between his belief in the just war and his advocacy of nonviolence almost to the point of pacifism should be left as one of the paradoxes of his thought. He himself admits: 'I have had to accept the fact that my life is almost totally paradoxical.' [21] On the other hand, the problem may be resolved in part by his statement: '*Nothing is lost by peace, yet everything may be lost by war.*' [22]

Protest Against Nuclear Weapons

The destructive totality of war came to be symbolized to Merton by the use and stockpiling of nuclear weapons. This more than anything led him to question the just war. In an important essay 'Target Equals City', he states:

It took five years for war to turn the Christian ethic of the 'just war' inside out. The years 1940 to 1945 completely revolutionized the moral thinking of the allies who were fighting totalitarianism with a *just cause* if there ever was one....

When the Japanese bombed Pearl Harbor, there was no

question about the morality of America's entering the war to defend its rights. Here was a very clear example of a 'just cause' for war. Few doubted the fact. Those who did so were regarded as foolish because they were against all war on principle. They thought war was intrinsically evil. Twenty years later one is tempted to wonder if they were not more wise than men believed them to be.[23]

What had happened, of course, was that the precision bombing of military targets had soon given way to the obliteration bombing of entire cities; 'the word "target" and the word "city" had become completely identified.'[24]

Merton was horrified by Hiroshima and Nagasaki, especially by the American selection of these two cities from a list of potential targets, and the inclusion on this list of the ancient city of Kyoto, a center of Japanese religious and cultural life. It was especially ironic that it was the United States—the defender—and not the aggressor—Japan—who used these terrible weapons of destruction. No wonder Merton remarked: 'There is one winner, only one winner, in war. The winner is war itself.'[25] Merton realized that with the advent of nuclear weapons war had taken on a totality never known before. Now no one was safe. If you lived in a city you were automatically a potential target, and if you lived in a rural area you would still be affected by fallout. Not even Merton in his hermitage was immune:

> Of course at three-thirty A.M. the SAC plane goes over, red light winking low under the clouds, skimming the wooded summits on the south side of the valley, loaded with strong medicine. Very strong. Strong enough to burn up all these woods and stretch our hours of fun into eternities.[26]

The most alarming fact for Merton was that nuclear weapons gave man the power to destroy himself. With this in mind he wrote *Original Child Bomb: Points for Meditation to be Scratched on the Walls of a Cave*.[27] The subtitle alone provides adequate evidence of Merton's uncertainty of man's fate should nuclear war occur. He was convinced that any total nuclear war would result in the total destruction of life; the possibility of man's living in caves was not at all unrealistic.[28]

His concern over nuclear weapons led Merton to begin to write essays and articles on the subject, and he soon found himself under harsh criticism from many Catholics. A policeman

in Chicago wrote that he was scandalized and he advised
Merton to start a 'spiritual Los Alamos project'.[29] Merton was
profoundly disturbed when a survey taken by *Fortune* revealed
'that half the respondents felt the decision to use the bomb on
Hiroshima and Nagasaki had been right, while nearly a quarter
of them *regretted that more atomic bombs* had not been used on
other Japanese cities!'[30] Most disturbing was that very few
American church leaders spoke out on the issue; in fact Merton
was told to be silent on such matters:

> I am told by a higher superior: 'It is not your place to
> write about nuclear war: that is for the bishops.' I am told
> by a moral theologian: 'How can you expect the bishops to
> commit themselves on the question of peace and war,
> unless they are advised by theologians?' Meanwhile, the
> theologians sit around and preserve their reputations.
>
> Pretty soon they will no longer have any reputations to
> preserve.[31]

Zahn relates an incident when Merton received a letter from a
woman he called a 'devout she-wolf'. This woman, a total
stranger to Merton, 'asked him to solicit the prayers of the
Gethsemani community that America might finally launch a
full-scale nuclear war against Russia!'[32] Such a position was
almost totally incomprehensible to Merton, especially in
someone who claimed to be a Christian.

Merton expressed concern over those who equate the West
with Christianity and the Communist world with the antichrist.
Too many churchmen used the phrase 'no price is too high' to
pay for freedom, especially religious freedom. For Merton, one
price was too high:

> The fact is that genocide *is* too high a price, and no one,
> not even Christians, not even for the highest ideals, has
> the right to take measures that may destroy millions of
> innocent noncombatants and even whole defenseless
> populations of neutral nations or unwilling allies.[33]

The Christian's task is not to fight in wars but 'to contribute
everything he can to help this great common work: *of finding
nonmilitary and nonviolent ways of defending our rights, our
interests, and our ideals.*'[34]

Merton directed his protest not only against the use of
nuclear weapons in warfare but also against nuclear testing,
especially in the earth's atmosphere. Despite concern over the

danger of radioactive fallout, which the bombings of Hiroshima and Nagasaki and the numerous tests had clearly revealed, there seemed to be little opposition to the continuation of nuclear tests and this weighed heavily upon Merton's mind:

> The high-altitude H-bomb explosion set off by the U.S.A. on July 9 of this year [1962] has permanently knocked out communication with several satellites sent up by us, and has also created a new radiation belt, 'a phenomenon that is not fully understood,' so we are told. Another fruitful contradiction emerging from the recesses of the military and scientific mind.[35]

Military policy decisions were being based upon existing scientific and technological data with no checks from experiments on possible ill effects.[36]

Merton also opposed the stockpiling of nuclear weapons, because he feared the possibility of an accidental war, which could result from technological failure or, more likely, a moral failure wherein human morality failed to keep pace with rapid technological development. There could be no turning back once someone launched nuclear warheads, 'the eschatological weapon'.[37]

Merton angered many by pointing out the guilt not only of military men and scientists, of those who in any way contributed to the manufacture of such weapons, who worked for companies who manufactured them.[38] Too often, he felt, we associate the interests of the West and NATO with the interests of the Church and thus contribute directly and indirectly to what is the most grievous of evils—modern warfare. To avoid facing up to the problem is impossible:

> To what extent can the individual claim to remain uncommitted when his government pursues a policy that leads directly to nuclear war?... If you go to work for Boeing with the impression that you will not have to build bombers, or for Chrysler missiles with a mental reservation that you won't manufacture anything with a warhead, you remain partly responsible for the nuclear war which you have helped to prepare, even though you may have had 'good intentions' and desired nothing but to make an 'honest living'.[39]

Merton went so far as to call for a general strike by all Catholics working in defense plants, and was strongly criticized.[40] Merton took the position that a global threat, such as nuclear war, re-sults in a global responsibility; no one can remain 'virgin' and claim innocence. We are all potential victims, and we are all potential aggressors; we can no longer leave the decisions to government officials and military leaders. We must look at the situation realistically and until we do, there can be no end to the threat of nuclear warfare.

His strongest protest, *Original Child Bomb*, written with stark simplicity clearly shows the naked reality of nuclear war. Better than any of his other statements the lines summarize his feelings on war in general and nuclear war in particular:

> 32: The bomb exploded within 100 feet of the aiming point. The fireball was 18,000 feet across. The temperature at the center of the fireball was 100,000,000 degrees. The people who were near the center became nothing. The whole city was blown to bits and the ruins caught fire instantly everywhere, burning briskly. 70,000 people were killed right away or died within a few hours. Those who did not die at once suffered great pain. Few of them were soldiers.

> 33: The men in the plane perceived that the raid had been successful, but they thought of the people in the city and they were not perfectly happy. Some felt they had done wrong. But in any case they obeyed orders. 'It was war.'...

> 35: Then the military governor of the Prefecture of Hiroshima issued a proclamation full of martial spirit. To all the people without hands, without feet, with their faces falling off, with their intestines hanging out, with their whole bodies full of radiation, he declared: 'We must not rest a single day in our war effort....We must bear in mind that the annihilation of the stubborn enemy is our road to revenge.' He was a professional soldier.[41]

Nonviolence and Revolution

Merton has been referred to as 'an active peacemonger', a term that would have delighted him.[42] Yet Merton's protest against war and nuclear weapons was not active in the sense that he participated in the political process or took part in various protest actions. His protest was limited to statements, essays, books, and several privately circulated mimeographed collections of essays and letters. Obviously his monastic vocation and contemplative orientation had a great deal to do with this limitation. All of this changed somewhat, however, with the war in Vietnam, for Merton, an overwhelming atrocity. He says: 'One thing is certain, the Vietnam war is a tragic error....' [43] He was so opposed to the Vietnam war that for the first time his protests went beyond statements and essays. He took limited action, meeting numerous figures involved in the peace movement, making a statement on behalf of the visiting Vietnamese Buddhist monk, Thich Nhat Hanh, and directing a retreat at Gethsemani in November, 1964 on 'The Spiritual Roots of Protest'. At least five participants who were later jailed for their antiwar activities attended. [44] He was so impressed by the 'Peace Hostage Exchange' project that he seriously considered becoming personally involved, although he later decided that it was out of the question for him. [45]

The Vietnam war enraged Merton especially because of his deep involvement in the life and thought of the Orient, and his statements reveal an interesting shift in emphasis, as Zahn points out:

> The spiritual and theological arguments which so completely dominated most of his discussions on war in general, the Bomb and deterrence, and, as we shall see below, Christian non-violence, seemed to give way at times to stress on practical, even pragmatic, political considerations. Some of his strongest statements are prefaced with a phrase like 'quite apart from moral considerations' or 'quite apart from questions of conscience.' To some extent, I suspect, this reflects Merton's extensive knowledge of, and affinity to, the cultures of the Far East. On matters concerning differences between East and West he was an expert and, as such, could bring to his analysis of the tragic conflict and its probable consequences a 'practical' perspective denied to others. [46]

It is possible that Merton, like so many others, found that the closer one gets to a situation like that of Vietnam, the more practical one becomes. On the other hand, as Zahn is careful to show, Merton's customary spiritual and theological perspective is still present even if not given the same emphasis as previously. [47] It may well be that Merton assumed his readers were already familiar with his more theological writings on war and therefore felt that a more practical perspective would be in order. In any event his activity against the Vietnam war raises some important questions concerning nonviolence and revolution.

In *Seasons of Celebration*, Merton declares: 'From the very first moment in which a man becomes a Christian and begins to express himself as a vocal and active member of the Body of Christ, the liturgy reminds him of his person and we might say "political" responsibility in the City of God.'[48] As Merton found out, the journey from the City of God to the City of Man is not very long, and as one becomes a vocal and active member of the society one soon finds that he has a 'political responsibility' to 'change relationships that are evil into others that are good, or at least less bad.'[49] To bring about such changes mankind must confront 'the encroachments and brutality of massive power structures which threaten either to enslave him or to destroy him, while exploiting him in their conflicts with one another.'[50] This does not mean that one must be a pacifist, for there are times when force is necessary, as Merton explains:

> There are situations in which the only way to protect human life and rights effectively is by forcible resistance against unjust encroachment. Murder is not to be passively permitted, but resisted and prevented—and all the more so when it becomes mass-murder. The problem arises not when theology admits that force can be necessary, but when it does so in a way that implicitly favors the claims of the powerful and self-seeking establishment against the common good of mankind or against the rights of the oppressed.[51]

There is no moral problem in using force to restrain an individual murderer who is killing innocent people, but Merton holds that the mass murderer must also be restrained. It is here that a problem arises.

Merton clearly states that 'violence today is *white-collar violence, the systematically organized bureaucratic and technological destruction of man*' and this violence must be resisted.[52]

> The theology of violence must not lose sight of the real problem which is not the individual with a revolver but *death and even genocide as big business*. But this big business of death is all the more innocent and effective because it involves a long chain of individuals, each of whom can feel himself absolved from responsibility, and each of whom can perhaps salve his conscience by contributing with a more *meticulous efficiency* to his part in the massive operation.[53]

There can be no doubt that he considered the American military-industrial complex genocide-as-big-business; therefore it was to be resisted.

Too often, Merton said, we apply our theology of nonviolence to the poor and the oppressed while we continue to make war. Thus, he says, 'A theology of love may also conceivably turn out to be a theology of revolution. In any case it is a theology of *resistance*, a refusal of the evil that reduces a brother to homicidal desperation.'[54] Merton expanded on this theme in speaking of his book *Faith and Violence:*

> It can at least provide a few materials for a theology, not of pacifism and non-violence in the sense of *non-resistance*, but for a theology of resistance which is at the same time *Christian* resistance and which therefore emphasizes reason and humane communication rather than force, but which also admits the possibility of force in a limit-situation when everything else fails....
>
> Instead of preaching the Cross *for others* and advising them to suffer patiently the violence we sweetly impose on them, with the aid of armies and police, we might conceivably recognize the right of the less fortunate to use force, and study more seriously the practice of non-violence and humane methods on our own part when, as it happens, we possess the most stupendous arsenal of power the world has ever known.[55]

We see here a change in Merton's thinking. He moved from a theological approach to strict nonviolence to a political resistance. Well aware of the dangers of using force, he never expressly advocated it, but he did leave open the possibility of force when all else failed. He cautioned, however, that 'he who resists force with force in order to seize power may become contaminated by the evil which he is resisting and, when he gains power, may be just as ruthless and unjust a tyrant as the one he has dethroned.'[56]

There is in nonviolent resistance the danger that, too often, the idealist fighting for peace by nonviolent methods may become a part of this violence by his own activism and overwork.

> The rush and pressure of modern life are a form, perhaps the most common form, of its innate violence. To allow oneself to be carried away by a multitude of conflicting concerns, to surrender to too many demands, to commit

oneself to too many projects, to want to help everyone in everything is to succumb to violence. More than that, it is cooperation in violence. The frenzy of the activist neutralizes his work for peace. It destroys his own inner capacity for peace. It destroys the fruitfulness of his own work, because it kills the root of inner wisdom which makes work fruitful.[57]

As a result one can easily become cut off from his own inner roots, the source of his strength and wisdom. Action may be separated from contemplation.

The act of protest itself may increase the war mentality rather than lessen it. Merton cites the burning of draft cards as an example: 'Much current protest simply reinforces the old positions by driving the adversary back into the familiar and secure mythology of force. Hence the strong "patriotic" reaction against protest in the United States.'[58] He argued that dissent must be responsible and that the 'important thing about protest is not so much the short-range possibility of changing the direction of policies, but the longer range aim of helping everyone gain an entirely new attitude towards war.'[59] This new attitude can come only by helping 'sincere and concerned minds to accept alternatives to war without surrendering the genuine interests of our own national community.'[60] Too often dissent shocks or horrifies and thus, understandably, turns many people away in disgust and bores those who have become immune to shock. In other cases dissenters catch the public eye for a few days or weeks and then are forgotten as other more interesting stories hit the news headlines. Merton points out that a violent society is characterized by a lack of communication: 'any society which is geared for violent action is by that fact systematically unreasonable and inarticulate.'[61] Dissent, therefore, must foster communication and implies 'belief in openness of mind and in the possibility of a mature exchange of ideas'.[62]

A further danger confronting protestors is that they can easily be used. Merton related an incident where a well-known couple, close friends of Martin Luther King, became involved in a protest march. They were caught up in the crowd, soon things got out of hand, and they found themselves under arrest. Merton comments: 'They had been forced to break a law they never intended to break and didn't want to break so that they could be used and the activists could say, "So-and-so was arrested on *our* side."'[63] He reflects: 'Even in protest one must be discreet, not only for the sake of saving one's skin, but above all for the sake of protecting the virginity of one's own protest against the salacious advances of the publicist, the agitator, or the political police.'[64]

Having said all this, Merton still felt there was a case for the use of force to resist what he called mass violence. He was indirectly involved in what was probably the most celebrated protest of this kind in recent years, the raids on the draft board offices by the Berrigan brothers and their associates in October 1967. Merton was a close friend of both Daniel and Philip Berrigan and had dedicated several of his books to them.[65] They had both been present at the November 1964 retreat which he led. There is little doubt that his reflections on nonviolence, protest, and resistance played an important part in the thinking and subsequent actions of the Berrigan brothers.[66]

Merton played no direct part in the raids; in fact he took part in no protest demonstrations of any kind after entering the monastery. At the same time, he did comment on the actions of the Berrigans and, although he reached no conclusions, he raised several serious questions concerning their actions. Merton felt that in some instances some forms of protest came very close to violence even though they could technically be called nonviolent. In his view, the action of the Berrigans 'bordered on violence and was violent to the extent that it meant pushing some good ladies around and destroying some government property.'[67] He also felt that 'the evident desperation of the Baltimore nine has, however, frightened more than it has edified....And it has long ago become automatic to interpret nonviolence as violence merely because it is resistance.'[68] Merton had no doubt that the Berrigans had acted in a prophetic manner, but he doubted the rest of the country would see it that way.[69] His concern almost certainly would have deepened had he lived to see the day when raids were being carried out on selective service offices across the nation.[70]

There are several clues to Merton's later thinking on actions of dissent. Daniel Berrigan, writing in January 1969 stated: 'At a time when political and social activism is the rage among western Christians, Merton had calmly turned his back (for a time, we trusted, and only to a degree) on all of that, and on all of us as well. He undertook a search for alternatives; rightly understood, it was a revolutionary decision.'[71] Merton, in one of his last statements before departing for Asia, explained at length this sudden turn:

> I want to talk a little bit more about community because in the Church today you have a very strong and active movement that you run into everywhere, in which a whole

lot of people—a minority but a very influential minority of whom I know many—say that there is only one real community in existence today and that is the community which is concerned with the problem of under-privileged people, that the only practical way of handling this is revolution and that, therefore, Christianity equals revolution.

People talk in this way and there is going to be trouble because they don't really know what they are talking about. They are all good, middle-class people who have become priests and nuns, and all of a sudden they are talking about revolution!...

In other words, when you start dealing with people of this sort you are not dealing with a community in the Christian sense, you are dealing with a bunch of operators and they have their reasons, but they are in power politics and this is dangerous. You are probably not going to run into much of this up here [in Alaska], but people in your position in the lower forty-eight states are going to meet Catholic activists, perhaps coming for a retreat or conference, and they are going to be fermenting with these ideas and we really have to know what the score is.

I personally think that we should be in between; we shouldn't be on the conservative side and shouldn't be on the radical side—we should be Christians. We should understand the principles involved in anything where there is not true Christian fellowship. You do have a lot of goodwill in these movements and you do have a kernel of desire for community, but power takes priority. The power play is the important thing and you come up against not love but loveless means. Most of them do not go out for naked violence yet, but they will. In other words, there are ways and means to force people to go in a certain direction. That is okay, that is politics, you might say. If you are a politician you need to know about it and deal with it, but we have to stay out of it....

We have to be where love is and it is really the harder position, but it is also the creative position and the constructive position. It is the kind of position taken by Gandhi.

It is not at all just an idealistic position because Gandhi took it. I edited and wrote a preface for a little book of quotations from Gandhi on non-violence, and perhaps it is good to remember it because it all tends to get lost now. Non-violence has become all fouled-up and is turning into a sort of semi-violence. But the basic thing Gandhi said, and it has proved absolutely right, is that you can't have any real non-violence unless you have faith in God. If it isn't built on God, it isn't going to work, it isn't going to be for real. Gandhi said this and Martin Luther King picked it up and carried it on. So there you have the spiritual approach and it was based on asceticism. Gandhi primarily used to fast and use spiritual means. So what we have to do is try to distinguish between the temptation to see community in all sorts of power movements, as so many are doing, and to maintain our position in a Christian community—a community built by God. [72]

Merton points out here two concepts basic to his understanding of social action and dissent. Firstly, one's primary orientation should be toward God. His turning away from certain kinds of dissent is not to be seen as a repudiation of all social action, but only of that action which places power or anything else above one's spiritual concern. Secondly, Merton was thoroughly convinced that his vocation was primarily contemplative, and that to become overly involved in political action was to be unfaithful to that vocation. He felt that many priests and nuns, whose vocations were essentially religious, were being unfaithful to their vocations by their involvement in social action. [73] A religious vocation does not need to be justified by involvement in social action, but is, in and of itself, important and vital for the life of the Church. He states that 'if prayer, meditation and contemplation were once taken for granted as central r alities, in human life everywhere, they are so no longer. They are regarded, even by believers, as somehow marginal and secondary: what counts is getting things done.' [74] As a result, he declares: 'We have more power at our disposal today than we have ever had, and yet we are more alienated and estranged from the inner ground of meaning and love than we have ever been....Far from being irrelevant, prayer and meditation and contemplation are of the utmost importance in America today.' [75]

Merton's firm commitment to Christian principles and to his vocation as a contemplative drew praise from Marco Pallis: 'The one thing Thomas Merton never did was to surrender his soul to the "activist" trend now in vogue, of which an anti-metaphysical, anti-contemplative, anti-traditional and anti-symbolical bias is now the sinister hallmark.' [76] At the same time he was not divorced from the social ills of mankind; Daniel Berrigan mentions how Merton's 'profound inner life' was connected with 'his compassionate, surgical skill in diagnosing man's illness'.[77] Perhaps the best evaluation comes from Merton himself:

> There is no revolution without a voice....The more the cry of the oppressed is ignored, the more it strengthens itself with a mysterious power that is to be gained from myth, symbol and prophecy. There is no revolution without poets who are also seers. There is no revolution without prophetic songs.[78]

Convinced of the need for peace, nonviolent protest, and social justice—revolution if you will—he believed that, as a contemplative, it was his task to be a voice for that revolution.

The Importance of the Persons

Underlying all Merton's thought concerning war and peace was his firm belief in the importance of the person. This is nowhere emphasized more forcefully than in the essay 'A Devout Meditation in Memory of Adolf Eichmann'. He begins the essay with these words: 'One of the most disturbing facts that came out in the Eichmann trial was that a psychiatrist examined him and pronounced him *perfectly sane*. I do not doubt it at all, and this is precisely why I find it disturbing.'[79] Sanity implies 'a sense of justice, with humaneness, with prudence, with the capacity to love and understand other people.'[80] Sane people have built and are prepared to use the nuclear missiles that could destroy the world. Sane people, like Eichmann, built and operated the concentration camps of Nazi Germany. Merton asks:

> What makes us so sure, after all, that the danger comes from a psychotic getting into a position to fire the first shot in a nuclear war? Psychotics will be suspect. The sane ones will keep them far from the button. No one suspects the sane, and the sane ones will have *perfectly good reasons*, logical, well-adjusted reasons, for firing the first shot. They will be obeying sane orders that have come sanely down the chain of command. And because of their sanity they will have no qualms at all. When the missiles take off, *it will be no mistake*.[81]

Merton then raises the question: 'What is the meaning of a

concept of sanity that excludes love, considers it irrelevant, and destroys our capacity to love other human beings, to respond to their needs and their sufferings, to recognize them also as persons, to apprehend their pain as one's own?'[82]

Sanity is basically a way of saying that someone has adjusted well to his society, but it in no way necessarily means the person is capable of love, for love is a religious concept. Merton asks: 'What business have we to equate "sanity" with "Christianity"?'[83] For him the 'worst error is to imagine that a Christian must be "sane" like everybody else, that we 'belong' in our kind of *society*.'[84] Too often we accept society as having been divinely constituted and we adjust to it, so that society ends up pushing us along. We forget that, in the final analysis, we are society. The results can be very dangerous:

> For social life, in the end, is too often simply a convenient compromise by which your pride and mine are able to get along together without too much friction. That is why it is a dangerous illusion to trust in society to make us 'balanced,' 'realistic,' and 'humble'. Very often the humility demanded of us by our society is simply an acquiescence in the pride of the collectivity and of those in power. Worse still, while we learn to be humble and virtuous as individuals, we allow ourselves to commit the worse crimes in the name of 'society'. We are gentle in our private lives in order to be murderers as a collective group. For murder, committed by an individual, is a great crime. But when it becomes war or revolution, it is represented as the summit of heroism and virtue.[85]

The individual's acquiescence to society is 'encouraged by social life itself when it is lived at a low level of spiritual intensity'.[86]

We need, according to Merton, a religious understanding of love not based on society's standards. Even here, there are two ways in which love can be corrupted. It can seek a perfect object, which does not exist, and thus irresponsibly avoid any committments to persons as they really are. Or it can admit that perfection is difficult and can be attained only by one means, forcing everyone into the same system. Merton himself had fallen into the first trap during his year at Cambridge. He had thought that to be well adjusted in love one had to be sexually promiscuous, thus avoiding any real and lasting commitments to others as persons.

The danger of totalitarianism, however, more immediately concerned Merton when he considered mass society and the various ways in which the person could become a part of the mass and lose all personal identity. In such societies, says Merton, 'every kind of pressure is brought to bear upon the individual to divest him of his true personality and of his normal social attachments'.[87] One gives up his personal responsibility and freedom, or has it taken from him, and this results in the atrocities done in 'good conscience' in police states.[88] One loses his concept of self-worth and personhood and accepts the values of society. Society, rather than the individual, becomes the deciding factor. Once one has lost his own soul he also loses sight of the soul in others, and massive dehumanization results. In such circumstances it is not surprising to hear of sane, well-adjusted men committing barbarous acts of torture and murder.

Merton took note that existentialists had been among the first to react against the modern concept of mass society which describes the authentic person as 'a rebel, an individualist, who, because he withdraws from the common endeavor of techno-logical society to brood on his own dissatisfactions, condemns himself to futility, sterility, and despair'.[89] The existentialists held that this view of mass society was actually an illusion; mass society really does not exist at all, since 'the public mind is a pure abstraction, a nonentity'.[90] Merton expands on this:

> The mythical being which thinks and acts for everybody, and does the most shameful of deeds without a moment of hesitation or of shame, is actually no being at all. Those who take part in its acts can do so insofar as they have abstracted themselves from themselves and have sur-rendered to the public void, which they believe to be fully and objectively real: this collective self whose will is the will of nobody, whose mind is the mind of nobody, which can contradict itself and remain consistent with itself.[91]

Merton, quoting Kierkegaard, pointed out that 'more and more individuals, owing to their bloodless indolence, will aspire to be nothing at all—in order to become the public.'[92]

How then does one escape this predicament? In commenting on the existentialism of Albert Camus, Merton says: 'The alienated man is one, who, though "adjusted" to society, is alienated *from himself*' but 'the basic choice by which one elects to have one's own personal, autonomous existence is a choice *of oneself as a freedom that has been gratuitously given by God.*'[93] He goes on to explain that this freedom to choose exists outside any form of social pressure: 'It is made in and proceeds from the inviolate sanctuary of the personal conscience.'[94] The individual—the person—makes the really important choices and decisions. In his booklet, *Albert Camus' The Plague*, Merton shows Camus' basic concern with the person, for he 'wanted to explore...the possibility of a new and authentic humanism based not on religious or political ideologies, to which the individual may all too easily be sacrificed, but on a deeply authentic relationship between living persons.'[95] Camus, like Merton, recognized that politics and religion were just other forms of society in which the individual was made to conform to external political or religious ideologies.

While Merton stressed the importance of the person he was not blind to the social nature of man.[96] Man cannot live by himself in his own private universe, in complete and total isolation from other persons. Community, says Merton, is a vital necessity for human life:

> The very condition of normal human life is community, communication, and 'conversation' in the old Latin sense of *conversatio*, exchange on the level of social living. The lives of all men are inextricably mixed together, and the salvation and damnation of souls is involved in this inescapable communication of freedoms. Either we will love and help one another or we will hate and attack one another, in which latter case we will all be one another's hell. Perhaps Sartre was not far wrong in saying that where freedom is absurd, society itself turns into hell. (*'L'enfer c'est les autres.'*) [97]

Therefore, Merton writes, 'freedom does not operate in a void... It should conform to a rational estimate of reality.... Freedom depends necessarily on man's concept of himself and of the situation in which he finds himself.'[98] A major part of that situation is the society in which we live.

'There is no genuine holiness without this dimension of human and social concern' [99] and, as a result, says Merton, the 'Church is obligated to protect man against the encroachment of a secularized society on his human dignity. She should defend him against a worldview in which money and power are held to be of greater importance than man himself.'[100] A society which will be made up not of faceless numbers but of persons can be realized only through spiritual means. 'The only cure is, and must be always spiritual.'[101] The evils of society are really the evils of individuals and 'in all their boastfulness they have become victims of their own terror, which is nothing but the emptiness of their own hearts.'[102] In commenting on a story of robbers told by the Hassidic rabbi, the Baal Shem Tov, Merton asks the question: 'What if we awaken to discover that *we* are the robbers, and our destruction comes from the root of hate in ourselves?'[103] Behind the problems of war and peace Merton perceived the far deeper issue of the person. The solution to the evils of society must be found within the inner being of each one of us. He concludes: 'The problem of the person and the social organization is certainly one of the most important, if not the most important problem of our century. Every ethical problem of our day—especially the problem of war—is to be traced back to this root question.'[104]

Racism and the American Indian

War and racism appeared similar to Merton in that both fail to view the person in the light of his inner spirituality. Both deny the worth of the human person and are become the twin scourges of human society.

Of special concern to Merton was the plight of the American Indian, both in its historical manifestations and as it exists in the present day.[105] The whites who settled the American frontier viewed the Indian as a 'savage' or a 'devil', and saw him as the enemy who was to be done away with. They considered the Indian inferior to the white man, and assumed that nothing in his culture was significant, important, or of value. This was especially true of his religion, which the early missionaries and later the United States government did all they could to eradicate. Everyone assumed that the white man was superior to the Indian, and therefore that whatever the white man did was right and whatever the Indian did was wrong. In failing to see the Indian as a person, the white man lost a good deal of his own personhood.

In his study of the American Indian, Merton found that while the modern techniques of warfare were new, genocide itself was not new at all:

> Genocide is a new word. Perhaps the word is new because technology has now got into the game of destroying whole races at once. The destruction of races is not new—just easier. Nor is it a speciality of totalitarian regimes. We have forgotten that a century ago white America was engaged in the destruction of entire tribes and ethnic groups of Indians. The trauma of California gold. And the

vigilantes who, in spite of every plea from Washington for restraint and understanding, repeatedly took matters into their own hands and went out slaughtering Indians. Indiscriminate destruction of the 'good' along with the 'bad'— just so long as they were Indians. Parties of riffraff from the mining camps and saloons suddenly constituted themselves defenders of civilization. They armed and went out to spill blood and gather scalps. They not only combed the woods and canyons—they even went into the ranch houses, to find and destroy the Indian servants and hired people, in spite of the protests of the ranchers who employed them.[106]

Behind this genocide lay the myth that America was an earthly paradise, a new land of opportunity, and a land of seemingly endless frontiers. According to Merton: 'When a myth becomes an evasion, the society that clings to it gets into serious trouble,' and this is precisely what happened in the case of the Indian.[107] Once there were no more frontiers 'America gradually became the prisoner of that curse, the historical memory, the total consciousness of an identity responsible for what had happened to the Indians....'[108] The Indian did not fit into the white man's myth of America so the white man had no alternative but the extermination of the Indian.[109] To do this he had to view the Indian as one who did not rightfully belong in this new American paradise:

> As long as there was merely the frontier, and one camp of pioneers here, another there, what happened to the Indians was, in a way, happening to the devil. It was at any rate heroic—and *well meant.* The Indian could somehow seem to be the serpent in Paradise, because he was outside the myth.[110]

At the present time, however, there are no more frontiers—at least not in America.

At this point Merton makes an incisive connection between the treatment of the Indians on the American frontier and the treatment of the Vietnamese in the recent war.

> One cannot help thinking today of the Vietnam war in terms of the Indian wars of a hundred years ago. Here again, one meets the same myths and misunderstandings, the same obsession with 'completely wiping out' an enemy regarded as diabolical. The language of the vigilantes had

overtones of puritanism in it. The backwoods had to be 'completely cleaned out', or 'purified' of Indians—as if they were vermin....

What is most significant is that Vietnam seems to have become an extension of our old Western frontier, complete with enemies of another, 'inferior' race. This is a real 'new frontier' that enables us to continue the cowboys-and-Indians game which seems to be a part and parcel of our national identity. What a pity that so many innocent people have to pay with their lives for our obsessive fantasies! [111]

For Merton, a long chain of events leads from the first skirmishes between immigrants and Indians to the war between Americans and the Vietcong and North Vietnamese.

The various ways in which the Indians reacted to the coming of the white man especially intrigued Merton: 'I am particularly interested in the ways in which an oppressed and humiliated "primitive" civilization seeks to recover its identity and to maintain itself in independence, against the overwhelming threat of a society which can rely on unlimited backing from the big powers, precisely because it is white.'[112] Most of the Indian tribes had led peaceful and trusting lives. Some tribes, the Navaho and the Hopi of the American southwest, were totally noncompetitive and viewed life in terms of the group rather than of the individual. The coming of the white man changed all this for the Indians found themselves face-to-face with a people who were extremely competitive, highly individualistic, and warlike toward strangers.

Merton greatly admired the Mayas of Central America, whom, with the Incas, he regarded 'as perhaps the most human of peoples and as those who, as far, have done the most honor to our hemisphere.'[113] In their contact with the white man, however, they possessed one fatal flaw:

> The Mayans failed because they did not know one of the main axioms of modern life, an axiom on which is based the American pragmatic imperative to push for the competitor's unconditional defeat. 'In war there is no substitute for victory.' The Mayans failed because they were still too willing to listen to the voice of peaceful and constructive human instinct—a voice which has to be silenced if efficiency is to be total.[114]

The Mayas and the Incas were not the only Indian tribes

to possess this trait. In 'Ishi: A Meditation,' Merton related how the white man had attempted to exterminate the Yana Indians who lived around the foothills of Mount Lassen in California. The Yana tribe, known as the Yahi or Mill Creek Indians, retreated into the forests where they hid for almost fifty years. Finally, when there were only about twenty-five survivors left, they straggled out of the woods, and Merton relates what happened:

> A delegation from the tiny remnant of the tribe appeared at a ranch to negotiate. In a symbolic gesture, they handed over five bows (five being a sacred number) and stood unarmed waiting for an answer. The gesture was not properly understood, though it was evident that the Indians were trying to recover their captives and promising to abandon all hostilities. In effect, the message was: 'Leave us alone, in peace, in our hills, and we will not bother you anymore. We are few, you are many, why destroy us? We are no longer any menace to you.' No formal answer was given. While the Indians were waiting for some kind of intelligible response, one of the whites slung a rope over the branch of a tree. The Indians quietly withdrew into the woods. [115]

For the next few years this tiny band lived in the hills keeping completely away from the white man, for they had decided that 'since coexistence was impossible, they would try to be as if they did not exist for the white man at all. To be there as if they were not there.' [116] Eventually the lone survivor, Ishi, surrendered to the white man in 1911. After being a curiosity for anthropologists in his unique role as 'the last wild Indian' Ishi died in 1916 of tuberculosis, a disease he picked up from the white man.

Two factors contributed to this small tribe's ability to survive under such conditions for as long as they did. In the first place they were totally convinced that they were right. Says Merton: *'Of very great importance to their psychic health was the circumstance that their suffering and curtailments arose from wrongs done to them by others. They were not guilt-ridden.'* [117] The tiny band had a reason for existing, and they had no doubts within themselves as to the validity of that reason. Closely related to this inner psychic unity of the Indians was their religious worldview, a view that greatly impressed Merton and to which he felt a deep affinity. The Yahi had a profound religious understanding of life, but they never discussed it. Each member of the tribe was given a name which remained his and was never revealed to others. 'In the end, no one ever found out a single name of the vanished community. Not even Ishi's. For Ishi means simply MAN.'[118] To the white man the Indian's religion was almost totally beyond comprehension, and for the most part he made no attempt to understand it and, in fact, did all that he could to destroy it.[119]

Characteristic of almost all Indian religion was a feeling of closeness to the earth and a profound respect for nature. Merton discusses this in some detail in an article dealing with the Mayan city of Monte Alban in Mexico. Monte Alban was built sometime between 1000 and 500 BC, by the Zapotecan Indians who knew writing, had a calendar, practised astronomy, and were among the first urban dwellers in America. The city's major purpose was to be not a center of trade and commerce but a center of worship. It was, in Merton's words, a sacred city. As such, it was also a city without war. The inhabitants of this city, unlike the inhabitants of modern cities, were not alienated. They had an identity which was an outgrowth of their religious point of view.

> This 'objective' identity seems to have been fully integrated into a cosmic system which was at once perfectly sacred and perfectly worldly. There was no question that the Indian in the 'sacred city' felt himself completely at home in his world and understood his place in it perfectly....The individual found himself, by his 'objective' identity, at the intersection of culture and nature, crossroads established by the gods, points of communication not only between the visible and invisible, the obvious and the unexplained, the higher and the lower, the strong and the helpless, but above all between complementary opposites that balanced and fulfilled each other (firewater, heat-cold, rain-earth, light-dark, life-death).
> 'Self -realization' in such a context implied not so much the ego-consciousness of the isolated subject in the face of a multitude of objects, but the awareness of a network of relationships in which one had a place in the mesh. One's identity was the intersection of cords where one 'belonged'. The intersection was to be sought in terms of a kind of musical or aesthetic and scientific synchrony—one fell in step with the dance of the universe, the liturgy of the stars.[120]

Merton believed that three things distinguished this sacred

city from contemporary cities: 'Indifference to technological progress, a lack of history, and the almost total neglect of the arts of war.'[121] All three were due to the Indian's concept of man, which was quite different from ours and from that of the white men who first came to America.

> It is a difference between a peaceful, timeless life lived in the stability of a continually renewed *present*, and a dynamic, aggressive life aimed at the future. We are more and more acutely conscious of traveling, or going somewhere, of heading for some ultimate goal. They were conscious of having arrived, of being at the heart of things. Mircea Eliade speaks of the archaic concept of the sanctuary as the *axis mundi*, the center or navel of the earth, for those whose lives revolve in the cycles of its liturgy....
>
> The 'reality' and 'identity' of archaic man was, then, centered in sensuous self-awareness and identification with a close, ever-present, keenly sensed world of nature.[122]

Their view was in total conflict with that of the white man who reinforced his sense of reality 'by acting on the external world to get ever new results. Primitive man did not understand this; he recoiled from it, striving to influence external reality by magic and self-identification.[123]

The result was predictable. The white man drove the Indian from his lands and by mass extermination did all that he could to destroy his culture and his way of life. The once fertile lands became barren, the cities were abandoned, and disease claimed untold millions of Indians. In Mexico alone the Indian population dropped by nineteen million in just eighty years. No wonder Merton declared: 'Contact with the Europeans was in many ways a human disaster for the Mexicans.'[124] And the same can be said for the Indians of the United States and Canada.

The Struggle of American Blacks

The same attitudes that resulted in the extermination and humiliation of the American Indian also came to the fore in the white man's relations with blacks. Unlike Indians, blacks were not native to America; they were brought here from Africa as slaves. As a result there are a number of circumstances—loss of cultural identity and a pattern of broken families—unique to blacks. But the white man's attitudes were the same. The black man was somehow less than human and he had value only to the extent that he could work on the plantation, cook and care for the house, or serve as a mistress for the plantation owner. The black was treated as an object, not much different from a horse or a cow, to be used and then discarded when he was no longer useful. Once slavery was abandoned, Americans found themselves with a large and growing black population, a population that was now obsolete and thus to be discarded. In *The Seven Storey Mountain*, Merton gives a vivid description of life in Harlem, a ghetto of discarded blacks:

> Here in this huge, dark, steaming slum, hundreds of thousands of Negroes are herded together like cattle, most of them with nothing to eat and nothing to do. All the senses and imagination and sensibilities and emotions and sorrows and desires of a race with vivid feelings and deep emotional reactions are forced in upon themselves, bound inward by an iron ring of frustration: the prejudice that hems them in with its four insurmountable walls. In this huge cauldron, inestimable natural gifts, wisdom, love, music, science, poetry are stamped down and left to boil with the dregs of an elementary corrupted nature, and thousands upon thousands of ‾souls are destroyed by vice and misery and degradation, obliterated, wiped out, washed from the register of the living, dehumanized. [125]

His rare gift of insight enabled Merton to see this situation and to describe it as early as 1948, long before national attention was being drawn to it.

More importantly, however, Merton, writing in 1948, was able to connect this picture of degradation and squalor with the life of ease and wealth of the white man.

> Now the terrifying paradox of the whole thing is this: Harlem itself, and every individual Negro in it, is a living condemnation of our so-called 'culture'. Harlem is there by way of divine indictment against New York City and the people who live downtown and make their money downtown. The brothels of Harlem, and all its prostitution, and its dope-rings, and all the rest are the mirror of the polite divorces and the manifold cultured adulteries of Park Avenue: they are God's commentary on the whole of our society.
>
> Harlem is, in a sense, what God thinks of Hollywood. And Hollywood is all Harlem has, in its despair, to grasp at, by way of a surrogate for heaven. [126]

Merton was convinced that the blacks were attempting, to the best of their ability, to imitate white culture simply because that was all they had; there was nothing else to imitate. He made yet another astute observation, that even though the blacks were imitating the white culture they knew deep in their hearts that it was worthless and that it was the cause of their own misery. Thus he remarked: 'No, there is not a Negro in the whole place who can fail to know, in the marrow of his own bones, that the white man's culture is not worth the jetsam of the Harlem River.'[127]

Merton himself had rejected American culture only a few years before writing *The Seven Storey Mountain* and this almost certainly influenced his views, yet at the same time he saw right to the heart of the racial problem in American society and he was able to articulate this in a vivid and unforgettable manner. Although he did not write on the racial problem again until the early 1960s, his views remained much the same and he was still concerned with the relationship between white culture and the prejudice shown toward American blacks. Those early words on American racism foretold even stronger words yet to come from Merton, words that would have a decisive influence on the attitudes and actions of many of those who were to become involved in the struggle for racial justice in America.

One of those influenced by Merton was the black revolutionary Eldridge Cleaver. In *Soul on Ice*, Cleaver tells how a prison teacher introduced him to Merton's life and work and made him promise that some day he would read Merton. That day came in 1963, when Cleaver was placed in solitary confinement at Folsom Prison. One of the books on the approved prison reading list was *The Seven Storey Mountain*. Cleaver describes his reactions to the book:

> I was tortured by that book because Merton's suffering, his quest for God, seemed all in vain to me. At the time, I was a Black Muslim chained to the bottom of a pit by the Devil. Did I expect Allah to tear down the walls and set me free? To me, the language and symbols of religion were nothing but weapons of war. I had no other purpose for them. All the gods are dead except the god of war. I wished that Merton had stated in secular terms the reasons he withdrew from the political, economic, military and social system into which he was born, seeking refuge in a monastery.
>
> Despite my rejection of Merton's theistic world view, I could not keep him out of the room. He shouldered his

way through the door. Welcome, Brother Merton. I gave
him a bear hug. Most impressive of all to me was
Merton's description of New York's black ghetto—Harlem.
I liked it so much that I copied out the heart of it in long-
hand. Later, after getting out of solitary, I used to keep
this passage in mind when delivering Black Muslim
lectures to other prisoners....

For a while, whenever I felt myself softening, relaxing, I
had only to read that passage to become once more a rigid
flame of indignation. It had precisely the same effect on
me that Elijah Muhammad's writings used to have, or the
words of Malcom X, or the words of any spokesman of the
oppressed in any land. I vibrate sympathetically to any
protest against tryanny.[128]

What most impressed Cleaver about Merton's critique of
American racism was Merton's clear vision of the sickness of
white society in its oppression of the blacks and of the blacks'
position at the absolute bottom of American society.

For many years the blacks were 'content' to do all in their
power to gain entrance into American society and become a part
of the white culture. In the early 1960s, however, a gradual
change began to come about among black leadership. Blacks
began to seek out their own identity, based not upon a sick
white culture but upon their own black culture. Merton had
foreseen this already in 1948, and he had been highly critical of
the civil rights movement in the 1950s and early 1960s when the
goal had seemed to be black assimilation into white culture. In
addition Merton had begun to question some of the basic
assumptions of the white liberal establishment. One of them is
that society must be kept running smoothly at all costs. It was at
precisely this point, according to Baker, that the American racial
situation was most tense and Merton recognized this:

Merton believed that the American white man, who has
afflicted the American Negro with his prejudice, is perhaps
even more unjust and violent than the white men in other
parts of the world because of his fear of imminent social
disruption. The British colonial could grant his slaves their
freedom and return home, leaving the land, if not the
money in their hands, but the white American shares his
own soil with his slaves.[129]

In other words, the black problem is primarily a white problem
and there can be no solution 'without a profound change of

heart, a real shake-up and deep reaching *metanoia* on the part of White America'.[130]

Merton held the opinion that the conservative white southerner's attitude on race relations was much closer to reality than that of the liberal northerner. The conservative knows that if he were to accept blacks as equals his way of life would be radically changed. The liberal, on the other hand, operates under the illusion that he can be totally in favor of civil rights while at the same time continuing to enjoy his comfortable way of life.[131] The liberal continues to believe that blacks want to be integrated into white society, when, in fact, the most perceptive blacks have long ago given up on white society altogether.[132] 'It is,' says Merton, 'simply taken for granted that, since the white man is superior, the *Negro wants to become a white man*. And we, liberals and Christians that we are, advance generously, with open arms, to embrace our little black brother and welcome him into white society.'[133] It is here that the crux of the problem is found, for all whites, including the liberals, live 'under a system that is unjust to the Negro and thus contributes to a social order that relegates him to an inferior station in life.'[134] White society is unable to face up to this fact, however, 'because white people cannot cope with their own drives, cannot defend themselves against their own emotions, which are supremely unstable in a rapidly changing and overstimulated society.'[135] To state it simply, most whites are unable to admit their own racism.[136]

At the same time the white man fears and needs the black man. Knowing—but not admitting—that to accept the black means changing his way of life, the white constructs a myth of the black, lazy, sexually potent, and violent, which is particularly important in the face of black power exhibited in riots and other forms of violence:

> The 'fear of attack' represents in actual fact a very serious earnest *desire to be attacked*. Not in order to be hurt, or to suffer, far from it: but in order to find the psychopathic myth verified, and all of its practical conclusions justified. Therefore when the National Guard is called out to 'keep order' it is recognized at least obscurely by all, both blacks and whites, that this act expresses an urgent and almost official need for disorder. It manifests a desire and a need bred by guilt, seeking to turn itself by every possible means into a self-fulfilling prophecy.[137]

The white man can then look at the black man and say, 'I told

you so.' Here, according to Merton, a strong emotional need of
the white man is being satisfied:

> Blaming the Negro (and by extension the Communist, the
> outside agitator, etc.) gives the white a stronger sense of
> identity, or rather it *protects* an identity which is seriously
> threatened with pathological dissolution. It is by blaming
> the Negro that the white man tries to hold himself
> together. The Negro is in the unenviable position of being
> used for *everything*, even for the white man's psycho-
> logical security. Unfortunately, a mere outburst of violence
> will only give the white man the justification he desires. It
> will convince him that he is for real because he is
> *right*.[138]

Unable to face his own inadequacy, the white man blames the
black man.

Merton believed that for a time, in the person of Martin
Luther King, there was the possibility of bringing about a
solution to the race problem, especially since the blacks were
seeking equality through nonviolent means. In order for such a
moment of *kairos* to be effective, however, the white man had to
respond to the blacks and thereby to lay a basis upon which to
build. If such a moment of *kairos* were ignored only destruction
and hatred would result.[139] Unfortunately events were such that
in 1968 Merton observed: 'At this present moment...we have
already passed a point of crucial decision. It can be said that the
classical approach to non-violence is no longer the dominant and
guiding force in radical efforts to achieve reform and conflict
resolution.'[140] It appears therefore that the moment of *kairos*
has passed and that a nonviolent solution to the problem is not,
at least at the present time, possible.

Although very pessimistic about the future of race relations
in the United States, Merton did hold to what he called 'the
classic way of religious humanism and non-violence exemplified
by Gandhi'.[141] In order for there to be any progress the whites
must first of all turn inward, a turning inward which is, by the
way, quite different from a turning away from the problem. The
white man must see the black man as he is. Says Merton: 'What
is demanded of us is not necessarily that we believe that the
Negro has mysterious and magic answers in the realm of politics
and social control, *but that his spiritual insight into our common
crisis is something we must take seriously*.'[142] The white man
must view the black man as an equal who has something to say
to him. 'If they are forced to listen to what the Negro is trying

to say, the whites may have to admit that their *prosperity is rooted to some extent in injustice and sin.*'[143] Such soul-searching would demand that the white man change not only his thinking but also his actions.

Merton was convinced that the two races—black and white—need one another and that a coming together is especially crucial for the whites.

> A genuinely Catholic attitude in matters of race is one which concretely accepts and fully recognizes the fact that different races are *correlative. They mutually complete one another.* The white man needs the Negro, and needs to know that he needs him....Our significance as white men is to be seen *entirely* in the fact that all men are not white. Until this fact is grasped, we will never realize our true place in the world, and we will never achieve what we are meant to achieve in it.[144]

In order to be free, however, the blacks will have to seek their freedom without the aid of the white man: 'the white man is so far gone that he cannot free the Negro because he cannot even free himself.'[145] The solution to the racial conflict between whites and blacks lies within the heart of every black man and every white man, and speaking as a white man Merton emphasized the need for whites to look within and to face the ugly reality there, for until white America faces up to this reality, the conflict, the violence, the injustice, and the degradation will continue.

American Foreign Policy as Racism

The great tragedy of racism in America is made worse by the extension of our racist attitudes far beyond our nation's borders. Merton was concerned about this as early as 1941, prior to Pearl Harbor, when the United States had still to decide its role in World War II. He was convinced that the United States considered itself superior to other countries and that a victory in World War II would result in an American attempt at world domination. He wrote: 'The big catch in our argument is the promise that if *we* won there would be peace and harmony in the world.'[146] He also predicted that the United States would end up in a role of world policeman, with its military forces scattered throughout the world 'to keep order'. The flaw in the American argument, according to Merton, was the tacit assumption that Americans were somehow morally superior to others and that only America could really do a proper job of running the world—which is another way of saying that the only valid peace is an American peace.

This attitude was closely related to the American myth and the constant need to widen ever further the scope of the frontier.[147] Americans were seen as the 'good guys' and whatever country America was fighting automatically became the 'bad guys'. This has been especially true, Merton pointed out, of American involvement in various wars:

> There have been foreign wars, in which America has been persuaded to take part only when convinced that we would ride into battle as cowboys. We took over Cuba from Spain. Why? Because we were roughriders, of course. Clear-eyed, independent, with the honesty that is bred by gazing out over great plains, we jumped on our horses and rode up San Juan Hill, to liberate the poor, defenseless, nonindependent Cubans. They, too, have plains, of course. But looking out over the small plains of Camaguey is somehow different.[148]

Merton further stated that 'after every war (which we, being the good guys, have always won) we have, with the utmost sincerity, exported just a little bit of our innocence, just a little bit of our paradisaical idealism, to the lands sunken in history and sin.'[149]

This form of racism can also be seen in American Christianity. It assumes that only Christians have a true understanding of God, and therefore all others of different religions— and of other nations, cultures, and races—are lost in a state of sin and are in need of a salvation which only the Christian West can bring. In a letter to a Jewish rabbi, Merton compares this racist Christ to Prometheus:

> When the Christians began to look at Christ as Prometheus...You see what I mean? Then they justified war, then they justified the crusades, then they justified pogroms, then they justified Auschwitz, then they justified the bomb, then they justified the Last Judgment: the Christ of Michelangelo is Prometheus, I mean the Christ in the Sistine Chapel. He is whipping sinners with his great Greek muscles. 'All right,' they say, 'if we can't make it to the wedding feast (and they are the ones who refused) we can blow up the joint and say it is the Last Judgment.'[150]

Such a theology easily goes hand-in-hand with the 'good guys versus bad guys' mentality that has characterized much of America's foreign policy, and it is perhaps no accident that whenever the missionaries arrived the armies and the businessmen were not far behind.[151]

Merton firmly believed that much of the talk about conversion of the heathen was motivated by political consideration rather than by a concern for the heathens' spiritual welfare. In regard to the once common practice among American Catholics of praying for the conversion of Russia after each Mass, he raised the question: 'Is this simply a desire that the Russians will stop menacing us, will stop being different from us, will stop challenging, will stop trying to get ahead of us?'[152] He went on to point out the harm to us if all the rest of the world were just like us and enclosed itself within our limitations:

> Until we recognize the right of other nations, races and societies to be different from us and to stay different, to have different ideas and to open up new horizons, our prayers for their conversion will be meaningless. It will be no better and no worse, perhaps, than the Russian Communist's idea that we will someday become *exactly like him*. And if we are not prepared to do so...he will destroy us. For he wants us to have his attitudes, his prejudices, and his limitations. Until we feel in our own hearts the sufferings, the desires, the needs, the fears of the Russians and the Chinese as if they were our own, in spite of political differences, until we *want* their problems to be solved in much the same way as we want our own to be solved: until then it is useless to talk about 'conversion' —it is a word without significance.[153]

'It is,' he says, 'when we insist most firmly on everyone else being "reasonable" that we become, ourselves, unreasonable.'[154]

Behind this insistence that others be reasonable lies a deep-seated racism. Indeed, it is this racism that lies behind much of our benevolence toward other countries, especially those we term 'underdeveloped'. Merton felt that this racist attitude was also a factor in the anti-americanism so often found abroad:

> The Congo: because Albert Schweitzer is there in the jungle, we are all firmly convinced that we are all bene-

volent, all brave, all self-sacrificing: that we have *all* loved Africa. That it is our very nature to love Africa, Asia, 'inferior races,' etc., etc. And that if they do not recognize this at once, it is proof that they are by nature inferior since they cannot appreciate the superior bene-volence and culture of the white race. This perversity, itself a sign of ingrained malice, predisposes them to Communism....

Whole continents and whole races do not take well to imaginary roles, roles assigned to them by minds they find it difficult to understand, and which look quite strange to them. Thus they finally insist, if necessary with violence, on asserting what is least imaginary—and least acceptable to our collective imagination. 'Here', they say, setting fire to a building, 'see what you can make of *this*!'[155]

Americans react to such violence by assuming it to be a Com-munist plot, and therefore using force to crush the rebellion, 'we drive them all into the arms of the Communists, since we have left them nowhere else to go!'[156]

In one of his most important essays on world affairs, 'A Letter to Pablo Antonio Cuadra Concerning Giants,' Merton discusses the conflict between Gog—the Soviet Union—and Magog—the United States:[157]

> Gog is a lover of power, Magog is absorbed in the cult of money: their idols differ, and indeed their faces seem to be dead set against one another, but their madness is the same: they are two faces of Janus looking inward, and dividing with critical fury the polluted sanctuary of dehumanized man....
>
> I for my part believe in the very serious possibility that Gog and Magog may wake up one morning to find that they have burned and blasted each other off the map during the night, and nothing will remain but the spasmodic exercise of automatic weapons still in the throes of what has casually been termed overkill.[158]

One possible result of such a conflict is the virtual destruction of western civilization, with the possible exceptions of Australia and New Zealand. It would be up to the nations of the southern hemisphere to rebuild civilization. Says Merton: 'It is conceivable that Indonesia, Latin America, Southern Africa and Australia may find themselves heirs to the opportunities and objectives which Gog and Magog shrugged off with such careless abandon.'[159]

For Merton, such an eventuality would have spiritual significance as a 'characteristic of these races is a totally different outlook on life, a spiritual outlook which is not abstract but concrete, not pragmatic but hieratic, intuitive and affective rather than rationalistic and aggressive.'[160] Most significant, however, is their understanding of man:

> Let me be quite succinct: the greatest sin of the European-Russian-American complex which we call 'the West' (and this sin has spread in its own way to China), is not only greed and cruelty, not only moral dishonesty and infidelity to truth, but above all *its unmitigated arrogance towards the rest of the human race....*
>
> Christ is found not in loud and pompous declarations but in humble and fraternal dialogue. He is found less in a truth that is imposed than in a truth that is shared ....
> God speaks, and God is to be heard, not only on Sinai, not only in my own heart, but in the *voice of the stranger.* That is why the peoples of the Orient, and all primitive peoples in general, make so much of the mystery of hospitality.[161]

Merton's opinion on this point is rooted in his understanding of the incarnation: 'Since the Word was made Flesh, God is in man. God is in *all men.*'[162] Indeed, the problem with the missionaries was that they failed to encounter the Christ already present in the ancient civilizations of the Incas, Mayas, Hindus, and others.[163] It is, says Merton, a tragedy that the Church has forgotten its New Testament roots when it learned from the Greeks and adapted itself to various cultures. What could, and should, have been a mutual sharing of spiritual experiences between cultures has become an imposition of western European values upon virtually all the other peoples of the world. Unlike the primitives, western man is unable to listen to and to accept the stranger.

Merton was especially critical of the western tourist with his cameras, exposure meters, and prepackaged tours. He travels at the suggestion of others, he sees what he has been told to see beforehand, and he totally ignores the possibility that he might learn something from the people of the country he is visiting.

> He cannot possibly realize that the stranger has something very valuable, something irreplaceable to give him: something that can never be bought with money, never

estimated by publicists, never exploited by political agitators: the spiritual understanding of a friend who belongs to a different culture. The tourist lacks nothing except brothers. For him these do not exist.[164]

With specific reference to the tourist in Latin America, Merton's words are harsh and biting: 'So the tourist drinks tequila, and thinks it is no good, and waits for the fiesta he has been told to wait for. How should he realize that the Indian who walks down the street with half a house on his head and a hole in his pants is Christ? All the tourist thinks is that it is odd for so many Indians to be called Jesus.'[165]

Merton was angered by what he called our 'unmitigated arrogance' toward the rest of the world. He was aware that these other cultures possessed a deep spirituality that could be shared with the West if westerners would only listen. Beyond this, however, was a deeper problem: people in these other cultures believe western propaganda and, in their desire to become western, renounce their own heritage. This is especially true in Asia, where a materialistic communism imported from the West is rapidly replacing much that is authentically Asian. Merton believed that one task of the Christian was to try to save the best in Asian cultural and spiritual traditions.

The Asians have renounced Asia. They want to be western, sometimes they are frantic about being western. They want to go places. They feel that there have been centuries of inertia and stagnation, and there is a reaction against the humiliations and misunderstandings of colonialism, calling for a defeat of the west at its own technological game. All this is dangerous but inevitable. Christianity of course has a crucial part to play in saving all that is valuable in the east as well as in the west.[166]

The West—its people, attitudes, culture, money, and technology—has become a god that is worshipped not only by westerners but by Asians, Africans, and Latin Americans. 'In order to disentagle Christian faith from the crisis and collapse of western culture, and open it to entirely new world perspectives,' says Merton, 'we have to be able to renounce the mighty spirit that has let himself be set up in the place of God: the Angel of the West.'[167]

1. *The Seven Storey Mountain*, pp. 142-45.

2. Ibid., pp. 310-16, 366-68.

3. Ibid., p. 402. See p. 404 for the poem which Merton wrote in John Paul's memory.

4. *New Seeds of Contemplation*, p. 87.

5. Ibid., p. 94.

6. *The Seven Storey Mountain*, pp. 311-12.

7. *Thomas Merton on Peace*, ed. Gordon C. Zahn, p. 44.

8. Ibid., pp. 44-45.

9. *The Sign of Jonas*, p. 312.

10. *The Sign of Jonas*, p. 312. Merton now realized that the evils of war did not justify his total withdrawal from people.

11. Ibid.

12. *Thomas Merton on Peace*, p. 21.

13. In a letter to Dorothy Day Merton stated that he was not theoretically a pacifist, and he held that it might be possible for a Christian to fight and even for a war to be just. For a discussion of this problem see Zahn, 'Original Child Monk: An Appreciation' in Ibid., pp. xvii-xx.

14. Ibid., p. 49.

15. Ibid.

16. Ibid., p. xix.

17. *Faith and Violence: Christian Teaching and Christian Practice*, p. 35.

18. Ibid., p. 36.

19. Ibid., p. 39.

20. *Emblems of a Season of Fury*, pp. 72-73.

21. 'First and Last Thoughts:An Author's Preface' in *A Thomas Merton Reader*, ed. McDonnell, p. ix.

22. *Thomas Merton on Peace*, p. 257.

23. Ibid., pp. 94-95.

24. Ibid., p. 99.

25.   Ibid., p. 94.

26.   *Raids on the Unspeakable*, p. 14.

27.   See Thomas Merton, *Original Child Bomb: Points for Meditation to be Scratched on the Walls of a Cave* (New York: New Directions, 1962).

28.   An interesting novel dealing with the possibility of a nuclear war and its aftermath is Walter M. Miller, Jr., *A Canticle for Leibowitz* (New York: Bantam Books, 1959). Miller writes of a future society of monks who preserve knowledge and learning in a new dark age following a nuclear war. The book was on Merton's list of suggested readings for the novices at Gethsemani.

29.   *Conjectures of a Guilty Bystander*, p. 271.

30.   *Thomas Merton on Peace*, p. 100.

31.   *Conjectures of a Guilty Bystander*, p. 271.

32.   *Thomas Merton on Peace*, p. xv.

33.   Ibid., p. 83.

34.   Ibid., p. 89.

35.   *Conjectures of a Guilty Bystander*, p. 230.

36.   A treaty by most of the world's nuclear powers has now been signed banning tests in the atmosphere. There are, however, several nations which did not sign the treaty, and there is an ever increasing danger of nuclear weapons being developed by more and more countries. Of special concern to many is the possibility that terrorist organizations may come into possession of nuclear weapons.

37.   Gordon C. Zahn, 'The Peacemaker', *Continuum* 7 (1969) 270.

38.   See Baker, *Thomas Merton Social Critic*, p. 96.

39.   *Thomas Merton on Peace*, p. 87. Although Merton did not carry this issue of responsibility further, the question of taxes does arise. Is it really possible to remain untouched by the responsibility for war? As a monk, Merton did not have to face the issue in the same way as a married man with a family to support and home to pay for. To withhold payment of taxes would undoubtedly mean a prison term and the man's family responsibilities could not be met. The extremely complex issue of responsibility for war must be understood within the context of a whole network of responsibilities.

40.   See Baker, *Thomas Merton Social Critic*, p. 96. For specific references see Merton, 'Christian Ethics and Nuclear War,' *Catholic Worker* 28 (March 1962) 2, 7, rpt. in Merton, *Thomas Merton on Peace*, pp. 82-87 and Merton, 'We Have to Make Ourselves Heard,' *Catholic Worker* 28 (May 1962) 4-5.

41.   *Original Child Bomb*, n. pag.

42. Zahn, 'The Peacemaker', p. 226.

43. *Faith and Violence*, p. 93.

44. Zahn in Merton, *Thomas Merton on Peace*, p. xiv. See pp. 259-60 where Merton gives an outline of this retreat.

45. Ibid., p. xiv. This project involved an exchange of Americans who were active in the peace movement for American prisoners of war.

46. Ibid., p. xxv.

47. Ibid.

48. *Seasons of Celebration*, p. 7.

49. Merton, ed., *Gandhi on Non-Violence: Selected Texts from Monhandas K. Gandhi's 'Non-Violence in Peace and War'* (New York: New Directions, 1965) p. 13.

50. *Faith and Violence*, p. 4.

51. Ibid., p. 5.

52. Ibid., p. 6.

53. Ibid.

54. Ibid., p. 9.

55. Ibid., pp. 9-10.

56. Ibid., p. 12. Cf. James W. Douglass, *Resistance and Contemplation: The Way of Liberation* (Garden City: Doubleday, 1972), p. 43 where he points out that 'non-violent liberation seeks the redemption of humanity from power itself, from all power *over* men, which is a power of domination and sin.'

57. *Conjectures of a Guilty Bystander*, p. 73.

58. *Faith and Violence*, p. 43.

59. Ibid.

60. Ibid.

61. *Gandhi on Non-Violence*, p. 7. See pp. 7-8 for a discussion of communication problems and violence in society.

62. *Faith and Violence*, p. 44.

63. Merton, 'Community, Politics, and Contemplation,' ed. Naomi Burton Stone, *Sisters Today* 42 (1971) 241.

64.   *Emblems of a Season of Fury*, p. 76.

65.   Merton's book *Faith and Violence* is dedicated to Philip Berrigan and James Forest (involved in a similar protest action in Milwaukee) and his booklet *Albert Camus' The Plague* is dedicated to Daniel Berrigan.

66.   For an example of this influence see Daniel Berrgian, *No Bars to Manhood* (New York: Bantam Books, 1970), pp. 125, 130-32, 139. This book is dedicated to Berrigan's father and to Thomas Merton whom Berrigan calls 'my brother'.

67.   *Thomas Merton on Peace*, p. 232.

68.   Ibid.

69.   See Gordon C. Zahn, 'Great Catholic Upheaval,' *Saturday Review* 54 (September 11, 1971) 24-27, 54-56.

70.   Zahn in Merton, *Thomas Merton on Peace*, p. xxxv, comments: 'It remains a matter of pure speculation, but one that can scarcely be avoided, how he would have reacted to the proliferation of these raids until by 1970 they numbered at least a dozen in major cities all over the nation. My own opinion, based on my reading of Merton, is that his disapproval would have grown more outspoken once it had passed beyond the "one or two reasonable" test he suggested for draft card burnings. A quite contrary opinion has been expressed by one of the participants in the Milwaukee action; it was his impression that Merton's attitude had shifted to the more favorable side following the appearance of the *Ave Maria* article. Unfortunately, there is nothing in the later Merton writings to confirm either point of view; most of the raids took place after his departure for Asia and his death there.' The article referred to is Merton, 'Nonviolence Does Not, Cannot Mean Passivity,' *Ave Maria* 108 (Sept 7, 1968) 9-10 rpt. as 'The Burning of Papers/The Human Conscience/And the Peace Movement,' *Fellowship* 35 (March, 1969) 7-8. This article is also rpt. as 'Note for *Ave Maria*' in Merton, *Thomas Merton on Peace*, pp. 231-33.

71.   Daniel Berrigan, 'Foreword' in Jean Marie Paupert, *The Politics of the Gospel* (New York: Holt, Rinehart & Winston, 1969) pp. vii-viii.

72.   Merton, 'Community, Politics, and Contemplation', pp. 241-43.

73.   For an account of what happened when one religious entered politics, see Aldous Huxley, *Grey Eminence: A Study in Religion and Politics* (New York: Harper & Row, 1966).

74.   *Contemplation in a World of Action*, p. 158.

75.   Ibid., p. 164.

76.   Marco Pallis, 'Thomas Merton, 1915-1968,' *Studies in Comparative Religion* 3 (1969) 140.

77.   Berrigan, 'Foreword' in Paupert, *The Politics of the Gospel*, p. xi.

78.   *Seeds of Destruction*, p. 72. Note that Merton was both a poet and a writer of prophetic songs. See C. Alexander Peloquin, 'To Remember,' *Liturgical Arts* 37 (1969) 52-53.

79.   *Raids on the Unspeakable*, p. 45.

80.   Ibid., p. 46.

81.   Ibid., p. 47.

82.   Ibid.

83.   Ibid.

84.   Ibid., pp. 48-49. Merton expands on this tendency in his essay 'Final Integration—Toward a "Monastic Therapy"' in *Contemplation in a World of Action*, pp. 205-17.

85.   *The New Man*, pp. 71-72.

86.   *The Behavior of Titans*, p. 83.

87.   *The Living Bread*, p. 128. This kind of pressure is not limited to secular societies but is also present in the Church as Merton points out in a letter to Dorothy Day quoted in *Seeds of Destruction*, p. 254.

88.   See *Disputed Questions*, pp. 107-08, and *Thomas Merton on Peace*, pp. 150-59.

89.   *Mystics and Zen Masters*, p. 265.

90.   Ibid., p. 264.

91.   Ibid., p. 267.

92.   Ibid.

93.   Ibid., pp. 268-69.

94.   Ibid., p. 268.

95.   Merton, *Albert Camus' The Plague*, Religious Dimensions in Literature, gen. ed. Lee A. Belford (New York: Seabury, 1968) pp. 9-10.

96.   Merton made a distinction between the individual and the person, as he explains in *Disputed Questions*, pp. ix-x: 'When I say I am concerned with the *person*, I do not mean that I am interested primarily in the *individual*. There is a great difference. Individualism is nothing but the social atomism that has led to our present inertia, passivism and spiritual decay....This individualism, primarily an economic concept with a pseudo-spiritual and moral facade, is in fact mere irresponsibility. It is, and has always been, not an affirmation of genuine human values but a flight from the obligations from which these values are inseparable. And first of all a flight from the obligation to *love*....The vocation of the *person*

is to construct his own solitude as a *conditio sine qua non* for a valid encounter with other persons, for intelligent cooperation and for communion in love.'

97.   *Seasons of Celebration*, pp. 222-23.

98.   *Seeds of Destruction*, p. 99.

99.   *Life and Holiness*, p. 132.

100.   Ibid., p. 133.

101.   *Thoughts in Solitude*, p. 14.

102.   *Emblems of a Season of Fury*, pp. 86-87.

103.   *Faith and Violence*, p. x. Merton relates the complete story on p. ix. Cf. Martin Buber, *Tales of the Hasidim: The Early Masters* (1947; rpt. New York: Shocken, 1968) I, 11-23.

104.   *Disputed Questions*, p. viii.

105.   The term 'American' refers not only to the United States and Canada but to all of Latin America as well.

106.   *Thomas Merton on Peace*, p. 248. This attitude can still be seen today in almost any television western. The most vivid example of this one-sided view that this writer has seen is the Custer Battlefield National Monument located in the center of the Crow Indian Reservation in southeastern Montana. The monument commemorates the white men, yet it was the Indians who won the battle. For a vivid account of the Indian wars see Dee Brown, *Bury My Heart at Wounded Knee: An Indian History of the American West* (New York: Holt, Rinehart & Winston, 1971).

107.   *Conjectures of a Guilty Bystander*, p. 23.

108.   Ibid., p. 25.

109.   Ibid. Merton mentions Daniel Boone as a notable exception who was able to accept the Indian into his world view.

110.   Ibid.

111.   *Thomas Merton on Peace*, p. 253. Undoubtedly the next frontier will be outer space. At least one writer, Ray Bradbury, in his futuristic novel *The Martian Chronicles* (Garden City: Doubleday, 1950), sees the Americans who land on Mars exterminating all the Martians and destroying their culture.

112.   Merton, 'The Cross Fighters—Notes on a Race War,' *Unicorn Journal* 1 (1968) 26.

113.   *Conjectures of a Guilty Bystander*, p. 280.

114.   'The Cross Fighters', p. 10.

115. *Thomas Merton on Peace*, p. 250. Merton's account is based upon Theodora Kroeber's book *Ishi in Two Worlds: A Biography of the Last Wild Indian in North America* (Berkeley and Los Angeles: University of California Press, 1961).

116. *Thomas Merton on Peace*, p. 250.

117. ibid., p. 252.

118. Ibid., p. 253.

119. The white man was especially opposed to the new religions which arose among Indians after his coming—religions that expressed the cultural upheaval among the Indians. Merton discusses one of these religions, the Ghost Dance, which developed among the Indians of the American west in the late 1800s in *The Geography of Lograire*, pp. 131-37.

120. Merton, 'The Sacred City,' *The Center Magazine*, 1 No. 3 (1968) 74; rpt. in *Ishi Means Man* (Greensboro, N.C.: Unicorn Press, 1976).

121. 'The Sacred City,' p. 76.

122. Ibid.

123. Ibid.

124. Ibid., p. 77.

125. *The Seven Storey Mountain*, p. 345.

126. Ibid.

127. Ibid., p. 346.

128. Eldridge Cleaver, *Soul on Ice* (New York: Dell, 1968) pp. 34-35.

129. Baker, *Thomas Merton Social Critic*, p. 100. A similar situation exists today in South Africa as is pointed out by Nicholas Wolterstorff, 'Calvinists in Potchefstroom,' *The Reformed Review* 25 No. 9 (1975).

130. *Seeds of Destruction*, p. 310. Such a *metanoia*—a conversion—would mean changes in education, housing, and employment, and a radical redistribution of wealth.

131. Ibid., pp. 8, 36, Merton explains the problem with the liberal position.

132. Ibid., pp. 58-59.

133. Ibid., p. 58.

134. Baker, *Thomas Merton Social Critic*, pp. 100-101.

135. *Conjectures of a Guilty Bystander*, p. 22.

136. See *Seeds of Destruction*, pp. 37-47. On pp. 45-46, Merton states: 'The purpose of non-violent protest in its deepest and most spiritual dimensions is then to awaken the conscience of the white man to the awful reality of his injustice and of his sin, so that he will be able to see that the Negro problem is really a *White* problem: that the cancer of injustice and hate which is eating white society and is only partially manifested in racial segregation with all its consequences, *is rooted in the heart of the white man himself.*'

137. Ibid., p. 51.

138. *Conjectures of a Guilty Bystander*, p. 23.

139. See *Seeds of Destruction*, pp. 69-70.

140. *Thomas Merton on Peace*, p. 228.

141. Ibid., p. 230.

142. *Seeds of Destruction*, p. 69.

143. Ibid., p. 48.

144. Ibid., p. 61.

145. Ibid., p. 89.

146. *The Secular Journal*, p. 208. See also pp. 205-10.

147. Merton discusses the myth of the frontier in *Conjectures of a Guilty Bystander*, pp. 23-29.

148. Ibid., p. 26.

149. Ibid., p. 27.

150. *Seeds of Destruction*, pp. 273-74.

151. This was especially true of Great Britain's foreign policy, but it is also true of the United States to some extent, particularly in Asia and Latin America. Many American missionaries in Asia have closer ties with the United States militarymen than they do with the Asian nationals.

152. *Conjectures of a Guilty Bystander*, p. 74.

153. Ibid.

154. *The Way of Chuang Tzu*, p. 32.

155. *Conjectures of a Guilty Bystander*, p. 21.

156. Ibid.

157. See *Emblems of a Season of Fury*, pp. 70-89. Pablo Antonio Cuadra is a leading intellectual figure in Nicaragua and one of his country's outstanding poets. His poetry reflects his mixed Spanish and Indian background.

158. Ibid., pp. 73, 76-77.

159. Ibid., p. 77.

160. Ibid., p. 78.

161. Ibid., pp. 78, 81, 82.

162. Ibid., p. 78.

163. See Ibid., p. 79.

164. Ibid., p. 85.

165. Ibid., p. 86.

166. *Seeds of Destruction*, pp. 287-88.

167. *Faith and Violence*, p. 198.

VI

THE WRITER AS SOCIAL PROPHET

The Pasternak Affair

MERTON began corresponding with the Russian writer Boris Pasternak in 1958. This, according to James York Glimm, was a turning point in his views on contemplation.[1] In his dialogue with Pasternak, Merton began to relate the subject matter of his earlier works to the social and political situation of the times. The real turning point came in 1959, when Pasternak won the Nobel Prize for literature and was pressured by the Russian government into refusing it.

The correspondence between Merton and Pasternak was contemplative and poetic, for both men were deeply spiritual and appreciative of each other's cultural and religious heritage. Herbert Burke points out that 'Merton's study of Pasternak reflected his understanding and love not only for the novelist and his work, especially *Doctor Zhivago*, but also for much else in the Russian novel, Russian poetry, philosophy, theology'.[2] Above all, he saw Pasternak as a contemplative. Yet Pasternak's spirituality had social and political implications:

> For one of the most important and most helpful signs of the times is in the turbulent, anarchic, but fully determined efforts of a small minority of men to recover some kind of contact with their own inner depths, to recapture the freshness and truth of their own subjectivity, and to go on from there not only to God, but to the spirit of other men. In the face of our own almost hopeless alienation, we are trying to get back to ourselves before it is too late. One of the most outstanding examples of this struggle is seen in the almost symbolic career of Boris Pasternak whose more recent poetry and prose can most certainly qualify in a broad and basic sense as *contemplative*....[3]

The contemplative is not just a man who sits under a tree with his legs crossed, or one who edifies himself with the answer to ultimate and spiritual problems. He is one who seeks to know the meaning of life not only with his head but with his whole being, by living it in depth....[4]

The key to Merton's understanding of Pasternak lies in those words 'living it in depth', for Merton was convinced that Pasternak did just that, and that he had, as a result, come into conflict with his government. In a moving tribute to Pasternak, Merton says: 'To me...one of the most persuasive and moving aspects of Pasternak's religious mood is its slightly off-beat spontaneity. It is precisely because he says practically nothing that he has not discovered on his own, that he convinces me of the authenticity of his religious experience.'[5] It was the spontaneity and freedom to discover life on his own—his life in its depths—that brought Pasternak into conflict with the official Marxist doctrines of the Russian government, which saw everything in terms of dialectical materialism. Pasternak opposed this static view of life, and his critique was often blunt and outspoken:

Now what is history? It is the centuries of systematic explorations of the riddle of death, with a view to over-coming death... Now you can't move in this direction without a certain faith. You can't make such discoveries without spiritual equipment. And the basic elements of this equipment are in the Gospels. What are they? To begin with, love of one's neighbor, which is the supreme form of vital energy. Once it fills the heart of man it has to overflow and spend itself. And then the two basic ideals of modern man—without which he is unthinkable—the idea of free personality and the idea of life as sacrifice. Mind you, all this is still extraordinarily new... It was not until the coming of Christ that time and man could breathe freely. It was not until after Him that man began to live toward the future. Man does not die in a ditch like a dog—but at home in history, while the work toward the conquest of death is in full swing; he dies sharing in this work.[6]

Merton believed, as Baker shows, that Pasternak 'provided the most accurate critique of Marxism when he pointed out the foolishness of seeking immortality in a stone, which has already been stamped lifeless and dead.'[7] Merton says: 'Communism, like all characteristically modern political movements, far from opening the door to the future is only a regression into the past, the ancient past, the time of slavery before Christ.'[8]

Pasternak's critique of Marxism, while it had political implications, was basically spiritual, for, as Merton states, 'those who have been struck by the religious content of his work have been responding, consciously or otherwise, not so much to a formal Christian witness as to a deep and uncompromising *spirituality*.'[9] This spirituality of which Merton speaks relates to everyday life, and Merton saw Pasternak as a defender of true spirituality:

> Pasternak stands first of all for the great spiritual values that are under attack in our materialistic world. He stands for the freedom and nobility of the individual person, for man the image of God, for man in whom God dwells. For Pasternak, the person is and must always remain prior to the collectivity. He stands for courageous, independent loyalty to his own conscience, and for the refusal to compromise with slogans and rationalizations imposed by compulsion....Over against the technological jargon and empty scientism of modern man, Pasternak sets creative symbolism, the power of imagination and of intuition, the glory of liturgy and the fire of contemplation.[10]

Immediately after the controversy over the Nobel Prize, western newsmen and politicians emphasized the political implications of Pasternak's works, especially his novel *Doctor Zhivago*. Yet, as Merton shows, 'the dimensions of Pasternak's world view are more existential and spiritual and are decidedly beyond left and right.'[11] Indeed, says Merton: 'It would seem that Pasternak's ability to rise above political dichotomies may very well be his greatest strength. This transcendence is the power and essence of *Doctor Zhivago*.'[12] Unlike most people of the West, Merton saw that Pasternak was speaking of the evils not only of the eastern communists but of the western capitalists as well. He comments:

> If Pasternak is ever fully studied, he is just as likely to be regarded as a dangerous writer in the West as he is in the East. He is saying that political and social structures as we understand them are things of the past, and that the crisis through which we are now passing is nothing but the full and inescapable manifestation of their falsity.[13]

In Pasternak Merton saw a new dimension of the contemplative life: that a true contemplative is a subversive; his values are in opposition to prevailing political structures. Pasternak's life provided a vivid example of the dangers of being a contemplative in the modern world. As his experiences have shown, the temptation to move from the realm of the spiritual to that of the political and thus lose the basis of one's contemplation is always present. It is this temptation which causes much of the difficulty for modern man. Speaking of this situation Merton concludes his essay 'The Pasternak Affair' with the words:

> For twenty centuries we have called ourselves Christians, without even beginning to understand one tenth of the Gospel. We have been taking Caesar for God and God for Caesar. Now that 'charity is growing cold' and we stand facing the smoky dawn of an apocalyptic era, Pasternak reminds us that there is only one source of truth, but that it is not sufficient to know the source is there—we must go and drink from it as he has done.
>
> Do we have the courage to do so? For obviously, if we consider what Pasternak is saying, doing and undergoing, to read the Gospel with eyes wide open may be a perilous thing! [14]

The Poets of Latin America

In the late fifties, Merton began an extensive study of Latin American poetry, and in the years that followed he not only read the works in the original Spanish and Portuguese, but he also made a number of his own translations of these works into English. [15] He contributed to *El Corno Emplumado*, an avant-garde literary journal published in Mexico City, and carried on an extensive correspondence with editors, writers, and poets from the various Latin American countries. Merton knew at least one of these poets personally, Ernesto Cardenal of Nicaragua. He had been received into the novitiate at Gethsemani in 1957, but poor health led him to leave and later to return to Nicaragua.

A good share of Merton's interest in Latin American poetry stemmed from his own vocation as a writer and a poet. Beyond this were the deeply religious, even contemplative, themes of Latin American poetry, particularly of poems by Cardenal describing his life at Gethsemani. Merton expressed his admiration of Cardenal's ability to communicate the contemplative experience through poetry:

> Never has the experience of novitiate life in a Cistercian monastery been rendered with such fidelity, and yet with such reserve. He is silent, as is right, about the inner and most personal aspects of his contemplative experience, and yet it shows itself more clearly in the complete simplicity and objectivity with which he notes down the exterior and ordinary features of this life. No amount of mystical rhetoric could ever achieve so just an appreciation of the unpretentious spirituality of this very plain monastic existence. Yet the poet remains conscious of his relation to the world he has left and thinks a great deal about it, with the result that one recognizes how the purifying isolation of the monastery encourages a profound renewal and change of perspective in which 'the world' is not forgotten, but seen in a clearer and less delusive light. [16]

In Cardenal's poetry Merton saw an expression and an extension of the contemplative life.

He was also deeply moved by the contemplative poetry of Jorge Carrera Andrade of Ecuador, who like most Latin American poets, was active in the literary and political life of his country. For a time he sided with the communists 'but the ambiguities of power politics making use of the humble and defenseless to increase its own power did not satisfy him. He broke away from Communism. He found himself more alone.' [17] This sense of aloneness fascinated Merton:

> Yet I do not think Carrera Andrade has built his hopes definitely on any earthly or political power. He has learned a new geography, the world which has to be discovered sooner or later by those who do not believe in power, violence, coercion, tyranny, war. 'I embarked for the secret country, the country that is everywhere, the country that has no map because it is within ourselves.'
>
> It is in this secret country that I have met Carrera Andrade, and here we have become good friends. Here without noise of words we talk together of the mountains of Ecuador, and of the silent people there who do not always eat every day. The secret country is a country of loneliness and of a kind of hunger, of silence, of perplexity, of waiting, of strange hopes: where men expect the impossible to be born, but do not always dare to speak of their hopes. For all hopes that can be put into words are now used by men of war in favor of death: even the most sacred and living words are sometimes used in favor of death. [18]

This secret country with its geography of the world Merton never forgot, for it formed the basic theme of his last and longest poetic work, *The Geography of Lograire*.[19]

By his interest in the Latin American poets Merton began, in a very real sense, to reach out to the world. Like Cardenal, Merton had not forgotten the world he left behind when he entered the monastery and, like Andrade, he was beginning to learn of a new geography of the world, a geography that arose from that secret country within himself. In the poetry of Latin America he was able to see the relationship between both worlds, and he began to understand the poet as someone who stood on the boundary of those worlds.

The Latin American poets were all very much involved in the social and political struggles of their people. The Peruvian poet Cesar Vallejo, a half Indian poet, knew the life of poverty as well as the intellectual life of the Left Bank in the Paris of the twenties. His involvement in the political struggles of his time was too much for him, and after going to Madrid during the Spanish Civil War he returned home 'broken and almost without hope, to die in 1938, torn apart by the inexorable forces that were plunging the world into disaster'.[20]

Pablo Antonio Cuadra, a Nicaraguan poet, was also half Indian, and his works reflect the indigenous Indian roots of Latin American culture, a culture which Merton said has produced 'the deepest and most authentic sources of Latin American poetic inspiration, in Mexico, Peru, Ecuador and other predominantly Indian countries'.[21] In commenting on Cuadra's poetry Merton elaborated on these roots deep in Indian culture:

> Cuadra's verse owes its vitality not to a sentimental and romantic meditation on the 'Indian past' of Central America, but to its roots in a grim and vital Indian present, in which the past still lives with an unconquerable and flourishing energy....
>
> Cuadra, then, absolutely refuses to regard the Indian heritage of Central America as a matter of archaeology or of lavish color pictures in *Life* magazine. It is to him something living, something that boils and fights for expression in his own soul, and in the soul of his people. Certain aspects of his verse are social and political. He cannot do otherwise than attempt, as so many others have attempted, to clarify contemporary aspirations in the language of ancient myth.[22]

In his early writings Merton had made numerous attempts to

clarify modern political realities by retelling the ancient Greek myths: in the late 1960s he began to publish essays concerning the various Indian cultures of the Americas.[23] There can be little doubt that the Latin American poets did much to influence Merton at this crucial time when he was beginning to relate the life of contemplation to the world of action outside the monastery walls.

He corresponded with poets from Venezuela, Columbia, and even Cuba, and he hoped to 'try to keep in contact with the poetic underground' of Cuba.[24] Of all the Latin American poets, however, none were comparable to those of Brazil. Their works Merton termed 'a whole new world'.[25] He was impressed with the beauty of the Portuguese language and called it 'a language of admiration, of innocence, of joy, full of human warmth and therefore of humor: the humor that is inseparable from love, that laughs at the uniqueness of each individual being not because it is comical or contemptible but because it is unique'.[26] The Brazilian poets also reflected a love of life and joy not to be found in other Latin American poets. Says Merton:

> There is in the Brazilians none of the hardness, none of the sour, artificial, doctrinaire attitudes which you find in so many of the Spanish-American poets, wonderful as they are. What a difference between Manual Bandeira, or Jorge de Lima, whose love is for *men*, and some of the Marxist poets writing in Spanish whose love is for a *cause*.[27]

Merton thought the poetry of Brazil, written in Portuguese, 'richly expressive and in its own way innocent'.[28]

While not attempting to ignore the problems of the world, Merton was certain that emphasis needed to be placed upon those things that were good, joyful, and healthy, and he spoke of this in a letter to the Brazilian poet Alceu Amoroso Lima:

> I believe it is very important that we exchange ideas from time to time. This is a crucial and perhaps calamitous moment in history, a moment in which reason and under-standing threaten to be swallowed up, even if man himself manages to survive. It is all very well for me to meditate on these things in the shelter of the monastery: but there are times when this shelter itself is deceptive. Everything is deceptive today. And grains of error planted innocently in a well kept greenhouse can become gigantic, deadly trees.
>
> Everything healthy, everything certain, everything holy:

if we can find such things, they all need to be emphasized and articulated. For this it is necessary that there be a genuine and deep communication between the hearts and minds of men, communication and not the noise of slogans or the repetition of clichés.[29]

Such communication is necessary for the survival of mankind:

For faith cannot be preserved if reason goes under, and the Church cannot survive if man is destroyed: that is to say if his humanity is utterly debased and mechanized, while he himself remains on earth as the instrument of enormous and unidentified forces like those which press us inexorably to the brink of nuclear war.[30]

It was of utmost importance to Merton that humanity preserve those things which distinguish man from the beasts, and in his view, the poet has much to share in accomplishing that task.

A meeting of new Latin American poets in February 1964 was, in Merton's words, 'not a highly organized and well-financed international congress, but a spontaneous and inspired meeting of young poets from all over the hemisphere, most of whom could barely afford to be there. One, for instance, sold her piano to make the trip from Peru.'[31] In a 'Message to Poets' which was read at this meeting, Merton discussed what he considered the role of the poet in contemporary society. In speaking of the 'Spirit of Life' which brought the group together, he explained their solidarity as a group by saying:

The solidarity of poets is not planned and welded together with tactical convictions or matters of policy, since these are affairs of prejudice, cunning, and design. Whatever his failures, the poet is not a cunning man. His art depends on an ingrained innocence which he would lose in business, in politics, or in too organized a form of academic life. The hope that rests on calculation has lost its innocence. We are banding together to defend our innocence.

All innocence is a matter of belief. I do not speak now of organized agreement, but of interior personal conviction 'in the spirit'. These convictions are as strong and undeniable as life itself. They are rooted in fidelity to *life* rather than to artificial systems. The solidarity of poets is an elemental fact like the seasons, like the rain. It is something that cannot be organized, it can only happen.[32]

Such solidarity is not the same thing as collectivity, for 'true solidarity is destroyed by the political art of pitting one man against another and the commercial art of estimating all men at a price'.[33]

The poet, in his view, should try to remian outside 'their' categories and, like the monks, 'remain innocent and invisible to publicists and bureaucrats'.[34] The poet should be caught up 'in the light of everyday existence. Poetry is innocent of prediction because it is itself the fulfillment of all the momentous predictions hidden in everyday life.'[35] What then is the task of the poet? Merton sums it up:

> We are not persuaders. We are the children of the Unknown. We are the ministers of silence that is needed to cure all victims of absurdity who lie dying of a contrived joy. Let us then recognize ourselves for who we are: dervishes mad with secret therapeutic love which cannot be bought or sold, and which the politician fears more than violent revolution, for violence changes nothing. But love changes everything.[36]

In obedience to the Spirit of Life which calls men to be poets, 'we shall,' says Merton, 'harvest many new fruits for which the world hungers—fruits of hope that have never been seen before. With these fruits we shall calm the resentments and the rage of man.'[37] In these words to a group of Latin American poets, Merton has shown not only that the contemplative life has much to offer modern man, but that its fruits are essential for humankind's survival.

Writing in a Monastic Milieu

As a writer and as a member of an enclosed religious order, Merton found himself in a unique position. His monastic vows cut him off from many of the resources normally available to writers—extensive travel, a vigorous social and cultural life, numerous friends, and the stimulation of the academic community. By his vow of obedience to the abbot, he had to submit his works to the censors of the Order for permission to publish, and he was not able to reap any financial profits from his published works. Such a life, for most writers, would impose an unbearable hardship, and there is every indication that, in some ways, Merton found it quite difficult.

On the other hand, there are advantages to a writer in a

monastic milieu, particularly to a hermit: the freedom of economic security, the time for writing. The contemplative life was especially suited to one who thought a great deal about the issues of contemporary life, and there was a certain advantage to being a nonparticipating observer. Living at the hermitage, he was able to meditate, read, and write at his leisure. There was no one to disturb him, and he was, for the most part, free to do as he wished.

When Merton first entered the monastery he resolved to give up writing, but the abbot, recognizing his ability, ordered him to continue. While correcting the proofs for one of his earliest books of poetry, *Figures for an Apocalypse*, a disgusted Merton asked permission to stop writing poetry. 'Father Abbot,' he notes, 'gave me a guarded and partial permission to stop writing poetry "if it is a burden." But he wants me to go on "reaching souls". It seems I do not have permission to drop poetry altogether.'[38] On another occasion the abbot selected Merton, over his protests, to prepare a one-hundredth anniversary book for the monastery. Merton's only comment was: 'And so I offer my pride to be slain on this particular altar.'[39] Especially disturbed over some of his "very bad" books, he made certain that his feelings were known to as many people as possible. These were books written at the request of the abbot and Merton says: 'At that time I thought I was upset by the fact that Dom Frederic, who was then Abbot, wanted me to write a lot of books. Perhaps I was less upset than I thought. But in any case, I did have to write a lot of books, some of which were terrible.'[41]

A special problem arose in submitting articles to magazines, particularly to avant-garde journals of limited circulation. In fact Merton was discouraged from even reading such magazines and he remarked that one issue reached him probably because 'Father Abbot did not look at it too closely'.[42] Even the Abbot General warned him to be especially cautious concerning magazines:

> Dom Gabriel told me not to let myself get roped in to any magazines as a *'collaborateur,'* i.e., not to get my name on the mast-head as a staff worker and be slow to accept any magazine work. They are all 'commercial'. They ruin you. He told me not to write book reviews.[43]

Merton relates still another facet of the problem in the following incident: 'A magazine called *Tiger's Eye* wants to give me ninety-six dollars for a poem. I do not think Saint Benedict would want me to take that much. However, by a peculiar irony, I am not allowed to decide. I have a vow of poverty which prohibits one from *refusing* money.'[44] In time things at the monastery changed. Merton found that most of his work was appearing first in magazines and journals and only later in books. He found himself editing an avant-garde magazine of his own. *Monks Pond* contained essays, poetry, art, and criticism and appeared in only four issues, but he thoroughly enjoyed the experience of editing his own magazine and having it printed at the monastery.[45]

As long as Merton wrote on spiritual themes he encountered few difficulties from the censors of the Order, but when his writing took on a more worldly orientation problems began to arise.[46] Rice discusses them:

> He returned over and over again, once he had found his new direction in the 1960s, to these basic themes: war and peace, violence and nonviolence, and Buddhism. He began to run into opposition from the Trappist censors on a scale never before encountered. They stopped a very innocuous article on Pierre Teilhard de Chardin at the time when every Catholic publication was writing about him, and they constantly held up or castrated articles on peace, as if a monk had no business writing about peace....When he addressed an open letter to the American hierarchy on peace and war in 1965 it was ignored. Later he wrote to his own bishop in Louisville in a very warm yet demanding letter to ask for a firm, Christian statement on the same subject, and never received a reply. He was forced to publish a book of essays by different contributors anonymously, with himself listed merely as another contributor and not as editor because of this hostility on the part of his superiors. A book called *Peace in the Post-Christian Era*, which states in the clearest, most Catholic, moral, unambiguous and responsible terms the role of the Christian in a nuclear age, was stopped dead by the censors. Another book, a collection of essays on peace, was also stopped though some of the material had already appeared in censored form.[47]

He was able, however, to circulate numerous essays and even books in mimeographed form provided they were not published and were circulated only among a few carefully chosen friends.[48] In fairness to the Cistercian Order, one must point out that much of this previously censored material has been published, especially since Merton's death.[49]

Merton was not always happy with this situation, and his criticism of those who censored his work was often harsh. At the same time he never complained publicly, and whenever he circulated an unpublished work he was always careful to advise his friends against quoting any part of it. He remained convinced of his monastic vocation. He freely chose to remain under the authority of the Order even when his freedom as a writer was thereby placed under limitations. From a writer's point of view, this is difficult to understand, but we must remember that Merton was first of all a contemplative monk and, as the following words show, he was well aware that such problems could arise:

> Art and asceticism. The artist must be free, otherwise he will be dominated by his material instead of dominating it. Hence, art demands asceticism. Religious ascetics have something to learn from the natural asceticism of the artist: it is unselfconscious, organic, integrated in his art. It does not run the risk of becoming an end in itself. But the artist also has something to gain from religious asceticism. It not only raises him above his subject and his material but above his art itself. He can now control everything, even his art, which usually controls him.
>
> Asceticism may involve a total sacrifice of art.[50]

For Merton, the contemplative life involved a renunciation of one's self, and for him that included his abilities as a writer. He was not dominated by his writing as this was not an ultimate value for him.

While Merton himself came to terms with his unique situation, much of his reading public did not and this caused no end of problems. Merton commented on public speculations about his life and work in the meditation 'Day of a Stranger':

> I do not consider myself integrated in the war-making society in which I live, but the problem is that this society *does* consider *me* integrated in it. I notice that for nearly twenty years my society—or those in it who read my books—have decided upon an identity for me and insist that I continue to correspond perfectly to the idea of me which they found upon reading my first successful book. Yet the same people simultaneously prescribe for me a contrary identity. They demand that I remain forever the superficially pious, rather rigid and somewhat narrow-

minded young monk I was twenty years ago, and at the same time they continually circulate the rumor that I have left my monastery. What has actually happened is that I have been simply where I am developing in my own way without consulting the public about it since it is none of the public's business.[51]

He goes on: 'the freedom of the artist is to be sought precisely in the choice of his *work* and not in the choice of the role as "artist" which society asks him to play, for reasons that will always remain very mysterious.'[52]

Merton was especially disturbed by speculations on his life as a hermit, particularly on his new-found freedom from the routine of monastery life. His life as a hermit gave him more time to write, but he was not about to be classified as some kind of special person with graces and gifts that were not available to others.

> In an age where there is much talk about 'being myself' I reserve to myself the right to forget about being myself, since in any case there is very little chance of my being anybody else. Rather it seems to me that when one is too intent on 'being himself' he runs the risk of impersonating a shadow.
>
> Yet I cannot pride myself on special freedom, simply because I am living in the woods like Thoreau instead of living in the desert like St John the Baptist. All I can answer is that I am not living 'like anybody.' Or 'unlike anybody.' We all live somehow or other, and that's that. It is a compelling necessity for me to be free to embrace the necessity of my own nature.[53]

Merton was a monk, a writer, a social prophet, and in his later years a hermit. He had difficulties in fitting into all these sometimes contradictory roles, and his life style was often paradoxical. Yet he insisted upon one thing: to be himself. And it is perhaps at this point that he was most prophetic, for he stood for the integrity of the person amid the dehumanizing forces of the twentieth century.

The Dangers of Technology

Merton was strongly critical of anything that might in any way limit the freedom and development of the human person—

the limitations from war, racism, totalitarianism, and censorship. There was yet another source of danger that was often overlooked: the rise and development of technology. Merton considered this one of the most important issues of our time, because technology has brought about a virtual revolution in society, a revolution which is continuing as technology influences our lives more and more.

Merton was not opposed to technology in and of itself. He saw it as neutral, a useful means of improving human life. He writes: 'There is nothing wrong with technology in itself. It could indeed serve to deepen and perfect the quality of men's existence and in some ways it *has* done this.'[54] In the days before he had electricity in the hermitage, Merton was cooking on his Coleman stove and musing about the place of technology in his life:

> Technology is here, even in the cabin. True, the utility line is not here yet, and so G.E. is not here yet either. When the utilities and G.E. enter my cabin arm in arm it will be nobody's fault but my own. I admit it. I am not kidding anybody, even myself. I will suffer their bluff and patronizing complacencies in silence. I will let them think they know what I am doing here.[55]

There was no doubt, even in Merton's mind, that an electric stove was better than a portable gas camping stove and electric lights easier to work by than a candle or gasmantle lantern. Indeed, he could not get along without books, his typewriter, eyeglasses, and the medical technology of his doctor in Louisville.

The problem arises when technology becomes the arena of man's sinfulness and folly. 'The real root-sin of modern man,' says Merton, 'is that, in ignoring and condemning *being*, and especially his own being, he has made his *existence* a disease and an affliction.'[56] This can be done no place as easily as in the realm of technology. In times past an evil king might send forth his armies to kill with the sword, but today a button is pushed and missiles rain destruction on entire cities. Technology has vastly increased man's capacity for both good and evil.

According to Merton, an even more serious danger is that man is continually 'proclaiming at every turn that he stands on frontiers of new abundance and permanent bliss. This ambiguity and arbitrariness appear most clearly in technology.'[57] Merton emphasizes this by a quotation from Lewis Mumford: 'Too many thought not only that mechanical progress would be a positive aid to human improvement, which is true, *but that mechanical progress is the equivalent of human progress*, which turns out to be sheer nonsense.'[58] The real danger of technology is that it can become a god of illusion, which when worshipped, turns out to be a vicious demon.

Merton was of the opinion that 'the central problem of the modern world is the complete emancipation and autonomy of the technological mind at a time when unlimited possibilities lie open to it and all the resources seem to be at hand.'[59] Technology has, in his view, become accountable to no one but itself. It has created its own ethics of expediency and efficiency so that 'what *can* be done efficiently *must* be done in the most efficient way.'[60] The result is a totalitarianism of technology over man.

> Actually, technology represents the rule of *quantity,* not the rule of reason (quality=value=relation of means to authentic human ends). It is by means of technology that man the person, the subject of qualified and perfectible freedom, becomes *quantified*, that is, becomes a part of a mass—mass man—whose only function is to enter anonymously into the process of production and consumption. He becomes on the one side an implement, a 'hand,' or better, a 'bio-physical link' between machines: on the other side he is a mouth, a digestive system and an anus, something *through which* pass the products of his technological world, leaving a transient and meaningless sense of enjoyment.[61]

The end of technological totalitarianism is the destruction of man.[62]

Technology takes on a demonic dimension when its ethics of efficiency are applied to modern warfare. 'For technology,' cautions Merton, 'what matters is efficiency first. What to the moralist is a crime against humanity is to the strategist simply the most efficient solution to a technical problem.'[63] Deep moral problems arise,[64] particularly crucial in the technology of war:

> Our sudden, unbalanced top-heavy rush into technological mastery has left us without the spiritual means to face our problems. Or rather, we have thrown the spiritual means away. Even the religious people have not been aware of the situation, not become aware until perhaps too late. And here we all stand as prisoners of our own scientific virtuosity, ruled by immense power that we ought to be

ruling and cannot. Our weapons dictate what we are to do. They force us into corners. They give us our living, they sustain our economy, they bolster up our politicians, they sell our mass media, in short we live by them. But if they continue to rule us we will also most surely die by them. [65]

A morality is needed able to come to grips with our technology, for, in Merton's words, 'technology can elevate and improve man's life only on one condition: that it remains subservient to his *real* interests; that it respects his true being; that it remembers that the origin and goal of all being is in God.' [66] James Douglass, quoting from Jacques Ellul, points out that 'haste is also one of the foremost characteristics of technique'. [67] Modern man is in such a hurry that he has lost sight of his real interests.

Technology has invaded virtually every aspect of human existence so that prayer—one's deepest relationship to God— has been reduced to a mere technique. This trend could be seen many years ago in the Jesuit formulas for prayer which set up all the right conditions to obtain the desired result. Technology has improved on this, says Merton, for now 'this concept has by now evolved into the simple pharmacology of contemplation: you take the right pill and you turn on.' [68] It is ironic, in Merton's opinion, that 'within this perspective of the technicizing of the spirit, "the pharmacology of contemplation" can in fact be seen as the potential revolutionary's final surrender to the rule of the technological society.' [69] Merton, of course, strongly opposed this kind of technological spirituality since, in his words, 'man cannot assent to a spiritual message as long as his mind and heart are enslaved by automation'. [70]

At the crux of the problem is not technology, but man. Man's mind and man's heart determine whether or not he will become a slave to technology, and any morality suited to the contemporary technological world must come from man for 'the materials for a synthesis of science and wisdom are not lacking'. [71] Merton believed quite strongly that 'technology is not in itself opposed to spirituality and to religion.' [72] He explains:

> Technology was made for man, and not man for technology. In losing touch with being and thus with God, we have fallen into a senseless idolatry of production and consumption for their own sakes. We have renounced the act of being and plunged ourself into *process* for its own sake. We no longer know how to live, and because we

cannot accept life in its reality life ceases to be a joy and becomes an affliction. And we even go so far as to blame God for it! The evil in the world is all our own making, and it proceeds entirely from our ruthless, senseless, wasteful, destructive, and suicidal neglect of our own being. [73]

Man needs a respect for the world that rests on an intuition of the act of being and a grateful, contemplative, and christian sense of being.

Unfortunately, man perceives being not as it really is, but rather as he would like it to be. This is a special problem when man, by means of technology, can partially create the world that he already idolizes in his dreams. Merton explains this in terms of man's false image of himself:

In my opinion the root of our trouble is that our habits of thought and the drives that proceed from them are basically idolatrous and mythical. We are all the more inclined to idolatry because we imagine that we are of all generations the most enlightened, the most objective, the most scientific, the most progressive and the most humane. This, in fact, is an "image" of ourselves—an image which is false and is also the object of a cult. We worship ourselves in this image. The nature of our acts is determined in large measure by the demands of our worship. [74]

Merton did not provide any easy answers to the problem of man's false image of himself, but he did say that 'the root of the answer is the love of Christ and the ground is the sinful heart of sinful man as he really is—as we really are, you, and I, and our disconcerting neighbor.' [75]

Marshall McLuhan has put forth the idea that the media are really extensions of man. It seems as if the same can also be said of technology, for technology enables man to extend himself, to further his influence, and to exercise control over his environment. The question that Merton raised is whether or not sinful man can use technology in any way other than sinfully, for technology is only an extension of man, and the actions of man are an extension of the heart.

Ecology

Man's technological actions often disrupt the balance of nature. A disturbed Merton went back to the church Fathers and their interpretation of the fall of man as told in Genesis. According to one theory sin is a perversion of man's active instincts so that 'the world is then exploited for the glory of man, not for the glory of God. Man's power becomes an end in itself. Things are not merely used, they are wasted, destroyed. Men are no longer workers and "creators" but tools of production, instruments for profit.'[76] Such a theological perspective has great significance for an industrial society in which work becomes drudgery whose only goal is a wage. Says Merton: 'In such a disordered social setting work loses this basically healthy character, and becomes frustrating or irrational.'[77]

Another, more recent, complication stems from the American frontier mentality, to which the natural environment is a thing, not to be respected and enjoyed, but to be used.

> The pioneer, the frontier culture hero, is a product of the wilderness, but at the same time he is a destroyer of the wilderness. His success as pioneer depends on his ability to fight the wilderness and win. Victory consists in reducing the wilderness to something else, a farm, a village, a road, a canal, a railway, a mine, a factory, a city—and finally an urban nation.[78]

According to Merton, this attitude to living things is the same:

> There are some men for whom a tree has no reality until they think of cutting it down, for whom an animal has no value until it enters the slaughterhouse, men who never look at anything until they decide to abuse it and who never even notice what they do not want to destroy. These men can hardly know the silence of love: for their love is the absorption of another person's silence into their own noise.[79]

It was Merton's observation that 'man's unhappiness seems to have grown in proportion to his power over the exterior world.'[80] He attributed the reason for this to the 'desecration and de-sacralization of the modern world' which has been brought about by the advent of technology.[81] Unlike the ancient Indians, who lived in harmony with nature and knew where they fit in the ecological balance, modern man has almost no knowledge whatsoever of the world of nature. What man needs is an ecological conscience or awareness, which Merton explains:

> The ecological conscience is centered in an awareness of *man's true place as a dependent member of the biotic community*. Man must become fully aware of his *dependence* on a balance which he is not only free to destroy but which he has already begun to destroy. He must recognize his obligations toward the other members of that vital community. And incidentally, since he tends to destroy nature in his frantic efforts to exterminate other members of his own species, it would not hurt if he had a little more respect for human life too. The respect for life, the affirmation of *all* life, is basic to the ecological conscience. In the words of Albert Schweitzer: *A man is ethical only when life as such is sacred to him, that of plants and animals as well as that of his fellow man.*'[82]

Man's importance in the ecological balance took on a theological dimension for Merton. As a contemplative he placed a great premium on silence and pleaded for solitude in which we can communicate with God alone, 'without words, without discursive thoughts, in the silence of our whole being'.[83] The noise of the modern world only defiles the silence of the natural world; contemplation becomes more difficult. Merton felt man needs to be alone to know the value of aloneness:

> A community that seeks to invade or destroy the spiritual solitude of the individuals who comprise it is condemning itself to death by spiritual asphyxiation....
> Solitude is so necessary both for society and for the individual that when society fails to provide sufficient solitude to develop the inner life of the persons who compose it, they rebel and seek false solitudes.[84]

The solitude provided in nature is one of man's most pressing needs and precious possessions.

Drawing from the thought of Henry David Thoreau, Merton stated: 'He warned that some wilderness must be preserved. If it were not, man would destroy himself in destroying nature.'[85] He comments:

> Thoreau had enough sense to realize that civilization was

necessary and right. But *an element of wilderness was necessary as a component in civilized life itself.* The American still had a priceless advantage over the European, one that would enable him to develop a greater and better civilization, if he did not miss his chance. He could, in Thoreau's words, 'combine the hardiness of the Indian with the intellectualness of civilized man.' For that reason, said Thoreau, 'I would not have every part of man cultivated.' To try to subject everything in man to rational and conscious control would be to warp, diminish and barbarize him. So too, the reduction of all nature to use for profit would end in the dehumanization of man. The passion and savagery that the Puritan had projected on to nature in order to justify his hatred of it and his fanatical combat against it, turned out to be within man himself.[86]

Thoreau based his thinking on the Chinese cosmology of the Yin and the Yang and 'preached an inner integration and proportion between conscious and unconscious that anticipated the discoveries of Freud and Jung'.[87] He recognized, as did Merton, that 'civilized man needed an element of irrationality, spontaneity, impulse, nature to balance his rationalism, his discipline, his controlled endeavor.'[88]

Merton understood this need in man very well. Speaking of the birds near his hermitage he wrote: 'I share this particular place with them: we form an ecological balance. This harmony gives the idea of "place" a new configuration. There is a mental ecology, too, a living balance of spirits in this corner of the woods.'[89] He summed up in the words of Aldo Leopold, an early American conservationist: *A THING IS RIGHT WHEN IT TENDS TO PRESERVE THE INTEGRITY, STABILITY AND BEAUTY OF THE BIOTIC COMMUNITY. IT IS WRONG WHEN IT TENDS OTHERWISE.'* [90]

Ethics in a Business Society

A discussion of technology and ecological concerns shows the relevance to our times of the biblical statement, 'the love of money is the root of all evil' (1 Timothy 6:10). A society dominated by the making and spending of money increasingly sees the worth of a person in terms of his wealth. Merton comments on this:

Leon Bloy remarked on this characteristic of our society:

A businessman will say of someone that he *knows* him if he *knows he has money.*

To say of someone 'I do not know him' means, in business, 'I am not so sure that he will pay.'

But if he has money, and proves it, then 'I know him.' So we have to get money and keep spending it in order to be known, recognized as human. Otherwise we are excommunicated. [91]

This tendency to see persons in terms of their wealth—or ability to produce wealth—is one of the most crucial social problems of our time, and it lies at the root of much of our racism and discrimination against the poor and the elderly. [92] Merton expands:

It seems to me that we have little genuine interest in human liberty and in the human person. What we are interested in, on the contrary, is the unlimited freedom of the corporation. When we call ourselves the 'free world' we mean first of all the world in which *business* is free. And the freedom of the person comes only after that, because in our eyes, the freedom of the person is dependent on money. That is to say, without money, freedom has no meaning. And therefore the most basic freedom of all is the freedom to make money. If you have nothing to buy or sell, freedom is, in your case, irrelevant. In other words, what we are really interested in is not *persons*, but *profits*. [93]

The rights of blacks, who are poor and cannot spend money and are also uneducated and therefore unable to make money, have been considered unimportant. Persons who are not productive members of the business community are considered nonpersons.

When the blacks spoke of their rights in terms of freedom and civil rights they were largely ignored by the white community. They were taken seriously when their demonstrations and boycotts hurt business. *'It was,'* says Merton, *'only when money became involved that the Negro demonstrations finally impressed themselves upon the American mind as being real.'* [94] Immediately, blacks had to be taken into account, and thereby the whites discovered that some real blacks did have money. 'When the Negro claims he wants to take his full part in American society as a *person*, we retort: "you are already playing your part as a person: Negroes over the years," we now declare, "have had a rapid rise in income."'[95]

Placing of profits above persons has also had its effect upon the foreign policy of the United States. The American economy is largely based upon what has been called the military-industrial complex. We actually make our money from producing weapons of death. Many justify this on the basis of destroying a system which is hostile to us—communism—a system which would prevent us from doing business as usual.[96] American business methods have had a seriously detrimental effect upon our relations with Latin America, as Merton wrote in a letter to the Nicaraguan poet Pablo Antonio Cuadra: 'Money has totally corrupted the brotherhood that should have united the people of America.'[97] Americans took an interest not in the people of Latin America, but in the profits that could be gleaned from the natural resources of the area. Even the anti-communism of the United States is movtivated by a desire to protect Latin American business interests.

Of special concern to Merton were those aspects of American business that touched him personally. As a resident of Kentucky he was very much opposed to the strip mining which turned vast areas of the state into a wasteland. Through his frequent trips to the doctor in Louisville he became aware of the high cost of medical care, and he showed special concern about the high cost of drugs. He accused drug companies of fixing the prices with no regard for those who could not afford to pay, and complained that people must either pay the high prices or die.[98]

Merton's observations of American business included illegitimate enterprises such as trafficking in illicit drugs, gambling, violation of liquor laws, and prostitution. Such activities thrive on a total disregard for the human person. But what really disturbed him was the fact that more money could often be made in illegitimate busines than in legitimate business, and as a consequence crime was flourishing.[99]

By the various forms of mass media, American business sells its products. Merton had only scathing denunciation for the media. He felt they provided the public false information that could lead to violence and even war.[100] He was convinced that 'one of the great problems of our time *is the lack of reliable and serious information and of sound perspective* in political and social affairs.'[101] If the media should choose to distort the facts, the average American would have no way of recognizing the distortion since the media provide many people's only access to

information. He was of the opinion that most people rely on the
mass media far more than is either necessary or healthy, and he
appealed for a breaking free from the influence of the media:

> That people may learn to open their eyes and *see*, instead
> of thinking that they see, looking only at what they have
> been told to see, or at what they imagine they ought to
> see. This may sound too simple, but the problem is
> enormous. We are a generation of men who have eyes and
> see not, ears and hear not, because we have let ourselves
> be so completely and abjectly conditioned by words,
> slogans and official pronouncements. [102]

The political implications of such blindness are both obvious and
frightening, but there are important business implications to the
problem as well.

In his criticism of the media Merton especially singled out
modern advertising, for it is there that the desire for profit is
most blatant. He says:

> There are various ways of being happy, and every man
> has the capacity to make his life what it needs to be for
> him to have a reasonable amount of peace in it. Why then
> do we persecute ourselves with illusory demands, never
> content until we feel we have conformed to some standard
> of happiness that is not good for us only, but for
> *everyone?* Why can we not be content with the secret gift
> of the world? Why do we insist, rather, on a happiness
> that is approved by the magazines and TV? Perhaps it is
> because we do not believe in a happiness that is given to
> us for nothing. We do not think we can be happy with a
> happiness that has no price tag on it. [103]

This kind of consumption never satisfies; it is like the con-
tinuous round of unsatisfied desires spoken of by St Gregory of
Nyssa. In the process of buying happiness one gains the whole
world but loses one's soul; the person becomes an empty shell
continually seeking what it can never buy.

In our desire for profit and material things we become
alienated not only from ourselves and from other persons, but
from God. The profit motive so dominates us that we are unable
to see others as persons, and we become so wrapped up in
things that we lose touch with our own spiritual depths. For
Merton, this is the real tragedy behind the materialism of
contemporary American society. We not only destroy others, we

destroy ourselves. We become mere automatons in the wheels of business, and as a consequence we become spiritually dead. Says Merton: 'It is not the life of the spirit that is real to us, but the vitality of the *market*. Spiritual values are to us, in actual fact, meaningless unless they can be reduced to terms of buying and selling.'[104] Indeed, the contemporary Church finds itself caught up in business and monetary concerns. And yet, says Merton: 'God gives us the freedom to make our own lives within the situation which is the gift of His love to us, and by means of the power His love grants to us....We are quite capable of being happy in the life He has provided for us, in which we can contentedly make our own way, helped by His grace.'[105] In effect, the profit motive comes between man and the greatest gift of all, God's grace.

The Alienation of Modern Man

Writing in *The Cistercian Spirit: A Symposium in Memory of Thomas Merton,* Basil De Pinto comments on one of Merton's chief interests, alienation:

> In the last decade of his life he openly expressed his increasing concern over the spiritual bankruptcy of modern man, whom he saw as the slave of a bastard society spawned on political unscrupulosity and technological overkill and producing in its turn the fruits of atomic war and racial hatred. He unerringly perceived and tirelessly denounced hypocrisy and demagoguery whether in religious or civil life. And yet his relentless realism never turned bitter and he retained a basic optimism in the power of man to be converted and live: the result of a vision that was radically biblical, and monastic in focus, but expressed in human terms that touched not only the heart of the matter he was dealing with, but the heart of his reader or listener as well, and caused thousands who never knew him personally to admire and look up to him.[106]

Merton was well aware of the complexity of the problem, which must be resolved before man can deal constructively with such other issues as war, racism, and technology. Yet at the same time he understood that these problems contributed to modern man's increasing sense of alienation.

Merton diagnosed the problem of alienation in words both

forceful and filled with insight, and he leaves little doubt as to its seriousness. As people in an age of science and technology, he asserted, we 'live precipitated outside ourselves at every moment, interiorly empty, spiritually lost, seeking at all costs to forget our own emptiness, and ready to alienate ourselves completely in the name of any "cause" that comes along.' [107] Alienation divides man against man and nation against nation so that 'the problems of nations are the problems of mentally deranged people, but magnified a thousand times because they have the full, straight-faced approbation of a schizoid society, schizoid national structures, schizoid military and business complexes, and, need one add, schizoid religious sects.' [108] What is more, 'man's drive to destroy, to kill, or simply to dominate and to oppress comes from the metaphysical void he experiences when he finds himself a stranger in his own universe.' [109]

Man's attempts to save himself from alienation compound the problem, all too often alienating him even more than before, for western culture itself has lost its own soul. [110] Thus Merton says: 'The alienated man is one who, though "adjusted" to society, is alienated *from himself.*' [111]

> How does this work? The collectivity informs and shapes your will to happiness ('have fun') by presenting you with irresistible images of yourself as you would like to be: having *fun that is so perfectly credible that it allows no interference of conscious doubt.* In theory such a good time can be so convincing that you are no longer aware of even a remote possibility that it might change into something less satisfying. In practice, expensive fun always admits of a doubt, which blossoms out into another full-blown need, which then calls for still more credible and costly refinement of satisfaction, which again fails you. The end of the cycle is despair....' [112]
>
> [The] inner life of the mass man, alienated and leveled in the existential sense, is a dull, collective routine of popular fantasies maintained in existence by the collective dream that goes on, without interruption, in the mass media. [113]

Merton spoke out forcefully against mass man in his poetic *Cables to the Ace.* [114] James York Glimm analyzes this work:

> Unlike Marshall McLuhan who revels in the vision of man united through mass-media communications, Merton sees

man caught in the web of electrical cables which manipulate him morally and destroy him spiritually. Modern man allows the 'news' to stand between him and his world; soon the news becomes his world. The greater his dependence upon the media the easier he is to manipulate and eventually to control. Merton saw the political implications: through mass-media the state is able to impose mass values upon society and make, in Merton's phrase, 'mass men' out of individual human beings. What troubled Merton most was that he saw man yielding to this imposition without even being aware of it. *Cables* is a warning.[115]

Again Merton's understanding of man centered on the person. Once the person becomes part of the mass man, he cannot hope to end his alienation, for its end can come only from within, never from external society.

Merton saw the freedom of the individual to decide for himself as a spiritual value, whose roots are ultimately religious.[116] One must look inward—into the depths of being—in order to truly find oneself. This is not a hopeless task, Merton believed, for 'we are not utterly condemned to think our way into an impasse from which the only issue is destructive violence. Human and reasonable solutions are still open to us. But they depend on our climate of thought, that is to say, on our ability to hope in peaceful solutions.'[117] Hopelessness is itself a form of delusion.

The danger of being deluded into believing that there is really no external threat, that if we turn inward everything will turn out all right in the end also threatens us. 'We must not strive to maintain a climate of optimism by the mere *suppression* of tragic realities.' Merton wrote, 'Christian optimism lies in a hope of victory that transcends all tragedy: a victory in which we *pass beyond* tragedy to glory with Christ crucified and risen.'[118] The solution to alienation rests upon a realistic view of life and of ourselves.

To overcome his alienation man must have an awareness of God's action in Christ, and this implies, says Merton, 'some awareness of history, not in the abstract, academic sense, but in the concrete: an awarenss of the crisis of our time in relation to Christ's plan for the salvation of man.'[119] In God we see ourselves in relation to him and to his task in the world. Thus Merton says: 'A Christian's consciousness is therefore a special kind of historical consciousness: an awareness of *kairos* (the providential time of crisis and judgement) and of *choice*.'[120] 'In this world from which he is alienated, man can come to find himself and recover his right relation to the world and to God, by the work which God has given him to do.'[121]

Our alienation does nothing to eliminate the presence of God in the world. We can do nothing to change the mystery of the Incarnation in itself, but 'we are able to decide whether we ourselves, and that portion of the world which is ours, shall become *aware* of His presence, consecrated by it, and transfigured in its light.'[122] We must choose:

> We have the choice of two identities: the external mask which seems to be real and which lives by a shadowy autonomy for the brief moment of earthly existence, and the hidden, inner person who seems to us to be nothing, but who can give himself eternally to the truth in whom he subsists. It is this inner self that is taken up into the mystery of Christ, by His love, by the Holy Spirit, so that in secret we live 'in Christ'.[123]

In the final pages of *Conjectures of a Guilty Bystander*, Merton discussed God's wrath in terms of saving and purifying power. 'True wrath' he says, 'is ontological. It reaches into the very depths of being.'[124] The wrath of God, mediated through Jesus Christ, can free us from false illusions which serve to alienate us from each other, from ourselves, and from God. Perhaps no better words can be found to describe this process than those Merton quotes from Karl Barth: 'To be a man, means to be situated in God's presence as Jesus is....'[125]

1.   See James York Glimm, 'Exile Ends in Satire: Thomas Merton's Cables to the Ace,' *Cithara* 11 (November, 1971) 31-40.

2.   Burke, 'The Man of Letters,' p. 279. See also *Selected Poems of Thomas Merton*, p. 110.

3.   *Selected Poems of Thomas Merton*, p. 110.

4.   Ibid., pp. 110-11.

5.   *Disputed Questions*, p. 34. Merton discusses Pasternak's Christian witness on pp. 20-22.

6.   Boris Pasternak, *Doctor Zhivago*, trans. Max Hayward and Manya Harari (New York: Pantheon, 1958) p. 10.

7.   Baker, *Thomas Merton Social Critic*, pp. 68-69.

8.   *Disputed Questions*, p. 60.

9.   Ibid., p. 35.

10.   Ibid. For a similar perspective see Alexander Solzhenitsyn, et al., *From Under the Rubble*, trans. under direction of Michael Scammell (Boston: Little, Brown, 1975). The views of Solzhenitsyn are similar to those expressed by Pasternak and Merton, and like Pasternak, Solzhenitsyn was unable to leave Russia to receive his Nobel Prize until his expulsion in 1974.

11.   *Disputed Questions*, p. 19.

12.   Ibid., p. 96.

13.   Ibid., p. 60.

14.   Ibid., pp. 60-61.

15.   Most of these translations with commentaries are found in Merton, *Emblems of a Season of Fury*, pp. 93-149. A listing of other translations can be found in Burke, 'The Man of Letters,' pp. 280-81.

16.   *Emblems of a Season of Fury*, p. 115.

17.   Ibid., p. 127.

18.   Ibid., pp. 127-28.

19.   *The Geography of Lograire* (New York: New Directions, 1969).

20.   *Emblems of a Season of Fury*, p. 136.

21.   Ibid., p. 93.

22.   Ibid., pp. 94-95.

23. See Burke, 'The Man of Letters', p. 283.

24. Ibid., p. 281.

25. *Conjectures of a Guilty Bystander*, p. 4. An informative account of contemporary Brazilian culture may be found in Gilberto Freyre, *New World in the Tropics: The Culture of Modern Brazil* (New York: Vintage, 1963).

26. *Conjectures of a Guilty Bystander*, pp. 4-5.

27. Ibid., p. 5.

28. *Seeds of Destruction*, p. 242.

29. Ibid., pp. 242-43.

30. Ibid., p. 243.

31. *Raids on the Unspeakable*, p. 155.

32. Ibid., p. 156.

33. Ibid., p. 157.

34. Ibid., p. 158.

35. Ibid., p. 159.

36. Ibid., p. 160.

37. Ibid.

38. *The Sign of Jonas*, p. 79.

39. Ibid., p. 80.

40. 'First and Last Thoughts: An Author's Preface' in *A Thomas Merton Reader*, ed. McDonnell, p. ix.

41. *The Sign of Jonas*, pp. 23-24.

42. Ibid., p. 83.

43. Ibid., p. 120.

44. Ibid., p. 56.

45. *Monks Pond*, edited by Merton and printed at Gethsemani during 1968, came out in four issues: spring, summer, fall and winter. As well as Merton's poetry each issue included photography, poetry, criticism, essays, and excerpts from diaries and journals. The magazine was distributed free of charge to all who were interested, and anyone was invited to submit manuscripts for possible publication. *Monks Pond* was, by Merton's own design, an experimental publication of which only four issues were planned, and at the end of the year publication ceased.

46.   Merton never wrote of the problems between the censors of the Order and himself. He did, however, speak of them in some of his private, unpublished letters.

47.   Edward Rice, *The Man in the Sycamore Tree*, pp. 81, 86.

48.   Included among these mimeographed unpublished works are *Peace in the Post-Christian Era, Cold War Letters,* and numerous essays and notes bound together in a number of folios under the title *Collected Essays.*

49.   The most important sections of *Peace in the Post-Christian Era* have since been published in *Thomas Merton on Peace*, pp. 20-62 and in *Seeds of Destruction*, pp. 93-183. A selection of the *Cold War Letters* appears in Merton's *Seeds of Destruction*, pp. 237-328. The essays, often in several different forms, have appeared and are now appearing in various journals and will eventually be collected and included in future books. Work on this is presently being carried out by the Merton Legacy Trust.

50.   *The Sign of Jonas*, p. 56.

51.   *Raids on the Unspeakable*, p. 172.

52.   Ibid., p. 173.

53.   *The True Solitude: Selections from the Writings of Thomas Merton,* ed. Dean Walley (Kansas City, MO.: Hallmark, 1969) pp. 48-49.

54.   *Conjectures of a Guilty Bystander*, p. 201.

55.   *Raids on the Unspeakable*, p. 13. When the utility company sent its first bill Merton noted that the hermitage had been classified as a 'lodge'.

56.   *Conjectures of a Guilty Bystander*, p. 201.

57.   Ibid.

58.   Ibid., p. 202.

59.   Ibid., p. 62. Merton wrote this in the 1960s.

60.   Ibid., p. 63.

61.   Ibid., p. 64.

62.   Ibid. On the same page he goes on to say: 'If technology remained in the service of what is higher than itself—reason, man, God—it might indeed fulfill some of the functions that are now mythically attributed to it. But becoming autonomous, existing only for itself, it imposes upon man its own irrational demands, and threatens to destroy him. Let us hope it is not too late for man to regain control.' For two opposing solutions to this problem see C.S. Lewis, *The Abolition of Man* (New York: Macmillan, 1957) and B.F. Skinner, *Beyond Freedom and Dignity* (New York: Knopf, 1971).

63.   *Redeeming the Time*, p. 89.

64.   Birth control, abortion, and automation are only the beginning of a host of awesome moral problems looming on the horizon. For an enlightening discussion of some of these problems see Alvin Toffler, *Future Shock* (New York: Random House, 1970).

65.   *Seeds of Destruction*, p. 265.

66.   *Conjectures of a Guilty Bystander*, p. 230.

67.   James W. Douglass, *Resistance and Contemplation: The Way of Liberation* (Garden City: Doubleday, 1972), pp. 125-26.

68.   *Contemplation in a World of Action*, p. 102.

69.   Douglass, *Resistance and Contemplation*, p. 121.

70.   *Thoughts in Solitude*, p. 14.

71.   *Gandhi on Non-Violence   Selected Texts from Mohandas K. Gandhi's 'Non-Violence in Peace and War'* (New York: New Directions, 1965), p. 3.

72.   *Conjectures of a Guilty Bystander*, p. 15.

73.   Ibid., p. 202.

74.   *Faith and Violence*, p. 154.

75.   Ibid., p. 164.

76.   *The New Man*, pp. 41-42.

77.   *Life and Holiness*, p. 124.

78.   'The Wild Places,' *The Catholic Worker* 34 No. 5 (June 1969) 4.

79.   *No Man is an Island*, pp. 192-93.

80.   *Disputed Questions*, p. 81.

81.   *Emblems of a Season of Fury*, p. 83.

82.   'The Wild Places,' p. 6.

83.   *No Man is an Island*, p. 190.

84.   Ibid., p. 185.

85.   'The Wild Places,' p. 4.

86.   Ibid.

87.   Ibid.

88.   Ibid.

89.   *The True Solitude*, p. 49.

90.   'The Wild Places,' p. 6.

91.   *Conjectures of a Guilty Bystander*, pp. 84-85.

92.   This is especially true of the treatment of the elderly in America. Shunted off to rest homes where they wait to die, they are unwanted because they have neither the money to buy goods nor the health to manufacture them.

93.   *Seeds of Destruction*, pp. 22-23.

94.   Ibid., p. 24.

95.   Ibid.

96.   See ibid., pp. 15-16, for a discussion of this conflict between the communist and the capitalist systems.

97.   *Emblems of a Season of Fury*, p. 85.

98.   Merton frequently spoke in his conferences at Gethsemani of this one area of social concern with which he had direct experience.

99.   *Faith and Violence*, pp. 3-8.

100.   See *Seeds of Destruction*, pp. 104-10.

101.   *Life and Holiness*, p. 143.

102.   *Disputed Questions*, pp. 122-23.

103.   *Conjectures of a Guilty Bystander*, p. 84.

104.   *Seeds of Destruction*, p. 24.

105.   *Conjectures of a Guilty Bystander*, p. 84.

106.   Basil De Pinto, 'Introduction' in Pennington, ed., *The Cistercian Spirit*, p. viii.

107.   *Selected Poems of Thomas Merton*, p. 109.

108.   *Gandhi on Non-Violence*, p. 3.

109.   *Albert Camus' The Plague*, Religious Dimensions in Literature, gen. ed. Lee A. Belford (New York: Seabury, 1968) p. 4.

110.   See *Gandhi on Non-Violence*, pp. 1-2. In a footnote on p. 77 Merton cites Laurens Van Der Post's *The Dark Eye of Africa* 'with its thesis that the white man's spiritual rejection and contempt for the African is the result of his rejection of what is deepest and most vital in himself. Having "lost his own soul," the materialist and cunning exploiter of the colonies destroyed the soul of the native.'

111. *Mystics and Zen Masters*, p. 268.

112. *Raids on the Unspeakable*, p. 16.

113. *Mystics and Zen Masters*, p. 268.

114. *Cables to the Ace: Or Familiar Liturgies of Misunderstanding.* Not one of Merton's more popular works, this has not had the audience it deserves.

115. Glimm, 'Exile Ends in Satire', p. 31.

116. *Raids on the Unspeakable*, p. 167.

117. *Seeds of Destruction*, p. 102.

118. *Seasons of Celebration*, p. 88.

119. 'The Historical Consciousness,' *Contemplative Review* 1 (May 1968) 2.

120. Ibid.

121. *Seasons of Celebration*, p. 162.

122. *New Seeds of Contemplation*, p. 229.

123. Ibid.

124. *Conjectures of a Guilty Bystander*, p. 318.

125. Ibid., p. 317.

VII

CONTEMPLATION IN A WORLD OF ACTION

The Impossibility of an Either/Or

MERTON entered the Abbey of Gethsemani expecting to leave forever the cares and attractions of the everyday world. As his train neared Louisville he thought to himself: 'I was free. I had recovered my liberty. I belonged to God, not to myself: and to belong to Him is to be free, free of all the anxieties and worries and sorrows that belong to this earth, and the love of the things that are in it.'[1] No longer did he have to worry about war and the aimlessness of life, for 'the only thing that mattered was the fact of the sacrifice, the essential dedication of one's self, one's will. The rest was only accidental.'[2]

Merton found he had no desire to return to the outside world.[3] Before long, however, he found certain similarities between life outside and life inside monastery walls:

> Now I saw the monastery from within, from the church floor, so to speak, not from the visitor's gallery. I saw it from the novitiate wing, not from the shiny and well-heated Guest House. No I was face to face with monks that belonged not to some dream, not to some medieval novel, but to cold and inescapable reality. The community which I had seen functioning as a unity, in all the power of that impressive and formal liturgical anonymity which clothes a body of men obscurely in the very personality of Christ Himself, now appeared to me broken up into its constituent parts, and all the details, good and bad, pleasant and unpleasant, were there for me to observe at close range.
> By this time God had given me enough sense to realize at least obscurely that this is one of the most important aspects of any religious vocation: the first and most

elementary test of one's call to the religious life...is the willingness to accept life in a community in which everybody is more or less imperfect.

The imperfections are much smaller and more trivial than the defects and vices of people outside in the world: and yet somehow you tend to notice them more and feel them more, because they tend to be so greatly magnified by the responsibilities and ideals of the religious state, through which you cannot help looking at them.[4]

Although thoroughly convinced of his monastic vocation, Merton was somewhat taken aback by the actions of many of his fellow monks. He found that outward appearances could often be deceiving: 'It can be said, as a general rule, that the greatest saints are seldom the ones whose piety is most evident in their expression when they are kneeling at prayer, and the holiest men in a monastery are almost never the ones who get that exalted look, on feast days, in the choir.'[5] Indeed, 'The people who gaze at Our Lady's statue with glistening eyes are very often the ones with the worst tempers.'[6] There were those usual petty jealousies, minor conflicts, and personality clashes that so often arise within a group. He was himself considered difficult to get along with by some of his fellow monks, and he reserved some of his harshest criticism for members of the Gethsemani community.[7]

The lack of solitude disillusioned him at first and he seriously considered going to a stricter monastery where he could remove himself even further from the world and its problems. The Carthusians, whose members lived in individual cells a hermitlike existence, rarely speaking to each other,[8] and the Camaldolese, a monastic order of hermits in Italy, attracted him. Another monk recalls:

He had very few inhibitions about discussing with students problems or disorders that arose, and one of the things that kept the boat rocking in the community of students at Gethsemani besides his social critique (which was a steady diet) was his open discussion of his recurrent temptations to leave Gethsemani and become a hermit someplace or other. I recall entering his office one day when he was reading a long letter. 'Look at this,' he said, showing me the letter. 'It just came from Cardinal Valeri (Prefect of the Congregation of Religious). He turned me down. Can't go to the Camaldolese. He quotes my own writings against it. [Cf. *No Man is an Island*, p. 138: 'Our Father in

Heaven has called each one to the place in which He can best satisfy His infinite desire to do us good.'] Pretty good, don't you think! That makes it *proxima fidei*, doesn't it?[9]

Merton's openness concerning his desire for more solitude caused the many rumors which persisted right up until his trip to Asia in 1968.

The temptation to leave Gethsemani presented Merton with an intense struggle. He remembers speaking to the abbot of it:

> I went and talked over the whole business of my vocation again with Father Abbot and he assured me once again, patiently, that everything was quite all right and that this was where I belonged. In my bones I know that he is quite right and that I am a fool. And yet, on the surface, everything seems to be all wrong. As usual, I am making too much fuss about it.[10]

On another occasion the abbot told him that 'I must remember that my desire to become a Carthusian is full of self-love and only some very extraordinary upheaval in my whole life would justify my leaving here for a Charterhouse.'[11] In time, Merton came to realize that his place was at Gethsemani and that to go elsewhere would merely be to run away from himself and from God. Gethsemani was to be the stage upon which the play of his life would be written and acted out.

The first seven years of Merton's monastic life were spent entirely within the walls of Gethsemani. 'Those were hard years, before the days when radiators were much in favor during the winter, when the hours of communal prayer were much longer, when the fasts were much stricter. It was a period of training, and a happy, austere one, during which I wrote little.'[12] At the end of the novitiate his health broke down and he was given the task of writing and doing translations from the French. In addition he was studying for the priesthood and reading in philosophy and theology. It was during this time, in 1946, that he wrote *The Seven Storey Mountain*, a book that was to bring him fame.

In August of 1948 an event occurred that changed Merton's life. His abbot, Dom Frederic Dunne, died while on a trip to Georgia, and the Vicar General of the Order, Dom Gabriel Sortais, came to Gethsemani for the funeral. Dom Gabriel spoke no English and Merton, fluent in French, was appointed to serve as his translator. He accompanied Dom Gabriel to Louisville to speak to a group of sisters and hear their confession. This trip to Louisville was Merton's first absence from Gethsemani in seven years, and in his journal he was careful to point out that it was an errand of charity and not a pleasure trip. He describes his feelings upon returning to the world:

> We drove into town with Senator Dawson, a neighbor of the monastery, and all the while I wondered how I would react at meeting once again, face to face, the wicked world. I met the world and I found it no longer so wicked after all. Perhaps the things I had resented about the world when I left it were defects of my own that I had projected upon it. Now on the contrary, I found that everything stirred me with a deep and mute sense of compassion. Perhaps some of the people we saw going about the streets were hard and tough—with the naive, animalistic toughness of the Middle West—but I did not stop to observe it because I seemed to have lost an eye for merely exterior detail and to have discovered, instead, a deep sense of respect and love and pity for the souls that such details never fully reveal. I went through the city, realizing for the first time in my life how good are all the people in the world and how much value they have in the sight of God.
>
> After that I returned to the peaceful routine of monastic life—I had only left it for six hours!—and the autumn descended upon Gethsemani.[13]

In that brief trip he had come to realize that the world was not really 'so wicked after all'.

On another trip to Louisville in January, 1949, he noticed the poverty of certain sections of the city.

> In winter the stripped landscape of Nelson county looks terribly poor. We are the ones who are supposed to be poor: well, I am thinking of the people in a shanty next to the Brandeis plant, on Brook Street, Louisville. We had to wait there while Reverend Father was getting some tractor parts. The woman who lived in the place was standing out in front of it, shivering in some kind of rag, while a suspicious-looking anonymous truck unloaded some boot-leg coal in her yard. I wondered if she had been warm yet this winter. And I thought of Gethsemani where we are all all steamed up and get our meals, such as they are, when meal time comes around, and where I live locked up in

that room with incunabula and manuscripts that you wouldn't find in the house of a millionaire! Can't I ever escape from being something comfortable and smug? The world is terrible, people are starving to death and freezing and going to hell with despair and here I sit with a silver spoon in my mouth and write books and everybody sends me fan mail telling me how wonderful I am for giving up so *much*. I'd like to ask them, what have I given up, anyway, except headaches and responsibilities.[14]

Having entered the monastery to find his place in the world, he now visited the world only to question his place in the monastery. His trips to Louisville were proving decisive.

He made another to attend to details of printing a new postulants' guide for the monastery.

In Louisville, at the corner of Fourth and Walnut, in the center of the shopping district, I was suddenly overwhelmed with the realization that I loved all those people, that they were mine and I theirs, that we could not be alien to one another even though we were total strangers. It was like waking from a dream of separateness, of spurious self-isolation in a special world, the world of renunciation and supposed holiness. The whole illusion of a separate holy existence is a dream. Not that I question the reality of my vocation, or of my monastic life: but the conception of 'separation from the world' that we have in the monastery too easily presents itself as a complete illusion: the illusion that by making vows we become a different species of being, pseudo-angels, 'spiritual men,' men of interior life, what have you.[15]

Merton left the world to escape the illusions of life in modern twentieth-century civilization. After years of living in the monastery, the perfect haven, safe and secure from all that would come between man and God, Merton realized that monks had their illusions too, and that the monastery could also serve as an escape from reality.

He had become convinced that the world was to be avoided at all costs and to believe that the people living in the world were evil and were at best inferior to those who were living the religious life. For seven years he had been cut off from all contact with the outside world—people, newspapers, movies, business, and politics. He had been steeped in philosophy and theology and the various aspects of the monastic life. Now, quite suddenly, he found himself making trips to the city and being forced to confront again that world which he had left.

From 1949 to 1950 several health problems necessitated frequent trips to Louisville and several periods of hospitalization. While in the hospital he had time not only to meditate but also to read newspapers, something he was not allowed to do in the monastery. Suddenly he became aware again of world affairs, and he began to realize that it was impossible for him to remain aloof from the world beyond the monastery walls. He writes: 'It is all very well for me to meditate on these things in the shelter of the monastery: but there are times when this shelter itself is deceptive. Everything is deceptive today. And grains of error planted innocently in a well kept greenhouse can become gigantic deadly trees.'[16] He admitted: 'Contemplation is not an end in itself. Contemplation is not sanctity.'[17] One cannot flee to the monastery to find salvation for oneself alone, for 'what every man looks for in life is his own salvation and the salvation of the men he lives with.'[18] Monastic spirituality may in fact become a bogus interiority, a pious sentiment.[19] Thus Merton states: 'The effectiveness of the monk's presence in the world and of his monastic witness to the Gospel of Christ will depend on his ability to see his place in relation to the world correctly.'[20]

In his early years as a monk Merton drew a distinction between action and contemplation. He had left the world to pray and to find God. There was little doubt in his mind that the religious life was vastly superior to the secular. This theme runs throughout *The Seven Storey Mountain*. Now Merton took great pains to correct what he considered the false image of himself presented in that book. In *The Sign of Jonas* he writes:

> I have become very different from what I used to be. The man who began this journal is dead, just as the man who finished *The Seven Storey Mountain*, when this journal began was also dead, and what is more the man who was the central figure in *The Seven Storey Mountain* was dead over and over. And now that all these men are dead, it is sufficient for me to say so on paper and I think I will have ended up by forgetting them....Consequently, *The Seven Storey Mountain* is the work of a man I never even heard of.[21]

In 'Poetry and Contemplation: A Reappraisal' Merton expanded on his changing views:

Contemplation is not to be thought of as a separate department of life, cut off from all man's other interests and superseding them. It is the very fullness of a fully integrated life. It is the crown of life and of all life's activities.

Therefore the earlier problem was, largely, an illusion, created by this division of life into formally separate compartments, of 'action' and 'contemplation'. But because this crude division was stated so forcefully and so frequently in my earlier writings, I feel that it is most necessary now to try to do something to heal this wound and draw together the two sides of this unfortunate fissure.[22]

The man who pretends that he can turn his back on Auschwitz or Viet Nam and act as if they were not there is simply bluffing. I think this is getting to be generally admitted, even by monks. [23]

It is impossible for us to leave the world, for 'by telling ourselves that we are not of this world,' Merton insisted, 'we have actually made it easier for ourselves to be worldly in a manner that is sometimes not only un-Christian but completely ineffective at the same time.'[24] An individualistic piety is no substitute for a true religious humanism.

Merton's change in thinking about the world changed his view of monasticism as well. He never turned his back on the monastic vocation, for he found that 'contemplation and action necessarily have their part in every religious Rule. The two always go together, because Christian perfection is nothing else but the perfection of charity, and that means perfect love of God and of man. This is only one love....It cannot be divided into two.'[25] He did not consider his seven years away from the world a waste of time, nor did he, upon returning to the world, feel drawn to leave the religious life. He found that he had not really left the world at all. 'The monk,' he wrote, 'searches not only his own heart: he plunges deep into the heart of the world of which he remains a part although he seems to have "left" it. In reality the monk abandons the world only in order to listen more intently to the deepest and most neglected voices that proceed from its inner depth.'[26]

In another sense we can say that the monk is more worldly than the city-dweller working in a factory, for the monk lives and works close to the land and is able to appreciate the spiritual values to be found in the world. Merton asserts that 'in modern times we have lost sight of the fact that even the most ordinary actions of our everyday life are invested, by their very nature, with a deep and spiritual meaning.'[27] There can be little doubt that it was the monastic vocation which gave Merton this understanding of life and of the world.

Most importantly, however, the monastic life provided the basis for Merton's turning to the world.

> As usual, one comes back to the old question: what do you mean by 'the world' anyway? In this, I don't think an abstract answer makes too much sense. My concrete answer is: what did I leave when I entered the monastery? As far as I can see what I abandoned when I 'left the world' and came to the monastery was the *understanding of myself* that I had developed in the context of civil society—my identification with what appeared to me to be its aims.[28]

His years in the monastery had given him a new understanding of himself and of his place in the world. This new self-understanding carried with it responsibilities toward others:

> Coming to the monastery has been for me exactly the right kind of withdrawal. It has given me perspective. It has taught me how to live. And now I owe everyone else in the world a share in that life. My first duty is to start, for the first time, to live as a member of the human race which is no more (and no less) ridiculous than I am myself. And my first human act is the recognition of how much I owe everybody else.[29]

What had happened to Merton in the monastery? He had looked within himself and found himself in God. The contemplative life became the means whereby he came to understand who he was in relation to God and in relation to others. He had discovered that the fruits of his contemplative life were to be shared.

This returning to the world meant that he could not live in an *either/or* situation. Life was not a matter of *either* contemplation *or* action, of *either* the religious life *or* the secular life. For Merton it meant that his monastic life must include elements of *both* contemplation and action. Commenting on a letter of Merton's in *L'Osservatore Romano*, Aldhelm Cameron-Brown observes the implications in Merton's views for all monastic life:

> There he says that people must find in monasteries 'both a *monastic* reality (simple and deep persons who have acquired monastic values by putting them into practice), and

an opening to the *social* reality of the twentieth century. It is possible that one or the other of these values may be realized in our present structures. *It is very difficult for both of them to be realized at the same time.'* If both of them are to be realized, the present monastic structures must be changed. The survival of monasticism requires that both should be realized.[30]

Monastic Renewal

Monasticism begins with vocation: 'To have a vocation is something quite different from following a career. Religious vocations are the work not of man, but of God.'[31] Furthermore, 'the one "called" must himself respond to his vocation by his own free, and deliberate choice.'[32] This is a difficult concept to understand, so difficult, in fact, that it cannot be explained, as Merton admitted: 'All the substance of the monastic vocation, therefore, is buried in the silence where God and the soul meet. The very essence of monasticism is hidden in the existential darkness of life itself. And life is inexplicable. It is only understood by being lived.'[33] Being a monk involves one's being entirely; 'the monk is important more for what he *is* than for what he *does*. This is true, in fact, of every Christian. "Being" always takes precedence over "doing" and "having".'[34]

The vocation to monastic life is not a call *'to any particular work'*.[35] Monasticism is not a career—not doing one's job; monasticism is a vocation—being in relationship to God. This does not mean that the contemplative monk does nothing; it is part and parcel of his vocation to center his being in God. Of his own tradition Merton observed:

> This still constitutes the peculiar function of the White Monks in the Church: to contemplate God as perfectly as it can be done by men living in common, to contemplate God day and night, winter and summer, all the year round, not merely as individuals in community but precisely as a community. And that is the Cistercian vocation.[36]

This element of community is of vital importance, for there can be no true contemplation without charity and no charity without the Mystical Body of Christ.[37] Even hermits must first have spent years living in community with their brothers. Contemplation alone is neither possible nor desireable. Merton emphasizes 'that for St Benedict *both action and contemplation are necessary in the monastic life*. Both go together.'[38] Comparing the monastic life to Marxism, Merton emphasized the monk's relatedness to his fellow men: 'His role in history, though more hidden, is just as decisive.'[39] The monk lives communism in its most extreme form: 'For a cenobite, sanctity resolves itself in the practice of the most ruthless communism ever devised....He gives up things a Marxist has never even heard of, things which no amount of human violence or political strategy could ever take away.'[40] The means for realizing this communistic community life is the rule.

All monastic orders, including the Cistercians, live according to a Rule or a book of instruction which carefully sets down each aspect of their life. These rules are generally based upon St Benedict's Rule for Monasteries.[41] The rule facilitates the life of prayer: 'If the rule is not austere enough, the monk will let himself get too soft for prayer and spiritual discipline, and will become, in fact, a comfortable (though perhaps anxious) citizen —another inert member of the middle class.'[42] In Merton's view laxity has practical implications:

> If we find buildings that are ugly, furniture ill-made, doors that do not close properly, vines and fruit trees clumsily pruned, materials and fodder going to waste, the lack of skill and care which these things represent might simply be the fruit of a wrong attitude toward work itself—a false orientation of the monastic spirit. [43]

For the monk contemplation and action are interconnected, and sloppiness in prayer shows itself in actions. The monk must, under the guidance of the rule and the community, discipline his life so that God is at its center and his actions reflect this God-centeredness.

Most rules were written hundreds of years ago and therefore contain many ideas no longer relevant today. As a result monks may observe various disciplines for their own sake rather than for the purpose of deepening their lives. As a twentieth-century monk, Merton found very difficult the traditional monastic attitude toward the world which he refers to as *contemptus mundi.*

> There is in Christianity...a tradition of *contemptus mundi* which needs to be re-examined and understood. Originally, no doubt, it was intended to give the believer a certain freedom of action, a distance, a detachment, a liberation from care without which any question of love for the people of the world would be completely irrelevant....
>
> The conservative position retains a certain element of traditional *contemptus mundi.* We keep up our cohesion and morale by fulminating against certain typical issues— especially lax sexual morals, birth control, divorce, pornography, which are not only obvious but also typological— that embody in themselves all that we means by 'the world' and 'sin'. (Here we tend to forget that they typify the 'flesh' rather than 'the world'. The world, in the triad of world-flesh-devil, represents greed for wealth and prestige, and this is seldom attacked. As a matter of fact it is

precisely here that, having 'satisfied' the Christian
conscience by anathemas directed at the flesh, we can
come to terms with the world which, let us admit it, offers
us a prestige which we believe to be essential for the dis-
semination of the Gospel. The message of the priest who
drives an Oldsmobile is surely more credible than that of
one who rides in the bus![44]

Contempt for the world can flourish in large wealthy
monasteries protected by government concessions and filled
with monks who observe the rule to the letter and retreat from
the world. In doing so, they are actually coming to terms with
the world, and in some situations become a rival power to the
worldly power struggle going on around them.

There is also involved with *contemptus mundi* a second
danger from the liberals in the Church. Recognizing that
contemptus mundi is an impossible position to hold in the latter
part of the twentieth century, liberals tend to identify with the
world and its struggles. Merton explains how they do this:

The liberal attitude, on the other hand, makes a
different choice of symbols. Less experienced on the
problems of the flesh, it concerns itself more with symbolic
social issues, and having taken an edifying stand
(somewhat late) in questions of civil rights (in the United
States) or labor (Europe) it explicitly declares that the
Church has much to learn from 'the world' in these
matters, and the insights of the most modern and
advanced social thought are more relevant to Christianity
than the platitudes of a theology that has still not caught
up with the twentieth century.

For the liberal, the message of the Church will become
credible to the modern world if the priest is seen on the
assembly line—or if he is arrested in a sit-in. There is no
question that this position is somewhat more relevant to
the times and implies a more real sense of man's need
than the position of those who reduce *contemptus mundi*
to anti-Communism and readiness to shower Russia with
H-Bombs in the name of Christ.

But does the ancient, ascetic idea of renunciation of the
world have no meaning at all in the present context?[45]

Both the conservative and liberal monks concern themselves
primarily with monastic renewal in an institutional sense. Yet as
Merton points out:

> In order to understand monasticism, it is important to
> concentrate on the *charism of the monastic vocation* rather
> than on the *structure of monastic institutions or the
> patterns of monastic observances.*
>
> Most of the ambiguities and distresses of the current
> renewal seem to come from the fact that there is too much
> concern with changing the observances or adapting the
> institution and not enough awareness of the charism which
> the institution is meant to serve and protect.[46]

Actually, the renewal of monasticism cannot have any real
meaning until it is seen as a renewal of the *wholeness* of
monasticism in its *charismatic* authenticity.[47]

The renewal of monasticism in its charismatic authenticity
begins within the inner man and has prophetic implications for
the world, both within and without the monastery walls.

> The charism of the monastic life is the freedom and peace
> of a wilderness existence, a return to the desert that is
> also a recovery of (inner) paradise. This is the secret of
> monastic 'renunciation of the world.' Not a *denunciation*,
> not a denigration, not a precipitous flight, a resentful
> withdrawal, but a liberation, a kind of permanent
> 'vacation' in the original sense of 'emptying.' The monk
> simply discards the useless and tedious baggage of vain
> concerns and devotes himself henceforth to the one thing
> really necessary—the one thing that he really wants: the
> quest for *meaning* and for *love*, the quest for his own
> identity, his secret name promised him by God (Apoca-
> lypse 2:17) and for the peace of Christ which the world
> cannot give (John 14:27). In other words the monk
> renounces a life of agitation and confusion for one of order
> and clarity. But the order and clarity are not of his own
> making; nor are they, so to speak, an institutional product,
> an effect of exterior regularity. They are the fruit of the
> Spirit. The monastic life is a response to the call of the
> Spirit to espousals and to peace in the wilderness (Hosea
> 2:19-20).[48]

Monastic renewal begins with the monk, the person, and what
takes place on the personal level determines what stance the
monk will take toward the world. The significant question is not
so much 'How shall I understand the world?' but 'How shall I
understand myself?'

The world cannot be a problem to anyone who sees that ultimately Christ, the world, his brother and his own inmost ground are made one and the same in grace and redemptive love. If all the current talk about the world helps people to discover this, then it is fine. But if it produces nothing but a whole new divisive gamut of obligatory positions and 'contemporary answers' we might as well forget it. The world itself is no problem, but we are a problem to ourselves because we are alienated from ourselves, and this alienation is due precisely to an inveterate habit of division by which we break reality into pieces and then wonder why, after we have manipulated the pieces until they fall apart, we find ourselves out of touch with life, with reality, with the world and most of all with ourselves.[49]

The task of monasticism is to produce men and women who are fully integrated, who know themselves, and who understand their relationship to God and to the world.

Merton firmly believed that monasticism has an important role to play in the modern world, but only if it fulfils its proper role. 'Monastic education is for experience. There is no reason for contemplative monasticism to exist if you are not able in a contemplative monastery to develop a different kind of consciousness from that experienced outside.'[50] He thought that a monastic or contemplative community should develop *unusual* people.[51] They should be people involved in finding themselves and drawing close to God, people whose lives protest against the illusions and falsehoods of the world, and above all, people who orient their lives contemplatively. There is more to monasticism than getting back to the land, making cheese, leaving the world 'as if, for instance, "leaving the world" were adequately summed up by those pictures of "the Trappist" with his cowl over his head and his back to the camera, looking at a lake.'[52] Merton was adamant: 'when a contemplative order ceases to produce a sizable proportion of contemplatives, its usefulness is at an end. It has no further reason for existing.'[53]

Within the renewal of monasticism, he saw the importance of the concept of diaspora, made popular by Karl Rahner.[54] We can little doubt that the world is rapidly becoming industrialized, urbanized, and secularized. The Church is losing wealth, power, influence, and membership. More and more the Christian finds himself one of a minority. Rahner considers this an irreversible trend; the task of the Church is not to stop secularization, therefore, but to adapt to it, and to learn to live and work in a diaspora situation. Merton admitted that religious life 'may become unrecognizable and it is quite likely that many religious institutes will simply cease to exist. In any case, diaspora or no diaspora, there can be no question that the religious life faces a crisis today.'[55]

In Merton's view monasticism is uniquely well suited to survive in a diaspora situation.

> The monk lives, at least theoretically, a contemplative life in which active works play only an incidental part or none at all. Provided he is allowed to work the land and make his own living, the monk can survive where schools are closed, the Catholic press is suppressed and other institutions are taken out of Catholic hands. There is no real need for the monk to be a cleric or a priest, and traditionally the monk is in fact not a cleric. The earliest monks were simply laymen living in solitude or in small informal communities of a somewhat charismatic nature, grouped around a holy and well trained hermit, a 'spiritual father.' So, traditionally, the monastic life does not require much organization....
>
> It is significant that Rahner, who has laid such stress on the importance of the *person* in the diaspora situation (rather than the organized group) should cite St Benedict as an example of one who admirably understood this kind of situation and adapted to it successfully. In all times of monastic crisis the monk instinctively looks back to the primitive simplicity of the origins, not in order to effect an archeological restoration of the past, but in order to see in what spirit renewal can be envisaged for the future.[56]

Merton even foresaw the time when all institutional monasticism may be impossible. In his last talk, given at the Bangkok conference on monasticism, he spoke of a Tibetan lama who had to flee the communists and was cut off from his monastic community:

> He sent a message to a nearby abbot friend of his, saying: 'What do we do?' The abbot sent back a strange message, which I think is very significant: 'From now on, Brother, everybody stands on his own feet.'
>
> To my mind, that is an extremely important monastic statement. If you forget everything else that has been said, I would suggest you remember this for the future: 'From now on everybody stands on his own feet.'

This, I think is what Buddhism is about, what Christianity is about, what monasticism is about—if you understand it in terms of grace. It is not a Pelagian statement, by any means, but a statement to the effect that we can no longer rely on being supported by structures that may be destroyed at any moment by a political power or a political force. You cannot rely on structures. The time for relying on structures has disappeared. They are good and they should help us, and we should do the best we can with them. But they may be taken away, and if everything is taken away, what do you do next?[57]

Merton answered his own question in part by referring to the Russian Orthodox theologians forced by the communists to leave Russia who now live in diaspora in Paris. They have developed the idea of 'monastery of heart' (*monachisme interiorisé*):

This is not merely a conventional notion of 'an interior life for the layman' but the idea of the lay-monk, hidden solitary and unprotected, without the benefit of distinguishing marks and outward forms, called to deepen his monastic vocation 'beneath the level of forms' and penetrating to the 'ontological roots, the mystical essence' of the monastic life on a 'ecumenical and transconfessional level.'[58]

In *monachisme interiorisé* Merton found 'a perfect summary of the current intuitions of the monk's place in the diaspora world....'[59] Here the monk is truly himself, he is a solitary and a man of prayer, poverty, and labor, and at the same time he is open to the world. He is unhampered by unchanging structures yet remains within the ancient monastic traditions of the Church.

Merton believed that the monk should be a prophet to the world and not one to condemn it, for 'it is better to prophesy than to deride. To prophesy is not to predict, but to seize upon reality in its moment of highest expectation and tension toward the new. This tension is discovered not in hypnotic elation but in the light of everyday existence.'[60] The monk stands between the past and the future. His is a life based upon roots deep in the past, among the hermits of the desert. Yet at the same time the monk is open to the future with its uncertainties and contingencies.[61] Here, in this relationship between the past and the future, the monk in the present can bring together contemplation and action. 'His horizons which are those of the

desert and of exile...should enable him to have a special understanding of his fellow man in an age of alienation.'[62] Contemplation gives the monk this perspective, and the understanding
which results is itself a very relevant form of action. It was
Merton's view that the monastic life, in its fullest and deepest
expression, is vitally important for the life of the Church, and
indeed for the life of the world.

The Eremitic Life

No aspect of monasticism concerned Merton more than
eremitism. The word derives from the Latin *eremus*, and
according to one Cistercian abbot 'expressed a certain physical
separation from the affairs of the world, but it is intended to
indicate an attitude.'[63] No better words could be used to
describe Merton's last years, for while a hermit, he was never
really separated from the affairs of the world. His writings on
social issues actually increased after he had withdrawn to the
hermitage.[64]

When Merton became a hermit, many people were surprised
and had difficulty understanding how anyone who had been so
outspoken on social issues could so completely withdraw from
the world. At least one writer suggested that this reaction
revealed something of himself to the surprised onlooker:

> Perhaps, after all, Thomas Merton's vocation does not tell
> us so much about him as it does about ourselves. That is
> to say, that the tolerance we exercise upon hearing it could
> well be a measure of what God means in our lives. The
> difference between openness and mere indifference is, of
> course, that the open man listens for the Spirit and
> searches to learn from others' decisions; the indifferent
> man shuts his ears.[65]

That Merton's action is important primarily in terms of others'
reactions to it is partially true, but Merton's decision to become
a hermit should not surprise anyone who views it in terms of
Merton's life and work. And his decision can only be fully
understood when it is viewed in this light.

'Solitude for Merton,' writes Dennis McInerny, 'was not only
essential to monasticism, it was essential to life.'[66] From his
earliest days in the monastery Merton expressed a desire to live
in complete solitude: he understood the solitary life as he did
the monastic life—as a vocation. One can 'and indeed must if it

were to prove efficacious for him, *choose* solitude.'[67] Merton
described the vocation to solitude:

> To deliver oneself up, to hand oneself over, entrust oneself
> completely to the silence of a wide landscape of woods and
> hills, or sea, or desert; to sit still while the sun comes up
> over that land and fills its silences with light. To pray and
> work in the morning and labor and rest in the afternoon,
> and to sit still again in meditation in the evening when
> night falls upon that land and when the silence fills itself
> with darkness and with stars. This is a true and special
> vocation. There are few who are willing to belong
> completely to such a silence, to let it soak into their bones,
> to breathe nothing but silence, to feed on silence, and to
> turn the very substance of their life into a living and
> vigilant silence.[68]

In an important essay, 'Notes for a Philosophy of Solitude',
he set forth several basic assumptions upon which any desiring
a life of solitude must build. They may be paraphrased as
follows:

1. All men are solitary and at the same time man cannot
   live without society.
2. The solitary has the disconcerting task of facing and
   accepting his own absurdity.
3. Interior solitude is the actualization of a faith in which a
   man takes responsibility for his own inner life.
4. Every man is a solitary, held firmly by the inexorable
   limitations of his own aloneness. Death makes this very
   clear, for when a man dies, he dies alone.
5. The solitary is called not to leave society but to
   transcend it.
6. The solitary life is able to grasp the meaning of crimes
   that are committed in the name of society by the mass
   man.
7. The solitary is one who is called to make one of the most
   terrible decisions possible to man: the decision to
   disagree completely with those who imagine that the call
   to diversion and self-deception is the voice of truth and
   who can summon the full authority of their own
   prejudice to prove it.
8. The solitary lives in unity. His solitude is neither an
   argument, an accusation, a reproach or a sermon. It is
   simply itself. It *is*.

9. The solitary is different from the individualist. What the
   individualist wants is not the hidden, metaphysical agony
   of the hermit but the noisy self-congratulations and self-
   pity of the infant in the cradle. Ultimately what he wants
   is not the desert but the womb. [69]

Two aspects of the solitary life stand out here. First, the solitary
must come to terms with himself. He must take upon himself
'the lonely, barely comprehensible, incommunicable task of
working his way through the darkness of his own mystery until
he discovers that his mystery and the mystery of God merge
into one reality, which is the only reality'. [70] The solitary must
be a contemplative. [71] Secondly, the solitary must understand
his true relationship to society. Merton avers that 'the true
solitary does not renounce anything that is basic and human
about his relationship to other men.' [72] In his view the Christian
can turn his back on society without hating society. Quite the
reverse:

> Withdrawal from other men can be a special form of love
> for them. It should never be a rejection of man or of his
> society. But it may well be a quiet and humble refusal to
> accept the myths and fictions with which social life cannot
> help but be full—especially today. To despair of the
> illusions and facades which man builds around himself is
> certainly not to despair of man. On the contrary, it may be
> a sign of love and of hope. For when we love someone, we
> refuse to tolerate what destroys and maims his personality. [73]

Becoming a solitary is itself an action.

Merton believed strongly in the place of solitaries in contemporary monasticism. [74] This context is important if the dangers
of eremitism are to be avoided, for a solitary cannot live without
human contact and retain his sanity. [75] He pointed out that 'no
matter how solitary a man may be, if he is a contemplative his
contemplation has something of a social character. He receives
it through the Church.' [76] The monk who lives alone is still a
monk and has responsibilities to his community. Problems can,
however, arise. No one enters a monastery and immediately
becomes a hermit. He must spend time, often years, learning to
live in the community and these years can be difficult. Merton
sheds some light from his own experience:

> There is no true intimacy between souls who do not know

how to respect one another's solitude. I cannot be united
in love with a person whose very personality my love tends
to obscure, to absorb, and to destroy. Nor can I awaken
true love in a person who is invited, by my love, to be
drowned in the act of drowning me with love.[77]

Members of the community may feel that the hermit does
not contribute his share to the community's life, yet Merton
contends that he makes a unique contribution: 'The elementary
obligation of the hermit is to renounce all arbitrary demands on
other people. The hermit's ability to live alone is his gift to the
community and his witness to the grace of Christ in his own
life.'[78] The hermit contributes as well to the life of the Church
at large. The hermit may function as a kind of desert father
who, having been acknowledged by others to be especially holy
and wise, is able to guide and direct others in the spiritual
life.[79] Even more essential to the eremitic life is prayer:

A Christian hermit can, by being alone, paradoxically live
even closer to the heart of the Church than one who is in
the midst of her apostolic activities. The life and unity of
the Church are, and must be, visible. But that does not
mean that the invisible and spiritual activities of men of
prayer are not supremely important. On the contrary, the
invisible and more mysterious life of prayer is *essential* to
the Church. Solitaries, too, are essential to her![80]

If the hermit is acknowledged as a spiritual director, other
members of the community may feel that their cenobitic life is
inferior to the eremitic life. Merton cautions that 'it should
always remain clear to cenobites that the hermit life is an
unusual way and is *not required for monastic perfection*....The
hermit vocation is always exceptional.'[81] The eremitic is a
difficult life, for the hermit has no one to depend upon, except
God and himself. As Merton says: 'He faces boredom squarely
with *no other resources than those he has within himself*—his
own capacities and God's grace.'[82] 'Indeed,' he writes, 'when a
solitary loses the true spirit of his vocation, his call is no longer
able to contain him. It casts him out, as the sea casts up a dead
body on the shore.'[83] Those who persevere in the eremitic life
are very few indeed.

What, then, does the hermit do and how does he live? He
seeks the silence of God:

It is the silence of God that forms the solid floor on which we fight our battles, and if His silence gave out beneath us we would all fall together with our cataclysms of sound into the depth of oblivion. And so, when the restless agitation of man falls still, and when his machines and his world turn over to go to sleep, everything is once again pervaded by the silence of God. Then those who remain awake—the monks and the solitaries—are able to tell by the sound of the mysterious song returning to their hearts, that all man's noise and all his works are unsubstantial: that every new thing that can stand up and shout about itself is an illusion, and that only the everlasting silence in things is real: for it is the silence of God, buried in their very substance, singing the song which He alone can hear.[84]

In silence the hermit hears God's voice and in silence he shares God's words with others: 'God does not give us graces or talents or virtues for ourselves alone. We are members one of another and everything that is given to one member is given for the whole body.'[85]

The Apostolatè of Prayer

The monk is not called to a particular job. Although he may find himself ploughing on a farm or printing books in order to earn his livelihood, this work is always secondary to his being in relationship to God. It is for this reason that a monk may, after proper preparation and with permission, become a hermit. It is for this reason that Merton was able to understand the contemplative vocation in terms of the diaspora and even to include within it those who might not be members of religious communities. Monasticism is, of course, the milieu out of which Merton speaks, but his words have meaning to those beyond the cloister.

It stands to reason that one whose vocation is centered in relationship to God will spend a great deal of time in prayer. Merton emphasizes the one basic reason for the monastic life—to pray without ceasing. When he notes that prayer may just be 'waiting on the Lord',[86] we realize that Merton's prayer is essentially contemplative. In his book *Merton's Theology of Prayer*, John J. Higgins expands on this:

For Merton, the term, *contemplative*, when applied to prayer, refers more to the *orientation* that one's life of prayer must take. Because all men have a need to listen to God in silence, man must develop a personal outlook or attitude of prayer and try to live consciously in an atmosphere of prayer. However, according to Merton, what matters in prayer is, not so much the witnessing for God, but the surrendering to God; for, the contemplative orientation lies essentially in emptiness. Man must descend into the depths of his own emptiness and await the word by which God will speak to him and create in him a new being—a being that is totally free insofar as it is like God. [87]

Prayer is more than repeating petitions from memory or from a book. Prayer, Merton reminds us, involves one's entire life:

> In the way of prayer, as described by the early monastic writers, *meditatio* must be seen in its close relation to *psalmodia, lectio, oratio*, and *contemplatio*. It is part of a continuous whole, the entire unified life of the monk, *conversatio monastica*, his turning from the world to God. To separate meditation from prayer, reading and contemplation is to falsify our picture of the monastic way of prayer. In proportion as meditation takes on a more contemplative character, we see that it is not only a *means* to an end, but also something of the *nature* of an end. Hence monastic prayer, especially in meditation and contemplative prayer, is not so much a way to find God as a way of resting in him whom we have *found*, who loves us, who is near to us, who comes to us to draw us to himself. [88]

In Merton's view prayer cannot be limited to one particular form or one kind of activity, for prayer is an orientation of the whole person toward God. There are, however, different kinds of prayer and there are steps which one can take to help build a deeper prayer life. One is the practice of meditation, which Merton describes as:

> ...simply the beginning of a process which leads to interior prayer and is normally supposed to culminate in contemplation and in affective communion with God. We can call this whole process (in which meditation leads to contemplation) by the name *mental prayer*. In actual practice, the word 'meditation' is quite often used as if it meant exactly the same thing as 'mental prayer.' But if you look at the

precise meaning of the word, we find that meditation is only a small part of the whole complex of interior activities which go to make up mental prayer. Meditation is the name given to the earlier part of the process, the part in which heart and mind exercise themselves in a series of interior activities which prepare us for union with God.[89]

By meditation one makes himself receptive to God and open to his voice. 'The first thing I must do if I want to practice meditation,' says Merton, 'is to *develop a strong resistance to the futile appeals which modern society makes to my five senses.* Hence I will have to mortify my desires.'[90] This is so that outside things do not distract one from the things of God. Merton asserts that 'meditation is spiritual work, sometimes difficult work....Meditation is almost all contained in this one idea: the idea of *awakening* our interior self and attuning ourselves inwardly to the Holy Spirit, so that we will be able to respond to His grace.'[91]

In meditating, one 'should not look for a "method" or "system", but cultivate an "attitude", an "outlook": faith, openness, attention, reverence, expectation, supplication, trust, joy.'[92] In order to achieve this, however, most people must learn *how* to meditate and this requires effort which is enlightened, well-directed and sustained. For most of us a spiritual director or guru is not only helpful but almost necessary if we are to deepen our life of prayer.

Of particular importance is the proper relationship between the interior life of prayer and the exterior life of activity in the world. One should accept reality without dividing it into two states in opposition to each other. Says Merton: 'Meditation has no point and no reality unless it is firmly rooted in *life.*'[93] In *The Sign of Jonas* he tells of an afternoon's meditation in which he recognized the division between the interior and exterior life as illusory:

> In the afternoon I went to the old horsebarn with the Book of Proverbs and indeed with the whole Bible, and I was wandering around in the hay loft, where there is a big gap in the roof, and one of the rotting floorboards gave way under me and I nearly fell through.
> Afterwards I sat and looked out at the hills and the gray clouds and couldn't read anything. When the flies got too bad, I wandered across the bare pasture and sat by the enclosure wall, perched on the edge of a ruined bathtub that has been placed there for the horses to drink out of. A

pipe comes through the wall and plenty of water flows into the bathtub from a spring somewhere in the woods, and I couldn't read there either. I just listened to the clean water flowing and looked at the wreckage of the horsebarn on top of the bare knoll in front of me, and remained drugged with happiness and with prayer. [94]

In these few words, he summed up his conviction that prayer is an attitude and an awakening.

Although meditation can be a step toward contemplation, Merton maintained that 'the ultimate end of meditation should be a more intimate communion with God not only in the future *but also here and now.*' [95] Opening oneself to God's grace not only aids one in attaining a deeper prayer life, but it also brings the prayer closer to God and makes him more receptive to God's grace in the many and varied experiences of everyday life. Thus Merton avers that 'all good meditative prayer is a *conversion of our entire self to God.*' [96]

Another aspect of prayer Merton called recollection, which he defined as 'a change of spiritual focus and an attuning of our whole soul to what is beyond and above ourselves'. [97] Recollection results in peace, interior silence, and tranquility of heart, but it does not require that one turn away from the world. Merton maintained that 'sometimes we are more recollected, quieter, simple and pure, when we see *through* exterior things and see God in them than when we turn away from them to shut them out of our minds. Recollection does not deny sensible things, it sets them in order.' [98]

Two elements are involved in becoming present to oneself according to Merton's recollection: the interior soul, concerned with contemplation: and the exterior soul, concerned with action. [99] He writes:

> When my practical and outward self is submissive and ordered to the deepest needs implanted in my inward being by nature and grace, then my whole soul is in harmony with itself, with the realities around it, and with God. It is able to see things are they are, and it enables me to be aware of God. This makes me 'present' to myself. That is to say that my outward self is alive to its true function as a servant of the spirit and of grace. It is aware of the mastery of grace, aware of the inward self, aware of its power to work among outward things, and by this work to help the inward transformation of the spirit by grace.... Recollection...brings the outward self into line with the

inward spirit, and makes my whole being answer the deep pull of love that reaches down into the mystery of God.[100]

Recollection involves a degree of detachment: 'The secret of recollected action is, first of all, detachment from ourselves and from the results either of our action or of our prayer. We must be detached from the anxiety that makes us plunge into action without restraint.'[101] 'Recollection...makes me present to whatever is significantly real at each moment of my existence.'[102]

Merton makes two significant points here. The two facets of one's personality, the inner, spiritual man and the outer, active man, must be in harmony if one is to be recollected and truly present to oneself. Second, recollection enables one to become detached from what is often misdirected and useless and this detachment prepares one for a closer, deeper union with God in contemplation.

'Contemplation,' explains Merton, 'is really simple openness to God at every moment, and deep peace.'[103] It 'is our personal response to His mystical presence and activity within us.'[104] Contemplation grows from both meditation and recollection, for meditation prepares one for God's grace, and recollection makes possible God's presence and activity united within us. Merton speaks of this in terms of penance and prayer:

> All contemplative life on earth implies penance as well as prayer, because in contemplation there are always two aspects: the positive one, by which we are united to God in love, and the negative one, by which we are detached and separated from everything that is not God. Without both these elements there is no real contemplation.[105]

Merton calls contemplation 'the highest expression of man's intellectual and spiritual life.'[106] 'Contemplation,' he says, 'is the awareness and realization even in some sense *experience*, of what each Christian obscurely believes: "It is now no longer I that live but Christ lives in me."'[107] One is lifted beyond oneself:

> Since contemplation is the union of mind and will with God in an act of pure love that brings us into obscure contact with Him as He really is, the way to contemplation is to develop and perfect our mind and will and our whole soul. Infused contemplation begins when the direct intervention of God raises this whole process of development above the

level of our nature: and then He perfects our faculties by seeming to defeat all their activity in the suffering and darkness of His infused light and love. [108]

One begins with meditation, moves to recollection and finally attains contemplation, and all of this is prayer. [109] What mattered for Merton was 'the *contemplative orientation* of the whole life of prayer.' [110]

In viewing prayer as one's orientation, Merton did not deny the importance and value of prayers of petition. 'We can and must use the prayer of petition,' he wrote, 'and this is even compatible, in a very simple and pure form, with the spirit of contemplation. One can pass from the prayer of petition directly into contemplation when one has a very profound faith and a great simplicity of theological hope.' [111] For Merton petition implies a strong reliance on God. 'What is the use of praying,' he asks, 'if at the very moment of prayer, we have so little confidence in God that we are busy planning our own kind of answer to our prayer?' [112]

To answer such a question one is driven back to the inner self. 'Prayer and identity go together.' Says Merton, 'Who is it that prays? What is our concept or our non-concept of ourselves praying? Who do we feel ourselves to be when we pray?' [113] Merton believed that our failure to pray with a contemplative orientation is the root cause of our lack of faith:

> The majority of people, even those who possess the gift of sanctifying grace, never enter into this inward self, which is an abode of silence and peace where the diversified activities of the intellect and will are collected, so to speak, into one intense and smooth and spiritualized activity which far exceeds in its fruitfulness the plodding efforts of reason working on external reality with its analyses and syllogisms. [114]

Indeed, Merton asserted, 'the highest form of prayer is, then, a prayer "without forms," a prayer in which there are no longer any images or ideas, and in which the spirit does not take any initiative of its own, for all the activity of the human mind and senses is here completely suppressed.' [115] This highest form of prayer is a contemplation in which one is united with God to the point where the self is lost in God and forms and images and even words become unnecessary.

Prayer itself involves action, for it does not come easily. Prayer requires years of learning, discipline, and practice. A personal prayer life brings about changes in the person, and Merton comments on this in reference to a spiritual director: 'in summary, one of the most important benefits a director can bring to the prayer life of his contemplative penitents is to help them reinforce their whole existence, as far as possible, on a simple, natural ordinary level on which they can be fully *human*. Then grace can work on them and make them fully sons of God.'[116] Prayer can result in definite action in the lives of those who pray. It can result in a contemplative orientation wherein one can fully realize what it means to be human.

Merton's understanding of prayer is not individualistic in the sense that the one who prays withdraws from the concerns and cares of the world. He emphasizes that 'contemplation, at its highest intensity, becomes a reservoir of spiritual vitality that pours itself out in the most telling social action.'[117] He goes on to stress that 'prayer does not blind us to the world, but it transforms our vision of the world, and makes us see it, all men, and all the history of mankind, in the light of God.'[118] This is reminiscent of the words of St Paul: 'From now on, therefore, we regard no one from a human point of view' (2 Cor 5:16).

Contemplative prayer is basic not only to the monastic life but to the Christian life as a whole for Merton, for without this contemplative orientation our action becomes futile and our religion useless.

> The most important need in the Christian world today is this inner truth nourished by this Spirit of contemplation: the praise and love of God, the longing for the coming of Christ, the thirst for the manifestation of God's glory, his truth, his justice, his Kingdom in the world. These are all characteristically 'contemplative' and eschatological aspirations of the Christian heart, and they are the very essence of monastic prayer. Without them our apostolate is more for our own glory than for the glory of God.
>
> Without this contemplative orientation we are building churches not to praise him but to establish more firmly the social structures, values and benefits that we presently enjoy. Without this contemplative basis to our preaching, our apostolate is no apostolate at all, but mere proselytizing to insure universal conformity with our own national way of life.
>
> Without contemplation and interior prayer the Church cannot fulfill her mission to transform and save mankind. Without contemplation, she will be reduced to being the servant of cynical and worldly powers, no matter how hard

her faithful may protest that they are fighting for the
Kingdom of God.

Without true, deep contemplative aspirations, without a
total love for God and an uncompromising thirst for his
truth, religion tends in the end to become an opiate.[119]

The life of prayer is perhaps the most important activity within
the Church, for without it the Church can only wither and die.

Detached Involvement

By its very nature, the contemplative life is lived in partial
withdrawal from the world and its concerns. Merton spent years
within the confines of Gethsemani, leaving only for trips to see
the doctor in Louisville, a trip to New York City where he met
with D.T. Suzuki, and his final journey to Asia. Aside from
these brief excursions he was one of the most stabilized monks
at Gethsemani.[120] He lived the last three years of his life as a
hermit, less frequently in contact with the rest of the monastic
community than most other monks. In fact Merton became
increasingly detached from the world around him.[121] Yet at the
same time his writings evinced more and more social concern.

At first glance we seem to see an inherent contradiction
here. How can one be detached from the world and yet be
deeply involved in its social concerns? Addressing this question,
another Cistercian writer quotes Merton's preface to the
Japanese edition of *The Seven Storey Mountain:*

My monastery is not a home. It is not a place where I am
rooted and established on the earth. It is not an environment in which I become aware of myself as an individual,
but rather a place in which I disappear from the world as
an object of interest in order to be everywhere in it by
hiddenness and compassion. To exist everywhere I have to
be No-one.[122]

Yet another Cistercian explains this in terms of irrelevance:

In regard to relevance Father Merton said something in
his second to last talk, the one given in Calcutta, which is
worth recalling. He had prepared a paper but he put it on
the table saying, 'You can read this paper if you want to,
but I suspect you have better things to do than read my
papers.' And then he gave an extemporaneous talk in

which he spoke about our irrelevance, that we monks should not attempt to be relevant.[123]

Merton held that the monk should not pattern his style of living after that of the world and thus make no attempt to be relevant. Merton himself wrote that detachment or *apatheia* is one of the marks of the mature christian soul.[124] Detachment begins not with the exterior world, however, but within the interior heart of man:

> The question of detachment depends it seems to me first of all on self knowledge. Or rather the two are mutually interdependent. One must know what are the real attachments in his soul before he can effectively work against them, and one must have a detached will in order to see the truth of one's attachments.[125]

One must become detached even from spiritual experiences for 'everything you love for its own sake, outside of God alone, blinds your intellect and destroys your judgement of moral values. It vitiates your choices so that you cannot clearly distinguish good from evil and you do not truly know God's will.'[126] If one seeks enlightenment or fulfillment one must become detached even from this desire:

> Hence it becomes overwhelmingly important for us to *become detached from our everyday conception of ourselves as potential subjects for special and unique experiences, or as candidates for realization, attainment and fulfillment.* [127]

The reason for this detachment is obvious; if one remains attached to something which is not God, his moral judgement will be impaired. His ambiguity as to God's will then spreads to the society until no social action can really be accomplished. Once one attains inner detachment, he is then prepared to become further detached from the world. It is primarily for this reason that monks desiring to become hermits must spend years living in community, for the solitary life of detachment from the world will be of no avail unless interior detachment has already been achieved.

A social critic has a distinct advantage in maintaining a degree of detachment from the world and its problems. Aldhelm Cameron-Brown writes that 'as a monk Merton was able to write on social topics with a detachment and truth sometimes difficult for those in the field, where compromise inevitably creeps in, or is avoided by erecting a sterilising hatred.'[128] There can be little doubt that Merton's position as a detached observer contributed much to his ability to diagnose correctly many of the social ills of contemporary society. Indeed he was disturbed by the fact that so few social critics are not detached enough from the world to see it as it really is. He writes:

> I wonder if there are twenty men alive in the world now who see things as they really are. That would mean there were twenty men who were free, who were not dominated or even influenced by any attachment to any created thing or to their own selves, or to any gift of God, even to the highest, the most supernaturally pure of His graces. I don't believe that there are twenty such men alive in the world. But there must be one or two. They are the ones who are holding everything together and keeping the universe from falling apart.[129]

According to Merton, detachment plays an important part in the development of charity, for one must become detached from selfishness: 'This is the great paradox of charity: that unless we are selfish enough to desire to become perfectly unselfish, we have not charity.'[130] Only by becoming unselfish can we truly love others and only through detachment can we avoid compromise and hatred.

Detachment for Merton meant involvement, but involvement from a different perspective than is common. Detachment helps one keep a degree of objectivity: one can look at a situation and see it as it really is and not as one wants it to be. One can be involved by doing nothing at all! 'One must be humble enough,' says Merton, 'to get along without such a lot of "doing" and simply "be" a son that is loved by the heavenly Father. Until one has made this discovery, he cannot really begin to be a monk.'[131] Detached involvement can be a strong form of social action in a society like that of contemporary America where the emphasis is on doing. In 'A Signed Confession of Crimes Against the State' Merton writes: 'My very existence is an admission of guilt....The very thoughts of a person like me are crimes against the state. All I have to do is think: and immediately I become guilty.'[132]

> I confess that I am sitting under a pine tree doing absolutely nothing. I have done nothing for one hour and firmly intend to continue doing nothing for an indefinite

period. I have taken my shoes off. I confess that I have
been listening to a mockingbird. Yes, I admit that it is a
mockingbird. I hear him singing in those cedars, and I am
very sorry. It is probably my fault. He is singing again.
This kind of thing goes on all the time. Wherever I am, I
find myself the center of reactionary plots like this one....
   I confess that there is nobody else around because I
came here on purpose to get away from the state. I avow,
in a frantic paroxysm of grief, that the state and I are
much better off where we have nothing to do with each
other. And I even confess that I (in contradistinction to the
state) believe that this separation is not only desirable but
even possible. Indeed it is, at least temporarily, an accomplished fact. I confess it. I confess it. The birds are singing
again, and I confess it.[133]

Although Merton is being satirical, there come to mind visions
of George Orwell's *1984*, where doing nothing was a crime
against the state.

Detachment, especially when it takes the form of disinterest,
can be a form of action with political implications. Disinterested
involvement where one does nothing is, Merton goes on to say,
the worst possible crime since one refuses to take sides:

You say that this is indeed horrible, but that it is not yet
horrible enough. I am sorry, I cannot improve on the truth.
That is a refinement I must leave to the state, which is
perfectly equipped to do a very good job of it. I am just
writing down what I have actually done, or rather what I
have not done. That is usually it: I just *don't do* the things
that they do on one side or the other. I am therefore
probably worse than all the rest, since I am neither a
partisan nor a traitor. The worst traitor is the one who
simply takes no interest. That's me. Here I sit in the
grass. I watch the clouds go by, and like it. Quisling.
Trotsky. Judas. [134]

It is one thing to support the system and another to rebel
against it. Yet, in both cases one shows an interest in the
system. Merton asserts that the worst crime of all is simply to
ignore the system.

Disinterested involvement not only shows contempt for the
system, it establishes one's independence and thus serves as an
important form of prophetic action. At least one writer is of the
opinion that Merton's disinterested involvement served to

criticize not only society but monastic life:

> He viewed the monk as the man who takes distance from
> his society, who because of his commitment rejects the
> prevailing structures of society and can, as the result,
> function credibly as its critic. Therefore, he did not see
> how an oppressively disciplined, rigoristic system which
> dehumanized the monk could be much better than the
> oppression that characterizes the technological society that
> the monk rejects today.[135]

Merton could criticize only within the context of disinterested
involvement and detachment. His unique position kept him from
taking one side or the other and so he was able to point out the
illusions of both. He could present a critique of society and of
monasticism. He could see his own illusions, and could say that
he had learned 'to let go of my idea of myself, to take myself
with more than one grain of salt....In religious terms, this is
simply a matter of accepting life, and everything in life as a gift
and clinging to none of it, as far as you are able.'[136]

Contemplation and Writing

When he entered Gethsemani he faced an identity crisis
between two persons—Father Louis the contemplative and
Thomas Merton the writer. 'There was this shadow,' he writes,
'this double, this writer who had followed me into the cloister.
He is still on my track. He rides my shoulders, sometimes, like
the old man of the sea. I cannot lose him.'[137] No matter how
hard he tried he could not escape the fact that he was a writer
and a very gifted one. Merton's superiors recognized this and
told him to write even when he did not know whether or not his
writing conflicted with his contemplative vocation.[138] As time
passed and he began to understand himself more fully, he
became reconciled to his dual vocation as a contemplative and a
writer. He speaks of this in his preface to a collection of his
works covering twenty-five years:

> If the monastic life is a life of hardship and sacrifice, I
> would say that for me most of the hardship has come in
> connection with writing. It is possible to doubt whether I
> have become a monk (a doubt I have to live with), but it is
> not possible to doubt that I am a writer, that I was born
> one and will most probably die as one. Disconcerting, dis-

edifying as it is, this seems to be my lot and my vocation.
It is what God has given me in order that I might give it
back to Him. [139]

As a contemplative monk, he had to work out a synthesis of
these two seemingly conflicting vocations.

He realized that the artist, the writer, is 'in some sense
already naturally prepared and disposed to remove some of the
principal obstacles to the light of infused contemplation.' [140] The
writer is also in the unique position of being able to share the
fruits the contemplative enjoys:

> What if one is morally certain that God wills him to con-
> tinue writing anyway? That is, what if one's religious
> superiors make it a matter of formal obedience to pursue
> one's art, for some special purpose like the good of souls?
> That will not take away distractions, or make God abrogate
> the laws of the spiritual life. But we can console ourselves
> with Saint Thomas Aquinas that it is more meritorious to
> share the fruits of contemplation with others than it is
> merely to enjoy them ourselves. And certainly, when it
> comes to communicating some idea of the delights of
> contemplation, the poet is, of all men, the one who is least
> at a loss for the means to express what is essentially
> inexpressible. [141]

Writing can serve as a means of sharing the contemplative
experience outside the monastery walls. It is a form of action
which springs from contemplation.

Reading, too, was important to Merton, who said that
'reading ought to be an act of homage to the God of all
truth.' [142] Books, like God, can speak to us and reading can give
God glory for 'when it is a more deeply vital act not only of our
intelligence but of our whole personality, absorbed and
refreshed in thought, meditation, prayer, or even in the
contemplation of God', reading becomes part of our being in
relationship to God. [143]

The very act of writing, quite aside from whether or not it is
done within a monastic framework, can be a form of
contemplation. Merton's biographer John Howard Griffin
discovered this while doing research in Merton's hermitage:

I need not tell you that I am blessed in my work, in being able to research Thomas Merton's life through the experience of the silence and solitude of his hermitage. Blessed also because Thomas Merton left magnificent materials. He literally meditated on paper. I have said that he could not scratch his nose without writing about it. That is not exactly correct, but it is very nearly so. Writing was so profoundly a part of his nature that, like some other writers, he thought, meditated on paper. This kind of writing is quite distinct from the structured writing of books, conferences, or articles. Those were done deliberately and formally. In his notebooks, things were tossed down, perhaps as a means of concretising experience, though I think probably not even that consciously—but rather because this action was simply a normal way of functioning for him.

Such writing, needless to say, has no value to the writer if he has any idea that anyone will ever see it. It has value and authenticity only when done in the complete freedom of privacy, where one has no need to be consistent, where there is no concern for proprieties that unconsciously begin to color the materials if one thinks that another will see them. These are meditations on paper, reactions, descriptions; and because there is no need to make them eloquent, sometimes they contain the greatest eloquence a man ever puts down on paper.[144]

Merton was a disciplined man, and he spent some three hours every morning in writing, apart from the other times when he would put his thoughts and poems down on paper. His writing was, in a very real sense, contemplation.

Writings spawned in contemplation can have social and political implications, however. By the mere setting down of something on paper, one puts it there for others to read, to criticize, and even to hold against the writer. In his 'Signed Confession', Merton comments:

I declare that everything that I am now about to write will be either true or false, and that neither I nor the state care which, so long as something is written. Everything that is written, anywhere, or by anybody, is a potential confession of a crime against the state. Including the official documents of the state itself, the official histories, etc., etc. Everything written down, whether defiant or servile, whether partisan or indifferent, turns in the end into a death warrant. I will mix defiance and servility in the desired proportions and my indifference will make me the partisan of all oppositions.[145]

In spite of this Merton continued to write, for writing and contemplation were inseparable; he needed both in order to live. Merton was a contemplative, for this was the way in which he could know God most fully, and he was a writer because this was the way in which he could express himself most fully. Sometimes the two merged and became virtually indistinguishable. In *My Argument with the Gestapo* he relates how the hero watches as his journal is taken from him, perhaps to be lost forever, and he closes the book with the following words:

> Yet here is the typewriter and a pile of new paper, white, untouched.
> I think suddenly of Blake, filling paper with words, so that the words flew about the room for the angels to read, and after that, what if the paper was lost or destroyed?
> That is the only reason for wanting to write. Blake's reason.[146]

The Desire to Know God

The monk spends a great deal of time in prayer. He may, if he is—like Merton—so inclined, venture forth as a perceptive social critic, always remaining detached from actual social involvement. Many monks find that they possess abilities, such as writing, which are enhanced by their contemplative vocation. It is not at all uncommon to find monks who are creative artists, outstanding farmers, who make excellent cheese, or who are known for their careful and skilled craftsmanship.[147] Such occupations go well with the contemplative vocation, but Merton cautions that for the contemplative 'the great thing is a more direct confrontation with God'.[148] For the Cistercian the supreme ideal is 'the contemplation of God in silence and detachment from all things.'[149]

Underlying Merton's spirituality of contemplation and action is his concept of God. 'No idea of God can have any value,' he wrote, 'if it is not strongly *based on a metaphysical sense of Being*.'[150] He explains what he means:

> The mere fact of treating God as a hypothesis amounts to treating him as an existent which might or might not

exist—as a *possibility*. But to begin with God as a *possibility* is to start on a road that leads away from him, since the whole meaning of "God" is that of *necessary* and *absolute* subsisting Being—a Being whose *essence is to exist.* To take God as a possibility that might exist and then say that he *does* in fact exist is to prove nothing whatever. [151]

Although Merton maintains that the created self is ontologically distinct from God, he does hold to a belief in a mystical union between God and man in contemplation. For him 'contemplation goes beyond concepts and apprehends God not as a separate object but as the Reality within our own reality, the Being within our being, the life of our life'. [152]

In an important essay entitled 'The New Consciousness' Merton discussed contemplation in greater detail. He pointed out that 'the consciousness of Being (whether considered positively or negatively and apophatically as in Buddhism) is an immediate experience that goes beyond reflexive awareness. It is not "consciousness *of*" but *pure consciousness*, in which the subject as such "disappears."' [153] He expands on this:

> Posterior to this immediate experience of a ground which transcends experience, emerges the subject with its self-awareness. But, as the Oriental religions and Christian mysticism have stressed, this self-aware subject is not final or absolute; it is a provisional self-construction which exists, for practical purposes, only in a sphere of relativity. Its existence has meaning in so far as it does not become fixated or centered upon itself as ultimate, learns to function not as its own center but 'from God' and 'for others.' The Christian term 'from God' implies what the nontheistic religious philosophies conceive as a hypothetical Single Center of all beings, what T.S. Eliot called 'the still point of the turning world,' but which Buddhism for example visualizes not as 'point' but as 'Void'. (And of course the Void is not visualized at all.)
>
> In brief, this form of consciousness assumes a totally different kind of self-awareness from that of the Cartesian thinking-self which is its own justification and its own center. Here the individual is aware of himself as a self-to be-dissolved in self-giving, in love, in 'letting go,' in ecstasy, in God—there are many ways of phrasing it.
>
> This self is not its own center and does not orbit around itself; it is centered on God, the one center of all, which is

'everywhere and nowhere,' in whom all are encountered, from whom all proceed. Thus from the very start this consciousness is disposed to encounter 'the other' with whom it is already united anyway 'in God'.[154]

To experience this kind of new consciousness one must rid oneself of all that is not God for 'only when we are able to "let go" of everything within us, all desire to see, to know, to taste and experience the presence of God, do we truly become able to experience that presence with the overwhelming conviction and reality that revolutionizes our entire inner life.'[155] What then is contemplation?

Contemplation is at once the existential appreciation of our own 'nothingness' and of the divine reality, perceived by ineffable spiritual contact within the depths of our own being. Contemplation is the sudden intuitive penetration of what really IS. It is the unexpected leap of the spirit of man into the existential luminosity of Reality Itself, not merely by the metaphysical intuition of being, but by the transcendent fulfilment of an existential communion with Him Who IS.[156]

The same holds true for life in community and the 'one thing the monk needs to live for is that *common will*—the will which is not peculiar to him alone, which does not seek its own momentary benefit or convenience, but which seeks the good of all in the will of God.'[157]

An ever-present danger is that one will begin with the self—the ego—rather than with Being which is God. According to Merton, contemplation built on self can lead nowhere but to ruin:

If we try to contemplate God without having turned the face of our inner self entirely in His direction, we will end up inevitably by contemplating ourselves, and we will perhaps plunge into the abyss of warm darkness which is our own sensible nature. This is not a darkness in which one can safely remain passive.[158]

If one is not careful, 'what is experienced as primary is not "being" or "isness" but individual *consciousness*, reflexive ego-awareness,'[159] quite different from the contemplation of God and produces a far different social action. Indeed, 'in true contemplation, there is no "reason why" emptiness would necessarily bring us face to face with God. Emptiness might just as well bring us face to face with the devil, and as a matter of fact it sometimes does. This is a part of the peril of this spiritual wilderness.'[160] Our only hope, says Merton, is our trust in God.

To guard against these dangers one should desire nothing but God for all other desires may fail. 'The only desire that is infallibly fulfilled is the desire to be loved by God.'[161] Most significantly, 'we come to "realize" and "know" ourselves when we are fully actualized as we are meant to be in the designs of God.'[162] As Merton goes on to say, 'the measure of our identity, our being (for here the two mean exactly the same thing) is the amount of our love for God'.[163] The desire to know God allows us also to know ourselves.

Yet knowing God and knowing oneself are not enough, for we are social beings who live in community with one another. We must also know our relationship to others. According to Merton such knowledge is derived from our consciousness of God. He stated this in terms of our discovery of the image of God within us and said that it is also 'our own definitive discovery of ourselves in one another and in Him'.[164] Thus our knowledge of God leads us to knowledge of ourselves and knowledge of others.

We must be able to discern the image of God in others. We can easily overlook it if we are not first of all aware of God's image in ourselves. Merton believed that all things carry within them an image of God:

> Everything that exists and everything that happens bears witness to the will of God. It is one thing to see a sign and another thing to interpret that sign correctly. However, our first duty is to recognize signs for what they are. If we do not even regard them as indicators of anything beyond themselves, we will not try to interpret them.[165]

If we fail to see God's image in other persons we may also fail to see in them anything beyond themselves. Such an attitude has serious implications for social action.

Merton strongly emphasized that contemplation goes beyond self and reaches out to others:

> Christian contemplation is existential not only in the sense that it experiences our own reality immersed in the reality of Him Who IS, but also in the sense that it is the participation in a concrete action of God in time, the climax of the divine irruption into human history which, because it

was an act of God as well as of Man, is capable of com-
municating itself over and over again in the lives of
individual men.[166]

Although his desire for union with God is the most fundamental
expression of man's revolutionary spirit, this certainly does not
render him incapable of social action in the world. 'It is not a
matter of *either* God *or* man, but of finding God by loving man,
and discovering the true meaning of man in our love for God.
Neither is possible without the other.'[167] Man's very being
demands he love both: *'there is no point at which it becomes
reasonable to abate your interior love for God or for other men,
because that love is an end in itself: it is the thing for which we
were created and the only reason why we exist.'*[168]

To know God and to live for God is the contemplative
vocation. Nothing takes precedence over this desire, for it is as
we discover God that God discovers us. Merton explains:

> Our discovery of God is, in a way, God's discovery of
> us. We cannot go to heaven to find Him because we have
> no way of knowing where heaven is or what it is. He
> comes down from heaven and finds us. He looks at us
> from the depths of His own infinite actuality, which is
> everywhere, and His seeing us gives us a superior reality
> in which we also discover Him. We only know Him in so
> far as we are known by Him, and our contemplation of
> Him is a participation in His contemplation of Himself.
> We become contemplatives when He discovers Himself
> in us.[169]

'If we believe in the Incarnation of the Son of God,' says Merton
elsewhere, 'there should be no one on earth in whom we are not
prepared to see, in mystery, the presence of Christ.'[170]

1. *The Seven Storey Mountain*, p. 370.

2. Ibid.

3. *The Sign of Jonas*, p. 23.

4. *The Seven Storey Mountain*, pp. 380-81.

5. Ibid., p. 382. In 'The Life That Unifies,' ed. Naomi Burton Stone, *Sisters Today* 42 (1970) 68-69, Merton tells of a monk who never came to Office or choir and yet was a saint.

6. *The Seven Storey Mountain*, p. 382.

7. See Bamberger, 'The Cistercian,' *Continuum* 7 (1969) 232; rpt. as 'The Monk' in Hart, ed., *Thomas Merton/Monk*, p. 44. Cf. comments on a similar theme in Edward Rice, *The Man in the Sycamore Tree*, p. 92.

8. Merton describes the Carthusians in his book *The Silent Life* (New York: Farrar, Straus and Cudahy, 1957) pp. 127-44.

9. Bamberger, 'The Cistercian,' pp. 232-33; rpt. *Thomas Merton/Monk*, p. 45. See Merton, *The Silent Life*, pp. 144-71, for a description of the Camaldolese. [An American Camaldolese monastery has since been established at Big Sur, California and Bloomingdale, Ohio—ed.]

10. *The Sign of Jonas*, p. 34.

11. Ibid., p. 28. See also pp. 78-79.

12. 'First and Last Thoughts: An Author's Preface' in *A Thomas Merton Reader*, ed. McDonnell, p. viii.

13. Ibid., pp. 97-98.

14. Ibid., p. 150. See *Thoughts in Solitude*, pp. 71-73, for further comments concerning poverty.

15. *Conjectures of a Guilty Bystander*, pp. 140-41.

16. *Seeds of Destruction*, pp. 242-43.

17. *The Ascent to Truth*, p. 281.

18. *No Man is an Island*, p. 11.

19. *The Climate of Monastic Prayer*, p. 145.

20. *Seeds of Destruction*, p. 203.

21. *The Sign of Jonas*, pp. 317-18.

22.   *Selected Poems of Thomas Merton*, pp. 108-09. Merton comments at length on this false division between the cloister and the world in his essay 'Is the World a Problem?' in *Contemplation in a World of Action*, pp. 143-56. See especially pp. 143-45, where Merton reflected on the changes that had taken place since the publication of *The Seven Storey Mountain*.

23.   *Contemplation in a World of Action*, p. 149.

24.   Quoted from a Merton letter in Leslie Dewart, 'A Post-Christian Age?' *Continuum* 1 (1964) 562.

25.   *The Waters of Siloe*, p. xxxiii.

26.   *The Climate of Monastic Prayer*, p. 35.

27.   *The Living Bread*, p. 126. Robert Farrar Capon discusses this idea of the spirituality of everyday life at length in his book *An Offering of Uncles: The Priesthood of Adam and the Shape of the World* (1967; rpt. New York: Harper Colophon, 1969).

28.   *Conjectures of a Guilty Bystander*, p. 36.

29.   *The Sign of Jonas*, p. 312. James Thomas Baker speaks of Merton's experience in the monastery in *Thomas Merton Social Critic*; note especially, p. 37.

30.   Aldhelm Cameron-Brown, 'Seeking the Rhinoceros: A Tribute to Thomas Merton,' *Monastic Studies* 7 (1969) 73; rpt. as 'Zen Master' in Hart, ed., *Thomas Merton/Monk*, p. 171.

31.   *Monastic Peace*, p. 52, rpt. *The Monastic Journey*, p. 79.

32.   Ibid., p. 54.

33.   *Silence in Heaven*, pp. 23-24.

34.   *Monastic Peace*, p. 9, rpt. *The Monastic Journey*, p. 44.

35.   Ibid., p. 10

36.   *The Waters of Siloe*, p. 299.

37.   *Bread in the Wilderness*, p. 19: 'Wherever Catholics have lived as solitaries the claims of their solitude have always yielded at certain times to the demands of the *synaxis*—the assembly of the hermits in communal, liturgical prayer. The lives of the Desert Fathers show that the liturgical and sacramental life of the Church played an essential part in their contemplation.

38.   *Monastic Peace*, p. 12, rpt. *The Monastic Journey*, p. 46.

39.   Ibid., p. 45.

40.   *The Waters of Siloe*, pp. 341-42.

41.   A handy translation is that of Leonard J. Doyle, *St Benedict's Rule for Monasteries*, (Collegeville, Minn.: Liturgical Press, 1948).

42.   *The Silent Life*, pp. 54-55.

43.   Ibid., p. 31.

44.   *Conjectures of a Guilty Bystander*, pp. 34-35.

45.   Ibid., pp. 34-35.

46.   *Contemplation in a World of Action*, p. 14.

47.   Ibid., p. 16.

48.   Ibid., pp. 16-17.

49.   Ibid., p. 156.

50.   'Prayer, Tradition, and Experience,' ed. Naomi Burton Stone, *Sisters Today* 42 (1971) 293.

51.   'The Life That Unifies,' p. 68.

52.   *Conjectures of a Guilty Bystander*, p. 37

53.   *The Waters of Siloe*, p. 31.

54.   Merton commented extensively on Rahner's concept of the diaspora in an essay entitled 'The Christian in the Diaspora' in *Seeds of Destruction*, pp. 184-220. This same essay is found in Thomas Merton, *Redeeming the Time* (London: Burns & Oates, 1966) pp. 93-119. See also Merton, 'The Monk in the Diaspora,' *Commonweal* 79 (1963-64) 741-45; and in *Blackfriars* 45 (1964) 290-302.

55.   *Seeds of Destruction*, pp. 199-200.

56.   Ibid., pp. 200-201.

57.   'Marxism and Monastic Perspectives,' in Moffit, ed., *A New Charter for Monasticism* (Notre Dame: University of Notre Dame Press, 1970) p. 78; rpt. in *The Asian Journal*, p. 338.

58.   *Seeds of Destruction*, p. 218.

59.   Ibid.

60.   *Raids on the Unspeakable*, p. 159.

61.   In a book review in *Monastic Studies* 1 (1963) 140-41, Merton speaks of the contingencies of modern life and their effect upon monasticism.

62.   *Seeds of Destruction*, p. 220.

63.   Edward McCorkell, 'Towards Conclusions: A Pre-position Paper' in Pennington, ed., *The Cistercian Spirit: A Symposium*, p. 260.

64.   See Baker, *Thomas Merton Social Critic*, p. 53: 'Merton's own attitude toward the world was paradoxical in that the more he learned to love man's society and the more effectively he addressed himself to its problems, the more he felt the need to withdraw from it.'

65.   Editorial, *Listening: Current Studies in Dialog* 1 (1966) 170.

66.   Dennis Quentin McInerny, 'Thomas Merton and Society: A Study of the Man and His Thought Against the Background of Contemporary American Culture,' Dissertation, University of Minnesota 1969, p. 219.

67.   McInerny, 'Thomas Merton and Society,' p. 220. This is quoted from Merton.

68.   *Thoughts in Solitude*, p. 129.

69.   *Disputed Questions*, pp. 139-44.

70.   Ibid., p. 141.

71.   See ibid., p. 139: 'A monk is, etymologically, a *monachos* or one who is isolated, alone. However, since 'monastic' now suggests not so much the man as the institution, I have seldom used the word 'monk' in these pages. I am speaking of the solitary spirit which is really essential to the monastic view of life, but which is not confined to monasteries. Nor is it limited to men and women who have consecrated their lives to God by vow.

72.   Ibid., p. 145.

73.   Ibid., p. 149.

74.   Merton built a strong historical case for the solitary life in 'The Case for a Renewal of Eremitism in the Monastic State' in *Contemplation in a World of Action*, pp. 294-327.

75.   An ever-present danger of an unhealthy solitary life is madness. See *The Silent Life*, p. 141.

76.   *The Ascent to Truth*, p. 145.

77.   *No Man is an Island*, p. 130.

78.   *Contemplation in a World of Action*, p. 249.

79.   See ibid., pp. 269-83 for the essay 'The Spiritual Father in the Desert Tradition'.

80.   *Disputed Questions*, pp. 149-50.

81.   *Contemplation in a World of Action*, p. 322.

82. Ibid., p. 244.

83. *The Silent Life*, p. 164.

84. *Silence in Heaven*, pp. 25-26.

85. *The True Solitude: Selections from the Writings of Thomas Merton*, ed. Dean Walley (Kansas City, Mo.: Hallmark, 1969) p. 18.

86. *Thoughts in Solitude*, p. 133.

87. Cistercian Studies Series, 18 (Spencer, Mass.: Cistercian Publications, 1971) pp. 50-51.

88. *The Climate of Monastic Prayer*, p. 42.

89. *Spiritual Direction and Meditation*, p. 45.

90. Ibid., p. 70.

91. Ibid., p. 98.

92. *The Climate of Monastic Prayer*, p. 49.

93. Ibid., p. 55.

94. *The Sign of Jonas*, pp. 221-22.

95. *Spiritual Direction and Meditation*, pp. 63-64.

96. *Thoughts in Solitude*, p. 37.

97. *No Man is an Island*, p. 164.

98. Ibid., p. 165.

99. Ibid., p. 166: 'I do not mean that there are two souls in man with two sets of faculties. Man's one soul acts in two different ways, when dealing with the outward works and inward contemplation.'

100. Ibid., pp. 166-67.

101. Ibid., p. 168.

102. Ibid., p. 167. Merton expresses a similar idea in relation to Zen in *Mystics and Zen Masters*, p. 25.

103. 'The Life that Unifies,' p. 65.

104. *Bread in the Wilderness*, p. 117.

105. *The Waters of Siloe*, p. 16.

106. *New Seeds of Contemplation*, p. 1.

107. Ibid., p. 4.

108. Ibid., p. 166.

109. See Higgins, *Merton's Theology of Prayer*, pp. 48-83, for an extensive discussion of prayer and the various terms used by Merton to describe it.

110. *The Climate of Monastic Prayer*, p. 152.

111. Ibid.

112. *Thoughts in Solitude*, p. 39.

113. 'Prayer and Conscience,' ed. Stone, *Sisters Today* 42 (1971) 409.

114. *Figures for an Apocalypse*, pp. 103-04.

115. 'The Humanity of Christ in Monastic Prayer,' *Monastic Studies* 2 (1964) 7, rpt., *The Monastic Journey*, p. 92.

116. *Spiritual Direction and Meditation*, p. 36.

117. 'The Contemplative Life: Its Meaning and Necessity,' *The Dublin Review* 446 (1949) 30.

118. *The Climate of Monastic Prayer*, p. 149.

119. Ibid., p. 154.

120. Although Merton's travels were well-publicized he left the monastery very infrequently. See Bamberger, 'The Cistercian' pp. 227-28, rpt. in Hart, ed., *Thomas Merton/Monk*, p. 38: 'Predictably, some journalistic accounts have spoken of him as having 'wandered back into the world' just as he had 'wandered into the monastery' in the first place. In reality, Merton was one of the most 'stabilized' monks in history.'

121. Rice, *The Man in the Sycamore Tree*, p. 131.

122. Charles Dumont *ocso*, 'A Contemplative in the Heart of the World—Thomas Merton,' *Luman Vitae* 24 (1969) 639; rpt. as 'The Contemplative' in Hart, ed., *Thomas Merton/Monk*, p. 132.

123. McCorkell, 'Towards Conclusions: A Pre-position Paper' in Pennington ed., *The Cistercian Spirit*, pp. 262-63.

124. *The Ascent to Truth*, p. 28.

125. *Seeds of Destruction*, p. 301.

126. *New Seeds of Contemplation*, p. 158.

127. *Zen and the Birds of Appetite*, pp. 76-77.

128. Cameron-Brown, 'Seeking the Rhinoceros', p. 166; rpt. in Hart, ed., *Thomas Merton/Monk*, p. 164.

129. *New Seeds of Contemplation*, p. 158.

130. *Bread in the Wilderness*, p. 102.

131. *Monastic Peace*, p. 15, rpt. *The Monastic Journey*, p. 49.

132. *The Behavior of Titans*, p. 65.

133. Ibid., pp. 68-69.

134. Ibid., p. 69.

135. James F. Andrews, 'Was Merton a Critic of Renewal?' *National Catholic Reporter* 6 (February 11, 1970) Lenten Supplement 14.

136. 'First and Last Thoughts,' *A Thomas Merton Reader*, p. x.

137. *The Seven Storey Mountain*, p. 410.

138. In *The Sign of Jonas*, p. 28, he relates how he looked forward to feast days when he was not under obligation to write.

139. 'First and Last Thoughts,' *A Thomas Merton Reader*, p. x.

140. *Figures for an Apocalypse*, p. 106.

141. Ibid., p. 111.

142. *Thoughts in Solitude*, p. 75.

143. Ibid.

144. John Howard Griffin, 'In Search of Thomas Merton,' *Thomas Merton Studies Center*, 1 (Santa Barbara: Unicorn Press, 1971) pp. 18-19.

145. *The Behavior of Titans*, p. 67.

146. *My Argument with the Gestapo*, p. 259.

147. See *Conjectures of a Guilty Bystander*, pp. 17-19.

148. 'The Solitary Life,' *Cistercian Studies* 4 (1969) 216.

149. *The Waters of Siloe*, p. xxxviii. In *Bread in the Wilderness*, p. 11. Merton elaborates: 'St Benedict of Nursia, writing his rule for monks, was writing for men who have no other purpose in life but God. After all, is there any other purpose for anyone? All men seek God, whether they know it or not?

150. *Redeeming the Time*, pp. 46-47.

151. Ibid., p. 13.

152. *The New Man*, p. 13. Merton makes no distinction between knowledge of God in a philosophical sense and the experience of God in mysticism. In his earlier works he maintained that the created self remains distinct from God even in mystical union.

153. *Zen and the Birds of Appetite*, p. 24.

154. Ibid., pp. 24-25. On pp. 22-23, Merton comments on the 'death of God' in relation to the Cartesian concept of God as an object.

155. Ibid., p. 111.

156. *The New Man*, pp. 9-10.

157. *The Waters of Siloe*, p 338. Cf. *Basic Principles of Monastic Spirituality*, p. 28: 'Without a true *metanoia*, a true conversion of one's whole life, monastic discipline is an illusion. There must be a total reorientation of our entire being from love of self to love of God, rpt. *The Monastic Journey*, p. 34.

158. *Thoughts in Solitude*, p. 59.

159. *Zen and the Birds of Appetite*, p. 27.

160. *The Climate of Monastic Prayer*, p. 125.

161. *No Man is an Island*, p. 29.

162. *The New Man*, p. 113.

163. *The Secular Journal of Thomas Merton*, p. 203.

164. *The New Man*, pp. 114-15. See also p. 113.

165. *No Man is an Island*, p. 59.

166. *The New Man*, p. 11.

167. *Redeeming the Time*, p. 40. In *The Ascent to Truth*, p. 167, he emphasizes that social action is motivated by faith and carried out by human decision.

168. *The Waters of Siloe*, p. 336.

169. *The True Solitude*, p. 27.

170. *New Seeds of Contemplation*, p. 229.

THE UNION OF CONTEMPLATION AND ACTION

The New Man

THE INCARNATION underlies Merton's understanding of
man. This is especially explicit within the context of
monasticism. He wrote that 'the whole meaning of
monastic life flows from the mystery of the Incarnation.'[1] The
doctrine of the Incarnation is itself difficult to comprehend, and
even more so when it is applied to the monastic life. Merton
likens it to a magnifying glass:

> As a magnifying glass concentrates the rays of the sun
> into a little burning knot of heat that can set fire to a dry
> leaf or a piece of paper, so the mystery of Christ in the
> Gospel concentrates the rays of God's light and fire to a
> point that sets fire to the spirit of man. And this is why
> Christ was born and lived in the world and died and
> returned from death and ascended to His Father in
> heaven: *ut dum visibilter Deum cognoscimus, per hunc in
> invisibilium amorem rapiamur.* Through the glass of His
> Incarnation He concentrates the rays of His divine Truth
> and Love upon us so that we feel the burn, and all
> mystical experience is communicated to men through the
> Man Christ.
> For in Christ God is made Man. In Him God and man
> are no longer separate, remote from one another, but
> inseparably one, unconfused and yet indivisible. Hence in
> Christ everything that is divine and supernatural becomes
> accessible on the human level to every man born of
> woman, to every son of Adam. [2]

The Incarnation, the perfect union of the human and the divine,
forms the basis for Christian mysticism.

Merton compares the mystical experience to the Incarnation

and points out that 'to live "in Christ" is to live in a mystery equal to that of the Incarnation and similar to it.'[3]

> For as Christ unites in His one Person the two natures of God and of man, so too in making us His friends He dwells in us, uniting us intimately to Himself. Dwelling in us He becomes as it were our superior self, for He has united and identified our inmost self with Himself. From the moment that we have responded by faith and charity to His love for us, a supernatural union of our souls with His indwelling Divine Person gives us a participation in His divine sonship and nature. A 'new being' is brought into existence. I become a 'new man' and this new man, spiritually and mystically one identity, is at once Christ and myself.[4]

This new man does not come into being until deep and important changes take place within the person. Merton outlines these in his book *The New Man* and he makes reference to the old and new Adam. He first speaks of the world as it existed prior to the fall of man:

> The world was, by the very presence of God in it, wonderful and sacred. But the sacred character of the world needed a witness and an interpreter. This was the function of the contemplative and active Adam, appointed to 'dress the garden of Paradise and to keep it.' By his morning and evening knowledge of God, Adam would know the Lord not only in contemplation but in action—not only in his own soul but in material creation. Everywhere he looked, Adam was beset by light, wonder and understanding. This, in the plan of God, was to have been our own condition.[5]

Adam was given to perform in the garden tasks which became 'an important aspect of his existential communion with the reality of nature and of the supernatural by which he was surrounded. It was a conversation with God, a moment of Adam's *parrhesia*.'[6] Adam's relationship to God was one of both contemplation and action.

Merton spoke of this *parrhesia* of Adam as 'the free spiritual communication of being with Being, Adam's existential communion with the reality around him in and through the Reality of God which he consequently experienced within himself.'[7] Basic to the union of man's soul with God which flows from this[8] is man's acceptance of reality—the reality of the world, the reality of God, and the reality of self. There was no illusion. Adam accepted God and the world openly.

With the fall of man, however, all of this changed; illusion was substituted for reality. Merton says:

> Adam's fall was therefore the willful acceptance of unreality, the consent to receive and even prefer a lie to the truth about himself and about his relationship to God. This lie robbed him of the innocence by which he saw nothing but good in himself, in things and in God and endowed him with the power to know evil, not only speculatively but by experience. The experience of falsity destroyed in him the instinctive taste for spiritual truth. Illusion entered in to spoil the existential flow of communication between his soul and God. *Parrhesia* was at an end not because God no longer consented to speak with Adam, but because Adam, stripped of his sincerity, ashamed to be what in fact he was, determined to fly from God and from reality, which he could no longer face without a disguise.[9]

Because Adam's work involved both contemplation and action, this change in his relationship with God became evident before long in his relationship to other men, taking the form of pride, in Merton's view 'a deep, insatiable need for unreality, an exorbitant demand that others believe the lie we have made ourselves believe about ourselves. It infects at once man's person and the whole society he lives in.'[10] This is the situation in which man found himself after the fall, and indeed, in which mankind finds itself today.

Merton speaks of the second Adam, Jesus Christ the incarnate Word of God. In Christ the union of God and man is restored, and the effect of Christ's coming 'is to manifest itself above all in the mystical union of all the transformed and deified members of regenerated humanity with one another and with God....'[11] In Christ we see the real meaning of self-realization:

> We come to 'realize' and 'know' ourselves when we are fully actualized as we are meant to be in the designs of God. We are fully 'alive' when we not only live perfectly in Him, but when we are aware of our life in Him—or, to put it more simply, fully aware of Him. Yet this awareness is arrived at through the plenitude of His Being reflected

in the plenitude of His life in ourselves. We are most truly
ourselves when our souls 'reflect as in a mirror the glory
of the Lord'. And when a mirror is full of light, you do not
see the glass—you are blinded by the light. [12]

Pride has no place here, for to be aware of our life in God
'means, in fact, to become humble, to throw away the illusion
that I am the center of everything and that other people only
exist to provide me with comfort and pleasure'. [13]

This dis-illusion cannot be achieved by man alone. Adam's
sin was the illusion that he could live on his own without the
light of God. As a result the mirror cracked and no longer
reflected any light at all. Thus Merton emphasizes our need of
God:

> But we are incapable of knowing and experiencing reality
> adequately unless we see things in the light of him who
> is All Being, all real. The Spirit of God, penetrating and
> enlightening our own spirit from within ourselves, teaches
> us the ways of freedom by which alone we enter into valid
> spiritual contact with those around us. In the contact we
> become aware of our own autonomy, our own identifica-
> tion. We find out who we really are. And having made the
> discovery we are ready for the love and service of
> others. [14]

Service to others comes only after we find out who we really are
in relationship to God.

Adam escaped from God by passing through the center of
himself. He turned his face from God and looked inward.
Unable to face who he really was, he 'mentally reconstructed
the whole universe in his own image and likeness'. [15] This
reconstruction he placed between God and himself and today
mankind reaps the results of this painful and useless labor.

> The labor of science without wisdom; the mental toil that
> pieces together fragments that never manage to coalesce
> in one completely integrated whole: the labor of action
> without contemplation, that never ends in peace or satis-
> faction, since no task is finished without opening the way
> to ten more tasks that have to get done. [16]

Merton felt there is only one way to return to God and to find
ourselves in him: we must reverse Adam's journey and go back
the same way he came. Merton avers that the path lies through

the center of our own soul:

> Adam withdrew into himself from God and then passed
> through himself and went forth into creation. We must
> withdraw ourselves (in the right and Christian sense) from
> exterior things, and pass through the center of our own
> souls to find God. We must recover possession of our true
> selves by liberation from anxiety and fear and inordinate
> desire. And when we have gained possession of our souls,
> we must learn to 'go out' of ourselves to God and to others
> by supernatural charity. [17]

In looking back on Merton's life we can see that this is
exactly what he in fact did. He withdrew from the world of the
city, the university and social life into the monastery, where he
passed through the center of his own soul and found God. Once
he had gained possession of his soul he went out to others in
action by prayer and writing. He was quite literally a new man.

Becoming a new man involves many things, one of the most
important of which is the development of a new consciousness.
'What is required of Christians,' says Merton, 'is that they
develop a completely modern and contemporary *consciousness*
in which their experience as men of our century is integrated
with their experience as children of God redeemed by Christ.' [18]
The new man is not complete unless he can intelligently and
creatively unite his relationship to God with his relationship to
the world.

New consciousness involves more than accepting the modern
viewpoint on consciousness which, in Merton's words, 'tends to
create this solipsistic bubble of awareness—an ego-self
imprisoned in its own consciousness, isolated and out of touch
with other such selves in so far as they are all "things" rather
than persons'. [19] Merton suggests four human needs that must
be met if this new consciousness is to have meaning in today's
world:

> *First:* His need for community, for a genuine relation-
> ship of authentic love with his fellow man. This will also
> imply a deep, in fact completely radical, seriousness in
> approaching those critical problems which threaten man's
> very survival as a species on earth—war, racial conflict,
> hunger, economic and political injustice, etc....
> *Second:* Man's need for an adequate understanding of
> his everyday self in his ordinary life. There is no longer
> any place for the kind of idealistic philosophy that removes

all reality into the celestial realms and makes temporal existence meaningless... Man needs to find ultimate sense here and now in the ordinary humble tasks and human problems of every day.

Third: Man's need for a whole and integral experience of his own self on all its levels, bodily as well as imaginative, emotional, intellectual, spiritual. There is no place for the cultivation of *one part* of human consciousness, *one aspect* of human experience, at the expense of the others, even on the pretext that what is cultivated is sacred and all the rest profane. A false and divisive 'sacredness' or 'supernaturalism' can only cripple man....

I might suggest a *fourth* need of modern man which is precisely liberation from his inordinate self-consciousness, his monumental self-awareness, his obsession with self-affirmation, so that he may enjoy the freedom from concern that goes with being simply what he is and accepting things as they are in order to work with them as he can.[20]

What we need is what James Douglass calls 'the acquiring of an absolutely new point of view toward life and the world'.[21] With this new point of view man becomes fully alive: 'Man, then, can only fully be said to be alive when he becomes plainly conscious of the real meaning of his own existence, that is to say when he *experiences* something of the fullness of intelligence, freedom and spirituality that are actualized within himself.'[22]

The new man is not a superman who is now above the problems of the everyday world. Merton makes this very clear: 'The "new man" is totally transformed, and yet he remains the *same person*. He is spiritualized, indeed the Fathers would say he is "divinized" in Christ.'[23] However, he is not perfect, and he must be aware of the ever-present danger of using illusion as a way of escaping life's responsibilities. In Merton's words we must assume 'full responsibility for our lives just as they are, with all their handicaps and limitations....'[24]

The new man has undergone a *metanoia*, a radical transformation of his being. He has returned through the depths of his inner soul to God and has found himself in contemplation. At the same time, however, he lives in the world, involved in myriad human relationships, each of which he now perceives differently than he did before. The new man, having distinguished reality from illusion, must also be able to initiate responsible action, for he is still very much a part of the world in which he lives. 'Though I often differ strongly from that "world,"' Merton writes, 'I think I can be said to respond to it. I do not delude myself that I am not still a part of it.'[25]

Events and Pseudo-Events

It is imperative that the new man face reality, beginning with his own inner self, for 'all falsity is disastrous in any relation with the ground of our own being and with God himself, who communicates with us through our own inner truth'.[26] If one is guilty of falsehood within himself its implications will extend to the rest of his life, including his relations with others. Merton emphasized the stripping away of all illusion from within as a prior condition to a search for and acceptance of the reality of the world at large.

Even if one has achieved this acceptance of reality in the inner man, he still faces the problem of separating reality from illusion in the world in which he lives. One may not be *of* the world but one must still live *in* the world. Merton found a problem here in making statements on various social issues. As a monk and as a hermit he was separated from the world, yet he found that he was compelled to speak out on matters of war and peace, racial injustice, the dangers of technology, and political oppression. At the same time he faced the difficulty of distinguishing between what he called events and pseudo-events. In Merton's view the monk's task is to deal with real events: 'A contemplative will, then, concern himself with the same problems as other people, but he will try to get to the spiritual and metaphysical roots of these problems—not by analysis but by simplicity.'[27]

In contemporary society, as Merton understood it, one may quite easily make pronouncements on issues of social concern but 'once one has taken a stand he is not necessarily obliged to come out with a new answer and a new solution to insoluble problems every third day'.[28] Unfortunately, most people seem to think they must come up with new answers all of the time, and this, he felt, can be dangerous spiritually:

> When one has too many answers, and when one joins a chorus of others chanting the same slogans, there is, it seems to me, a danger that one is trying to evade the loneliness of a conscience that realizes itself to be in an inescapably evil situation. We are all under judgement. None of us is free from contamination. Our choice is not

that of being pure and whole at the mere cost of formulating a just and honest opinion. Mere commitment to a decent program of action does not lift the curse. Our real choice is between being like Job, who *knew* he was stricken, and Job's friends who did not know that they were stricken too—though less obviously than he. (So they had answers!)[29]

Often our condemnation of social evils masks our own sinfulness, which we are unwilling to face. As a result, social statements become pseudo-events dealing with illusion rather than events dealing with reality.

An obvious example of this can be found in the mass media's presentation of the daily news. Merton, of course, rarely read newspapers and watched television only twice in his entire life. News reached him long after the events which made up the news had taken place. He declares:

Certainly events happen and they affect me as they do other people. It is important for me to know about them too: but I refrain from trying to know them in their fresh condition as 'news'. When they reach me they have become slightly stale. I eat the same tragedies as others, but in the form of tasteless crusts. The news reaches me in the long run through books and magazines, and no longer as a stimulant. Living without news is like living without cigarettes (another peculiarity of the monastic life). The need for this habitual indulgence quickly disappears. So, when you hear news without the 'need' to hear it, it treats you differently. And you treat it differently too.[30]

From his perspective Merton discovered that 'nine tenths of the news, as printed in the papers, is pseudo-news, manufactured events. Some days ten tenths.'[31]

In Merton's opinion, 'the root of our trouble is that our habits of thought and the drives that proceed from them are basically idolatrous and mythical.'[32] He expands in terms of political news:

Instead of taking care to examine the realities of our political or social problems, we simply bring out the idols in solemn procession. 'We are the ones who are right, *they* are the ones who are wrong. We are the good guys, *they* are the bad guys. We are honest, *they* are crooks....'

Thus in support of realism and objectivity we simply determine beforehand that we will be swayed by no fact whatever that does not accord perfectly with our own preconceived judgement. Objectivity becomes simple dogmatism.[33]

Events are fabricated, statements made and later denied, and it becomes almost impossible to tell the real from the false. Society becomes so caught up in this cycle that it leaves to a select few decisions that affect all of us. Most people believe what they are told with no thought to the morality of the situation or the truth of the matter. 'Our Salvation,' says Merton, 'cannot be sought in the realm of images and idols, of fabricated events and unclear meanings.'[34]

Another aspect of this web of events and pseudo-events is what Merton calls the myth of being contemporary: 'We imagine that we are of all generations the most enlightened, the most progressive and the most humane. This, in fact, is an "image" of ourselves—an image which is false and is also the object of a cult.'[35] Merton commented at length on the influence of this myth upon contemporary society:

If we examine this concept of 'being contemporary' we find that it is a pure myth and in fact one of the central myths of our society. The myth of contemporariness, like the myth of progress of which it is a special development, calls for more profound study than we could possibly attempt here. It is certainly a by-product of our extreme technological virtuosity. The affluent marketing mentality of the capitalist West, in which the individual identity of the consumer is conditioned, to a great extent, by his ability to come up with the latest model in cars, clothes, and TV sets just at the right moment, has created the proper atmosphere. If one is not 'right' in his outlook, his tastes, his decisions (manifested by the right kind of possessions), one feels that his very existence is somehow diminished. One's image has begun to fade. One is on the point of losing reality. Contemporariness is, in fact, status, and status is identity, reality. To be contemporary is to be recognizable as quite up to date in a fast moving world where not only tastes but whole world-views in art, science, philosophy, literature and religion are revolutionized every three to five years. A slight error in timing and one is no longer perfectly 'contemporary'. One goes under. One drowns in the flux of ephemeral decisions and is superseded by others who have the skill to stay contemporary.[36]

He added that the myth of being contemporary is even more important in communist countries, for 'here one's precise shade of rightness may mean life or death. It pays to be up to date and "truly contemporary."'[37]

As a result of this cult of the contemporary we find it extremely difficult to distinguish event from pseudo-event, for what is 'in' today may suddenly be 'out' tomorrow. What was important on one day may suddenly be rendered insignificant by the events of the following day. Many people live their lives almost totally in this fabricated, constantly changing world of pseudo-events and they never face themselves and the world. One can become so caught up in the desire to be contemporary that he thinks only in terms of himself, and this, says Merton, leads only to disaster: 'To consider persons and events and situations only in the light of their effect upon myself is to live on the doorstep of hell'.[38]

A further ramification of this problem lies in the area of man's ability to create artificial environments.[39] In many situations man has become so alienated from himself that he lives on a purely sensual level of external stimuli:

> Men have come to live so exclusively on the surface of their being that life has become a mere quest of rudimentary pleasures and a flight from physical and mental pain. We are left at the mercy of external stimuli, and stimulation has even come to take the place of what used, at one time, to be occupied by thought and reflection and understanding. [40]

Man has so lost touch with his own personhood that he cannot relate to himself or to others. He reacts only to those pseudo-events which give him pleasure and ease his pain.

Merton was emphatic in stating that 'the Church has an obligation *not* to join in the incantation of political slogans and in the concoction of pseudo-events, *but to cut clear through the deviousness and ambiguity of both slogans and events by her simplicity and love.'*[41] Not that the Church should fail to take the changing times into account and pretend to live in the Middle Ages. Merton pointed out that 'there should be a reasonable adaptation to the times—though the obvious danger is not a lack of adaptation to, but submersion in, the spirit of these times.'[42] By the same token we must beware of the tendency '*to identify the human with the secular.*'[43] If we do, the Church becomes suspicious of the human and neglects or condemns the human in favor of 'the spiritual'.

We should also beware of what Merton called spiritual excitement. 'Our life must be based first of all on simple and human truth,' he wrote, 'not on a willful determination to make things come out the way we have decided, in a moment of spiritual excitement, that they ought to be.'[44] The danger of pseudo-events in the spiritual life as well as in secular life, is evidenced by the cults, sects, and movements which spring up around various emotional religious experiences.

Although Merton was strongly opposed to the myth of being contemporary, he was well aware that the world is changing and says that for a contemplative the deep realization that passing things are provisional, not definitive, is of fundamental importance.[45] One must adjust to the times, concurrently realizing that the times come and go and cannot be regarded as definitive. Merton made this distinction between traditions 'living and active', and convention 'passive and dead....Convention is accepted passively, as a matter of routine. Therefore convention easily becomes an evasion of reality.'[46] Tradition concerns events; convention pseudo-events. Merton thought it unfortunate that so many monasteries which consider themselves traditional merely follow in fact a set of conventions held over from the Middle Ages.

There is a particular danger here to monasticism, for the monastic vocation and charism are easily confused with the institutional forms of the life. The monastic vocation is a real event and a valid tradition in the Church. The institutional structures, however, are transitory and provisional and can easily become mere conventions or pseudo-events.

> Before we can properly estimate our place in the world, we have to get back to the fundamental Christian respect for the *transiency* of both the world and the institutional structure of the Church....But if we despise the transient world of secularism in terms which suggest an ecclesiastical *world* that is not itself transient, there is no way to avoid disaster and absurdity.[47]

Where then does one find real events? The Church, Merton avers, 'is concerned with real events: saving events, the encounter of man and Christ in the reconciliation of man with man. In a sense, there is no other kind of event that matters and there is no other news that matters. To abandon this news is to become implicated in the manufacturing of pseudo-events....'[48] But the genuine saving event is not newsworthy because such an event is not usually sufficiently visible. This does not mean that it is not important. Merton illustrated this by speaking of the monasteries on Mount Athos:

> It is perhaps true that Athos is out of touch with our times, far more so than any monastery in the Western world. But precisely because of this it has much to teach us, since our salvation consists not in keeping up with the times but in transcending them or, as St Paul would say, in redeeming them.[49]

The monks of Mount Athos are living a saving event. The fact that it is not newsworthy, that it is not contemporary, or that it is out of touch is simply not important. The reality of Athonite monasticism depends upon its relationship to the encounter of man and Christ in the reconciliation of man with man. Real events center around redemption and reconciliation.

Action and Activism

Well aware of the confusion of real events and pseudo-events, Merton emphasized that the two are different and must not be mixed up if Christian action is to be significant. 'No matter how you doctor it,' he insisted, *'the pseudo-event cannot be turned into a saving and reconciling event.'*[50] This means that one must be discerning in choosing which events are worthy of action.

The contemplative, of all people, must learn to act in response rather than in reaction, for it is at this point that events are differentiated from pseudo-events. Merton's new man is able to respond to the world around him and do more than repeat formulas and statements given to him by society at large. 'Response involves the whole being of man in his freedom and his capacity to "see" and "move on"', Merton wrote. Reaction is nothing more than the mechanical, perhaps astutely and dishonestly improvised, answer of one's superficial self.'[51] The responsive man can see reality and therefore deal with real events. The man who reacts finds himself involved with pseudo-events.

Too much contemporary social action is based on reaction rather than on response, particularly when large numbers of people are involved. Merton felt that the mass movement makes it virtually impossible for one to respond to what is taking place around him.

> We are not saved *en masse*. Masses indeed may be called, but only individuals are chosen because only individuals can respond to a call by free choice of their own. The Church is not, and has never been merely for the mass-man, the passive, inert man who drifts with the crowd and never decides anything for himself.[52]

> ...from its very birth, Christianity has been categorically opposed to everything that savors of the mass-movement.[53]

Why did Merton take a stand against mass movements? To begin with there is always the danger of fanaticism which, in his words, 'is never really spiritual because it is not *free*'.[54] Caught up in the emotionalism of the mass, the fanatic is no longer in control of his actions and responds only minimally; reaction takes control.

He saw a further danger in mass movements: 'a mass movement always places the "cause" above the individual person, and sacrifices the person to the interests of the movement.'[55] In his terms, a cause would be a pseudo-event; the person a real event:

> Do not ask me to love my brother merely in the name of an abstraction—'society,' the 'human race,' the 'common good.' Do not tell me that I ought to love him because we are both 'social animals.' These things are so much less than the good that is in us that they are not worthy to be invoked as motives of human love....
>
> We need abstractions, perhaps, in order to *understand* our relations with one another. But I may understand the principles of ethics and still hate other men. If I do not love other men, I will never discover the meaning of the 'common good.' Love is, itself, the common good.
>
> There are plenty of men who will give up their interests for the sake of 'society,' but cannot stand any of the people they live with.[56]

To love another person in terms of a cause is extremely dangerous, for once the person no longer suits the cause there is no further reason for loving him.[57] Loving another as a person, however, means that causes are unimportant and the person is all important. One loves the person because of the person, not because of the causes with which that person may be associated.

A hidden, subtle danger in mass movements is perhaps most significant of all; the mass movement itself may become an illusion by which the person evades his own inner reality. There is the danger, in Merton's words, 'of being sidetracked by the "many things," that is, the activities of Martha....Yet the "one thing necessary" in our life must be the lived experience of God.'[58] The mass movement, he pointed out, gives one a certain degree of anonymity; he does not have to face his inner self in relation to his actions:

> The member of the mass-movement, afraid of his own isolation and his own weakness as an individual, cannot face the task of discovering within himself the spiritual power and integrity which can be called forth only by love. Instead of this, he seeks a movement that will protect his weakness with a well of anonymity and justify his acts by the sanctions of collective glory and power.[59]

All too often it has become evident that the basic spiritual problems still remain long after the mass movement has achieved its goal.

A preoccupation with pseudo-events can create within the Church a situation of activistic, secular, and anti-mystical bias.[60] As a result the Church itself takes on the form of a mass movement, and its members react to the world rather than respond to it. The Church then comes to be understood in terms of its reaction to contemporary social issues and not in terms of its response to the event of God's salvation to man. All too commonly the Church is used as a hiding place from both God and one's inner reality.

Merton knew that contemplatives could fall into this dangerous situation. Whenever activism has taken precedence over contemplation, he noted, monasteries have encountered difficulty and time after time failed to survive.[61] When the monastery loses its contemplative orientation and becomes involved in the cultural, economic, and political struggles of the society surrounding it, the monks lose their ability to speak prophetically to that society. Reaction to the needs and desires of society takes the place of a response to the call of God.[62] This does not mean that the contemplative is to withdraw totally from the world:

> It must be said at once that the active life is essential to

every Christian....Here action is not looked at in opposition to contemplation, but as an expression of charity and as a necessary consequence of union with God in baptism.... Even the cloistered 'contemplative' is inevitably implicated in the crises and problems of the society in which he is still a member (since he participates in its benefits and shares its responsibilities). Even he must to some extent participate 'actively' in the Church's work, not only by prayer and holiness, but by understanding and concern.[63]

The contemplative vocation is a call to real events, and the contemplative seeks to respond to God's saving action in those events. At the same time he must be able to distinguish the real from the illusory, beginning with himself and working outward to others and to the world. Of this difficult task, James Douglass states: 'Solitude is my home but I flee from it. I am not prepared to deal with its truth. Few men are. And the great temptation of resistance is that I will resist to avoid dealing with the truth of solitude.'[64] Much social activism today is nothing more than a means of avoiding one's own solitude and what one might find within oneself. Writing as one living and working outside the cloister, James Forest relates how Merton spoke to those involved in active social protest of the need for silence and solitude:

> He talked on the need for silence and the uncluttering of the mind, even more important for us than for monks: the imperative to protect the spirit from ambushes of busyness and schedules. 'Inside of yourselves, you shouldn't be running all the time,' he said, knowing well the kind of momentum which had been within us.[65]

Mere busy work, activity to keep one from facing himself, or attempts to be contemporary, were, for Merton, not action at all but activism.[66] In *Life and Holiness*, Merton distinguished between them:

> Is it strange that in this book on the active life the emphasis is not on energy and will power and action so much as on grace, and interiority? No, for these are the true principles of supernatural activity. An activity that is based on the frenzies and impulsions of human ambition is a delusion and an obstacle to grace. It gets in the way of God's will, and it creates more problems than it solves. We must learn to distinguish between the pseudo-spiritu-

ality of activism and the true vitality and energy of
Christian action guided by the Spirit.[67]

Any action that does not take into account the inner man and
the saving event of God's grace is not action at all but activism,
which separates man from his own inner being and from God.
Contemplation thus becomes a necessity for action. The two are
interrelated and cannot be separated if one is to live the
spiritual life in all of its fullness and vitality.

Living With Paradox

In the preface to *A Thomas Merton Reader*, Merton reflected
back on twenty-five years and said: 'I have had to accept the
fact that my life is almost totally paradoxical....It is in the
paradox itself, the paradox which was and still is a source of
insecurity, that I have come to find the greatest security.'[68]
This lays the cornerstone of Merton's understanding of
spirituality: we must accept ourselves as we are in reality and
not as we would like to be in illusion. Looking at himself Merton
found a virtual seedbed of contradiction and paradox, but he
learned to accept it, live with it, and turn it into an asset. He
wrote:

> I have become convinced that the very contradictions in
> my life are in some ways signs of God's mercy to me: if
> only because someone so complicated and so prone to con-
> fusion and self-defeat could hardly survive for long without
> special mercy. And since this in no way depends on the
> approval of others, the awareness of it is a kind of
> liberation.
> Consequently I think I can accept the situation with
> simplicity. Paradoxically, I have found peace because I
> have always been dissatisfied. My moments of depression
> and despair turn out to be renewals, new beginnings. If I
> were once to settle down and be satisfied with the surface
> of life, with its divisions and its clichés, it would be time
> to call in the undertaker, except that in the monastery we
> do without the ministrations of an embalmer. So, then,
> this dissatisfaction which sometimes used to worry me and
> has certainly, I know, worried others, has helped me in
> fact to move freely and even gaily with the stream of
> life.[69]

Out of his intense dissatisfaction grew Merton's understanding of the relationship between contemplation and action. It was still growing and developing at the time of his death.

Contradiction and paradox touched Merton at many levels of experience, but the contradiction between the ideal and the real most disturbed him. He wrote that 'the question itself is basic: how shall we face the contradiction between the ideal and the real in our society, the ideal and the concrete in ourselves?[70] He knew, for instance, that in society the ideal would be peace, but that the reality was war and violence. Most significantly, he also knew that the solution to the problem of war, or any other social problem, began when one faced the reality within the self: 'only when we have become able to accept the basic contradictions in our own self, can we have the humility to understand the contradictions in others and in society.'[71]

Accepting the contradictions within self leads to further paradox and contradiction. If one seeks wisdom one finds that 'wisdom manifests itself, and is yet hidden'.[72] Yet this seeming contradiction is, in reality, a pathway to renewal, for wisdom can be gained only by seeking it out and finding it. The same is true of love, for 'all love necessarily involves hate...choice demands exclusion.'[73] If one is to love God, one must hate the world.[74] If one chooses the contemplative life, one must exclude the life of worldly society. What at first appears as a contradiction later reveals itself as a liberation. However, one must first accept and face the reality of these contradictions, for if one tries to escape them he will find that 'we can overlay the contradiction with statements and explanations, we can produce an illusory coherence, we can impose on life our intellectual systems and we can enforce upon our minds a certain strained and artificial peace. But this is not peace.'[75]

The spiritual life, he believed, thrives on contradiction and paradox. He pointed out that 'there is no spiritual life without persistent struggle and interior conflict.'[76] Indeed, 'the spiritual life is a kind of dialectic between ideals and reality.'[77] He was careful to point out that dialectic is quite different from compromise, for compromise is but another way of seeking refuge in illusion. Compromise is another way of saying that there really is no contradiction. Dialectic, on the other hand, admits the reality of the contradiction and works from that starting point. For Merton this had important practical implications:

> The difference between the moral life and the mystical life is discovered in the presence of contradiction. When we

move ourselves as men, morally, *humano modo* we end up by hanging ourselves on the horn of the dilemma and hoping for the best. But when we are moved by God, mystically, we seem to solve the dilemma in ease and mystery, by choosing at the same time both horns of the dilemma and no horn at all and always being perfectly right. For instance in choir: orders are to keep up the pitch and make a pause of two beats at the mediant of the psalm verse: but the cantors drop the pitch and rush through the mediant with one beat. Moral activity: either (a) follow the cantor with a pure intention or (b) shut up and concentrate on praying, also with a pure intention. Mystical activity: the dilemma suddenly ceases to matter. You both follow the cantor and pray and find God and suddenly if God wills the contradiction disappears, and some attempt begins to be made to keep the rules the legislators have broken. [78]

There are several important things to note here. To begin, contradiction is not resolved until one accepts the reality of the contradiction. Then one does not resolve the contradiction by concentrating on it; rather, one focuses on one's relationship to God. The implications here for social action are obvious, and Merton makes this very clear by stressing that social action is vain unless one has first of all faced himself and his relationship to God.

This tension within us is also true of the relationship between life and death. 'Life and death are at war within us,' writes Merton. 'As soon as we are born we began at the same time to live and to die.'[79] Life consists largely of working out the tensions between life and death:

Man is truly alive when he is aware of himself as the master of his own destiny to life or to death, aware of the fact that his ultimate fulfilment or destruction depends on his own free choice and aware of this ability to decide for himself. This is the beginning of true life.[80]

Society would have us believe that one half of the paradox, death, is unreal, but by ignoring death one is not free to make decisions for himself since society decides for him. And when death comes it is more often than not brought about violently by a society that promised life. 'True peace,' according to Merton, 'is the "hidden attunement of opposite tensions"—a paradox and a mystery transcending both sense and will, like the ecstasy of the mystic.'[81]

These words 'hidden attunement of opposite tensions' are important for an understanding of Merton's view of contemplation and action. Although difficult for a westerner to understand, this concept is basic to the Chinese philosophy of Taoism and is symbolized in the yin-yang:

This symbol refers to the opposites—male-female, light-darkness, good-evil, etc. The two colors show that contradiction exists, yet each side flows into the other and at the heart of each is a small portion of the other. Taken separately each side appears to be contradictory; taken as a whole they come together smoothly in a dynamic unity.[82]

In *Resistance and Contemplation: The Way of Liberation*, James W. Douglass comments on this symbol as it relates to contemplation and action or resistance:

> The yin of contemplation is an encounter on the dark side of the mountain, in the soul....The yang of resistance, on the bright slope, is the struggle to stand against the murderous collective self and to express communally the living unity of all men in the One....
>
> The contemplative yin and resistance yang are coordinate powers of change which reinforce each other on a single way of liberation: liberation from a divided and divisive self in both its individual and collective forms, liberation into the One, where person, community, reality realize their ultimate identity. Yin becomes yang, contemplation passes into resistance, for the struggle on the dark side has forced me to recognize in the sunlight the murderousness of the collective self or my own self written large.[83]

The significant point here is the connection between the condition of the person and the condition of the society at large.

In order to deal with the problems of society one must first deal with the problems within himself and to discover the reality within one must go beyond himself to God. Merton asserted that 'contemplation is the highest and most paradoxical form of self-realization, attained by apparent self-annihilation'.[84] One finds himself by losing himself, and he finds others by finding himself, with the result that life 'is lived and experienced in its completeness, that is to say in all the ramifications of its spiritual activity'.[85] Merton summarizes this in the following words:

> To exist and function in the world of opposites while experiencing that world in terms of a primal simplicity does imply if not a formal metaphysic, at least a ground of metaphysical intuition. This means a totally different perspective than that which dominates our society—and enables it to dominate us.[86]

This, then, is what the union of contemplation and action is really all about—a different perspective, a new consciousness, a new man, a way of perceiving not illusion but reality. In the words of Merton: 'It might be good to open our eyes and *see*.'[87]

1. *Basic Principles of Monastic Spirituality*, p. 8, rpt. *The Monastic Journey*, p. 15.

2. *New Seeds of Contemplation*, p. 117.

3. *New Seeds of Contemplation*, p. 123.

4. Ibid.

5. *The New Man*, p. 40.

6. Ibid., p. 55.

7. Ibid., p. 53.

8. Ibid.

9. Ibid., pp. 53-54. Merton was greatly influenced by the thought of the Swiss philosopher Max Picard, who deals with man's flight from God in his book *The Flight From God* (Chicago: Henry Regnery, 1951).

10. *The New Man*, p. 70.

11. Ibid., p. 113.

12. Ibid., pp. 113-14.

13. Ibid., p. 71.

14. Ibid., pp. 47-48.

15. *The New Man*, p. 82.

16. Ibid., pp. 82-83.

17. Ibid., p. 83.

18. *Redeeming the Time*, p. 36.

19. *Zen and the Birds of Appetite*, p. 22. Merton elaborates on this idea of personhood in *Faith and Violence*, p. 111.

20. *Zen and the Birds of Appetite*, pp. 30-31.

21. James W. Douglass, *Resistance and Contemplation: The Way of Liberation* (Garden City: Doubleday, 1972) p. 60.

22. *The New Man*, p. 5.

23. *Life and Holiness*, p. 60.

24. Ibid.

25. *Conjectures of a Guilty Bystander*, p. vii.

26. *The Climate of Monastic Prayer*, p. 120.

27. *Faith and Violence*, p. 147.

28. Ibid., p. 145.

29. Ibid., pp. 145-46.

30. Ibid., p. 151.

31. Ibid. Merton explains what he means by pseudo-news on p. 152.

32. Ibid., p. 154.

33. Ibid., pp. 154-55. See p. 159, where Merton refers to the Berlin and Cuban crises as situations that can be 'turned on and off' to support our own preconceived judgements concerning international affairs.

34. *Faith and Violence*, p. 160.

35. Ibid., p. 154.

36. *Redeeming the Time*, pp. 30-31.

37. Ibid., p. 31.

38. *No Man is an Island*, p. 34.

39. Modern man has an intense desire for experience, but much of it is vicarious. He would rather visit Disneyland or Disneyworld than an African jungle. Films and television are more interesting than real life. The world of manufactured environments removes man from the real environment. The ultimate rejection of the real is found in the use of drugs where all external environments are rejected in favor of an artificial inner environment.

40. 'The Contemplative Life: Its Meaning and Necessity,' *The Dublin Review* 446 (1949) 27.

41. *Faith and Violence*, p. 161.

42. *Disputed Questions*, p. 69.

43. Book Review, *Monastic Studies* 1 (1963) 139.

44. Ibid.

45. See 'Notes From Meeting of Contemplatives,' notes taken by a nun on a talk by Thomas Merton given in December 1967 at Gethsemani, Kentucky, mimeographed, p. 4.

46. *No Man is an Island*, p. 120.

47. *Conjectures of a Guilty Bystander*, p. 42.

48. *Faith and Violence*, p. 162.

49. *Disputed Questions*, p. 62.

50. *Faith and Violence*, p. 163.

51. *Mystics and Zen Masters*, p. 250.

52. *Disputed Questions*, p. 104.

53. Ibid., p. 105.

54. Ibid.

55. Ibid.; p. 106. See Merton's essay 'Blessed Are the Meek' in *Faith and Violence*, pp. 14-19.

56. *No Man is an Island*, p. 132.

57. Cf. *Disputed Questions*, p. 106: 'Contrast this with the teaching of Christ, for whom the soul of the individual was more important than the most sacred laws and rites, since these exist only for the sake of persons, and not vice versa. 'The sabbath was made for man and not man for the sabbath' (Mark 2:27).

58. McCorkell, 'Towards Conclusions: A Pre-position Paper' in Pennington, ed., *The Cistercian Spirit*, p. 257.

59. *Disputed Questions*, p. 106.

60. *Zen and the Birds of Appetite*, p. 17.

61. See *The Waters of Siloe*, pp. 3-82.

62. The monk is not cut off from the world, as Merton explains in *Life and Holiness*, p. ix: 'Even in contemplative monasteries productive work is essential to the life of the community, and such work generally represents a service to society at large. Even contemplatives are, then, implicated in the ecomony of their nation. It is right that they should understand the nature of their service, and some of its implications. This is all the more true when the monastery offers to man the "service"—a very essential one indeed—of shelter and recollection during times of spiritual retreat.'

63. *Life and Holiness*, pp. vii-viii.

64. Douglass, *Resistance and Contemplation*, p. 141.

65. James H. Forest, 'The Gift of Merton,' *Commonweal* 89 (1969) 464.

66. McInerny, 'Thomas Merton and Society', p. 72.

67. *Life and Holiness*, pp. ix-x.

68. 'First and Last Thoughts,' in *A Thomas Merton Reader*, ed. McDonnell, p. ix.

69. Ibid., pp. ix-x. Cf. Matthew Kelty, 'Some Reminiscences of Thomas Merton,' *Cistercian Studies* 4 (1969) 175; rpt. as 'The Man' in Hart, ed., *Thomas Merton/Monk*, pp. 34-35.

70. *Monastic Peace*, p. 45, rpt. *The Monastic Journey*, p. 74.

71. Ibid., p. 46.

72. *Silence in Heaven*, p. 21.

73. 'Notes from Meeting of Contemplatives,' p. 12.

74. Merton uses the term 'world' in reference to the world system, political, social, economic, etc. He is not referring to the physical world of nature or of material objects.

75. 'First and Last Thoughts,' *A Thomas Merton Reader*, p. xi.

76. *Life and Holiness*, p. 158.

77. Ibid., p. 29.

78. *The Sign of Jonas*, p. 273.

79. *The New Man*, p. 3.

80. Ibid., pp. 7-8.

81. *The Behavior of Titans*, p. 76.

82. For further reflections on Taoism and the yin-yang symbol see Merton's essay 'A Study of Chuang Tzu' in his *The Way of Chuang Tzu* (New York: New Directions, 1965) pp. 15-32.

83. Douglass, *Resistance and Contemplation*, pp. 68-70. The views of Douglass were greatly influenced by those of Merton.

84. *The New Man*, p. 13.

85. Ibid., pp. 13-14.

86. *Zen and the Birds of Appetite*, p. 140.

87. Ibid., p. 141.

IX

DIRECTIONS FOR THE FUTURE

The Need for Contemplation in Today's World

TWENTY-SEVEN of Merton's fifty-three years of life were spent as a monk in Kentucky. During this half-life-time he wrote close to fifty books and well over three hundred articles. He made numerous tapes and carried on a correspondence with persons the world over. In all of this he spoke as a contemplative, as one who was called by God to a life of prayer, meditation, and union with Himself. He saw the contemplative life as a necessity, not a luxury, and wrote that 'since the direct and pure experience of reality in its ultimate root is man's deepest need, contemplation must be possible if man is to remain human'.[1] It was out of his contemplative experience that Merton looked to the future and charted new directions for the spiritual life.

One question Merton constantly asked was: What is the role of the contemplative in today's world? In the late 1950s he wrote: 'There are signs that a revival of solitary life in its various forms is of great importance for the Church today.'[2] The need for a turning inward, it seemed to him, was becoming more and more evident, particularly as Christians were confronted with racism, war and peace, and a fast changing quality of life. It was becoming apparent that many Christians were not responding to these issues with Christian action but were reacting within the context of their social and cultural situations. Merton became convinced that much of modern life was built upon illusion and that this illusion would have to be replaced by reality if change were to take place.

According to Merton the contemplative is in a unique position. In speaking of the contemplative life he writes: '*We have been called out of ordinary routines* in order to be explorers of areas which other people will never enter.'[3] Merton felt called to discover himself as he found himself in God, called to discover the ground of his being, in himself and in others. He declares: 'The Christian life—and especially the contemplative life—is a continual discovery of Christ in new and unexpected places. And these discoveries are sometimes most profitable when you find Him in something you had tended to overlook or despise.'[4] The contemplative life is generally lived within the context of monasticism, although there are notable exceptions, especially among artists, poets, and writers. Monasticism can be seen as a counterculture, for it is a form of social protest against the larger society and is therefore a form of social action. Becoming a hermit, as Merton did, further emphasizes the contemplative protest against the illusions of the world.

Merton did not believe in a total withdrawal from the world. He speaks of the need for contemplatives outside the cloister, beyond the rigidly fixed patterns of religious life, 'contemplatives in the world of art, letters, education, and even politics'.[5] In his opinion the world *needs* contemplatives. The world needs persons who are willing to understand the value of 'holy leisure'—*otium sanctum*, for, says Merton, 'perfection is found in the purity of our love for God, and this pure love is a delicate plant that grows best where there is plenty of time for it to mature'.[6]

Contemporary society needs a means whereby each person is given the opportunity to cultivate this holy leisure, so that each one can discover his being in all of its depth. Merton explains how this was accomplished among certain American Indians:

> I have studied some of our own Indians' spiritual training. In almost any tribe the young Indian had to go through a kind of novitiate. He was sent off into the mountains, into some rugged place perhaps on top of a cliff, to fast and pray. He was given instructions beforehand on what to do and he would mark out an area with the points of the compass, which made it into a cross-shaped place, and he had to stay within that area. While he was there fasting and praying he was supposed to have a vision (that was the object of his being there), and this vision would be his own spirit-person. It was really a discovery of one's own deepest self. When the boy returned to the tribe he would obey this spirit-person in important matters such as hunting and fighting and be guided by it. Obviously he was not talking to a spirit, but there was something in himself that had been released by this period of fasting and praying alone. He had access to a deeper level of his own being, a sort of sixth sense. This is

really interesting for us because we don't have anything like this anymore.[7]

This same kind of experience takes place in Asian countries where people can enter a Buddhist monastery or Hindu ashram on a temporary basis for a few weeks, months, or even years. It is this monastic experience that enables many persons to be in an environment conducive to holy leisure and self-discovery.[8]

We can little doubt that contemporary American society is in great need of the contemplative experience. Ours is a society of doing, and persons are pushed from school into marriage, career, military service, or further schooling with almost no opportunity for self-discovery. Little is done to provide for a person's spiritual development. The result is evident in a technology gone wild, an economy based upon war, and a social system that produces emotional and psychological cripples. Even more disturbing, the Church does little to provide an environment conducive to spiritual growth and development. This has not always been so, however, for there was a time when the spiritual director played an important role in the Church.[9] Throughout his life Merton stressed the importance of the monastic charism, of the person called to the contemplative life, perhaps even to the vocation of a spiritual father or director in the tradition of the ancient desert fathers. There is a place today for those who are able to lead others in the way of contemplation and self-discovery, as William Johnston points out:

> It seems to me that Christians must put some effort into forming their own directors or *roshi*. This means fewer Ph.D.s and more gurus; less study and more meditation; fewer universities and more meditation halls. Ordinarily speaking, enlightment is passed on from Master to disciple and on and on, but when a link is missing in the chain relationship, some people must be driven by the Spirit into the desert to fast and pray to hear the voice of God. And others, then, must stop badgering them about getting into classrooms and teaching mathematics.[10]

Modern man must learn to cultivate holy leisure and to emphasize self-discovery if he is to find himself and his place in the world.

Alvin Toffler, in his book *Future Shock*, maintains that society is changing at such a rapid rate that it is virtually impossible for people to cope adequately with this change.

Therefore, says Toffler, society needs 'enclaves of the past—communities in which turnover, novelty and choice are deliberately limited.'[11] Here 'people faced with future shock can escape the pressures of overstimulation for weeks, months, even years, if they choose.'[12] Toffler views such communities as a necessity for mankind's survival:

> Such communities not only should not be derided, they should be subsidized by the larger society as a form of mental and social insurance. In times of extremely rapid change, it is possible for the larger society to make some irreversible, catastrophic error. Imagine, for instance, the widespread diffusion of a food additive that accidentally turns out to have thalidomide-like effects. One can conceive of accidents capable of sterilizing or even killing whole populations.
>
> By proliferating enclaves of the past, living museums as it were, we increase the chances that someone will be there to pick up the pieces in case of massive calamity.[13]

I doubt that Merton would have approved Toffler's view, for Merton was opposed to rapid change simply for its own sake, especially when that change endangers human lives. Contemplation, if taken seriously by enough people, would make such enclaves of the past unnecessary, at least in terms of social insurance. And yet on the practical level this is exactly a role which monasteries have played in the past and are continuing to play in the modern world.[14] It was the monasteries that preserved the flame of knowledge and learning in the Dark Ages, and it is largely the monasteries that are keeping alive the charism of the contemplative life in the modern world. If nothing else, they provide places of retreat from the noise, confusion, and pressures of modern life. Merton's own monastery, Gethsemani, is filled every weekend with retreatants, persons who flee the city to a place where they can relax, read, think, meditate, and pray. The need for retreat houses today is evident and the monasteries share the fruits of contemplation by providing such places of refuge.

The contemplative life is by no means dead. As structures and forms and institutions change new and creative experiments are being tried. Merton always dreamed of a 'western Athos'—a community of monks in a monastic society made up of many different orders, perhaps including Protestants, Eastern Orthodox, and non-Christian monks. Asks Merton: 'Is this a heresy? Is this a dream? Have we reached the point where all dreams are regarded as dangerous and forbidden? When life has no more risk in it and no more dreams, it is no longer life.'[15] The possibilities he saw for the expression of the contemplative life are almost limitless.

What then is the role of the contemplative today? Merton answers succinctly:

> The mission of the contemplative in this world of massive conflict and collective unreason is to seek the true way of unity and peace, without succumbing to the illusion of withdrawal into a realm of abstraction from which unpleasant realities are simply excluded by the force of will. In facing the world with a totally different viewpoint, he maintains alive in the world a presence of a spiritual and intelligent consciousness which is the root of true peace and true unity among men.[16]

The Ecumenics of Spirituality

The mission of the contemplative is to seek unity and peace, and yet this is perhaps the quality most lacking in relationships between the world's religious traditions. Christian missionaries have often been especially guilty on this point.[17] Along with the Gospel the missionary brought western culture, business, money and sometimes military might. He often took a superior attitude toward the natives and their religion and held them to be pagan and inferior, never considering the possibility that westerners needed to learn spiritually from other races and cultures.[18] Merton observed that 'everyone knows that the Orient has venerated Christ and distrusted Christians, since the first colonizers and missionaries came from the West.'[19]

Merton took it upon himself to do something about this problem—not, at the time, a popular thing to do. He relates some of the difficulties he encountered in his dialogue with non-Christian religions:

> The Christian dialogue with Oriental religions, with Hinduism and especially with Zen, is considered rather suspect, though of course since dialogue is 'progressive' one must never attack it openly as such.
>
> It may however be pertinent to remark here that the term 'ecumenism' is not held to be applicable to dialogue with non-Christians. There is an essential difference, say the progressive Catholics, between the dialogue of Catholics with other Christians and the dialogue of

Catholics with Hindus or Buddhists. While it is assumed that Catholics and Protestants can learn from each other, and that they can progress together toward a new Christian self-understanding, many progressive Catholics would not concede this to dialogue with non-Christians. Once again, the assumption is that since Hinduism and Buddhism are 'metaphysical' and 'static' or even 'mystical' they have ceased to have any relevance in our time. Only the Catholics who are still convinced of the importance of Christian mysticism are also aware that much is to be learned from a study of the techniques and experience of Oriental religions. But these Catholics are regarded at times with suspicion, if not derision, by progressives and conservatives alike.[20]

Merton knew this criticism firsthand and he was often subjected to accusations that he was practising Zen in secret or that he had converted to Buddhism.

Merton specifically emphasized the techniques and experiences of other religions as a basis for dialogue. This does not mean that he considered doctrine and theology unimportant; they are of crucial importance, but they constitute only one basis for ecumenical dialogue. Merton chose to base his ecumenism upon experience, specifically upon the contemplative monastic experience. Such a basis for dialogue with non-christian religions causes apprehension among those whose basis for dialogue is instead doctrine and theology. Differences in doctrine are many, whereas there seems to be a great similarity among contemplative and mystical experiences.[21]

For Merton, ecumenism, like social action, must begin within the individual person: 'If I do not have unity in myself, how can I even think, let alone speak, of unity among Christians? Yet, of course, in seeking unity for all Christians, I also attain unity within myself.'[22]

The more I am able to affirm others, to say 'yes' to them in myself, by discovering them in myself and myself in them, the more real I am. I am fully real if my own heart says *yes* to *everyone*.

I will be a better Catholic, not if I can *refute* every shade of *Protestantism*, but if I can affirm the truth in it and still go further.

So, too, with the Muslims, the Hindus, and the Buddhists, etc. This does not mean syncretism, indifferentism, the vapid and careless friendliness that accepts everything by thinking of nothing. There is much that one cannot 'affirm' and 'accept,' but first one must say 'yes' where one really can.

If I affirm myself as a Catholic merely by denying all that is Muslim, Jewish, Protestant, Hindu, Buddhist, etc., in the end I will find that there is not much left for me to affirm as a Catholic: and certainly no breath of the Spirit in which to affirm it. [23]

Merton emphatically stated that this form of dialogue is not syncretism, that is, a blending of all religions on the assumption that they all lead to the same place though the various paths may be different. While the experiences may be similar, the theology framing these experiences may be quite different. Merton speaks of this problem in terms of the Christian goal of union with God:

> Can one tentatively say what these various traditions have in common? Here we immediately encounter difficulties, for it cannot be said that they all culminate in union with a 'personal God.' For the Moslem there is no question that God is a person, but He is so completely and totally transcendent that the idea of union with Him poses doctrinal problems (which, however, the Sufis, in the main, ignore). For the Hindu, union with God on an 'I-Thou' level is admitted in *bhakti*, which is, however, considered an inferior form of union. In Buddhism, the 'impersonality' of God is pushed to the point of *anatta*, in which not even the *Atman* or supreme self of Hinduism is admitted. But, on the other hand, as soon as one looks a little deeper into the question, one finds that it is extremely complex and that the whole notion of *personality*, whether divine or human, will require considerable clarification before a real dialogue with the East can begin. Note, however, that all this is on the level of doctrine or of metaphysics. [24]

Theologically, Merton made it clear that he, as a Christian, believed in a personal God. At the same time, however, he admitted that a great deal remained to be done in clarifying exactly what we mean by the word 'God'.

At the point of contemplative experience it becomes difficult to distinguish between Christianity in its mystical, apophatic form and Zen, and to maintain the subject-object relationship between God and man. In a talk given in Calcutta in 1968 Merton expanded on this in terms of the monastic life:

Its orientation is in a certain sense supra-personal. It goes beyond a merely psychological fulfilment on the empirical level, and it goes beyond the limits of communicable cultural ideals (of one's own national, racial, etc. background). It attains to a certain universality and wholeness which have never yet been adequately described—and probably cannot be described—in terms of psychology. Transcending the limits that separate subject from object and self from not-self, this development achieves a wholeness which is described in various ways by the different religions; a self-realization of *Atman*, of Void, of life in Christ, of *Fana* and *Baqa* (annihilation and reintegration according to Sufism), etc. [25]

Merton is dealing with a real problem here; the world religions do have similar mystical and contemplative experiences, albeit mediated through vastly different cultural and theological systems. The question is: are these experiences the same or is the Christian experience unique and superior to the others?

In his later writings on this subject Merton evaded the issue. On the one hand he opposed syncretism and held to the uniqueness of the Christian experience, yet on the other he said that he required further study before he could make any definite statement. [26] In speaking specifically of Zen, he stated that it is possible for a Christian to practise Zen if the theological doctrines surrounding it are discarded. [27] In another context he stated that Christ is already present in Hinduism and Buddhism. [28] Here we find Merton caught in a paradox; on the one hand he claims a uniqueness for the Christian faith and the biblical understanding of a personal God, and on the other hand he is open to the possibility that the mystical experiences found in the world religions may in their essence be the same. Clearly there is an unresolved problem here with which Merton, at the time of his death, was grappling. We have no choice but to accept Merton's work as it stands, unfinished and containing many unresolved problems.

The most serious difficulty here is that of the subject-object relationship between God and man. Merton speaks of it throughout his book *Zen and the Birds of Appetite*. [29] The mystics have claimed down through the ages that the transcendent experience cannot be explained—it can only be experienced. Merton says basically the same thing although he does attempt to define terms:

What is meant by *transcendent experience*...? It is an experience of metaphysical or mystical self-transcending and also at the same time an experience of the 'Transcendent' or the 'absolute' or 'God' not so much as object but Subject. The Absolute Ground of Being (and beyond that the Godhead as 'Urgrund' i.e. as infinite and uncircumscribed freedom) is realized so to speak 'from within'—realized from within 'Himself' and from within 'myself,' though 'myself' is now lost and 'found' 'in Him.' These metaphorical expressions all point to the problem we have in mind: the problem of a self that is 'no-self,' that is by no means an 'alienated self' but on the contrary a transcendent Self which, to clarify it in Christian terms, is metaphysically distinct from the Self of God and yet perfectly identified with that Self by love and freedom so that there appears to be but one Self. Experience of this is what we call 'transcendent experience' or the illumination of wisdom (*Sapientia, Sophia, Prajna*).[30]

In other words, Merton maintains a Christian distinction between subject and object on the metaphysical level while asserting that such a distinction disappears on the experiential level.

Merton fully realized the problems inherent in such a position, and he made no attempt to avoid them:

Mysticism will probably always be a disturbing subject.... There is no infallible way of guaranteeing the mystic against every mistake: he can never be perfectly sure of any human technique....In mystical union God and man, while remaining no doubt metaphysically distinct, are practically and experientially 'one Spirit' in the words of St Paul (I Cor. 6:16) quoted in this sense by Christian mystics down the centuries. But because there are also other 'spirits' and because man does not possess within himself a natural faculty which can by its own powers pass final judgement on the transcendent experiences taking place within him, a counterfeit mysticism is not only possible but relatively common.[31]

The ecumenics of spirituality present great uncertainty and challenge. It is a field which few persons are prepared to enter and capable of entering. Yet Merton was willing to enter even though it entailed great risk and even possible error. Even more significantly, he was willing to live with unresolved difficulties in the hope that someday the unity for which he longed would finally be achieved.

In a moving tribute to Merton, his personal secretary wrote of his ecumenical concern:

> In addressing the Asian monastic leaders at Bangkok a few weeks later on the subject of Marxism and monastic perspectives, Merton concluded his remarks with a frank appreciation of the monastic values of the East as a complement to our Western Christian monasticism:
> 'I believe that by openness to Buddhism, to Hinduism, and to these great Asian traditions, we stand a wonderful chance of learning more about the potentiality of our own traditions....The combination of the natural techniques and the graces and the other things that have been manifested in Asia, and the Christian liberty of the gospel should bring us all at last to that full and transcendent liberty which is beyond mere cultural differences and mere externals....'
> This was Thomas Merton's last ecumenical statement to the world, and it was uttered in all seriousness only two hours before his accidental death in a small Bangkok cottage room. Never in my life have I known a man more dedicated to his own monastic vocation of Christian witness and who was at the same time completely open to the Spirit in whatever way it might be made manifest.[32]

The Marxist-Christian Encounter

That Merton's last public statement was entitled 'Marxism and Monastic Perspectives' indicates his vital concern with Marxism and its implications for the contemplative life. At first glance such an interest may seem strange, but the relationship between Marxism and monasticism is much closer than it appears at first glance. Both make radical demands on their members and both reject the traditional forms of mass society. And, even more important, both point to a similar human problem: man's inner conflict. Merton, writing in *Monastic Peace*, explains how Marx diagnosed the problem of man:

> Karl Marx believed that religion had its roots in man's inner conflict with himself—the basic disproportion between man's idea of himself and his concrete reality, the contradiction of the ideal and the real in man's society. Since Marx diagnosed the cause of this disproportion as an

economic one, he also prescribed an economic cure.[33]

In understanding man's religious problem as an inner conflict, Marx was not far from the view of Christian monasticism; in prescribing an economic cure, however, Marx parted from monasticism, which prescribes an inner, spiritual cure.

Marx criticized the society of his day for its hypocrisy and falsehoods, a criticism also levelled by monks. Again, Marx prescribed an economic solution which monasticism rejects. That the basic Marxist critique of society, even the critique of religion, is valid, Merton points out: .

> Seeing all around him the hypocrisy and fake humanism of the early nineteenth century bourgeoisie, Marx believed that the problems which confronted all religious people were simply the indication that they had manoeuvered themselves, by their own spiritual dishonesty and incompetency, into an intellectual blind alley, where there was nothing left but to give their hopelessness a transcendental justification. The society which they had made for themselves by their own greed was indeed unjust: but what could be done about it? It was the 'will of God.'[34]

All too often the religion of society has accepted as its own the illusions of society; it is little wonder Marx referred to religion as an opiate.

Marx's solution to the problem 'was dictated by what he believed to be his own superior honesty and acumen; solve your problems, he said, by transforming your world.'[35] The monastic solution to the problem begins with a transformation of self and then a moving out into the world, for unless one is transformed from within there is no hope for transforming the world. To bring about this change in society Marx advocated a dictatorship. Strangely enough, says Merton, this is also a temptation among monks:

> The Marxian approach to this problem has been to take away all freedom from the individual, and place all responsibility in the hands of a few who remain themselves accountable to mysterious laws of history—laws whose action they themselves think they can determine. There exists for the monk a temptation remarkably like the Marxian solution: the tempation to *renounce his freedom*, to remain inert and apathetic in the hands of others who themselves pass on the responsibility to higher Superiors

and—to Divine Providence. But that is not the true
solution. [36]

Man must accept responsibility for his own situation and not
pass his responsibility on to others, be it the state, the Church,
or even God. The Marxist and the monk may end up making the
same mistake—succumbing to the temptation to renounce his
freedom.

Merton was convinced that an inner spiritual potential lay
hidden within Marx's critique of society. [37] He explained this in
the following manner:

> The subordination of man to the technological process is
> not something that Marx accepts with unqualified
> satisfaction. On the contrary it is, for him, the danger and
> challenge of a technology based on profit. He thought that
> the ultimate challenge was for man to free himself from
> his machines and gain control over them, thus breaking
> the bonds of alienation and making himself the master of
> his history. [38]

From these observations Merton concluded that a Marxist-
Christian dialogue was imperative:

> If there is to be a collaboration between the Christian
> humanist and the technological humanist, based on the
> latter's eventual realization of the need for wisdom, this is
> going to require as of now a living and radical dialogue
> between Christian thinkers of the west and revisionist
> Marxists in the east. How this is to be brought about the
> Lord alone knows. It is however vitally important. [39]

Merton was speaking, of course, of the thought and mystique of
Marxism among western and eastern European intellectuals.
Although fully aware of Marxist political tactics and oppression,
Merton maintained the need for dialogue, but he recognized
that it cannot take place at the level of politics and power
blocs. [40]

He was drawn to such Marxist thinkers as Herbert Marcuse,
Roger Garaudy, and some of the young student revolutionaries.
He was particularly impressed by Marcuse and the argument he
puts forth in his book *One Dimensional Man* that 'all highly
organized technological societies, as we have them now, all
so-called managerial societies, as found both in the United
States and in the Soviet Union, end up by being equally

totalitarian in one way or another.'[41] Underlying Marxist teaching is alienation, and Merton believed that this is also basic to Christian thinking.[42] Herein lies the basis for a Marxist-Christian understanding. Marcuse's view and the Christian view are similar in that both are concerned with the integrity and value of the human person. Indeed, in Marcuse one can find a striking similarity to Merton's own views on contemplation and action. Marcuse begins his work *One Dimensional man* with two value judgements:

1. the judgement that human life is worth living, or rather can be and ought to be made worth living. This judgement underlies all intellectual effort; it is the *a priori* of social theory, and its rejection (which is perfectly logical) rejects theory itself;
2. the judgement that, in a given society, specific possibilities exist for the amelioration of human life and specific ways and means of realizing these possibilities.[43]

By secular terminology, Marcuse is saying that man must find meaning in life—contemplation—and then realize this meaning in society—action.

In recent years there has been a growing sense of dialogue between Christians and Marxists, particularly in eastern Europe and Latin America. This dialogue has arisen partly because both Christian monasticism and revolutionary Marxism share a radical nature. Writing in *Christianity and Crisis* Rosemary Ruether avers that monasticism is really revolutionary in its social ethics:

A radicalism that identified with the poor was renewed continuously in the Middle Ages among the various brotherhoods, such as the Waldensians and the Franciscans. Again and again it was monastic spirituality, however domesticated by the institutional church, that provided the seedbed for radical brotherhoods that aligned themselves with the poor and did not scruple to attack the ecclesiastical and social hierarchies in language drawn from the apocalypse.[44]

Ruether traces the radical Catholic movement today to two sources: the Catholic Worker movement and the monastic spirituality of Thomas Merton.[45] Merton was closely allied with many of those involved in the Catholic Worker movement, so these twin roots really intertwine. Merton took the position that the true Marxist and the true monk were both struggling for the personhood of man and that both were in opposition to the vast political powers that would crush the individual and snuff out human freedom. Both are also subject to the same totalitarian temptation to take away the responsibility of the individual person. In Merton's view, an encounter between the two is not only desirable but inevitable.

There is, however, a problem here that Merton leaves unsolved, and it is basic to his views on contemplation and action. Merton admits that the Christian and the Marxist may both correctly diagnose the problem of man and society, yet their solutions to that problem differ. The Christian insists that the source of the problem is man's relationship to God; the Marxist is content to see the problem from a purely human perspective. The Marxist-Christian encounter raises the possibility that this entire problem be viewed within a secular rather than a religious context. We have already seen Eldridge Cleaver expressing this desire with he first read Merton:

> I was tortured by that book because Merton's suffering, in his quest for God, seemed all in vain to me. At that time, I was a black Muslim chained in the bottom of a pit by the Devil. Did I expect Allah to tear down the walls and set me free? To me, the language and symbols of religion were nothing but weapons of war. I had no other purpose for them. All the gods are dead except the god of war. I wished that Merton had stated in secular terms the reasons he withdrew from the political, economic, military and social system into which he was born, seeking refuge in a monastery.[46]

In Marxism Merton saw that what he expressed in religious terms could now be expressed in secular terms. We must ask the question: Is Merton merely fascinated by a secular statement of what he considered spiritual truths, or are the revisionist Marxists actually drawing closer to a Christian position?

Merton did not answer this question directly, but one has the feeling that he believed the Marxist and the Christian are really talking about the same thing, the integration of the human personality on both the individual and the social levels. For the Christian, God is the source of this integration, but it is not clear whether this is so for the Marxist. The Marxist would, of course, deny any working of God, but that would not rule out God's anonymous presence. The exact place of God in this situation Merton never made clear, and such a lack of clarity at this point is unfortunate.[47] A possible solution to this problem may lie in Merton's comments concerning the need among world religions for adequate definitions of personality both in a divine and in a human sense. Merton's thinking at this point was tentative. He was dealing more with the realm of possibility than with that of certainty. He is to be commended for his willingness to enter this sensitive and difficult area and there can be little doubt that his work will provide a foundation upon which others will build in the future.

The Importance of the Inner Man

Marcuse and other revisionist Marxists attempt to deal with man's being out of touch with human experience. This was also a central concern of Merton and he pointed out that we live in a society where 'life and death today depend upon everything except what you *are*'.[48] This is a personal problem, but it also involves society for, in Merton's words; 'This wound cannot be healed merely by solving each individual conflict, one at a time. The problem has to be solved by society itself, and it is not at all evident that society is ready with a solution.'[49] The problem is not with life but with man. As McInerny states: 'The universe for Merton was not meaningless, and therefore a man's absurdity was provisional; it was *his* absurdity not that of the universe, the result of his sins (the wrong decisions he made) and not simply "the way things are."''[50]

Merton was gratified that the Church was beginning to emphasize the importance of man. 'The Second Vatican Council,' he wrote, 'while continuing to develop and clarify the theology of the Church, manifested a wholly new concern-*man himself*.'[51] Although this emphasis was fresh and new in the Church at large, it was not new to Merton; man had long been his concern. 'Christianity is not the religion of a *law* but the religion of a *person*,'[52] he asserted. He was referring to the person of Christ, but the statement has important implications as well for the human person. Merton believed that true humanism depends upon a concept of the person that is incarnational in the sense that one holds the idea of subjectively becoming the other person.[53]

Merton defines person in terms of freedom. The person who is in tune with the ground of his being is a free person, a person free from falsehood and illusion. This implies responsibility, which Merton says is 'responsibility *to* other persons, responsibility *for* other persons'.[54] He writes:

Personalism and individualism must not be confused. Personalism gives priority to the *person* and not the individual self. To give priority to the person means respecting the unique and inalienable value of the *other* person, as well as one's own, for a respect that is centered only on one's individual self to the exclusion of others proves itself to be fraudulent. [55]

Therefore, 'the progress of the person and the progress of society...go together.' [56]

Keeping this relationship between person and society in mind, Merton maintained that each person must first become aware of his inner self. This awareness of the inner man is a prerequisite if one is to understand the relationship between person and society. Merton was convinced that society is not able to fill mankind's deepest inner needs:

The life of every man is a mystery of solitude and communion: solitude in the secrecy of his own soul, where he is alone with God; communion with his brethren, who share the same nature, who reproduce in themselves his solitude, who are his 'other selves' isolated from him and yet one with him. On the natural level, man's life is more of a solitude than a communion. Man fears solitude, yet the society in which he seeks refuge from his aloneness does not protect him adequately from his own insufficiency. [57]

A society which neglects the inner man and his needs is a society in deep trouble.

Contemporary society's danger lies in its emphasis upon the mass-man and its utter contempt of the person. Such a society cannot foster communion among its members for 'a communion between persons implies interiority and depth. It involves the whole being of each person—the mind, the heart, the feelings, the deepest aspirations of the spirit itself....But it also...safeguards the autonomy and character of each as an inviolate and solitary person.' [58] Freedom for the one implies a corresponding freedom for the many.

'Every man,' says Merton, 'has a vocation to *be* someone: but he must understand clearly that in order to fulfill this vocation he can only be one person: himself.' [59] He cannot allow himself to be lulled into believing that consumption of material goods will bring him happiness. Each person must face himself, in solitude, and find himself:

But in the last analysis the individual person is responsible for living his own life and for 'finding himself.' If he persists in shifting the responsibility to somebody else, he fails to find out the meaning of his own existence. You cannot tell me who I am, and I cannot tell you who you are. If you do not know your own identity, who is going to identify you? Others can give you a name or a number, but they can never tell you who you really are. That is something you yourself can only discover from within.[60]

This is the essence of what it is to be human, to know yourself and to discover who you are. Merton maintained that 'no matter how ruined man and his world may seem to be, and no matter how terrible man's despair may become, as long as he continues to be man his very humanity continues to tell him that life has a meaning.'[61]

As a contemplative, Merton felt he filled a special role in the world, a vocation which involved knowing himself in his inner ground of being and being able to see that same ground of being in others. In the following statement he shows contemplation and action united in a spiritual life of a profoundly prophetic nature:

The solitary cannot survive unless he is capable of loving everyone, without concern for the fact that he is likely to be regarded by all of them as a traitor. Only the man who has fully attained his own spiritual identity can live without the need to kill, and without the need of a doctrine that permits him to do so with a good conscience. There will always be a place, says Ionesco, '*for those isolated consciences who have stood up for the universal conscience*' as against the mass mind. But their place is solitude. They have no other. Hence it is the solitary person (whether in the city or in the desert) who does mankind the inestimable favor of reminding it of its true capacity for maturity, liberty and peace.[62]

1. *Faith and Violence*, p. 215.

2. *Disputed Questions*, p. 198.

3. 'The Solitary Life,' *Cistercian Studies* 4 (1969) 214.

4. *The Sign of Jonas*, pp. 275-76.

5. *Selected Poems of Thomas Merton*, p. 120. An outstanding contemplative of recent times, Dag Hammarskjöld, lived in the world of politics and statesmanship yet his spiritual life was one of great depth and insight. See Hammarskjöld, *Markings*, trans. Leif Sjöberg and W.H. Auden (New York: Knopf, 1965).

6. *Spiritual Direction and Meditation*, p. 76.

7. 'Prayer, Tradition, and Experience,' ed. Naomi Burton Stone, *Sisters Today* 42 (1971) 289-90.

8. See 'Community, Politics, and Contemplation,' ed. Stone, *Sisters Today* 42 (1971) 243-44, for comments on the hippies who came to a monastery to help the monks with manual labor and to deepen their own self-awareness.

9. Spiritual directors were especially important among fourth-century desert fathers. In the Russian Orthodox Church they came to be known as *startsi*. Spiritual directors in Zen Buddhism are referred to as *roshi*, and among Hindus and some Buddhists they are known as *gurus*.

10. William Johnston, *Christian Zen* (New York: Harper and Row, 1971) p. 92.

11. Alvin Toffler, *Future Shock*, (1970- rpt. New York: Bantam, 1971) p. 390.

12. Ibid., p. 391.

13. Ibid.

14. Monasteries are not the only enclaves of the past in our society. In an essay entitled 'Pleasant Hill: A Shaker Village in Kentucky' in *Mystics and Zen Masters* (1967; rpt. New York: Dell, 1969) pp. 193-202, Merton describes how the Shakers preserved a way of life that has now almost passed out of existence. At the time of this writing there are still thirteen Shakers living. Other groups, such as the Amish and the Hutterites are similar in that they live a communal life style and preserve a way of unity akin to that of the past.

15. *Disputed Questions*, p. 69. M. Basil Pennington in 'Atop a High Mountain,' *Monastic Exchange* 3 (1971) 103, points out that 'Merton dreamed of some place where the different contemplative traditions could dwell side by side—so that they could communicate—share their fragments of light and truth.'

16. *Faith and Violence*, p. 221.

17. There were a number of exceptions, especially among the early Jesuit missionaries to China. See Merton's essay 'The Jesuits in China' in *Mystics and Zen Masters*, pp. 80-90.

18. See *Seeds of Destruction*, p. 63 and *Emblems of a Season of Fury*, pp. 70-89.

19. *Seeds of Destruction*, p. 225.

20. *Zen and the Birds of Appetite*, pp. 20-21. On p. 15, Merton comments on openness toward non-christian religions: 'In some respects, progressive Christians were never *less* disposed to this kind of openness. True, they approve all forms of communication and inter-religious dialogue on principle. But the new, secular, "post-Christian" Christianity, which is activistic, antimystical, social and revolutionary, tends to take for granted a great deal of the Marxist assumptions about religion as the opium of the people. In fact, these movements aspire to a kind of Christian repentance on this point, and seek with the greatest fervor to prove that there is no opium about *us*! But, knowing little or nothing about Asian religions, and associating Asia with opium anyway (conveniently forgetting that it was the West that forced opium into China by means of war!) they are still satisfied with the old cliches about "life-denying Buddhism," "selfish navel-gazing," and *Nirvana* as a sort of drugged trance.'

21. See ibid., pp. 43-44, where Merton cautions against the assumption that Zen and Christianity are the same.

22. *Conjectures of a Guilty Bystander*, p. 128.

23. Ibid., p. 129.

24. *Mystics and Zen Masters*, p. 210.

25. 'Monastic Experience and the East-West Dialogue' in Finley P. Dunne, ed., *The World Religions Speak on the Relevance of Religion in the Modern World* (The Hague: Dr. W. Junk N.V. Publications, 1970), pp. 72-73; rpt. in *The Asian Journal of Thomas Merton*, p. 310.

26. See *Zen and the Birds of Appetite*, pp. 43-44.

27. Ibid., pp. 44-45. Merton has been criticized by some scholars for having failed to take into account the importance of the Buddhist theology implied in Zen. See especially R.C. Zaehner, *Concordant Discord: The Interdependence of Religions* (Oxford: The Clarendon Press, 1970).

28. Merton, *Emblems of a Season of Fury*, p. 79. For a theological exposition of this view see Karl Rahner, 'Anonymous Christians' in his *Theological Investigations*, 6 (Baltimore: Helicon, 1968) pp. 390-98.

29. See especially Merton's essay 'Transcendent Experience' in *Zen and the Birds of Appetite*, pp. 71-78.

30. Ibid., pp. 71-72.

31. Merton in the foreword to William Johnston, *The Mysticism of the Cloud of Unknowing: A Modern Interpretation*, p. ix.

32. Brother Patrick Hart, 'The Ecumenical Concern of Thomas Merton,' *The Lamp: A Christian Unity Magazine* 70 (December 1972) 23; rpt. as 'Ecumenical Monk' in Hart, ed., *Thomas Merton/Monk*, p. 217.

33. *Monastic Peace*, p. 43; rpt. *The Monastic Journey*, p. 73.

34. Ibid., pp. 43-44.

35. Ibid., p. 44.

36. Ibid., p. 47.

37. See *Seeds of Destruction*, p. 271.

38. Ibid.

39. Ibid., p. 272.

40. 'Marxism and Monastic Perspectives' in Moffitt, ed., *A New Charter for Monasticism*, p. 69; rpt. in *The Asian Journal of Thomas Merton*, pp. 327-28.

41. 'Marxism and Monastic Perspectives in Moffitt, p. 75; rpt. in *The Asian Journal*, pp. 334-35. See Herbert Marcuse, *One Dimensional Man: Studies in the Ideology of Advanced Industrial Society* (Boston: Beacon Press, 1964).

42. See 'Marxism and Monastic Perspectives' in Moffitt, pp.75-76; rpt. in *The Asian Journal*, pp. 335-36.

43. Marcuse, *One Dimensional Man*, pp. x-xi.

44. See Rosemary Ruether, 'Monks and Marxists: A Look at the Catholic Left,' *Christianity and Crisis* 33 (1973) 75. The question of radicalism and revolution is one that Merton found difficult to deal with, especially in view of the number of Catholic religious active in Latin American struggles. Merton was sympathetic to the revolutionaries and their cause but had serious reservations toward their use of violence. See Merton 'Toward a Theology of Resistance' in *Faith and Violence*, pp. 3-13.

45. See Ruether, 'Monks and Marxists', p. 76: 'Thus in the monastic spirituality of Thomas Merton, traditional Christian rejection of "this world" took on a new and concrete meaning, not as a struggle against flesh and blood, but as a struggle against the powers and principalities of the great empires, with America as their most recent representative. Here monastic spirituality was connected with its apocalyptic root.'

46. Eldridge Cleaver, *Soul on Ice* (New York: Dell, 1968) p. 34.

47. See *Faith and Violence*, pp. 189-287.

48. *Emblems of a Season of Fury*, p. 74.

49. *Monastic Peace*, p. 45; rpt. *The Monastic Journey*, p. 74.

50. McInerny, 'Thomas Merton and Society: A Study of the Man and His Thought Against the Background of Contemporary American Culture,' p. 220.

51. *Redeeming the Time*, p. 7.

52. *The New Man*, p. 128.

53. *Redeeming the Time*, pp. 91-92.

54. Ibid., p. 65.

55. *The Way of Chuang Tzu*, p. 17.

56. *Redeeming the Time*, p. 67. This union of the person and society is pointed out by Merton in an article 'Prayer and Conscience,' ed. Stone, *Sisters Today* 42 (1971) 412.

57. *The Living Bread*, p. 141.

58. *Disputed Questions*, p. 96.

59. *No Man is an Island*, p. 58. See *The New Man*, p. 166, where Merton states that 'the law of our life can be summed up in the axiom "be what you are."'

60. *No Man is an Island*, pp. 9-10. Gordon W. Allport says much the same thing in *The Individual and His Religion: A Psychological Interpretation* (1950) rpt. New York: Macmillan Paperback, 1960) p. 161.

61. *No Man is an Island*, p. 9.

62. *Raids on the Unspeakable*, p. 22.

X

A SIGN OF GOD

THE CHURCH throughout the centuries has produced mystics. A great number of them have faded into oblivion and are no longer remembered except for their esoteric practices and the difficulties they caused the Church. Some became the founders of schismatic groups through their charismatic leadership and the circumstances of their day; others are remembered by a few followers as a patron saint or as the founder of a religious order. The majority are remembered only by scholars who study their writings in obscure libraries and by those whose interests lie in the esoteric.

Within the Church there is a mystical tradition quite different, a tradition that has produced outstanding men and women remembered not only for their spirituality but for their effect upon the overall life and work of the Church. Their lives made a difference in the lives of others and they made substantial contributions not only to the Church but also to the society in which they lived. There can be no doubt that Thomas Merton belongs to this latter group, for his spirituality touches the lives of many and his work continues to make an impact upon the Church and the world.

What is the difference between those false mystics who are all but forgotten and those saints who are remembered? It lies primarily in the relationship of contemplation and action. It is here that spirituality stands or falls, for, in the words of Jesus, 'you will know them by their fruits' (Mt 7:20). The false mystics failed to keep a proper balance between contemplation and action. Their concern was with mystical visions, esoteric doctrines, and charismatic personalities. The true mystics, on the other hand, maintained a balance between their contemplative experiences and their service to the Church and their fellows.

Augustine wrote that there are three kinds of life: 'One which, not lazily, but in the contemplation and examination of the truth is leisured; another which is busied in carrying on human affairs; and a third which combines both of these.'[1] Each involves action, and the saint emphasized that the leisured life of contemplation is not one of idleness but of the leisure of thought. Even this leisured life of contemplation produces action. 'It is aflame with the love of generating,' Augustine says, 'for it desires to teach what it knows.'[2]

St Gregory the Great, following Augustine's teachings closely, also stressed the importance of action.[3] Without action, in fact, he felt no one could come to contemplation.[4] The mystical experience is preceded by years of study, discipline and concerted action. No one, in fact, can live a life of complete contemplation.[5] Providing the simple necessities of life involves action.

Bernard of Clairvaux insisted as well that those who work for the spiritual good of others, must themselves be spiritual men, exercising prayer and contemplation.[6] An active life spiritually motivated will be contemplative as well; what results is, in reality, a mixed life, as life of both contemplation and action. Bernard warned against a false mysticism which neglected action and discipline.[7] Merton commented on this:

> The subject of 'pure love' takes us at once to the heart of St Bernard's theology. It sets forth the principle that the 'immaculate law of God' is charity, and that there is no mystical liberation, no transformation in Christ, for the soul that has not been elevated, by the Spirit of God above the law of selfishness and cupidity to the realm of divine charity.[8]

> Bernard, the contemplative, was a great man of action because he was a great contemplative. And because he was a contemplative he never ceased fearing to be a mere man of action.[9]

Beneath Bernard's understanding of contemplation and action lay the concept of spiritual fecundity. The saint often compared the mystical state to that of marriage. Just as the good marriage produces offspring, so an authentic and healthy contemplative experience produces fruits. Butler points out that 'the effect of contemplation is to generate a love that makes such a one a good and worthy pastor of souls; thus the last three stages are: prayer, contemplation, spiritual fecundity.'[10]

A survey of the great contemplatives of the Church down through the ages manifests this 'spiritual fecundity'. Gregory of Nyssa was a bishop, a defender of the faith, a theologian, and 'the true Father of Christian apophatic mysticism'.[11] Bernard of Clairvaux was a mystical writer, a theologian, the leader of the Cistercian Order, and a well-traveled preacher.[12] Thomas Aquinas was a great philosopher, a theologian, and a contemplative whose influence is still felt today in philosophical and theological circles.[13] Teresa of Avila and John of the Cross reformed the Carmelites and by their writings continue to influence Christian mysticism even today.[14] Catherine of Siena was known for her sanctity and thus was able to mediate a peace between the Florentines and Pope Urban VI in the fourteenth century.[15] Ignatius Loyola had mystical visions which led him to dedicate his life to God and the Church by founding the Jesuits.[16] The list could go on to include countless other saints and contemplatives, all of whom contributed their lives of service and love to the Church and the world, and all of whom combined contemplation and action in a living and influential spirituality.

In reality all of these great contemplatives lived mixed lives of both contemplation and action, even when they held contemplation to be superior to activity. This is especially clear in the mystical writings of Meister Eckhart, as Georgia Harkness comments:

> Like Augustine and Bernard, he lived a very active life. He was a Dominican monk, the prior of his order at Erfurt, provincial vicar of Thuringia, and later vicar-general of Bohemia. He travelled widely, preached frequently in German both in the cloisters and to the multitudes who heard him eagerly, and wrote learned treatises both in Latin and German.[17]

Eckhart was never officially declared a saint, largely because of doctrinal difficulties in some of his writings, but he is widely revered as an outstanding mystic.[18] His mysticism was integrated into a spirituality which involved action. Harkness continues:

> He had no place for raptures and ecstasies as a substitute for human service, as is seen in his often quoted statement, 'Even if one were in a rapture like St Paul's and there was a sick man who needed help, I think it would be far better to come out of the rapture and show

love by serving the needy one.' He loved silence and
meditation, too seldom available for long in his busy life,
but he believed that the true test of the inward life is
found in its outward expressions. On this basis he ranked
Martha above Mary. Said he, 'God's purpose in the union
of contemplation is fruitfulness in works; for in contemplation thou servest thyself alone, but the many in good
works.' Yet he was as sure as Luther was to be later that
good works alone would not impart salvation. 'God is no
more to be found in any bodily exercise than He is to be
found in sin....The beginning of the holy life is to be found
in the inner man, in vision and in loving.'[19]

Eckhart realized that the spiritual life involved the whole man
and that the foundations of a truly holy life must be laid within
the inner man and not in the society at large.

Thomas Merton follows in this great tradition of mystics who
brought together contemplation and action. He maintained that
'if we experience God in contemplation, we experience Him not
for ourselves alone but also for others.'[20] His spirituality
integrated contemplation and action into a life of service. Thus
he wrote: 'God does not give His joy to us for ourselves alone,
and if we could possess Him for ourselves alone we would not
possess Him at all. Any joy that does not overflow from our
souls and help other men to rejoice in God does not come to us
from God.'[21]

Furthermore, he contended that 'the highest vocation in the
Kingdom of God is that of sharing one's contemplation with
others and bringing other men to the experimental knowledge of
God that is given to those who love Him perfectly'.[22] This
sharing may take a number of different forms:

He finds himself speaking of God to the man in whom he
has recognized the light of his own peace, the awakening
of his own secret: or if he cannot speak to them, he writes
for them, and his contemplative life is still imperfect
without sharing, without companionship, without communion.[23]

By his writings Merton shared his contemplation with others,
and in his situation contemplation would have been incomplete
had he not been able to write. His life and work witness to that
highest vocation of which he speaks, for he shared freely with
others what he had found in God.

Ours is an age of extremes. We have activists who appear to

be totally divorced from their own inner depths, and we have mystics who are engrossed in various forms of mystical experience to the almost total neglect of pressing social problems around them. We need today an authentic spirituality which encompasses both contemplation and action. We seek a spirituality by which persons may be vitally concerned with the inner man and his relationship to God and yet care deeply enough about the problems of mankind to do something about them. We need an integrated spirituality; a spirituality of the whole person which takes into account both contemplation and action and is at the same time aware of its own limitations and contradictions.

The spirituality of Thomas Merton is a spirituality for our time. It grew out of the conflicts and struggles of the twentieth century, and it speaks forcefully to us of the need for a union between the contemplative and the active life. Although Merton has died, his spirituality lives on through his books, 'for the saint does not represent himself, or his time, or his nation: he is a sign of God for his own generation and for all generations to come.'[24]

NOTES

1.   *The City of God*, 19.1, cited by Dom Cuthbert Butler, *Western Mysticism* (New York: E.P. Dutton, 1924) p. 206.

2.   *Contra Faustum*, 22, 54; Butler, p. 220.

3.   Butler, p. 218.

4.   Ibid., p. 217.

5.   Ibid., p. 247.

6.   Ibid., p. 248. See Bernard, Sermon 18 on The Song of Songs [=SC] (CF 4:133-9).

7.   See ibid., p. 250 for Butler's comments on Bernard, SC 46, 5 (CF 7:243-4).

8.   Thomas Merton in the foreword to Henri Daniel-Rops, *Bernard of Clairvaux: The Story of the Last of the Great Church Fathers*, trans. Elizabeth Abbott (New York: Hawthorn, 1964) p. 7.

9.   Ibid., pp. 5-6.

10.   Butler, p. 249. See Bernard, SC 18, 6 (CF 4:139).

11.   See *The Ascent to Truth*, pp. 319-21.

12.   Ibid., pp. 321-22. See also pp. 23-44.

13.   See *The Ascent to Truth*, pp. 323-25.

14.   Ibid., pp. 327-28 and 329-31. This book is largely based on the theology of St John of the Cross.

15.   See Williston Walker, *A History of the Christian Church*, rev. ed. (New York: Scribners, 1959) pp. 266, 284-85.

16.   Ibid., pp. 376-77.

17.   Georgia Harkness, *Mysticism: Its Meaning and Message* (Nashville/New York: Abingdon, 1973) pp. 103-04.

18.   See *Conjectures of a Guilty Bystander*, pp. 42-43.

19.   Harkness, *Mysticism*, pp. 104-05.

20.   *New Seeds of Contemplation*, p. 209.

21.   Ibid., p. 208.

22.   Ibid., p. 210.

23. Ibid., p. 209. On pp. 208-09 Merton says: 'But do not think that you have to see how [contemplation] overflows into the souls of others. In the economy of his grace, you be sharing his gifts with someone you will never know until you get to heaven.'

24. *The Last of the Fathers*, p. 27. Merton expands upon this idea of the sign and its significance to him personally in *The Sign of Jonas*, pp. 20-21.

This bibliography lists only those works cited. Many of the articles by Merton have been reprinted in one or more collections of his essays, and wherever possible, these collected essays have been cited as they are more readily available than the individual journals. Complete bibliographies of Merton's works can be found in: Marquita Breit, *Thomas Merton: A Bibliogrpahy*. ATLA Bibliography Series, 2. Metuchen, New Jersey: Scarecrow Press and The American Theological Library Association, 1974; Frank Dell'Isola, *Thomas Merton: A Bibliography*. New York: Farrar, Straus and Cudahy, 1956; and Frank Dell'Isola, *Thomas Merton: A Bibliography*. Revised and Expanded Edition. Kent, Ohio: Kent State University Press, 1975.

WORKS BY THOMAS MERTON

Books and Pamphlets

Albert Camus' The Plague: Introduction and Commentary.
Religious Dimensions in Literature, General Editor Lee A. Belford. New York: Seabury, 1968.

The Ascent to Truth.
New York: Harcourt, Brace, 1951.

The Asian Journal of Thomas Merton.
Eds. Naomi Burton, Brother Patrick Hart, and James Laughlin. Consulting Editor Amiya Chakravarty. New York: New Directions, 1973.

Basic Principles of Monastic Spirituality.
Trappist, Kentucky: Abbey of Gethsemani, 1957.

The Behavior of Titans.
New York: New Directions, 1961.

Bread in the Wilderness.
New York: New Directions, 1953.

Breakthrough to Peace.
Ed. with an Intro. by Thomas Merton. New York: New Directions, 1962.

Cables to the Ace: or Familiar Liturgies of Misunderstanding.
New York: New Directions, 1968.

The Climate of Monastic Prayer.
Cistercian Studies Series, Number 1. Cistercian Publications: Spencer, MA., 1969.

The Conjectures of a Guilty Bystander.
Garden City: Doubleday, 1966.

Contemplation in a World of Action.
Garden City: Doubleday, 1971.

Disputed Questions.
   1960; rpt. New York: Mentor Omega, 1965.

Emblems of a Season of Fury.
   New York: New Directions, 1963.

Faith and Violence: Christian Teaching and Christian Practice.
   Notre Dame: University of Notre Dame Press, 1968.

Figures for an Apocalypse.
   Norfolk, Conn.: New Directions, 1947.

Gandhi on Non-Violence: Selected Texts from Mohandas K. Gandhi's
   'Non-Violence in Peace and War'.
   Ed. with an Intro. by Thomas Merton. New York: New Directions, 1965.

The Geography of Lograire.
   New York: New Directions, 1969.

Ishi Means Man.
   Greensboro, North Carolina: Unicorn Press, 1976.

The Last of the Fathers: Saint Bernard of Clairvaux and the Encyclical Letter,
   Doctor Mellifluus.
   New York: Harcourt, Brace, 1954.

Life and Holiness.
   New York: Herder and Herder, 1963.

The Living Bread.
   New York: Farrar, Straus and Cudahy, 1956.

Marthe, Marie et Lazare.
   Trans. J. Charles-Dubos. Paris: Desclee de Brouwer, 1956.

The Monastic Journey. Ed. with a Foreword by Brother Patrick Hart. Kansas
   City: Sheed Andrews & McMeel, 1977.

Monastic Peace.
   Trappist, Kentucky: Abbey of Gethsemani, 1958.

My Argument with the Gestapo: A Macaronic Journal.
   Garden City: Doubleday, 1969.

Mystics and Zen Masters.
   1967; rpt. New York: Dell, 1969.

The New Man.
   London: Burns and Oates, 1962.

New Seeds of Contemplation.
   London: Burns and Oates, 1962.

No Man is an Island.
   1955; rpt. Garden City: Doubleday Image, 1967.

Opening the Bible.
Collegeville, MN: Liturgical Press, 1971.

Original Child Bomb: Points for Meditation to be Scratched on the Walls of a Cave.
Illustrated by Emil Antonucci. New York: New Directions, 1962.

Praying the Psalms.
Collegeville, MN: Liturgical Press, 1956.

Raids on the Unspeakable.
New York: New Directions, 1966.

Redeeming the Time.
London: Burns and Oates. 1966.

Seasons of Celebration.
New York: Farrar, Straus, and Giroux, 1965.

The Secular Journal of Thomas Merton.
1959; rpt. New York: Dell, 1960.

Seeds of Contemplation.
1949; rpt. New York: Dell, 1960.

Seeds of Destruction.
New York: Farrar, Straus and Giroux, 1964.

Selected Poems of Thomas Merton.
New York: New Directions, 1959.

The Seven Storey Mountain.
1948; rpt. Garden City: Garden City Books, 1951.

The Sign of Jonas.
1953; rpt. Garden City: Doubleday Image, 1956.

Silence in Heaven: A Book of the Monastic Life.
New York: New York: Studio Publications in association with Thomas Y. Crowell, 1956.

The Silent Life.
New York: Farrar, Straus and Cudahy, 1957.

Spiritual Direction and Meditation.
Collegeville, MN: Liturgical Press, 1960.

Thomas Merton on Peace.
Edited with an Introduction by Gordon C. Zahn. New York: McCall, 1971.

A Thomas Merton Reader.
Edited by Thomas P. McDonnell. New York: Harcourt, Brace and World, 1962.

Thoughts in Solitude.
    1958; rpt. New York: Dell, 1961.

The True Solitude: Selections From the Writings of Thomas Merton.
    Selected by Dean Walley. Kansas City, MO.: Hallmark, 1969.

The Waters of Siloe.
    New York: Harcourt, Brace, 1949.

The Way of Chuang Tzu.
    New York: New Directions, 1965.

*The Wisdom of the Desert: Sayings from the Desert Fathers of the Fourth
    Century.*
    Translated by Thomas Merton. New York: New Directions, 1960.

Zen and the Birds of Appetite.
    New York: New Directions, 1968.

Articles in Books and Journals

'Action and Contemplation in St Bernard.'
    Collectanea Ordinis Cisterciensium Reformatorum 15 (1953) 26-31, 203-216.

'The Burning of Papers/The Human Conscience/And the Peace Movement.'
    Fellowship 35 (March 1969) 7-8.

'Christian Ethics and Nuclear War.'
    Catholic Worker 28 (March 1962) 2, 7.

'Christ in the Desert.'
    in *Monastery of Christ in the Desert*. Abiquiu, New Mexico: Monastery of
    Christ in the Desert, n.d., n. pag.

'Community, Politics and Contemplation.'
    Ed. by Naomi Burton Stone. *Sisters Today* 42 (1971) 241-46.

'Concerning the Collection in the Bellarmine College Library.'
    in *The Thomas Merton Studies Center*, 1. Santa Barbara: Unicorn Press,
    1971, pp. 13-15.

'Contemplation and the Dialogue Between Religions.'
    Sobornost 5 (Winter-Spring 1969) 562-70.

'The Contemplative Life: Its Meaning and Necessity.'
    The Dublin Review 446 (1949) 26-35.

'The Cross Fighters—Notes on a Race War.'
    Unicorn Journal 1 (1968) 26-40.

Foreword to *Bernard of Clairvaux: The Story of the Last of the Great Church Fathers* by H. Daniel-Rops.
Trans. by Elisabeth Abbot. New York: Hawthorn, 1964.

Foreword to *The Mysticism of the Cloud of Unknowing: A Modern Interpretation* by William Johnston. New York: Desclée, 1967.

'The Historical Consciousness.'
Contemplative Review 1 (May 1969) 2-3.

The Humanity of Christ in Monastic Prayer.'
Monastic Studies 2 (1964) 1-27.

'The Life That Unifies.'
Ed. Naomi Burton Stone. *Sisters Today* 42 (1970) 65-73.

'Marxism and Monastic Perspectives.'
in *A New Charter for Monasticism*. Ed. John Moffitt. Notre Dame: University of Notre Dame Press, 1970, pp. 69-81.

'Monastic Experience and the East-West Dialogue.'
in *The World Religions Speak on the Relevance of Religion in the Modern World*. Ed. Finley P. Dunne. The Hague: Dr. W. Junk N.V. Publications, 1970, pp. 72-81.

'The Monk in the Diaspora.'
Blackfriars 45 (1964) 290-302.

'The Monk in the Diaspora.'
Commonweal 79 (1963-64) 741-45.

Monks Pond.
Quarterly ed. Thomas Merton. Nos. 1-4, Spring-Winter, 1968.

'Nonviolence Does Not, Cannot Mean Passivity.'
Ave Maria 108 (September 7, 1968) 9-10.

'Prayer and Conscience.'
Ed. Naomi Burton Stone. *Sisters Today* 42 (1971) 409-18.

'Prayer, Tradition, and Experience.'
Ed. Naomi Burton Stone. *Sisters Today* 42 (1971) 285-93.

'The Sacred City.'
The Center Magazine 1 No. 3 (March 1968) 73-77.

'The Solitary Life.'
Cistercian Studies 4 (1969) 213-17.

'The Wild Places.'
Catholic Worker 34 No. 5 (June 1969) 4-6.

'The Zen Revival.'
Continuum 1 (1964) 523-38.

Unpublished Materials

'Cold War Letters.' Mimeographed.

'Collected Essays.' 6 folios. Mimeographed.

'Conference on Contemplative Living in the Contemporary World. Mimeographed.

'Nature and Art in William Blake: An Essay in Interpretation.' MA Thesis, Columbia University 1939.

'Notes From Meeting of Contemplatives.' Notes taken by a nun on a talk by Thomas Merton given December 1967, at Gethsemani, KY. Mimeographed

'Peace in the Post-Christian Era.' Mimeographed.

WORKS ON THE LIFE AND THOUGHT OF THOMAS MERTON

Books

Baker, James Thomas. *Thomas Merton Social Critic.* Lexington: University Press of Kentucky, 1971.

Bailey, Raymond. *Thomas Merton on Mysticism.* Garden City, New York: Doubleday, 1975.

Griffin, John Howard. *A Hidden Wholeness: The Visual World of Thomas Merton.* Photographs by Thomas Merton and John Howard Griffin. Text by John Howard Griffin. Boston: Houghton Mifflin, 1970.

Hart, Brother Patrick, ed. *Thomas Merton/Monk: A Monastic Tribute.* New York: Sheed and Ward, 1974.

Higgins, John J. SJ. *Merton's Theology of Prayer.* Cistercian Studies Series 18. Spencer, MA: Cistercian Publications, 1971.

Kelly, Frederic Joseph SJ. *Man Before God: Thomas Merton on Social Responsibility.* Garden City, New York: Doubleday, 1974.

McInerny, Dennis Q. *Thomas Merton: The Man and His Work.* Cistercian Studies Series, 27. Kalamazoo, Michigan: Cistercian Publications, 1974.

Nouwen, Henri J.M. *Pray to Live, Thomas Merton: A Contemplative Critic.* Translated by David Schlaver. Notre Dame, Indiana: Fides, 1972.

Pennington, M. Basil OCSO, ed. *The Cistercian Spirit: A Symposium in Honor of Thomas Merton.* Cistercian Studies Series, 3. Spencer MA: Cistercian Publications, 1970.

Rice, Edward. *The Man in the Sycamore Tree: The Good Times and Hard Life of Thomas Merton.* Garden City: Doubleday, 1970.

Süssman, Cornelia, and Sussman, Irving. *Thomas Merton: The Daring Young man on the Flying Bell Tower.* New York: Macmillan, 1976.

Articles in Books and Journals

Andrews, James F. 'Was Merton a Critic of Renewal?' *National Catholic Reporter* 6 (February 11, 1970) Lenten Supplement 1, 12-15.

Bamberger, John Eudes *ocso.* 'The Cistercian.' *Continuum* 7 (1969) 227-41.

'A Homily.' *Continuum* 7 (1969) 226.

Berrigan, Daniel. Foreword to *The Politics of the Gospel* by Jean Marie Paupert. Trans. by Gregor Roy. New York: Holt, Rinehart and Winston, 1969, pp. vii-viii.

Burke, Herbert C. 'The Man of Letters.' *Continuum* 7 (1969) 274-85

Burton, Naomi. 'A Note on the Author and This Book,' in *My Argument with the Gestapo: A Macaronic Journal* by Thomas Merton. Garden City: Doubleday, 1969, pp. 7-11.

Cameron-Brown, Aldhelm. 'Seeking the Rhinoceros: A Tribute to Thomas Merton.' *Monastic Studies* 7 (1969) 63-73.

De Pinto, Basil. 'In Memoriam: Thomas Merton 1915-1968,' in *The Cistercian Spirit: A Symposium in Honor of Thomas Merton.* Cistercian Studies Series 3. Ed. M. Basil Pennington *ocso.* Spencer, MA: Cistercian Publications, 1970, pp. vii-x.

Dewart, Leslie. 'A Post Christian Age?' *Continuum* 1 (1964) 556-67.

Dumont, Charles *ocso.* 'A Contemplative in the Heart of the World—Thomas Merton.' *Luman Vitae* 24 (1969) 633-46.

Editorial. *Listening: Current Studies in Dialog* 1 (1966) 170-71.

Forest, James H. 'The Gift of Merton.' *Commonweal* 89 (1969) 463-65.

Glimm, James York. 'Exile Ends in Satire: Thomas Merton's *Cables to the Ace.*' *Cithara* 11 (November 1971) 31-40.

Griffin, John Howard. 'In Search of Thomas Merton,' in *Thomas Merton Studies Center,* 1. Santa Barara: Unicorn Press, 1971, pp. 17-24.

Hart, Patrick. 'The Ecumenical Concern of Thomas Merton.' *The Lamp: A Christian Unity Magazine* 70 (December 1972) 20-23.

Hinson, E. Glenn. 'Merton's Many Faces.' *Religion in Life* 42 (1973) 153-67.

Kelty, Matthew. 'Some Reminiscences of Thomas Merton.' *Cistercian Studies* 4 (1969) 163-75.

Lentfoehr, Sr M. Thérèse. 'The Spiritual Writer.' *Continuum* 7 (1969) 242-54.

MacCormick, Chalmers. 'The Zen Catholicism of Thomas Merton.' *Journal of Ecumenical Studies* 9 (1972) 802-18.

Marty, Martin E. 'To: Thomas Merton. Re: Your Prophecy.' *National Catholic Reporter* 3 (August 30, 1967) 6.

Mason, H. 'Merton and Massignon.' *Muslim World* 59 (1969) 317-18.

Mayhew, Alice. 'Merton Against Himself.' *Commonweal* 91 (1969-70) 70-74.

McCarthy, Colman. 'Thomas Merton.' *The Critic* 31 (July-August 1973) 35-39.

Mohs, Mayo. 'Review of *The Man in the Sycamore Tree: The Good Times and Hard Life of Thomas Merton*, by Edward Rice.' *Time* 96 (December 7, 1970) 59.

Pallis, Marco. 'Thomas Merton, 1915-1968.' *Studies in Comparative Religion* 3 (1969) 138-46.

Peloquin, C. Alexander. 'To Remember.' *Liturgical Arts* 37 (1969) 52-53.

Pennington, Basil. 'Atop a High Mountain.' *Monastic Exchange* 3 (1971) 101-06.

Saword, Sr Anne *ocso*. 'Tribute to Thomas Merton.' *Cistercian Studies* 3 (1968) 265-78.

Shannon, James P. 'Thomas Merton's New Mexico.' *New Mexico* 49 (May-June 1971) 18-23.

Steindl-Rast, David. 'Recollections of Thomas Merton's Last Days in the West.' *Monastic Studies* 7 (1969) 1-10.

Stevens, Clifford. 'Thomas Merton, 1968: A Profile in Memoriam.' *American Benedictine Review* 20 (March 1969) 7-20.

Wintz, Jack *ofm*. 'Thomas Merton Lives!' *St. Anthony Messenger* 82 No. 3 (1974) 18-27.

Zahn, Gordon C. 'Great Catholic Upheaval.' *Saturday Review* 54 (September 11, 1971) 24-27, 54-56.

——. 'The Peacemaker.' *Continuum* 7 (1969) 265-73.

Dissertations

Baker, James Thomas. 'Thomas Merton: The Spiritual and Social Philosophy of Union.' PhD Dissertation, Florida State University 1968.

McInerny, Dennis Quentin. 'Thomas Merton and Society: A Study of the Man and His Thought Against the Background of Contemporary American Culture.' PhD Dissertation, University of Minnesota 1969. Published with revisions as *Thomas Merton: The Man and His Work.* Cistercian Studies Series, Number 27. Washington, DC: Cistercian Publications, 1974.

Works of Related Interest
Books

Allport, Gordon W. *The Individual and His Religion: A Psychological Interpretation.* 1950; rpt. New York: Macmillan, 1960.

Anson, Peter F. *The Call of the Cloister: Religious Communities and Kindred Bodies in the Anglican Communion.* London: SPCK, 1964.

Arasteh, Reza. *Final Integration in the Adult Personality.* Leiden: E.J. Brill, 1965.

Armstrong, A.H. *An Introduction to Ancient Philosophy.* London: Methuen, 1947.

Berrigan, Daniel. *No Bars to Manhood.* New York: Bantam Books, 1970.

Bradbury, Ray. *The Martian Chronicles.* Garden City: Doubleday, 1950.

Barth, Karl. *Church Dogmatics*, I/2. Trans. G.T. Thomson and Harold Knight. Edinburgh: T. & T. Clark, 1956.

_____ . *Church Dogmatics*, II/1. Trans. T.L.H. Parker, et al. Edinburgh: T. & T. Clark, 1957.

_____ . *Church Dogmatics*, IV/2. Trans. G.W. Bromiley. Edinburgh: T. & T. Clark, 1958.

_____ . *Christ and Adam: Man and Humanity in Romans 5.* Trans. T.A. Smail. 1956; rpt. New York: Macmillan, 1968.

_____ . *The Humanity of God.* Trans. Thomas Wieser and John Newton Thomas. Richmond: John Knox, 1960.

_____ . *The Word of God and the Word of Man.* Trans. Douglas Horton. 1928; rpt. New York: Harper & Row Torchbook, 1957.

Bloesch, Donald G. *Centers of Christian Renewal.* Boston/Philadelphia: United Church Press, 1964.

_____ . *The Christian Witness in a Secular Age: An Evaluation of Nine Contemporary Theologians.* Minneapolis: Augsburg, 1968.

_____ . *The Ground of Certainty: Toward an Evangelical Theology of Revelation.* Grand Rapids: Eerdmans, 1971.

. *The Evangelical Renaissance.* Grand Rapids: Eerdmans, 1973.

. *The Reform of the Church.* Grand Rapids: Eerdmans, 1970.

. ed. *Servants of Christ: Deaconesses in Renewal.* Minneapolis: Bethany Fellowship, 1971.

. *Wellsprings of Renewal: Promise in Christian Communal Life.* Grand Rapids: Eerdmans, 1974.

Biot, Francois OP. *The Rise of Protestant Monasticism.* Trans. W. J. Kerrigan. Dublin/Baltimore: Helicon, 1963.

Bonhoeffer, Dietrich. *Letters and Papers from Prison.* Trans. Reginald H. Fuller. 1953; rpt. New York: Macmillan Paperback, 1962.

Bouyer, Louis. *Introduction to Spirituality.* Trans. Mary Perkins Ryan. New York: Desclee, 1961.

Brown, Dee. *Bury My Heart at Wounded Knee: An Indian History of the American West.* New York: Holt, Rinehart & Winston, 1971.

Bruns, J. Edgar. *The Christian Buddhism of St John: New Insights into the Fourth Gospel.* New York/Paramus, New Jersey/Toronto: paulist Press, 1971.

Buber, Martin. *Tales of the Hasidim: The Early Masters,* 1. 1947; rpt. New York: Shocken, 1968.

Butler, Dom Cuthbert. *Western Mysticism.* New York: E.P. Dutton, 1924.

Capon, Robert Farrar. *An Offering of Uncles: The Priesthood of Adam and the Shape of the World.* 1967; rpt. New York: Harper Colophon, 1969

Chavchavdze, Marina, ed. *Man's Concern with Holiness.* London: Hodder & Stoughton, 1970.

Cleaver, Eldridge. *Soul on Ice.* New York: Dell, 1968.

Cox, Harvey. *The Secular City: Secularization and Urbanization in Theological Perspective.* New York: Macmillan, 1965.

D'Arcy, M.C. *The Mind and Heart of Love.* New York: Meridian, 1956.

de Rougemont, Dennis. *Love in the Western World.* Rev. Ed., Trans. Montgomery Belgion. Greenwich, CT: Fawcett Publications, 1956.

Daniélou, Jean. *From Glory to Glory: Texts from Gregory of Nyssa's Mystical Writings.* Trans. and ed. Herbert Musurillo. New York: Scribner's, 1961.

Daniel-Rops, H. *Bernard of Clairvaux: The Story of the Last of the Great Church Fathers.* Trans. Elizabeth Abbott, New York: Hawthorn, 1964.

Dooyeweerd, Herman. *A New Critique of Theoretical Thought*, 1. Trans. David H. Freeman and William Young. Amsterdam: H.J. Paris/Philadelphia: Presbyterian and Reformed, 1953.

Douglass, James W. *Resistance and Contemplation: The Way of Liberation*. Garden City: Doubleday, 1971.

Freyre, Gilberto. *New World in the Tropics: The Culture of Modern Brazil*. New York: Vintage, 1963.

Gandhi, M.K. *Gandhi's Autobiography: The Story of My Experiments with Truth*. Trans. Mahadev Desai. Washington, D.C.: Public Affairs Press, 1948.

Gilson, Etienne. *History of Christian Philosophy in the Middle Ages*. New York: Random House, 1955.

. *The Spirit of Medieval Philosophy*. Trans. A.H.C. Downes. New York: Scribner's, 1936.

Hammarskjöld, Dag. *Markings*. Trans. Leif Sjöberg and W.H. Auden. New York: 1965.

Happold, F.C. *Prayer and Meditation: Their Nature and Practice*. Harmondsworth: Penguin, 1971.

Harkness, Georgia. *Mysticism: Its Meaning and Message*. Nashville/New York: Abingdon, 1973.

Heiler, Friedrich. *Prayer: A Study in the History and Psychology of Religion*. Trans. Samuel McComb. New York: Oxford University Press, 1932.

Henle, R.J. *Saint Thomas and Platonism: a Study of the Plato and Platonici Texts in the Writings of Saint Thomas*. The Hague: Martinus Nijoff, 1956.

Heschel, Abraham Joshua. *God in Search of Man: A Philosophy of Judaism*. New York: Farrar, Straus and Cudahy, 1955.

Hordern, William E. *A Layman's Guide to Protestant Theology*. rev. Ed. New York: Macmillan, 1968.

Huxley, Aldous. *Ape and Essence*. New York: Bantam Books, 1948.

. *The Doors of Perception and Heaven and Hell*. Harmondsworth: Penguin Books in assocation with Chatto & Windus, 1959.

. *Ends and Means: An Inquiry into the Nature of Ideals and into the Methods Employed for Their Realization*. New York: Harper, 1937.

. *Grey Eminence: A Study in Religion and Politics*. New York: Harper & Row, 1966.

. *Island*. New York: Bantam Books, 1962.

Inge, W.R. *Christian Mysticism.* 1899; rpt. Cleveland/New York: Living Age Meridian, 1956.

Jaspers, Karl. *Man in the Modern World.* Trans. Eden and Cedar Paul. London: Routledge and Kegan paul, 1951.

Johnston, William. *Christian Zen.* New York: Harper & Row, 1971.

———. *The Mysticism of the Cloud of Unknowing: A Modern Interpretation* New York: Desclee, 1967.

———. *The Cloud of Unknowing and The Book of Privy Counseling.* Garden City: Doubleday Image 1973.

Jung, Carl G., et al. *Man and His Symbols.* Garden City: Doubleday, 1964.

Knowles, David. *Christian Monasticism.* London: Weidenfeld & Nicolson, 1969.

Kroeber, Theodora. *Ishi in Two Worlds: a Biography of the Last Wild Indian in North America.* Berkeley and Los Angeles: University of California Press, 1961.

Lewis, C.S. *The Abolition of Man.* New York: Macmillan, 1957.

Littell, Franklin H. *The Anabaptist View of the Church: An Introduction to Sectarian Protestantism.* Studies in Church History, 3. New York: American Society of Church History, 1952.

Marcuse, Herbert. *One Dimensional Man: Studies in the Ideology of Advanced Industrial Society.* Boston: Beacon Press, 1964.

Maritain, Jacques. *Art and Scholasticism.* Trans. J.F. Scanlan. New York: Scribner's, 1930.

———. *The Degrees of Knowledge.* Trans. Gerald B. Phelan. New York: Scribner's, 1959.

Maslow, Abraham H. *Religion, Values, and Peak Experiences.* Columbus: Ohio State University Press, 1964.

Miller, Walter M., Jr. *A Canticle for Leibowitz.* New York: Bantam Books, 1959.

Neihardt, John G. *Black Elk Speaks: Being the Life Story of a Holy Man of the Oglala Sioux.* Lincoln: University of Nebraska Press, 1961.

Nygren, Anders. *Agape and Eros.* Trans. Phillip S. Watson. Philadelphia: Westminster, 1953.

Otto, Rudolf. *The Idea of the Holy.* Trans. John W. Harvey. 1923; rpt. New York: Oxford Galaxy, 1958.

Pasternak, Boris. *Doctor Zhivago.* Trans. Max Hayward and Manya Harari. New York: Pantheon, 1958.

Payne, Robert. *The Life and Death of Mahatma Gandhi.* New York: E. P. Dutton, 1969.

Picard, Max. *The Flight From God.* Chicago: Henry Regnery, 1951.

. *The World of Silence.* Chicago: Henry Regnery, 1952.

Praeger, Lydia, ed. *Frei fur Gott und die Menschen.* Stuttgart: Quell-Verlag, 1959.

Quell, Gottfried and Stauffer, Ethelbert. *Love, Bible Key Words from Gerhard Kittel's Theologisches Worterbuch zum Neuen Testament.* London: Black, 1949.

Rahner, Karl. *Theological Investigations,* 6. Baltimore: Helicon, 1969.

and Herbert Vorgrimler. *Theological Dictionary.* Trans. Richard Strachan. New York: Herder and Herder, 1965.

Robinson, John A.T. *Honest to God.* Philadelphia: Westminster, 1963.

Röper, Anita. *The Anonymous Christian.* New York: Sheed and Ward, 1966.

Roszak, Theodore. *The Making of a Counter Culture: Reflections on the Technocratic Society and Its Youthful Opposition.* Garden City: Doubleday Anchor, 1969.

Sachs, Maurice. *Witches' Sabbath and The Hunt.* Trans. Richard Howard. New York: Ballantine, 1965.

St Thomas Aquinas. *On Prayer and the Contemplative Life.* Ed. Hugh Pope *op.* London: Washbourne, 1914.

. *Summa Theologica.* 2. Trans. Fathers of the English Dominican Province. New York: Benziger, 1947.

St Benedict. *St. Benedict's Rule for Monasteries.* Trans. Leonard J. Doyle. Collegeville, Minn.: Liturgical Press, 1948.

St John of the Cross. *The Ascent of Mount Carmel,* 1. *The Complete Works of St. John of the Cross.* Trans. Allison Peers. London: Burns & Oates, 1934.

Skinner, B.F. *Beyond Freedom and Dignity.* New York: Knopf, 1971.

Snyder, Gary. *Earth House Hold: Technical Notes and Queries to Fellow Dharma Revolutionaries.* New York: New Directions, 1968.

Solzhenitsyn, Alexander, et al. *From Under the Rubble.* Trans. under the direction of Michael Scammell. Boston: Little, Brown, 1975.

Spencer, Sidney. *Mysticism in World Religion.* Baltimore: Penguin, 1963.

Suzuki, D.T. *Mysticism: Christian and Buddhist, The Eastern and Western Way.*
1957; rpt. New York: Macmillan, 1969.

. *Zen Buddhism: Selected Writings of D.T. Suzuki.* Ed. William
Barrett. Garden City: Doubleday Anchor, 1956.

Teilhard de Chardin, Pierre. *Hymn of the Universe.* Trans. Gerald Vann *op.*
1965; rpt. New York: Harper Colophon, 1969.

TeSelle, Eugene. *Augustine the Theologian.* New York: Herder and Herder,
1970.

Tillich, Paul. *the Future of Religions.* Ed. Jerald C. Brauer. New York: Harper
& Row, 1966.

. *Perspectives on 19th and 20th Century Protestant Theology.* Ed.
Carl E. Braaten. New York: Harper & Row, 1967.

. *Theology of Culture.* Ed. Robert C. Kimbell. 1959; rpt. New York:
Oxford Galaxy, 1964.

Toffler, Alvin. *Future Shock.* 1970; rpt. New York: Bantam Books, 1971.

Trungpa, Chogyam, as told to Esmé Cramer Roberts. *Born in Tibet.* Baltimore:
Penguin, 1971.

von Huegel, Baron Friedrich. *The Life of Prayer.* London: Dent, 1960.

von Kortzfleisch, Siegfried. *Mitten Im Herzen Der Massen.* Stuttgart: Kreuz-
Verlag, 1963.

Walker, Williston. *A History of the Christian Church.* Rev. Ed. New York:
Scribner's, 1959.

Williams, Daniel Day. *The Spirit and Forms of Love.* New York: Harper & Row,
1968.

Williams, George H. *Wilderness and Paradise in Christian Thought.* New York:
Harper, 1962.

Wills, Gary. *Bare Ruined Choirs: Doubt, Prophecy, and Radical Religion.*
Garden City: Doubleday, 1972.

Wyon, Olive. *Living Springs.* Philadelphia: Westminster, 1964.

Zaehner, R.C. *Concordant Discord: The Interdependence of Faiths.* Oxford:
Clarendon Press, 1970

. *Mysticism Sacred and Profane: An Inquiry into Some Varieties of
Praeternatural Experience.* 1957; rpt. New York: Oxford Galaxy, 1961.

Articles in Books and Journals

Bloesch, Donald G. 'The Ideological Temptation.' *Listening: Current Studies in Dialog* 7 (Winter 1972) 45-54.

Egan, Eileen. 'Crossing India.' *Catholic Worker* 37 No. 2 (1971) 7.

Hicks, Richard R. 'The New Mood of College Students: A Black Viewpoint.' *The Christian Century* 90 (1973) 538-41.

Jones, W. Paul. 'Monasticism as Counterculture.' *The Christian Century* 89 (1972) 628-30.

Riesenhuber, Klaus *sj*. 'Afterword: The Anonymous Christian According to Karl Rahner' in *The Anonymous Christian* by Anita Roper. New York: Sheed and Ward, 1966, pp. 145-79.

Ruether, Rosemary. 'Monks and Marxists: A Look at the Catholic Left.' *Christianity and Crisis* 33 (1973) 75-79.

Wimmersberger, Keith H. Letter to the Editor. *The Christian Century* 90 (1973) 517-18.

Wolterstorff, Nicholas. 'Calvinists in Potchefstroom.' *The Reformed Review* 25 No. 9 (November 1975) 8-13.

Zylstra, Bernard. Introduction to *Contours of a Christian Philosophy: an Introduction to Herman Dooyeweerd's Thought* by L. Kalsbeek. Ed. Bernard and Josina Zylstra. Toronto: Wedge Publishing Foundation, 1975, pp. 14-33.

CISTERCIAN PUBLICATIONS

Titles Listing

1979

THE CISTERCIAN FATHERS SERIES

THE WORKS OF BERNARD OF CLAIRVAUX

Treatises I (Apologia to Abbot William,
  On Precept and Dispensation)   CF 1
On the Song of Songs I   CF 4*
On the Song of Songs II   CF 7*
Treatises II (The Steps of Humility, On
  Loving God)   CF 13
Treatises III (In Praise of the New
  Knighthood, On Grace and Free
  Choice)   CF 19*
Five Books on Consideration   CF 37*
The Life of Saint Malachy   CF 10

THE WORKS OF WILLIAM OF ST THIERRY

On Contemplating God, Prayer, and
  Meditations   CF 3*
Exposition on the Song of Songs   CF 6
The Enigma of Faith   CF 9
The Golden Epistle   CF 12*
The Mirror of Faith   CF 15
Commentary on the Letter to
  the Romans   CF 27†

THE WORKS OF AELRED OF RIEVAULX

Treatises I (On Jesus at the Age of
  Twelve, Rule for a Recluse, The
  Pastoral Prayer)   OP
Spiritual Friendship   CF 5*

THE WORKS OF GUERRIC OF IGNY

Liturgical Sermons I & II   CF 8, 32

OTHER CISTERCIAN WRITERS

The Letters of Adam of
  Perseigne   CF 21
John of Ford, Sermons on the Final
  Verses of the Song of Songs I   CF 29
Gilbert of Hoyland, Sermons on the
  Song of Songs I   CF 14
The Way of Love   CF 16*
Idung of Prufening, Cistercians and Clu-
  niacs: The Case for Citeaux   CF 33
Three Treatises on Man:
  Cistercian Anthropology   CF 24
Magnificat: Homilies in Praise of the
  Blessed Virgin Mary   CF 18
Isaac of Stella, Sermons I   CF 11
John of Ford, Sermons on the Final
  Verses of the Song of Songs II   CF 36†

* Available in paperback
OP Temporarily out of print
† Projected

THE CISTERCIAN STUDIES SERIES

EARLY MONASTIC TEXTS

Evagrius Ponticus: Praktikos and Chap-
  ters on Prayer   CS 4
The Rule of the Master   CS 6
Dorotheos of Gaza: Discourses
  and Sayings   CS 33*
The Sayings of the Desert
  Fathers   CS 59*
Gregory of Nyssa: The Life
  of Moses   CS 31

MONASTIC STUDIES

The Climate of Monastic Prayer
  by Thomas Merton   CS 1
The Abbot in Monastic
  Tradition   CS 14
Why Monks?   CS 17
Silence: Silence in the
  Rule of St Benedict   CS 22
One Yet Two: Monastic Tradition
  East and West   CS 28
The Spirituality of Western
  Christendom   CS 30
Russian Mystics   CS 26
In Quest of the Absolute:
  The Life and Work of
  Jules Monchanin   CS 51*
The Name of Jesus
  by Irenee Hausherr   CS 44
Community and Abbot in the
  Rule of St Benedict
  by Adalbert de Vogue   CS 5

CISTERCIAN STUDIES

The Cistercian Spirit   CS 3
The Eleventh-Century Background
  of Citeaux   CS 8
Contemplative Community   CS 21
Cistercian Sign Language   CS 11
Thomas Merton: The Man and
  His Work   CS 27
Merton's Theology of Prayer   CS 18
Saint Bernard of Clairvaux: Essays
  Commemorating the Eighth
  Centenary of His
  Canonization   CS 28
William of St Thierry: The Man
  and His Work
  by J. M. Dechanet   CS 10
The Monastic Theology of Aelred
  of Rievaulx   CS 2
The Golden Chain: The Theological
  Anthropology of Isaac of
  Stella   CS 15
Christ the Way: The Christology of
  Guerric of Igny   CS 26
Studies in Medieval Cistercian
  History [I]   CS 13
Studies in Medieval Cistercian
  History II   CS 24*
Cistercian and Monastic Essays
  by Odo Brooke   CS 37*†

BY DOM JEAN LECLERCQ

Bernard of Clairvaux and the
  Cistercian Spirit   CS 16*
Aspects of Monasticism   CS 7*
Contemplative Life   CS 19*
A Second Look at St Bernard   CS 39†
Bernard of Clairvaux: Studies
  Presented to Jean Leclercq   CS 23